South Asian Literature, Culture and Society

A Critical Rumination

Edited by
Goutam Karmakar

ATLANTIC
PUBLISHERS & DISTRIBUTORS (P) LTD

Published by
ATLANTIC
PUBLISHERS & DISTRIBUTORS (P) LTD
7/22, Ansari Road, Darya Ganj, New Delhi-110002
Phones : +91-11-40775252, 40775214, 23273880, 23275880
Fax : +91-11-23285873
Web : www.atlanticbooks.com
E-mail : orders@atlanticbooks.com

Branch Office: Chennai
Phones : +91-44-48531784, 28291383
E-mail : chennai@atlanticbooks.com

Disclaimer

- The author and the publisher have taken every effort to the maximum of their skill, expertise and knowledge to provide correct material in the book. Even then if some mistakes persist in the content of the book, the publisher does not take responsibility for the same. The publisher shall have no liability to any person or entity with respect to any loss or damage caused, or alleged to have been caused directly or indirectly, by the information contained in this book.
- The author has fully tried to follow the copyright law. However, if any work is found to be similar, it is unintentional and the same should not be used as defamatory or to file legal suit against the author.
- If the readers find any mistakes, we shall be grateful to them for pointing out those to us so that these can be corrected in the next edition.
- All disputes are subject to the jurisdiction of Delhi courts only.

Printed & bound in India by Atlantic Print Services

Foreword

South Asian Literature has always been a somewhat neglected branch of post-colonial literature, which is better represented by African and Caribbean Literature as far as invader colonies are concerned, and Australian and Canadian Literature as far as settler colonies are concerned. Goutam Karmakar's edited volume, exclusively on South Asian Literature, Culture, and Society, is a welcome addition to the scant body of existing critical writing on the subject.

Karmakar's book is unique in that it does not artificially differentiate between writing in English and that in the native tongues. Here, Jhumpa Lahiri, Amitav Ghosh, Kamala Markandaya, Namita Gokhale, and Mohsin Hamid rub shoulders with 'vernaculars' like Ashapurna Debi, Nirmal Bose, Orijit Sen, and even the iconic among them, like Vijay Tendulkar, Badal Sircar, and Taslima Nasrin. Privileging hybridity, Karmakar jettisons the idea of genre purity, and includes essays not just on the novelists, but also on poets like Kamala Das and Eunice de Souza, and playwrights like Asif Currimbhoy. Section II of Karmakar's book goes beyond literature to take up issues concerning culture and society, such as archaeology, religion, mythology, health, gender, ecology, modernity, and tribes.

R. Raj Rao
Poet, Novelist,
Former Professor and Head,
Department of English,
University of Pune.

Preface

South Asia has an immense importance in the socio-political, cultural, and literary landscapes of the world, and any discussion on it inevitably encompasses social, cultural, and literary issues of world's one-fourth population as it includes the South Asian countries of India, Pakistan, Bangladesh, Nepal, Bhutan, Maldives, Sri Lanka, and Afghanistan. The historical legacy of South Asian countries holds much importance to the development of the region, whereas cultural affinity and geographical proximity provide commonality among them. The literature of this region has flourished under the shared European (primarily British) colonial legacy and eventually, the writers of these regions have adopted English as a medium of expression. Migration to the First World English speaking countries in the post-independence era has resulted in a body of diasporic literature. The regional and national languages of the South Asian countries further add variety to the rich literary culture of the region. Further, the translations of the regional texts have enriched the South Asian body of literature with its global recognition and representation. The South Asian literature is rich with its cultural multiplicity, historical complications, colonial legacy, and disowning the legacy, indigenous groups, environmental diversity, and diasporic global entanglement, have interested numerous scholars, historians, sociologists, and ethnographers around the world to explicate South Asian socio-culture and complexities, manifested in the livelihood of inhabitants of South Asia.

This anthology of thirty-seven chapters attempts to showcase the nuances of South Asian literature, culture, and society. It is an attempt to reflect and reverberate varied aspects of the subcontinent. It tries to give a global perspective where readers, scholars, and academicians can read, understand, realize, and appreciate the socio-cultural and literary traits of South Asia.

The book has been divided into two parts. The first part, namely "Mapping South Asian Literature" contains twenty-nine research articles which vividly explicate some noteworthy literary works of this region. The second part of this volume, namely "Glimpses of South Asian Culture and Society" consists of eight scholarly articles which define a few traits of South Asian society and culture. Despite many socio-cultural, political, religious, and economic problems, unity is there among South Asian countries and this book confirms to what Vina Mazumdar says in her article "Women and Development: The South Asian Experience and Expectations" published in the book *Emerging South Asian Order: Hopes and Concerns* edited by Sankar Ghosh and Soumen Mukherjee. The book discusses the writings in English and that in the native tongues of prominent authors such as Jhumpa Lahiri, Amitav Ghosh, Kamala Markandaya, Namita Gokhale, Mohsin Hamid, Ashapurna Debi, Nirmal Bose, Orijit Sen, Vijay Tendulkar, Badal Sircar, and Taslima Nasrin. It includes essays not just on the novelists, but also on poets like Kamala Das and Eunice de Souza, and playwrights like Asif Currimbhoy. Second part of the book goes beyond literature to take up issues concerning culture and society, such as archaeology, religion, mythology, health, gender, ecology, modernity, and tribes.

All the contributors to this anthology are experts of English literature and belong to prestigious institutions of India. The book will be useful for graduate and post graduate students of English literature of South Asian universities. It will also be helpful to the researchers and teachers of English literature dealing with South Asian literature.

Goutam Karmakar

Acknowledgements

Praise is to the Almighty, the most compassionate and the most merciful, for giving me persistence and potentiality to accomplish this project.

I would like to express my gratitude to my parents, other family members and friends for their constant support and encouragement. They all kept me going and this book would not have been possible without them. I wish to present my special thanks to my mother for guiding me throughout this project in spite of the time it took away from her busy schedule.

I would like to pay my regards to R. Raj Rao, poet, novelist, and former Professor of English at University of Pune, for writing the foreword of this book. I am thankful to those professors and writers who guided, supported, motivated and directed me, gave suggestions, offered comments, and allowed me to quote their remarks. Thanks to all the contributors, without them this book would never find its way to the web and I appreciate your patience. I would like to pay my regards to the reviewers for reviewing the papers. Their help and sympathetic attitude at every point during this project helped me to finish my work in time. I am thankful to Ms. Somasree Sarkar for assisting me in editing and proofreading of the manuscript. I would like to especially thank and warmly appreciate all those who extended their support morally and emotionally.

Last but not least, I beg forgiveness of all those who have been with me over the course of the years and whose names I have failed to mention.

May the Almighty bless all of you.

Goutam Karmakar

Contents

Contributors

Alak Kumar Syamal is Head at the Post Graduate Department of Physiology, Hooghly Mohsin College, Hooghly, West Bengal, India.

Anamika Ghosh teaches English at Acharya Jagadish Chandra Bose College, University of Calcutta, West Bengal, India. She has obtained her M. Phil. degree from Visva Bharati University. Her area of interest covers Post-colonialism, Post-colonial Environmentalism, Feminism, and Dalit Literature.

Anindita Chowdhury is an Assistant Professor of English at Seshadripuram First Grade College, Bengaluru, India.

Anirban Kahali teaches English at Kulti College, Kazi Nazrul University, Asansol, West Bengal, India.

Anna Lynn Tom is an Assistant Professor of English at St. Joseph's College of Commerce, Bengaluru, India. Her research interests include gender and identity, feminist theories, and creative writing.

Basudhara Roy is an Assistant Professor at the Department of English, Karim City College, Jamshedpur, Jharkhand, India.

Chaitali Bose is a Ph.D. Research Scholar at the Post Graduate Department of Physiology, Hooghly Mohsin College, Hooghly, West Bengal, India.

Debajit Paul is a Lecturer of English at Vidyasagar University, West Bengal, India. His interests include Comparative Philology (Linguistics), Comparative Literature, Translation Studies, Literary criticism, Indian Writing in English, and English Poetry and Novel. He is a member of Comparative Literature Association of India.

Dechhen Dolma teaches at Khuruthang Middle Secondary School, Punakha, Bhutan. She is also a researcher. Her fourteen years of teaching experience includes expertise in English language teaching and leadership roles as Staff Secretary, HoD for English Department, and literary coordinator for the school literary programmes.

Deepayan Das is an Assistant Professor of English at Muzaffar Ahmed Mahavidyalaya, Salar, Murshidabad, West Bengal, India. His areas of interest include Indian writing in English and post-colonial literature.

Durga Patva is an Assistant Professor of English at City Public Mahila Degree College, Nekpur Kalan, Farrukhabad, Uttar Pradesh, India.

Guni Vats is a Ph.D. Research Scholar at the Department of English, University of Lucknow, Lucknow, Uttar Pradesh, India.

Hemanga Dutta is an Assistant Professor in the Department of Linguistics and Contemporary English, The English and Foreign Languages University, Hyderabad, India. His research interests include Phonetics phonology interfaces, Phonological theories, and Sociolinguistics.

Indrani Chakraborty is an Assistant Professor and Head of the Department of English at Prabhu Jagatbandhu College, Jhorehat, Andul-Mouri, Howrah, West Bengal, India. She has done her M. Phil. on Selected Texts of Amitav Ghosh, analysing his style of representing the Subaltern. Her special area of interest is Fin-de-siècle Speculative Fiction.

Juhi Gupta is an Assistant Professor at Centre for Women's Studies, Aligarh Muslim University, Uttar Pradesh, India.

Kauser Tasneem is an Assistant Professor at the Department of History, Karim City College, Jamshedpur, Jharkhand, India. Her areas of interest include Modern Indian History, World History, Cultural History, and Gender Studies.

K.B.S. Krishna is an Assistant Professor of English at the Central University of Himachal Pradesh, Kangra, Shahpur, Himachal Pradesh, India.

K. Subapriya is an Assistant Professor of English at Pachaiyappa's College, Chennai, Tamil Nadu, India. Her area of specialization is Multi-ethnic literature and Indian writing in English. She is interested in bilingual poetry writing, creative writing, and translation.

Madhu Kamra is an Assistant Professor at the Department of English, Durga Mahavidyalaya, Modha Para Raipur (C.G.), Chhattisgarh, India.

Mahamadul Hassan Dhabak is a Ph.D. Research Scholar at the University of Kalyani, West Bengal, India. He is having an ongoing thesis in English Literature on Dalit Masculinity. He has done M.Phil. in Women's Studies on "Representation of Women in Ismat Chughtai's Select Short Stories" in 2017 from University of Kalyani.

Malini Chongder is a Ph.D. Research Scholar at the Department of English, Raiganj University, Raiganj, West Bengal, India. She has also worked as a Guest Lecturer at the Department of English (P.G.), Malda College, Malda, and Chanchal College, Singia, Malda, West Bengal, India.

Nabanita Dhali teaches English at Gobardanga Hindu College, Jamdani, Gobardanga, and Sree Chaitanya College, Prafullanagar, Habra, under West Bengal State University. She is also a M. Phil. Research scholar at Calcutta University, Kolkata. She is working on the idea of Heterotopic Spaces and its role in the transformation of human conscience portrayed by Virginia Woolf.

Pankaj Luchan Gogoi is an Assistant Professor of English at Digboi Mahila Mahavidyalaya, Digboi, Assam, India.

Paulomi Banerjee is a Ph.D. Research Scholar at Techno India University, West Bengal, India. She is pursuing her research on Dalit and subaltern studies.

Pragnya Parimita Chayani is a Teaching Assistant at the Department of Humanities and Social Sciences, Indian Institute of Technology, Dharwad, Karnataka, India.

Prakash C. Balikai is an Assistant Professor of English, Central University of Karnataka, Kalaburagi, India.

Pratibha Patel is an Assistant Professor at the Department of English, Ramashray Baleshwar College, Dalsingsarai, Samastipur, Bihar, India.

Ramprasad Dutta teaches English at Acharya Sukumar Sen Mahavidyalaya, Gotan, West Bengal, India. His areas of interest include postmodern literature, comics and graphic novels, American literature, and gender studies.

Rimpa Roy is an Assistant Professor at the Department of English, Subhas Chandra Bose Centenary College, Lalbagh, Murshidabad, West Bengal, India. Her areas of interest include Indian writing in English and post-colonial literature.

Ritushree Sengupta is an Assistant Professor at the Department of English, Patrasayer Mahavidyalaya, Patrasayer, West Bengal, India.

S. Barathi is an Assistant Professor at the Department of English, Srinivasa Ramanujan Centre, SASTRA (Deemed to be University), Kumbakonam, Tamil Nadu, India.

S. Chitra is a faculty at the Department of English, Yonphula Centenary College (a constituent college of Royal University of Bhutan), Trashigang, Bhutan. Currently, she teaches the Masters Programme in English, supervises the research scholars, and serves as Programme Leader. She holds nearly two decades of tertiary teaching experience. Her service record includes teaching expertise in areas of English literature and language along with a contribution to curriculum development.

Sucheta Kapoor is a Ph.D. conveyor at Techno India University, Kolkata, West Bengal, India. She was also the ex-faculty member at the Department of Modern Languages and Cultures, Liverpool University, UK.

Sayani Nayak teaches English at Triveni Devi Bhalotia College, Raniganj, West Bengal, India. Her areas of interest include modernism, post-modernism, post-colonial literature, and cultural studies.

Shamaila Amir is a Teaching Assistant at Hamdard Institute of Education and Social Sciences (HIESS), Hamdard University, Karachi, Pakistan.

Soma Mandal is a former Research Scholar at the Department of Humanities and Social Sciences, Indian Institute of Technology,

Patna, and former guest faculty at the Department of English, Durgapur Women's College, Durgapur, West Bengal, India. Her areas of interest include Dalit Literature, Women's Studies, and literature from the margins.

Subhajeet Singha is an Assistant Professor and Head of the Department of English at Deshapran Mahavidyalaya, Purba Medinipur, West Bengal, India.

Subhankar Dutta is a Teaching Assistant at the Department of Humanities and Social Sciences, Indian Institute of Technology, Bombay, India.

Subhasnata Mohanta is an Assistant Professor of English at the Institute of Engineering and Industrial Technology, Durgapur, West Bengal, India.

Syed Foyez Ahmed is a Teaching Assistant at the Department of English, Aliah University, Kolkata, West Bengal, India. His areas of interest include Indian English Drama, Diaspora Studies, performance studies, and partition literature.

V.P. Singh is a Professor of English at the Department of English, University of Lucknow, Lucknow, India.

Vishali Sharma is an Assistant Professor of English at Sharda University, Delhi, India.

Introduction

It is an established fact that South Asia has succeeded to gain an immense importance in the socio-political, cultural, and literary landscapes of the world; and any discussion on South Asia inevitably encompasses social, cultural, and literary issues of world's one-fourth population as it includes the South Asian countries of India, Pakistan, Bangladesh, Nepal, Bhutan, Maldives, Sri Lanka, and Afghanistan. While the historical legacy holds much importance to the development of this region, cultural affinity and geographical proximity provide commonality among the countries of this region. South Asian literature has flourished under the shared European (primarily British) colonial legacy and eventually, the writers of these regions have adopted English and practice in the language. Migration from these countries to the First World English speaking countries in the post-independence era has also resulted in the production of a body of diasporic literature. The regional and national languages of the South Asian countries further add variety to the rich literary culture of the region. Further, the translations of the regional texts have enriched the South Asian body of literature with its global recognition and representation. The literature of South Asia is rich with its cultural multiplicity, historical complications, colonial legacy and disowning the legacy, indigenous groups, environmental diversity, and diasporic global entanglement, have interested numerous scholars, historians, sociologists, and ethnographers around the world to explicate South Asian socio-culture and complexities, manifested in the livelihood of inhabitants of South Asia.

One important factor that binds the cultural history of South Asia is its shared colonial past under the British. The people of South Asia have had to break away from their colonial bondage that not only enslaved them through oppression but also colonized its culture and history. The period of colonization can be seen as a state of paralysis when the people were unable to act and react freely and they were unable to cherish the rich cultural diversity of their native lands. But, with a consistent show of resistance, the writers of these countries have voiced their opinions and ideas, sometimes in the regional languages to mobilize the mass and sometimes in the adopted language of English to threaten the colonizers in their own language. South Asian literature, highlighting the socio-cultural issues, history, demands, problems, challenges of the vast region called South Asia, is comparatively a recent development in the field of literary practice. This particular genre has been instrumental in gradually making people aware of the South Asian cultural plurality and diversity and of the fact that the division of 'Orient' and 'Occident' is mere fantasy and a political strategy of the West to continue the colonial enterprise.

South Asian literature forms a part in the gamut of "New Literatures in English" along with Australian literature, Caribbean literature, Canadian and African Literature. The term "New Literature" denotes the literature outside the paradigm of canonical British literature and the word 'new' indicates its relatively new emergence in the oeuvre of literary engagements. This genre of literature is also sometimes referred to as "Third World Literature" as it is primarily the outcome of thinking and creative endeavour of writers and poets originating in the less developed Asian countries or 'Third world' countries. Literature of this region attempts to reestablish its distinct identity in the global context by decolonizing the colonial past along with delineating the experience of colonization, as the writers have asserted "themselves by foregrounding the tension with the imperial power and by emphasizing their differences from the assumptions of the imperial center" (Ashcroft et al., *The Empire Writes Back: Theory and Practice in Post-colonial Literatures,* 1989: 01). Literature here has gone through the process of imitation, experimentation, tensions of the colonial relationship, resistance and the formation of identity, regionalism, and nationalism. But, at the same time, writers face difficulties while asserting nationalism in their works and at a conference in Leeds, Balachandra Rajan talks on this issue. He opines: "In newer literatures, the pressures of literary nationality can be compulsive and the writer writes according to specifications which can be subtly tempting when the writer himself is committed to them as a citizen.... [There is] the patriotic [view] in which the writer becomes the voice of nationhood and the achievement of an Indian writer, for example, is judged by the intensity of his Indianness" (qtd. in Meenakshi Mukherjee, *Considerations,* 1964: 1).

Owing to its colonial past and increased migration to the English-speaking countries (as stated earlier), English has become one of the major languages through which South Asian literature flourishes and expands. English language links the vast region of South Asia with each other and also connects the region to the rest of the world. However, Bangladesh, Pakistan, and Sri Lanka have also given ample emphasis on their regional languages which have also been translated in English for global readers. In this context Fakrul Alam (2007) aptly says in his article "Imagining South Asian Writing in English from Bangladesh", "After Independence, the countries of South Asia would adopt varying policies regarding the English language. These policies invariably impacted on the development of the literature written in English in each country" (*South Asian Review* 27.1: 42). At the same time, South Asian writers seek to decolonize the language by mixing regional words, idioms, and phrases with the English language. While the linguistic courtesy provides English with a scope to mingle with other regional languages, globalization makes the English language culturally and geographically proximate. English amalgamated with vernacular and regional linguistic peculiarities becomes an instrument through which writers of South Asia showcase resistance. This language alternation or code-switching not only makes the language a subject to change but also creates a wave of linguistic globalization where these writers become the major voices of modern iconoclastic lexicography. English interwoven with regional languages refers to the *chutnification* of language, as coded by Salman Rushdie. South Asian novelists, dramatists, short-story writers, and poets, practicing in English, mould, enhance, and shape the English language to fulfill their cross-cultural needs. While dealing with proliferating issues in ethical, sociological, cultural, and geographical milieus, writers expand the English language by providing the regional peculiarity and eccentricity which delineate that English is no longer the prerogative of colonial fathers, but has emerged as a language, flexible enough to adapt and adept. This experimentation with language along with intriguing narrative, South Asian culture and literature have invited global readers and researchers to enquire into the idiosyncrasy of the subcontinent. South Asian fictions in English unquestionably map the distinctive nature and behaviour of this subcontinent. Paul Brians in his book *Modern South Asian Literature in English* (Greenwood Press, Westport 2003) aptly says:

> The worlds visible through these fictional windows are wildly varied. Rohinton Mistry and Bapsi Sidhwa portray the tiny Parsi community, Khushwant Singh depicts Sikhs, and others concentrate on the dominant Muslim, Hindu, and (in Sri Lanka) Buddhist cultures. We meet street urchins, gangsters, prostitutes, peasants, small merchants, wealthy industrialists, and saints. Writers create satire, humor, tragedy, social criticism, and romance. Some write in experimental styles that require careful decoding; others are happy to lay out their tales in a traditional fashion that keeps the casual reader interested. Both, men and women write movingly of the lives of South Asia's women and girls. Many write about the world of their childhood, others try to depict contemporary reality, and an increasing number are writing historical novels ranging back a century and more. It would be absurd to refer to "the South Asian reality." There is no such thing. South Asian literature is a colorful kaleidoscope of fragmented views, colored by the perceptions of its authors, reflecting myriad realities—and fantasies. One of the most inviting ways to overcome the biases in any particular work is to read more, and a growing audience seems eager to do just that. (6)

Literature popularly claims to mirror the society and South Asian literature without being an exception, gives its readers and enquirers the scope to view how contemporary writers assert their identity, authority, ethos, and culture of their native land in their works and, thus, their works reflect the socio-realistic issues of this region. The literature of the region covers a wide spectrum of South Asian pattern of belief and livelihood, enabling the readers to understand what motivates an educated woman to wear a hijab, what instigates a poet or a novelist to write on war and ecology, what inspires an academician to show the naked truth of society, what allows an activist to speak on migration. The body of literature also probes into the issues related to border politics, challenges, and resilience of the marginalised section of the society, phobia and prejudice based on religious discrimination, the unsolved political tiff over a landmass in the northern tip of the subcontinent, named Kashmir, gigantic history of struggle for independence and wars of liberation, the problem of forced migration owing to the pathetic and devastating partition, immigration to other countries, and complex relationship with the neighbouring countries. The literature depicting multiculturalism, multilingualism, and multi-ethnicity, despite the apparent cultural similarities, help the readers to shape a unified psychology, both collectively and constructively towards South Asia. In his article "Introduction. Imaginations and Constructions of South Asia: An Enchanting Abstraction?", Arif Mohammad highlights the shared cultural and religious practices of the region by saying, "Commonalities in social and cultural practices find their roots in centuries-long cultural encounters. Such commonalities are numerous and varied ranging from marriage customs to material cultures and culinary habits" (*South Asian Multidisciplinary Academic Journal* 10 [2014]: 4).

South Asian poetry, fiction, short story, and drama have dealt with the profundity of experiences and issues, distinctive to South Asian communities across the continents. Writers hailing from South Asian communities have indulged in the thematic examination of various aspects of life, peculiar to South Asia. Many writers, for instance, have expressed diasporic sensibilities, patriarchal society of South Asia, gender and queer issues, politics of border, bordered lands, and no man's land. A profoundly disoriented scenario has witnessed eviction and expulsion of many people from various regions in South Asia as their lives are entangled in a cosmo-political web of cause and effect. The causes can be asserted as growing ethnic conflicts, violation of human rights, identity assertions, and the 9/11 attack on Twin Towers. All these events have compelled a body of enriched literature, dealing with the complications and conundrum on the landmass. Their works, more precisely an isometric development of fictional narratives, not only combat the stereotypical images of South Asian countries but also discuss how boundaries shape and reshape the identities of the displaced people of those affected regions. The fictions show the problems of displaced people living in an alien land and by linking the power-politics of those regions with a special plurality, they attempt to create counter-narratives where the dissolution of boundaries can be seen. Apart from the borderland issues, Muslims living in South Asia and other regions have faced an identity crisis since 9/11, owing to the prejudice meted out to the people belonging to this particular religious belief. With almost 2974 casualties, 9/11 terrorist attack still remains the biggest trauma of the 21st century, and an inveterate fear and unpredictability drastically have alternated a particular community living in the USA. This particular religious group, more precisely, people affiliated to Islam have come under strict observation, scrutiny, and verification in various Western countries. This altered condition of the 'Other' affects the notion of 'Self'. Muslim writers rise on this occasion to show their fractured identity, their untiring attempt to validate their existence in disconnection with any religious terror groups and religious radicalism in and outside of the USA. In order to show how the identity crisis and the subsequent trajectory of the Muslims from a hybrid identity to a unified identity, South Asian writers make an attempt to show in their writings the journey of the fictitious Muslim characters who represent the entire community with its dilemma and confusion. Reading the works of Pakistani and Afghanistani writers delineate how Muslims are exhausted because of their constant negotiations with their identities. Their works show how the Muslims have become undesirable, have been reduced to an object of doubt and disbelief, and have been identified as a destructive power. Post 9/11 South Asian fictions, highlighting the Islamic sensibility, reflect that islamophobia has created an existential crisis for the South Asian Muslim community and their culture and society, threatening their identity in general. Their works also become the counter-narratives to American imperialism and Western narcissism. Regarding the significance of these writings and the motifs of the writers, Pei-Chen Liao aptly comments in the book *'Post'- 9/11 South Asian Diasporic Fictions: Uncanny Terror* (UK: Palgrave Macmillan, 2013):

> Having their novels set across the worlds between South Asia and the West and in multiple temporalities, these novelists question the linear development of the sequentially pre-9/11, 9/11, and post-9/11 stages and, by exploring the repression and repercussions of 9/11, divert attention from the binary axis of time to that of power relations between terrorism and counter-terrorism. Moreover, they do not see '9/11' as a determining marker to which other cultures and countries are subordinated. Instead, they juxtapose the violence inherent in both 9/11 and the War on Terror with sexual and racial discrimination, ethnic cleansing, the Holocaust, the anti-immigration movement, and global capitalism. By doing so, these diasporic writers rethink the broader meanings of 9/11 and the War on Terror in light of the ambivalent link between violence and identity. (154-55)

While South Asia tends to become one of the leading regions in terms of economic development, inter and intraregional conflicts over religion, border, and ethnicity and resources don't allow peace and harmony to settle here. Regional cooperation is needed and potential academic deliberations are required to understand the regional connectivity, development, humanitarian and economic aspects, intra-regional conflicts, regionalism and globalization, movement of citizens across the borders, connectivity projects and regional integration, statelessness, protection policies of refugees, displacement, the idea of peace and stability, and the potentialities of this region. Through literature, films, theatre, performing and visual arts, Foundation of SAARC Writers and Literature (FOSWAL) helps to understand issues like ethno-religious feuds and radical nationalism, cross-cultural bonding, tribal issues, instability and the reasons behind the terrorist activities, diplomatic and political agendas of the government, colonial legacy, and decolonial activities. Writers here attempt to build a bridge of friendship across the territories and, thus, literature of this region produce cultural coalescence across the borders.

Another trait that binds the South Asian countries is its patriarchal system of society. Men here are fed with chauvinist and misogynist ideas, and they domesticate, subjugate, and exploit women that demolish the authority and power of women. In countries like Pakistan and Afghanistan, women are given very little opportunity to flourish as they are principally guided by the *Saria* code of conduct for women. Women have been doubly colonized by whites and native men in the society during the colonial rule, and in the post-colonial era, women continue to be colonized, dominated and oppressed by men of their own community. Hence, not changing much of their situation even after acquiring political freedom from their colonizers. In this context, Sue Ellen Charlton aptly says in the article "Development as History and Process", "Regardless of the precolonial status of women in a particular society the immediate impact of colonial control was either to remove the primary focus of decision-making from the local level to the regional colonial capital or to superimpose colonial decision-making mechanisms on the traditional ones. In either case, the decision-makers were male, as was the colonial administrators" (Visvanathan et al., *The Women, Gender and Development,* 1997: 10). Gender discrimination is the common issue here and women's subordination shows the patriarchal paradigm of South Asian society.

Ecological challenges and global climate changes are other issues that find a place in the writings of South Asian writers. With the advent of ecocriticism, the interconnectedness between man and the environment is realized and examined through culture, economics, race, class, and gender; and all these come into focus as the green movement raises the issue of ecosocial justice—a way to recognize the suppressed voice of non-human entities. In case of South Asian countries, notions of third world environmentalism, the fundamental interconnectedness between different life forms, gradual perish of natural resources for the sake of development, and deep-ecological concerns, place the writers somewhere in between Anthropocentrism and Ecocentrism. The ecosystem is heavily imbalanced due to the irrational attitudes, and Eco-Marxist approach has led to the commodification of nature that ultimately brings forth ecological senility as an outcome of Green criminology. Eco-aesthetic and humanistic enquiries are needed, and Non-Western writers take a postmodern ecocentric stance to portray how humans exploit the non-human entities to cater to their own needs. Writers of South Asia have laid importance on the global environmental concern and have expressed their sense of local place along with the entire planet. They have endowed themselves with a glocal environmental sensibility which alludes both to local and global consciousness for ecological sustainability. The exploitation of natural resources have begun from the colonial rule which has continued to bear an impact on the environment of South Asia. Feminism, socialism, and democratic movements have internalized the environmental movements of this region. While the environmentalist and historian Ramachandra Guha talks about a sustainable lifestyle, ecofeminists and ecologists like Bina Agarwal and Vandana Shiva show how women and nature are subjected to exploitation and subjugation in the patriarchal society. They suggest a few ways in which women and nature should work hand in hand to meet the demands of the society without compromising their importance. In her article "The Gender and Environment Debate", Vina Agarwal rightly points out:

> An alternative approach suggested by feminist environmentalism, needs to be transformational rather than welfarist—where development, redistribution, and ecology link in mutually regenerative ways. This would necessitate complex and interrelated changes such as in the composition of what is produced, the technologies used to produce it, the process by which decisions on products and technologies are arrived at, the knowledge system on which such choices are based, and the class and gender distribution of products and tasks. (Menon, *Gender and Politics in India* 1999: 96)

A close look at the growth and development of South Asian culture and society shows the paradoxes and complexities of state power, the art of governance and the rationality of governmental policies, material qualities of South Asian countries, meditation and circulation of socio-political, cultural, economic and religious memes, bureaucracy and its relation to state power, the control of states over migration, mobilities of labours and refugees, policies of states on citizenship, political and physical space of castes, historical and ethnographic perspectives of different castes along with socio-economic and political dominance over those castes, activities of South Asian countries to inculcate notions of nationalism through education, knowledge and other activities. At the same time, repression of free speech and a few policies of the governments raise various socio-political issues in South Asia. So, cultural differences are there and a few recurrent and distinctive features of South Asian culture are discernible. South Asian countries have borrowed many indigenous elements from the cultures of migrants and intruders like Indo-European Aryans, Europeans, Persians, Greeks, Mongols, Mesopotamians, and Arabians. Unity in diversity can be found here in religious beliefs, local customs, ethos, cuisine, regional languages, and dress. Languages like Hindi, Punjabi, Marathi, Gujarati, Bengali, Tamil, Telegu, Malayalam, Kannada, Urdu, Nepali, Hindi-Urdu, and many others are spoken and through English and Hindi-Urdu languages, inter-regional communication is enhanced. The vast geographical expanse of South Asia harbours diverse religions like Buddhism, Hinduism, Sikhism, Jainism, Brahmanism, Islam, Christianity, and Zoroastrianism. It is the birthplace of religions like Hinduism, Buddhism, Jainism, and Sikhism and also has seen several devotional movements like *Bhakti* movement and *Sufism*. The region has witnessed the birth of several religious exponents and reformers on one hand, and on the other hand, Communism has also found its ground in certain parts of the subcontinent. In terms of the economic system in South Asia, the countries maintain an amiable economic collaboration and relation, interdepending on each other for agricultural products, indigenous market produce, import and export of raw materials. Economic activities among the neighbouring countries are conducted and economic assistance is extended if necessary at the time of crisis owing to natural and man-made disasters.

With its peculiarities, socio-political and religious similarity and differences, South Asia, as a region, carry many significant characteristics. Through this volume *South Asian Literature, Culture and Society: A Critical Rumination*, an attempt has been made to reflect and reverberate varied aspects of the subcontinent. The first part of this book, namely "Mapping South Asian Literature" carries twenty-nine research articles which vividly explicate some noteworthy literary works of this region. The beginning article "Liminality and Second Generation Indian Migrant's Subject Position in Jhumpa Lahiri's *Nobody's Business*" written by Dr. Pankaj Luchan Gogoi takes "Nobody's Business", one of the stories of Jhumpa Lahiri's collection of short stories *Unaccustomed Earth* (2008) as the subject of his study. Like the other stories of the collection, the story, too, deals with Indian diaspora in liminality or "in-betweenness" in the U.S. Interestingly, the story is predominantly concerned with the second generation Indian migrants as seen in the portrayal of Sangeeta Biswas. The text in its concern with the second generation migrants deals with issues like ethnicity, alienation, multiculturalism, transnationalism, and the like. It places Sangeeta among the people of different nationals, and hence, an attempt is made to reveal as to how his liminal subjectivity being formed by her exposure to different people. A post-colonial study on the story carried out with a special focus on diaspora studies goes a long way in illuminating the second generation Indian migrant's subject position in America. This volume also explores some of the notable works of Bengali writers. Dr. Basudhara Roy and Dr. Juhi Gupta critically examine the works of Ashapurna Debi. Indian literature has always drawn attention worldwide, and when it comes to Indian women authors, they have consistently raised some pertinent issues through their works. Ashapurna Debi is one of the most celebrated feminist authors in Bengali Literature. In her novels, the protagonist women are always strong women who have their own desires and courage to pursue their dreams. Her writings give a clear picture of the patriarchal Indian Society and the sufferings of Indian women and their struggle for emancipation. She became the voice of those who were destined to die unheard because they committed the sin of being born as women. While Dr. Roy in her article "Of Potent Matchboxes: Reading Women, Space, and Power in Ashapurna Debi's *Wealth* ('Oishorjo')" portrays the condition of women in *Wealth*, Dr. Gupta in her article "Ashapurna Debi and her Literary Contribution to Feminism in India" attempts to highlight the contribution of Ashapurna Debi to the feminist movement through vernacular literature.

Subhasnata Mohanta in her article "The Age-old Relationship between Man and River: A Study of *Padma Nadir Majhi* and *The Hungry Tide*" attempts to work on a relatively less studied fictional sub-genre produced from Bengal, i.e., river narrative. Bengal is a land of rivers, a number of rivers flow through this intersection between earth and water-flows. The influence of these rivers on human life is therefore inevitably visible in culture, art, and craft of people who inhabit this sensitive area. In this typical geographical area, common people's destinies are always at the mercy of the rivers—they play the role of the preserver as well as the destroyer. In this paper, the peculiarities and features of the culture of this river centric land are studied with the help of two fictional works treating the same region—*Padma Nadir Majhi* (1936), a novel originally written in Bengali by Manik Bandopadhyay and later translated into English by Ratan K. Chattopadhyay, and *The Hungry Tide* (2004) by Amitav Ghosh. These novels reflect on a particular ecological relationship between man and environment and the river centric life of Bengal. In his novel *The Hungry Tide*, through Nirmal Bose's diary, Amitav Ghosh presents the Marichjhapi episode. Marichjhapi is an island in Sundarbans that has long been hidden from public knowledge. If the diary would not have been found by Nilima, wife of Nirmal Bose, the massacre of Marichjhapi would not have perhaps appeared in the novel. There are many important characters in this novel like the protagonist Kanai Dutta, his aunty Nilima, Kusum, and Horen who are closely related to the contents of the diary. Horen is chiefly responsible for Nirmal's involvement in the events of Marichjhapi and Syed Foyez Ahmed's article "Exploring Nirmal Bose's Diary as a Social Document in Amitav Ghosh's *The Hungry Tide*" aims to explore the significance of Nirmal's diary in the context of the novel. Contemporary South Asian Literature witnesses the growth and development of graphic narratives. Orijit Sen is one of the established graphic novelists who shows many socio-realistic issues in his works and Ramprasad Dutta explores a few socio-cultural issues in his article "The Prism of Paranoia: A Kaleidoscopic Representation of the Cultural Schizophrenia and Rhizomatic Dialectical Materialism in Orijit Sen's Graphic Narrative *The River of Stories*".

Short stories can be a source of learning discourse. By analyzing the narrative structure one could gain more information about the story. K.V. Dominic's short story entitled "Burn Your Horoscope" from the anthology, *Sanchita Karma,* is taken for analysis. The story deals with the lives of the two young people whose lives were disturbed due to their horoscopes. The method of narration in the story intrigues readers. So, the study tries to analyze the story from a narratological point using Labov's model. The reason for selecting Labov's model is that it fits for both oral as well as written narratives. Dr. S. Barathi's paper "A Narratological Study of K.V. Dominic's *Burn Your Horoscope*" brings out the aspects that are hitherto unknown to ordinary readers. In comparative literature, comparison and contrast are possible between two more kinds of literature. Especially giving emphasis upon common and unique quality, the comparatists with sincerity and seriousness, elicit comparative elements, from literary pieces, though there are some technicalities of comparison of literature that are the theme and genre. Based on various angles of vision, comparatists travel in the gold mine of literature to gather gems and jewels, that are skillfully and artistically placed in the heart of comparative literature to shed light on the quality of uniqueness, which is as equivalent as ambrosia. Debajit Paul makes a comparative study of a few Bengali and English novels in his paper "A Comparative Perspective: A Case Study of Bengali and English Novels of Indian Writers". Generally considered as one of the prominent stalwarts in the contemporary theatre, Asif Currimbhoy purports to expose and question certain political, social, psychological, and economic issues, and he takes innovative stances to explore all these. He uses theatrical devices like radios, pantomime, loudspeakers, puppets, radios, and shadow cut-out to produce lyrical effects in his works. Various symbolic properties like storm-scenes, poetic speech, monologue, and choruses are used by him to create a lasting impact over the audience. And at the same time, all these bring the quintessential "realism" that moved Faubion Bowers so intensely. Indrani Chakraborty's paper "Asif Currimbhoy and the Question of Representing Authenticity" intends to examine how the two plays of Currimbhoy, *The Doldrummers* (1961) and *Goa* (1965) indeed project Asif Currimbhoy as "India's first authentic voice in the theatre". All human beings are interconnected with one another in society with a link which is called connectivity. This connectivity results in the term relationship either it is social or political. Among all human relationships, the relationship between man and woman play a significant part in the soothing governance of society. One's existence cannot be imagined in the absence of others. Deploying the concept of man-woman relationship in *A Silence of Desire* by Kamala Markandaya, Dr. Durga Patva's paper "Tracing Man-Woman Relationship of the Victorian Era: A Study of Kamala Markandaya's *A Silence of Desire*" aims to explore how the Victorians views regarding the man-woman relationship are applicable in contemporary Indian society.

Theatre as a socio-cultural platform has been propagating ideas that influenced the epistemological manoeuvre of society and life. In the paper "Breaking the Barriers: Space and Time in Badal Sircar's *Basi Khabar* (The Stale News, 1979)", Subhankar Dutta takes the mise-en-scene of *Basi Khabar* (*Stale News*, 1979); a joint venture of Badal Sircar and Shatabdi Group. Sircar, initially an engineer by profession, is an influential Indian dramatist and theatre director who pioneered an egalitarian theatre, known as 'Third Theatre'. Taking the Santhal Rebellion at the centre of the plot, Sircar in *Basi Khabar* is trying to re-engage us in the perpetual questions related to the oppressor and oppressed in a new light. In one hand, he is re-looking at the past acts of social oppressions as deep truth of social segregations; on the other, he is contemporizing the very structure to suggest the situationality of acts beyond the historical time-frame of events. In this paper, Dutta looks at how Badal Sircar's *Stale News* presents the ideas of space and time in theatre, and in the life of Santhals with a focus on Sircar's life-like theatre pursuit and his engagement with "third theatre". So, the paper analyzes the ways in which Sircar has changed the earlier 'grammar' of theatre and presented public arena as a theatrical space. Anirban Kahali in his paper "Motherhood and Profession: A Comparative Study of Mahasweta Devi's *Breast-Giver* and Vijay Tendulkar's *Silence! The Court is in Session*" shows how in Mahasweta Devi's *Breast-Giver*, Jashoda's motherhood becomes her identity and when her husband becomes incapable to earn them two square meals, her motherhood becomes their source of income. She becomes a wet nurse and, thus, turns into the universal mother. On the contrary, Kahali also shows how in Vijay Tendulkar's *Silence! The Court is in Session*, motherhood becomes a curse for Benare and is forced to commit an act of "infanticide". Dr. K.B.S. Krishna's paper "Who Wants Murder? Solving Mystery to Confront Nostalgia in M.M. Kaye's *Death in the Andamans*" is an attempt to look at how even murder can set off a diasporic community on a nostalgic trip by a study of M.M. Kaye's *Death in The Andamans* (1985), and thereon show how such nostalgia—and nostalgia generally, can be addressed to find and create a secure home without craving for something that is past and/or lost. Anindita Chowdhury takes the famous translated Dalit women autobiographies namely, Bama Faustina's *Karukku*, Urmila Pawar's *The Weave of My Life: A Dalit Woman's Memoirs*, and Baby Kamble's *The Prisons We Broke*, to show hegemonic caste system and marginalized condition of Dalits in her paper "Marginalized Victimhood: Doubly Subjugated and Triply Marginalized with a Detached Subhuman Existence by Hegemonic Caste System: A Study of Select Dalit Narratives". In the cultural set-up of the post-nineties, women have given expression towards their existence as a human being. In the world of women's literature, women's voices have been given recognition as well as veneration. Dr. Pratibha Patel's paper "A Representation of Unexplored Existential Consciousness in Namita Gokhale's *The Book of Shadows*" reveals the keen concern of a woman's life who confronts to survive in order to attain her existence once again. The paper is a close introspection of experiences of an acid victim who struggles for self-realization as an individual out of unfavourable circumstances amid nature to sustain her urge for living.

Who is a mother and who is a daughter? The answers to these questions are easy and they are related to biology. What is motherhood and what is daughterhood? No book of biology can define them to their depth. These questions have difficult and complex answers. When we try to define motherhood and daughterhood in a socio-cultural context, the answers are embedded in the conventional social structure. On the other hand, when we try to explore them on the socio-political terms, our narratives are mostly shaped by feminism. The definitions are never apolitical. In this context, Anamika Ghosh's paper "Torn Apart and Tied Up in Relations: Exploration of the Theme of Motherhood and Daughterhood in the Select Poems of Kamala Das and Eunice de Souza" seeks to study selective English poems of Kamala Das and Eunice de Souza to probe into issues related to motherhood and daughterhood. Anamika attempts to map the stereotypical and feministic, cultural and political implications of motherhood and daughterhood in the context of Indian society. The psychic and physical worlds of mothers and daughters are explored here from the perspectives of these two women poets of contemporary India. Ritushree Sengupta's paper "Interrogating the Female Poetic Voice: A Comparative Study of Sylvia Plath and Kamala Das" makes a comparative study between Kamala Das and Sylvia Plath to show how these two poets become confessional to depict the pathetic condition of women in society. It has been seen through generations that writers articulating emotions in any language has to return to its roots—roots of the nation, roots of the culture, or to the roots of its origin. Toru Dutt is not an exception, her return was obvious, but she has to struggle to fit herself in the gendered logic of nationalism as her voice was colonial. Deepayan Das's paper "Gendered Logic of Indian Nationalism and the Voice of Toru Dutt" attempts to explore the issues in Toru Dutt, who had to prove her authenticity for she transgressed the limits bound by male culture being women and being a writer in English.

The September 2001 attack on America's Twin World Trade Centre established terrorism as 'no-ignore' issue. Further, like a staircase to terrorism, it made violence leap up with demonic strides and stature. Does the Chinese maxim—"Kill one and frighten ten thousand", validate terror as extreme violence? Is terrorism an illness of 'have-nots' or the greed-tool of 'want-mores'? Symptomatically, the periphery is much limited for diagnosis as the reasons are not any more obscure as Terrorists and Naxalites are equally vocal in their say of needs. Dr. Madhu Kamra's paper "'The Triumph of Humanity': A Stylistic Appraisal of B.K.S. Ray's *Terror Must Die!*" observes the purpose and mode of B.K.S. Ray's *Terror Must Die!* as well as to understudy and to define, interpret, and assess Terrorism/Naxalism as a fatal malady. This implies that terrorism is much more than "a system of weapons", the poet, therefore, has much to say. A hero is representative of the community and his action is centred on events. In this paper, the hero under analysis is the Indian legendary hero from the Jammu region of Jammu and Kashmir, popularly known as Bawa Jitto, the dogra peasant hero who sacrificed his life for the rights of tillers against landlords five hundred years ago. Bawa Jitto lived five hundred years ago in a feudal society when the relationship between the 'jagirdar' and the peasant was that of the exploiter and the exploited. Dr. Vishali Sharma's paper "Hero in Transition: A Study of Dogra Peasant Hero in Ramnath Shastri's *Bawa Jitto*" intends to trace the transition of hero from "the humble, self-deprecating man" to "the compulsive rebel" who in the end becomes the scapegoat and random victim for the redemption of society. Guni Vats and Dr. V.P. Singh in their paper "The Reverberating Phonemes: A Post-structuralist Study of Rashid Jahan's Select Works" explicate the works of Rashid Jahan from a post-structuralist perspective.

Being victimized and subjugated by the fascism of Islamic fundamentalists, Taslima Nasrin launches a crusade against authoritarianism, be it social or patriarchal. In her 'heretical' writings like *French Lover* and *Lajja*, she intends to demoralise the gender intolerance of Islamic society along with its narrow-minded constructs. Not only this, her novels delve deep into the fact of how social discrimination becomes a bi-product of the religious and patriarchal scheme of marginalisation. *Lajja* and *French Lover*, being a critique of the social representation of women as a passive product or an object to possess and master subtly, advocates the author's liberal humanistic outlook. Infusing the issue of patriarchal and religious bigotry in *Lajja* and juxtaposing the dichotomies and contradictions of eastern and western culture in *French Lover*, she yearns to make readers realize that exploitation of the "weaker sex" is relevant to every possible earthly phenomenon. Paulomi Banerjee and Dr. Sucheta Kapoor's paper "Lack of 'musawa': The Issue of Gender Favouritism in Taslima Nasrin's *Lajja* and *French Lover*" analyses the issue of gender prejudice and its consequence of curbing the free-flow of the protagonists in the two eminent works of Taslima Nasrin, namely *Lajja* and *French Lover*. Partition not only charts down cartographical domains but entails a plethora of charting down metaphorical boundaries of social, political, and religious belief in lingual, cultural, communal, and psychological arenas. Seeing through the lens of Bhabha and Rushdie, Sayani Nayak's paper "'A Bit of Earth which had No Name, Lay Toba Tek Singh': A Critique of Individual's Identity in the *No-Man's Land*" explores the tangibility of borders, nation's role in consolidating one's identity, the hypocrisy of sane minds in the gruesome act of partition, and the identity of an individual in a no-man's land.

Rimpa Roy's paper "Burdened by Border: Mohsin Hamid's *Exit West*" hints at the discourse of borders and boundaries, the definition of identity and the dark magical doors which serves as artifice. The boundaries and migration forms a part of the collective identity and brings a sense of 'us' versus 'you'. The breach of the border always leaves a scar and narratives portray the mental trauma of how the border burdens the identity both national and individual. It is the border which acts upon the individual and is "both like dying and like being born" and clarifies the fact that "we are all migrants through time". The protagonists Nadia and Saeed in Mohsin Hamid's *Exit West* felt the same burden of the border during the period of war and, thus, gets connected to each other within the same vicinity. As they found the doors to go out of their burdened life, their strings got attached to other people. The idea of the border plays a big role in their relationship and the novel shows how the unmaking of the border makes their choices free. Socio-religious reforms have been the main concern of Sufi poets of Pakistan. These Sufi poets of the region through centuries have identified problems of society that ultimately turn into ailments and become harmful to society in general and the persons of a region or religion in particular. They have been suggesting reforms and cures which reveal that stress is laid upon reforms generated from inside. Their teachings are based on their belief that strength, sagacity, and sensibility that a society needs for reformation are present within the minds and the souls of the persons of that society. Shamaila Amir's paper "Suggested Socio-Religious Reforms by Regional Sufi (Mystic) Poets: An Analysis of the Select Poets of Punjab, Sindh, Khyber Pakhtunkhwa, and Baluchistan", explores the contents of selected poets of various regions of Pakistan to determine problematic aspects of society which can be reformed through socio-religious aspects of humans. This paper also determines chief characteristics which are essentials to be present in human nature for reforms in the society. *Seasonal Adjustments* (1994) by Adib Khan shows how Iqbal Chaudhuri, the protagonist of the novel, left Bangladesh for Australia soon after the war with Pakistan and after eighteen years has returned to his native land accompanied by his daughter Nadine. Iqbal's return to his home is precipitated by his marital crisis. Iqbal's journey is the author's own journey. There are moments when Iqbal felt re-connected, dislocated, and further realized his in-betweenness all at once. Throughout the novel, Iqbal is in the process of ever-transformation, continuous perambulation, and reconciliation. Adib Khan's frequent usage of flashbacks, description of specific events from Iqbal's life, sustains the notion that life cannot be separated into individual, isolated threads but "must remain interwoven in a complex texture". After spending nearly two decades in Australia, Iqbal has discovered that fitting in simply does not work out for him and just like seasonal changes he is constantly shaped through the difficulties of being outsider across different social spaces. Malini Chongder's paper "'Where are you going and where have you been?': A Reading of Adib Khan's *Seasonal Adjustments*" explores Iqbal's constant problem with his homeland, his sense of belongingness, ambivalent identity, etc. within a restricted extent.

Socio-political instability has been one of the most challenging problems of democratic governments across the world. The cultivation of extremist propaganda, the rising cult of popular religious fanaticism, and a right-wing shift towards identity politics with a misplaced sense of unity based on one nation, one religion, one identity, and one country has become an archaic and universal trope for the rising intolerance, generalized precarity, a neoconservative revival, and the persecution of what constitutes 'the other', 'the unfamiliar', 'the outsider'. The banality of homocentric religion as a culminating force for the persecution of heterogeneous ethnicities and other religious communities has assumed monstrous proportions. Taking a cue from the present spectre of incessant destruction and post-holocaust annihilation of humanity, Soma Mandal's paper "Cultivating Terror, Persecuting Humanity: The Fallacy of Insurgency and the Anxiety of Islam in Khaled Hosseini's Land of Kite Runner(s)" shows how Khaled Hosseini's *The Kite Runner* presents a sordid metaphor of a world where kite flying is no more allowed and the final destination of humanity is destined to be doomed and deadly like hell. The ban on socio-cultural traditions, rituals, and literary texts has led to the rise of fascist forces across the world. As the world undergoes several kinds of anxieties ranging from citizenship, nationality(-ies) and religion, Hosseini's narrative exemplifies that his narrative is not about the thousand splendid suns and the kites that are flown in Afghanistan but a sense of loss and lamentation for humanity amidst a world on the brink of collapse. The term "Bacha Posh" derived from the Dari language, a local language of Afghanistan, means a "girl dressed like a boy". This is a hidden phenomenon practising since ancient time. Mahamadul Hassan Dhabak's paper "Bacha Posh Tradition and Contradictions of Patriarchy in Nadia Hashimi's *The Pearl That Broke Its Shell*" examines the bacha posh tradition, an ancient tradition and how it functions within the extremely patriarchal society. It also explores the gendered structure in Afghanistan and how Nadia Hashimi demonstrates the bacha posh tradition, gender performance, and emotional turmoil during and after the gender transformation. "The Application of Folklore Principle to Study the Select Folktales of India and Bhutan" written by Dr. S. Chitra and Dechhen Dolma is the last article of this section and this paper makes a critical study of the select folktales of India and Bhutan.

The second part of this volume, namely "Glimpses of South Asian Culture and Society" consists of eight scholarly articles which define a few traits of South Asian society and culture. The beginning article of this section "The Innovation of the Sacred: The Movement of the "Sacredness" of Folk Religious Rituals and the Archaeological Process of Adaptation of Performances" by Anna Lynn Tom and Dr. Hemanga Dutta examines the archaeological movement within the performances that are inspirations for the adaptive procedure; the texts that speak of such performative moments and the adapted performances themselves. This is done, within the purview of Indian folk traditions and performative adaptations. Accordingly, the first section will trace the singular sacredness situated within certain theatrical and oral folk narratives of South Indian religious rituals. The second section examines how these folk traditions are inculcated into the movements of the performative adaptation of O.V. Vijayan's novella *Khasakkinte Itihasam* by Deepan Sivaraman, and also examines the later changes of layers of meanings associated to these folk narratives within the texts themselves and how this maps the relationship between the text, the performance, and the archaeological moment of adaptation; the third and final part examines the consequent meaning that such a transformation of performance means within the social level and the layers that are ascribed to the multiplicities of the old sacred in its movement towards a new, richer sacred. Dr. Prakash C. Balikai makes an ecological study of the river Tunga in his paper "River Tunga—The Mother of Malenadu: An Ecological Perspective". Born to a Scottish-Irish family and influenced by none other than the great teacher, Swami Vivekananda, himself, Margaret Elizabeth Noble occupies an imperative position in the sphere of Indian Philosophy and History of Indian freedom-struggle. Whereas the Indians perceived the nation-state as a matriarchal institution and conceived India as the "Motherland", the Europeans believed nation as a masculine political identity. Margaret Noble was also a product of this Western education, but Sister Nivedita or Bhagini Nivedita imbibed the impulses of Oriental learning and she transformed her thoughts accordingly. The objective of the paper, "The Oneness in The Other: Re-evaluating the Role of Sister Nivedita" by Subhajeet Singha is to focus on the difference between the Nation as a patriarch in the eyes of West and how it changed when Sister Nivedita equipped the opposite and transformed herself. This is a journey from one framework of History to another, altering the dimension altogether. This dichotomy of the two selves, the presentation of thesis and antithesis, has been shown by Subhajeet Singha in his paper.

Childhood obesity has become a global epidemic in recent years. The World Health Organization (WHO; 2017) reported that the obesity rate which was <1% among children and adolescents in 1975 has become almost 8% in boys and 6% in girls in 2016. Obesity in childhood is likely to bring obese adulthood and associate co-morbidities like diabetes mellitus, insulin resistance, cardiovascular disease, fatty liver, gout, and osteoarthritis. Obesity in children affects their physical, social, and emotional wellbeing; and also results in poor scholastic performance, overall such children experience low spirited lives. Asian countries have been contributing a lot to extend childhood obesity throughout the world. Like other developing countries, India, Bangladesh, Pakistan, or other South Asian countries have been suffering from both obesity and malnutrition. Changed dietary habit and physical inactivity among people of these countries are the causative factors behind this epidemiological transition. A judicious choice of nutrient-dense foods and physical activities is assumed to play a pivotal role to overcome such a crucial health problem. In this context, Chaitali Bose and Dr. Alak Kumar Syamal's paper "Childhood Obesity in South Asia" is aimed to unveil the obesity or overweight seen in South Asian countries in recent years and also to note some preventive measures like lifestyle modification which can be adopted at home or school level, as the modest way to control body weight. Patriarchal society denies gender equality. Ethnic and religious groups strongly rally against any progressive step to bring about gender equality as they find it threatening. It is the patriarchal structure of a community that decides the course of gender. Males subjugate women by controlling all avenues of power. Sometimes this suppression and exploitation takes violent forms such as domestic violence, rape, honour killings, etc. In patriarchal societies, masculine and feminine qualities are condoned which makes women the most vulnerable and marginalized section of society. Dr. Kauser Tasneem's paper "Patriarchy and Female Subordination: Exploring the Equality Debate" attempts to analyze patriarchy and female subordination and how patriarchy benefits from the marginalization of women from the agencies of power. While Dr. K. Subapriya presents a socio-cultural study of Narikuravar tribes in her paper "Story of Progress: A Study of Narikuravar Tribes in Eraiyur Village at Perambalur District of Tamil Nadu", Nabanita Dhali's paper "Scroll Paintings of Naya: A Study of the Cultural Shift from Myth to Modernity" talks about scroll paintings of Naya. The concluding paper of this volume "Ritual, Body, Ecology-Interrogating Politics involved in the Celebration of 'menstruation' in the *Raja* Festival of Odisha" written by Pragnya Parimita Chayani seeks to analyse the rituals of 'Raja' in order to undertake a critique of the popular Odia belief that 'Raja' celebrates womanhood. At the same time, the paper agrees with Simone de Beauvoir's assertion that a "woman is made", and endeavours to show how through the practice of modern myths and rituals of the Earth (Gaia), the Odia women are subjugated.

The volume makes a humble attempt to showcase the nuances of South Asian literature, culture and society. Furthermore, this book can give a global perspective where readers, scholars, and academicians can read, understand, realize, and appreciate the socio-cultural and literary traits of South Asia. Despite many socio-cultural, political, religious, and economic problems, unity is there among South Asian countries and this book confirms to what Vina Mazumdar says in her article "Women and

Development: The South Asian Experience and Expectations" published in the book *Emerging South Asian Order: Hopes and Concerns* (1995) edited by Sankar Ghosh and Soumen Mukherjee:

> Despite many differences in ideology, there is a clear trend towards unity on major issues and efforts to cut across class, community, and religious divides—in opposing the negative impacts of globalization, the environment—population debate, fundamentalism-communalism of various hues, and violence—against women, and others—from the domestic to the social, economic, and political arena. Unity is also clear in the choice of alternative strategies for development, in the selection of key areas for organizing and advocacy, and the increasing emphasis, even dependence on poor omen at the grassroots as the most powerful force and agency in breaking the hardened mould of the hierarchy-patriarchy combine that continues to dominate the social system. (310-11)

Goutam Karmakar

Section I

Mapping South Asian Literature

Chapter 1

Liminality and Second-Generation Indian Migrant's Subject Position in Jhumpa Lahiri's *Nobody's Business*

Pankaj Luchan Gogoi

"Nobody's Business", a constituent story of Jhumpa Lahiri's short-story collection *Unaccustomed Earth* and narrated by the third person omniscient narrator, seems to be exclusively concerned with the liminality or "in-betweenness" of the second-generation Indian diaspora. For this, the story puts the second-generation Indian diaspora Sangeeta Biswas alias Sang, in liminality in the U.S. She is away from her parents, relatives, and compatriots, and finds herself amongst the foreign nationals of other countries. Under such circumstance, she has to lead her life characterized by alienation, struggle, and uncertainty which define her subjectivity in liminality. Prior to the nuanced analysis of the character of Sangeeta, it is imperative to talk about her family. The story is deliberately silent upon the details of her family, unlike the other stories of the collection; but is limited to the cursory reference to it. There are only two passing references to her parents and three references to her sister. Parents' first reference comes at the beginning of the story in terms of her marriage as they "desperately wanted her to be married" (Lahiri, 175), and the second reference comes towards the end of it when Sang is absent at the time of payment of her rent at the Brookline house. Similarly, the first reference to her sister comes when she visits her sister in London as "Her sister had had a baby boy recently" (191). The second reference comes when Sang visits her after the breakdown of her relationship with Farouk. The third reference to her sister comes when Paul and Heather, Sang's housemates in Brookline, think of calling her in London when the payment of the house rent is due at Sangeeta's absence. From the parents' references, it is assumed that they are in America but away from Brookline where Sangeeta lives. There is not a single mention of India, their ancestral land which further reinforces their stay in the U.S. only. Ed Minus notices this absence of India in immigrant Indians in *Unaccustomed Earth* and comments: "I was struck by how seldom thoughts of their mother country impinge on the consciousness of Lahiri's immigrants except in the most personal and incidental terms. Many of them annually return home, and they communicate with family and friends left behind, but India as a vital geopolitical phenomenon seems hard to exist for them" (Knoph, lxxxiv). Her sister is in London with her family, and there is no mention of parents either living or visiting her. Hence, Sangeeta is all alone in Brookline where she experiences her liminality all alone. Interestingly, housemates of Sangeeta are also foreign nationals, but their nationality is not disclosed. Paul, though initially appears to be Bengali, does not turn out to be so. For, had he been a Bengali he would not have got puzzled with her name or complexion: "what sort of name Sang was, half expecting a Japanese woman. It wasn't until she wrote out a check for her security deposit at the end of her visit that he saw that her official name was Sangeeta Biswas" (77).

Besides, they have never spoken in Bengali, and Paul does not have even the "far-fetched connection" (175) that Sangeeta's Bengali suitors have. Therefore, Sangeeta's subjectivity in Brooklyn is completely shaped and reshaped by foreign nationals and foreign environment; be it Heather and Paul, whose nationalities are not established, and Farouk, the Egyptian, and Deirdre, the Canadian. The liminal subject positions of two second-generation Indians, viz. Sangeeta and her sister are shown through further displacement. Sangeeta is displaced within the U.S. away from her parents and she hardly feels any tilt towards her ethnic Bengali or in larger sense Indian roots as strikingly seen in her refusing the marriage proposals of well-established Bengali bachelors. Similarly, her sister's has moved to another continent Europe to live in London with her family, although the text is silent on whether she has gone to England to secure career or for her marriage, and also silent on the nationality of her husband in London. Lahiri has deliberately adopted these silences just to accentuate the immeasurable depths of liminality which define today's second-generation Indian diaspora, leaving the readers to gauge the depths on their own. From the experience of the Lahirian world of *Interpreter of Maladies*, *The Namesake*, and the other stories of *Unaccustomed Earth* the readers are certainly aware of the liminal discourse of the author, and hence can sense its presence in different dimension in "Nobody's Business" as attempted to be projected through the character of Sangeeta.

In "Nobody's Business", liminality is not obvious as the other stories of the collection. Here, it is hidden and only a keen reading digs out its the deeply embedded layers in the story. On the surface, the story seems to be a love story of a young girl, but below the surface lies liminality that unsettles the characters in their subject positions. The story is circled around two triangles; one the housemate triangle in the Brookline house where three unknown persons Paul, Heather, and Sang, with different priorities of their lives, become housemates, and the love triangle of Sangeeta, Farouk, and Deirdre. Their nationalities, ethnicities, and priorities of life are different, and they are the children, the second generation of their parents. They meet each other as co-incidence in Brookline experiencing displacement from their homes. The first triangle sets the story in motion whereas the second one becomes the climax of it with Sangeeta as the meeting point of both. Sangeeta is the central character of the story, and through her, the liminality of the second-generation Indian diaspora is brought to the fore. Sangeeta's liminal subjectivity is highlighted through Paul's observation on the one hand, and on the other, her academic and professional career, and her personal life.

The action of the story begins when Sangeeta Biswas or Sang is at her marriageable age of thirty. She has a number of suitors, mostly Bengali settled in different parts of America like Partha Mazoomdar from Cleveland or elsewhere like Ashim Bhattacharya from Geneva. It appears that the Bengali suitors wish to get married with a Bengali girl because they, too, have got entrenched in liminality, and wish to have some semblance of roots on foreign soil. It is because of their liminal subject positions, that they have a hazy idea on Sang despite sharing the same ethnic origin. Their inaccurate information on Sangeeta vis-à-vis her profile is reflective of inadequacy that is inherent in liminality:

> Every so often a man called for Sang, wanting to marry her. Sang usually didn't know these men. Sometimes she had never even heard of them. But they'd heard that she was pretty and smart and thirty and Bengali and still single, and so these men, most of whom also happened to be Bengali, would procure her number from someone who knew someone who knew her parents, who, according to Sang, desperately wanted her to be married. (174)

Sang is a graduate from NYU in philosophy and is a dropout of Harvard after the first semester. But due to limited connection, the suitors procure inappropriate information on Sang and hence consider her to be a graduate from Columbia in physics and a doctorate from Harvard. It is assumed that the Bengali suitors are also second-generation migrants, and therefore, they are not interested in marrying a Bengali girl situated in their ancestral land India, instead, from the Bengali diasporic community.

Lahiri, time and again, seems to portray liminality as a zone for exploring one's future regardless of its derived results. All the characters portrayed in the text are situated in Brooklyn to shape their future in a present characterized by liminality. Paul is pursuing his PhD in English and European Literature, Heather is pursuing Law, Sangeeta is working a part-time job at a bookstall after having got dropped out of Harvard, Farouk is serving as a professor of Middle Eastern history at Harvard, and Dierdre is pursuing interior design. In all their careers, it is seen they are all struggling hard to survive in the U.S. which calls for intense hard work in pursuit of one's dream, and the way in which this dream subjectifies their liminal subjectivity is seen in Sang's parents' reaction to her failure, and also preparation of Sang and Farouk:

> She told him that after she dropped out of Harvard a year ago, her mother locked herself up in her bedroom for a week and her father refused to speak to her. She'd had it with academia, hated how competitive it was, how monkish it forced one to become. That was what her boyfriend did, always blocking off chunks of his day and working at home with the phone unplugged, writing papers for the next conference. (Lahiri, 181)

In the liminal subject position, there is a clash between interest and preference amongst the people of the same ethnic group. They may either like or dislike their roots, and the choice is driven by the reality they experience in liminality. This is noticeably shown in the marriage proposals to Sang and her response to them. Despite the frequency of good proposals, Sang does not show any interest in them. For, the proposals are driven by some considerations like degree, job, and ethnicity; but not love. In liminality, Sang is ridden by loneliness, and she is starved for love. She does not find her love in her ethnicity, but in multiculturalism, and hence she rejects the offers of Bengali suitors. It is undoubtedly a case of alienation and unsettlement on the part of the Sang in her host country. She develops an affair with Farouk, the Egyptian who is a professor of Middle Eastern History at Harvard. It is for her search of love she rejects the lucrative offers much to the surprise of Paul and Heather, her housemates. On being told by Heather about the prospective proposals as "romantic" (176), Sang says: "It's not love" (176), and proudly declares: "I have a boyfriend" (176). It is a kind of her "sexual rebellion" (Koshy, 360) against her parents and the concept of arranged marriage on the line of ethnicity. Sang knows that the proposals made by the suitors are not driven by love, but by gossip based on misinformation and communication gap. The prospective Bengali grooms in their liminal subjectivity have little knowledge or understanding of their prospective Bengali brides, and it is this sense of incompleteness even in the understanding of their own people is what characterizes the unsettled life of the migrants abroad:

> They were interested in a mythical creature created by an intricate chain of gossip, a web of wishful Indian community

> thinking in which she was an ageing, overlooked poster child for years of Bharatanatyam classes, perfect SATs. Had they any idea who she actually was and how she made a living, in spite of her test scores, which was by running a cash register and arranging paperback books in pyramid configurations, they would want nothing to do with her. (176)

In order to further elaborate Sang's liminal subjectivity, Lahiri takes recourse to metaphors—Penelope and Madame Defarge. In this regard, the character of Paul plays a crucial role in underlining the uncertainty that looms over her marriage. Given the incessant flow of proposals, it is Paul who calls her Penelope, the Odysseyan beauty of Homer. Like Penelope, who refuses the proposals of her suitors by weaving and unweaving the same shroud, Sang too, refuses the proposals of her suitors by one excuse or the other. While talking to them Sang sometimes writes down the names of suitors, or their hobbies. She asks them whether they have job satisfaction or not. To each of them, be he is an economist, doctor, or metallurgical engineer, she raises this question just to negate the process, and keep them at abeyance. Ironically, the question about job satisfaction is related to their existence in liminality. However, it is seen that in her liminal subject position, talking to her suitors reflects two aspects of her life. First, a time well spent in which feels herself to be an important one in an otherwise tedious life of working in a part-time job at a bookstall, away from parents, and living with two unknown persons Paul and Heather with whom she does not have too much intimacy. Secondly, it reflects her indecisiveness in choosing her life partner with whom she can spend a meaningful life:

> Her excuse to these men, her rebuttal to their offers to wine and dine her, was always the same white lie: she was busy at the moment with classes, it's being Harvard and all. Sometimes, if Paul happened to be sitting at the table, she would write him a note in the middle of the conversation: "He sounds like he's twelve" or "Total dweeb" or "This guy threw up once in my parents' swimming pool, waving the pad for Paul's benefit as she cradled the phone to her ear". (175)

After having observed these rejections by her, Paul resembles her to *Odyssey*'s Penelope: "You're like Penelope" (176). Sang's reply to this observation of Paul is also worth noticing: "Penelope. Only I can't knit" (177). Here, she inappropriately uses the word "knit" instead of "weave" that is soon corrected by Paul. It symbolizes her incapacity to relate to the people in her subject position and understanding them in the right context. Her desperate attempt to relate to the people is evident in her question: "Then, who's the woman who knits?" (177). Paul replies to her that it is Madame Defarge of Dicken's *A Tale of Two Cities*. Through the question, she refuses to be Penelope whom she more resembles in actual sense and tries to relate herself to Madam Defarge given her love affair with Farouk.

Sang's love affair with Farouk seems to be the greatest irony of her life. Despite the warmth in the relation as marked in regular calling and meeting, she has limited knowledge of Farouk. Here, her plight is no less than her suitors. Actually, the inadequacy of knowledge vis-à-vis the person with whom one is forging tie or the circumstance in which one is operating is what defines one's liminality. That is why, Sang is incapable of knowing Farouk in spite of having intimacies at all levels—"we're a serious couple, too" (198). Her ignorance of Farouk's affair with Dierdre, a Canadian woman, bears testimony to it. The moment Sang comes to know about the affair there is acrimony between them leading to the breakup of her relationship with Farouk. This break up stands for the persistent uncertainty of life in liminality. It renders Sang into the fit of loneliness and frustration:

> Sang gets trapped in a masochistic relationship with Farouk, an Egyptian-American academic. Ironically, her quest for sexual self-determination and recognition in a romantic relationship, the overdetermined site of liberal autonomy and the putative antithesis of arranged marriages, propels her into an abject feminine role more conventional and confining than the one she sought to escape in her parent's match-making efforts. The tropes of escape and entrapment run into each other in the story, figuring the dizzying ambiguities of internationality and consent in the minefields of sexual and generational rebellion. (Koshy, 361)

There are some sporadic hints off and on; but Sang fails to read out the situation due to her immaturity, gullibility, and away from parental guidance. She has to make her own decision and is herself to suffer its consequence. Nobody is around her; even she has not intimated the events to her parents. There is not a single instance in which it is shown that she is consulting the matter with her parents or sister. Besides, she does not consider her housemates Paul and Heather as close confidantes with whom she can share her inner feelings. This is evident in the observation of Paul vis-à-vis Sang, "They were friendly, but they were not friends" (199). Lahiri situates these characters away from the influence of parents and kins, and hence negotiation with the vicissitudes of life in liminality is one's own business and nobody's business. In the other stories of the collection, Lahiri has shown umpteen times the presence of parental influence, recommendation, guidance in the matter of their children's marriage. It is this consideration of one's own matter as one's exclusive zone puts subjectivity in real test. And tragedy lies in the fact that one does not fully know the nature of one's own business until its fallout comes to the fore. Farouk has been infidel to Sang throughout the affair with her; but, her understanding of him is limited to accusations only: "She was accusing: Why didn't he ever want to meet her friends? Why didn't he invite her to his cousin's house for Thanksgiving? Why didn't he like to spend the night together? Why, at the very least, didn't he drive her home?" (189).

She considers the affair with Farouk as "abnormal" (189) given Farouk's not dropping her home, and not living in the same house. She asks: "How are we ever going to get married? [...] Are we supposed to live in separate houses forever?" (189). These valid questions provoke him to the extent that he calls Sang "hysterical" (189) and warns her "I will not spend my life with a woman who makes scenes" (189). This altercation simply reflects that everything in her liminal subjectivity is defined by make-shift, provisional arrangement devoid of certainty. Like her relationship with Paul and Heather, her part-time job, her casual response to some well-placed suitors with the same ethnicity and nationality, her hazardous relation with Farouk all embody uncertainty and unsettlement of liminality.

Besides, the telephonic conversation in which Deirdre confesses to Paul, and Sang listens to it by different phone connection that Deirdre has an affair with Farouk, is also misunderstood by her. She does not even believe that Farouk can have an affair with Dierdre, and hence suspects Paul of having framed the fictitious story of Farouk and Dierdre just to win her as his beloved: "I mean, it's one thing for you to like me, Paul," she continued. "It's one thing for you to have a crush. But to make up a story like that—"She stopped, her mouth now straining into something that was not a smile. "It's pathetic, really. Pathetic!" (206).

To Sang, the real love affair between Farouk and Dierdre is, thus, a case of fiction hatched by Paul. Dierdre case too reflects Sang's half-knowledge with which she befools herself by giving a clean chit to both Farouk and Dierdre: "They talk, like, once a year. Farouk mentioned my name to her years ago when we first got together when he lived in another apartment, and she remembered it. She was trying to get in touch with him because she's getting married, and she wanted to send Farouk an invitation. She didn't have Farouk's new address or his number, and he's not listed. That's why she tried here" (205).

This assertiveness notwithstanding, Sang is going to be severally disturbed at heart. Because, she has rejected so many suitors just for Farouk, and the person turns out to be untrustworthy. It takes little time for her to discover the fickle nature of Farouk that resulted in a fight and eventual break-up of the tie. Her wish to have a permanent relationship with her own predilection seems to be a mirage in the liminality. Her visit to London to meet her sister is a virtual escape on her part from the pangs of her liminal subject position in Brookline, and a desperate attempt on her attempt to survive by clinging somehow to her roots whereas her sister is herself rootless in England negotiating her liminality on her own. Though the text does not provide the details of the sister, it can be assumed that she is a success story in liminality in England. For, she rears a family there and also provides refuge to her disheartened sister who has flown across the Atlantic to join her there. Therefore, success or failure in liminal subjectivity depends a lot upon the individual's own sensibility, intuition and resilience as Lahiri has shown in the preceding story "Only Goodness".

"Nobody's Business" is an ordeal for the second-generation Indian migrant in liminality. The story traces Sangeeta, the second-generation Indian migrant away from her parental supervision and clearly shows the different path she treads upon as per her understanding and need of her luminal subject position. The story is a true testimony to the second-generation migrant's subjectivity being formed by uncertainty and unsettlement of liminality in a foreign country.

REFERENCES

Bertens, Hans. *Literary Theory: The Basics*. London: Routledge, 2007. Print.

Bhabha, Homi K. *The Location of Culture*. New York: Routledge, 1994. Print.

Blackwell, Wiley. *A Concise Companion to Postcolonial Literature*. West Sussex: John Wiley & Sons Ltd., 2014. Print.

Das, Bijay Kumar. *Twentieth-Century Literary Criticism*. New Delhi: Atlantic Publishers & Distributors, 2010. Print.

Harte, Leah. "The Borderlands of Identity and a B-Side to the Self: Jhumpa Lahiri's 'When Mr. Pirzada Came to Dine,' 'The Third and Final Continent' and 'Unaccustomed Earth.'" *Passages: Movements and Moments in Text and Theory*. Eds. Maeve Tynan, Maria Beville and Marita Ryan. UK: Cambridge Scholars Publishing, 2009. 63-75. Print.

Koshy, Susan. "Neoliberal Family Matters." *American Literary History*, 25.2 (Summer 2013). 344-80. Print.

Lahiri, Jhumpa. *Interpreter of Maladies*. New Delhi: HarperCollins Publishers India, 1999. Print.

—. *Unaccustomed Earth*. New Delhi: Penguin Random House, 2013. Print.

Maxey, Ruth. *South Asian Atlantic Literature*, 1970-2010. Edinburgh: Edinburgh University Press, 2012. Print.

Minus, Ed. "Passages from India." *The Sewanee Review*, 116.4 (Fall 2008): lxxxiv-lxxxv. Print.

Chapter 2

Of Potent Matchboxes: Reading Women, Space, and Power in Ashapurna Debi's *Wealth* ('Oishorjo')

Basudhara Roy

The name of Ashapurna Debi needs no introduction to the world of Bengali letters, for in the mostly male-dominated sphere of Bengali literary writing in the early nineteenth century, she distinctly stands out as a pioneering female presence. In more than seventy-odd years of her robust literary career, spanning both colonial and post-independent times, Ashapurna Debi (1909-95) published more than 300 books which included around 176 novels in addition to a large number of short stories, articles, poems, and children's books, making a mark for herself as a writer not merely by her prolificacy and the staggering bulk of her literary output, but more significantly, by the delicacy of her art, the finesse of her sensibility, and by her indefatigable literary commitment to the issues affecting women of her time. A recipient of the Sahitya Akademi Award and the first Indian woman to be honoured by the Jnanpith Award, Debi's works while recording considerable commercial success, have also afforded frequent comparisons with the two great doyens of Bengali literature—Sarat Chandra and Tagore, whose sensitivity and craft as fiction-writers, Debi has indubitably matched, if not excelled. However, detractors of her work, too have galored. Ashapurna Debi has frequently been taken to task by critics for what are generally perceived to be the unforgivable limitations of her fictional canvas—her narrow thematic preoccupation with home, women, and middle-class domesticity; her apparently apolitical, even conservative stance as a writer; and the lack of an engagement of her work with the wider and more significant social issues of her turbulent times. Criticism such as this has attempted to thwart attention from the maturity of Debi's fictional art and the socio-political relevance of her work, leading to the establishment of her reputation as a writer of non-serious popular fiction with the result that her oeuvre has largely been scanted in serious academia and has, as Jhumpa Lahiri puts it, run the risk of being not only "misunderstood as a dubious representative of 'third-world feminism' but also of being exiled to the ancillary realm of regional literature" (xxii).

That Debi's fiction locates itself primarily within the middle-class Bengali homes of Calcutta is a fact that needs not be denied for every writer is nourished by the milieu s/he inhabits and Ashapurna Debi, in living out the conventional life of the typical early nineteenth-century Bengali woman, picked up her entire fictional material from the substance of her lived experiences. Born in colonial Bengal in 1909, married at the age of fifteen and denied like most women of her time, an opportunity of formal education, Ashapurna Debi was, however, inspired by her artist father and book-loving mother to a deep and abiding love for literature and had been encouraged to self-teach herself to read and write, publishing her first poem in a children's magazine at the early age of thirteen. This love for writing was, fortunately, encouraged by her husband Kalidas Gupta which led to Debi's establishment of a flourishing literary career "within her own home, in conjunction with her duties as a wife, mother, and member of a traditional Bengali joint family" (Lahiri, xvi). It is this middle-class life of Bengali domesticity lived within the four walls of an urban Calcutta home which becomes the permanent insular milieu of Debi's fiction. Lahiri writes:

> Although Calcutta's presence—its diversity, adversity, incongruities, and energies—unmistakably shape Debi's imagined world, the stories themselves take place almost exclusively behind drawn curtains and locked doors, inside the city's millions of flats, quarters, bungalows, and other dwellings. It is Debi's tendency to isolate a small spatial unit, such as an apartment, a neighbourhood, or a city

> block, and to explore in microscopic detail the manner of life identified with that place. To read Ashapurna Debi is to cross the thresholds of Calcutta's inhabitants, to witness intimately their private scenes and struggles, and to encounter life in the city from a distinctly interior perspective. (xii)

This "interior perspective" becomes Debi's very own six inches of Austen-like ivory and though it constitutes a spatial limitation to her work, it does not in any way inhibit the force and power of her writing. Debi's short stories, in the rich variety of plot, narrative, and characters that they offer, can neither be accused of thematic monotony, nor of stylistic jadedness, and nor can they be read as conservative pieces that end up reifying the existing structures of patriarchy. Tharu and Lalita are of the opinion that the critical dismissal of much of Ashapurna Debi's writing stems from the overt absence of radicality in it and they find Debi wanting as a serious writer in what they perceive as:

> the apparently conservative posture her narratives promote. Rebellion, defiance, anger, resentment, and passion are portrayed to evoke our sympathy. But [...] order, somewhat chastened no doubt, is always carefully restored. It is as if, given the scheme of the Ashapurna world, a rebellion that stubbornly insists on its fruits is an escapist dream. (476)

Manisha Roy, also accusing Debi of conservatism, argues that her popularity as a writer stems from her conformity to traditional values and roles for women so that her novels "which emphasize the glory of conjugal love in an urban setting, are frequently given to brides as wedding presents" (57). The fact, however, remains that Debi writing from within and about the thick of domestic life is a writer politically aware and insurgent in her own way. The insularity of her fictional world, as Lahiri points out, has denied her the kind of critical attention that her contemporary Bengali writer, Mahasweta Devi has received in full measure. As Lahiri remarks, "Mahasweta Devi's work, linked to such theoretical hotbeds as gender, ethnicity, caste, and class, fits conveniently into contemporary academic agendas and their pursuit of 'socially' based texts" (xxii). However, as she defiantly argues, "just as Mahasweta Devi's writing is appreciated for its resistance and rebellion on a public and political level, so must Ashapurna Debi's be read as exemplary of the insurgency on the private, domestic level" (xxii). The potential for radicality, for challenging, upsetting and subverting intact structures of power may be difficult to discern in Ashapurna Debi's stories at first glance, but the motivation fueling her aims as a writer remains clearly and consistently transgressive. As Dipannita Datta emphasizes, "In trying to adopt an alternative strategy to be heard, Ashapurna Debi chose to explore her marginalized position and voice it in her writings. Her agenda was to create a space for women where their plight would be voiced and consequently, be transmitted, in order to be heard" (10).

Debi's stories, in all that they project, essentially give voice to the status, identity, trials, and tribulations of the women of nineteenth-century Bengal and this fostering of a literary space for the depiction of the realistic, workaday, private world of women within the nationalistic and male-dominated discourse that was widely building in the period constitutes in itself an act of transgression, a political demand for expression, cognizance, and reception. The conflicts around which Debi's plots build themselves are potent ideological issues that bring out the tug-of-war between tradition and modernity that waged throughout the nineteenth century and her stories throw poignant light on the pros and cons of the Woman Question—on women's right to education, creativity, privacy, property, equity, and justice quite ahead of her times.

Though Debi is no loud feminist, seeking attention by her visible radicality of opinion or position, her work clearly, does not suffer in-depth, breadth or significance from the spatial limitations of her experience and fictional material. Rather as Lahiri states:

> In Debi's work, domesticity constitutes the very means by which resistance and a struggle towards reform are articulated. The characters' relationships to physical space are representative, on a concrete level, of an individual's relationship to liberty, both personal and public. The home

> serves as a locus for dramatizing not only constraints placed upon women, but upon men, children, the elderly, servants, and even the homeless. While culturally specific and bound to a restricted sense of place, Debi's stories resonate beyond both architectural and national borders. (xxiii)

This paper shall take up for critical study from the small volume of Ashapurna Debi's translated work in English, her short story "Oishorjo" or "Wealth" and shall attempt to read in the socio-cultural context of the nineteenth century its insular family drama as a substantiation of the writer's literary subversion of the patriarchal ideas on Bengali wifehood. "Wealth" constitutes the first tale in the collection of twenty-one stories of Debi translated into a "Bengali English" by Prasenjit Gupta. Almost all of the stories in this volume have been taken from Debi's *Sunirbachita Sreshtha Galpa* (*Self-selected Best Stories*) published by the Model Publishing House in Calcutta in 1988. The translator has aptly chosen to title the collection—*Matchbox*, and though the story which gives its name to the volume is simple enough, even ostensibly concluding on a restoration of patriarchal order, it memorably leaves behind a powerful feminist image of transgression—that of the matchbox or *deshlai baksho* which both thematically and ideologically looms large over the volume as a whole. In her story "Matchbox"/*Deshlai Baksho*, Debi writes:

> This—this is precisely why I compare women to matchboxes. Even when they have the means within themselves to set off many raging fires, they never flare up and burn away the mask of men's high-mindedness, their large-heartedness. They don't burn up their own colourful shells. They won't burn them—and the men know this too. That's why they leave them scattered so carelessly in the kitchen, in the pantry, in the bedroom, here, there, anywhere. And quite without fear, they put them in their pockets. (108)

The above extract effectively encapsulates both Debi's inclination and reserve towards and against feminism and offers a keen insight into her ideological position on the woman question. Her women, though they choose to remain within the fold of patriarchy, are potent matchboxes that could spark off much rebellion if they decided to. Debi is of the opinion that women, voluntarily and by choice, retreat into silence in the face of patriarchal power, but their silence must in no way be interpreted as docility, powerlessness, or acquiescence for women find their own subjective ways to emotionally voice their resistance and make byways within patriarchal highroads. As Debi herself says: her female characters despite their commonplaceness, remain exemplary in militating against the unjust dictates of patriarchy:

> I have written about women within the middle-class households. But I have written about those who have not been able to accept the intolerable situations within the homes. If the situation demands—then they give up home or their husbands. All along within my mind there was an element of uncompromising rebellion, but that was never apparent. You may even call it the desire for women's liberation. But that urge was not a personal one. It was directed towards the progress of society and the community as such. (qtd. in Dasgupta, 48)

"Wealth" pictures a typical upper-middle-class Bengali family in which live two married brothers, Srikumar and Shukumar; their respective wives, Oporna and Abha; and their children. The plot circles around Srikumar's habit of visiting the *kotha* every evening, a practice that is being carried on for the last eighteen years under the arrangements of his wife, Oporna, and the responses of the various members of the family to this. Srikumar, as the third-person narrative informs us, royally goes out to register his attendance for two hours every evening at "a Bai's house to hear her sing" (8). In the socio-cultural world of the story represented by the ritualistic younger brother, Shukumar, his wife Abha, and their guest, the widowed cousin Nonda, this constitutes an act of gross family dishonour. Perceived, in general, to be a blot on family respectability, Srikumar's act is also interpreted to be one that should ideally cause a deep disgrace to his wife and should belittle her identity and status in a grave way. However, for Srikumar's wife, Oporna, the case is different. She, who in Abha's words "should have sunk into the earth with this black mark of fortune" appears, on the other hand, to be forever mocking the world "with that sharp instrument, her invisible smile" (5). Oporna's imperturbability despite her position as the second woman in her husband's affections constitutes the cause of Abha's perpetual discontent:

> [...] is there only one reason for Abha's burning anger? Oporna? That special cast of Oporna's lips? Why cannot Abha look directly at her? Why does standing in front of Oporna make her feel somehow smaller, and—yes, nothing's hidden from the mind—inferior?... What source of contentment keeps Oporna always so pleased? As she thinks about this, Abha grows restless and unhappy. (5)

The plot of the story revolves around this emotive complex—Abha's vehement dislike for Oporna owing to her failure to assess and understand the latter's calm composure in the face of the disreputable conduct of her husband, and her marvel at the source of Oporna's relentless complacence. The story's title "Wealth", in fact, relates to the glory of no material possession, but to Oporna's wealth of a mature mind, a trusting heart, and a secure affection, all of which, as the story's conclusion establishes, Abha abysmally lacks in, with the result that she fails to summon any faith in the integrity of her husband despite his strict practices of ritualistic religiosity.

In "Wealth", Debi despite the presence of men seems to focus exclusively on her women for both Srikumar and Shukumar remain, beyond their function in the plot, a part merely of the narrative's backdrop. Under close narrative focus are four women—the two married women in the story, Oporna and Abha; and the two women who stand out of the marital fold—the widowed cousin, Nonda, and the courtesan, Kanchon, who though physically absent from the narrative, constitutes an inseparable part of it. The story thematically locates itself in the dense confluence of the nineteenth-century discourse on Bengali womanhood and converges on the cultural opposition set up between the colonial figure of the courtesan on the one hand and on the other, that of the gentle-woman or the *bhadramahila* generated by the progressive-reformist nationalistic discourse of the period, to the idea of which marital identity was pre-requisite. Built into the conflict of values within the story is a teeming crucible of problems, both sociological and emotional, that range from the experience of home as a site of inequality and victimization; the altered cultural signification of the status and vocation of the courtesan in colonial India; the inhibition of patriarchally coded gentility on the *bhadramahila*; the socio-cultural marginalization of widows; the omnipresent threat of the 'other woman' in middle-class conjugality given the practice of the early marriage of girls; the layers of hypocrisy under which social respectability is shrouded; and the difficulties of acquiring and keeping love in life.

Though the narrative describes Srikumar's evening ritual of going out through unmistakable cultural signifiers—

> Srikumar descended the stairs and walked across the courtyard, and the air filled with the scent of expensive cologne. Wearing a Panjabi of glossy addhi cotton frilled by hand, the pleats of his dhuti—of the finest quality, and also hand-frilled—skimming the ground, expensive leather Grecians on his feet, silver-cased walking-stick in his hand, walking rapidly, Srikumar went out. (1)

It remains an act socially unmentionable within the so-called respectable world of the story: "Where he goes—that is not unknown, certainly, but unspoken. Everyone knows it, but no one says it clearly, out loud. They don't say it—perhaps to preserve the honour of the master of the house, or perhaps the mistress's!" (2).

Once a figure of high respectability and great wealth, power, and social position allied to the creation, safeguarding, and the connoisseurship of the arts of music and dance in pre-colonial India, the social perception of the courtesan under the colonial administration had dwindled into that a woman of dubious character, almost to that of a prostitute. The socio-cultural reception of Srikumar's habit within the story is, thus, a moral judgement passed on his integrity of character on the one hand, and on the other, on his wife's inability to 'keep' him 'completely tied to her *anchol*'. Uninterrogated in the public sphere, Srikumar constitutes within the private household spaces of the bedroom, kitchen, and the courtyard, the primary subject of gossip and rumour, and significantly, even Oporna on being directly questioned about her husband, has no words to describe, justify, or legitimize his habit other than the statement that he has a rendezvous. Even in discussing the matter directly with Srikumar, the courtesan is civilly brushed aside. Unnamed, she remains unindividualized and is at Oporna's best, a "fellow-creature", the concern for whose well-being prompts her to let her husband's bachelor practice go on but the very mention of her name by Srikumar rouses the genteel housewife to a sharply admonishing cry of "Chhi". Thus, in establishing Kanchon as a signified without a signifier, as a gap in signification that though allowed and interpreted, must not be named or interrogated, Debi narratively emphasizes the courtesan's social and cultural marginality in the nineteenth century. And yet, the judgement on Srikumar's character is in no way the final judgment of the story, for as Debi narratively emphasizes, character, honour, and respectability are all cultural constructs devoid of identifiable meaning and preserved only linguistically. Abha's husband Shukumar who, in accordance with his family's respectability, has no immoral habits and engages in the ritualistic practise of Brahmanical faith, eating strictly vegetarian meals and observing fasts and celibacy regularly, is no more 'respectable' than his brother as the bitter irony of the concluding lines establish: "When she (Abha) imagines the train compartment with no third person present (her husband and his cousin, the widowed Nonda being the other two), she feels like hitting her head against the wall and dying. Who knows her husband better than she does?" (15).

Debi's narrative appears to emphasize the ubiquity of unequal hegemonic codes on women of her times. While dutiful housewives like Oporna and Abha must cater to unfaithful husbands and to homes that they feel unable to feel at home in, the relative freedom of the widow Nonda and the courtesan Kanchon is equally deceptive for out of the marital fold, their situation on the social-ladder is far worse. The final revelation of the story that Shukumar, despite his ritualistic devotion to religion is no better than a libertine in the knowledge of his wife, leaves the critical reader pondering over the symbolism of the story's title. Does the title symbolize the wealth of Oporna's faith in her husband that gives her, as Abha feels, "this wealth of foolhardiness" (13), allows her "to send her husband into the tigress's cage, to leave him before the she-snake's outspread hood?" Does it symbolize the wealth of love that allows Oporna to love Srikumar, despite the knowledge that she must share him with someone else, for as she says: "[...] to assert your right over a tree, do you have to uproot it entirely and bring it home with you? Is that the sensible thing to do? I don't have the all-consuming hunger that would make me claim everything [...]" (11). Or does the title of the story constitute a telling irony upon the impoverishment of women's condition in the nineteenth century as a whole?

My reading of the story endorses this latter interpretation of the story's title as irony. Irony dominates the entire narrative of 'Wealth' and is central to the story's understanding. Oporna's invisible ironical smile mocking the world around her grants her a sense of empowerment over people like Abha, Nonda, and Shukumar who regard her as an object of pity. Oporna, in fact, appears to be Ashapurna Debi's prime agent of subversion in the narrative for, in allowing her husband to keep up his old practice of going to the *kotha* for a couple of hours every evening, and in accepting the possible reality of the courtesan as 'the other woman' in her conjugal life, she actually empowers herself in her domestic sphere in contrast to the likes of Abha who must constantly be fearful for their husband's faithlessness and betrayal. A reading of the politics of space and power in the play calls for a comparison between Oporna and Kanchon on the one hand and between Oporna and Abha on the other. Well-versed in the politics of space, Oporna evinces acute consciousness of the centrality of the wife in the middle-class domestic world of the *bhadralok* and rests securely in it. Though colonial India had witnessed a steep decline of courtesans from their high esteem in society, historically, the wife and the courtesan were always meant to occupy and inhabit clearly different social spaces. While the wife languished within the four walls of the home and had the burden of wifehood and domesticity to bear, the courtesan clearly symbolized independence and freedom from patriarchal servitude. Oporna by accepting the courtesan as an equal and by endorsing her right to her own social space, a space in which her husband too is, at best, a visitor, holds firm sway over her own. She claims for herself all the entitlements of the wife without sacrificing her self-esteem as Abha does. Debi here, not only presents an empathetic acceptance of the courtesan's emotions on Oporna's part but also puts forward new, selfless ethics of love in the image of a tree whereby love is regarded as synonymous with belonging rather than possessing. This contrast between belonging and possession is more emphatically established in the story's conclusion where Abha may claim complete possession over her husband, but he fails to belong to her.

Wealth, incredibly humanizing its female characters, succeeds in dismantling several stereotypes of its times concerning the role, behaviour, and position of women in society. The housewife, the widow, and the courtesan, one realizes on reading Debi, are all flesh and blood beings who refuse to remain inhibited by patriarchally scripted roles. The courtesan may fall in love and be duly loved in return; the widow may be garrulous and feel as carefree as a little girl at times; the wife may accept the presence of another woman in her husband's life without regarding the fact in any way as belittling her own worth and she may, again, appear to be very proud of her husband's morality while still being unable to trust him alone with another woman. On the whole, Debi seems to suggest that in a world where women are dependent upon men, where men might be unfaithful and will have their way, wealth lies in the peace of mind, in seeing and knowing things as they are instead of dwelling in wishful worlds of fantasy. The emotional wealth of women, in the world of Debi's fiction, is not under any circumstance to be found with a man but within her own self-sufficiency, and it is her own being rather than anything else, that must be effectively explored, developed, and nourished for her personal, social, and cultural health.

REFERENCES

Dasgupta, Sanjukta. "A Tri-Generational Odyssey: Ashapurna Devi's Trilogy: Reading Pratham Pratisruti, Subarnalata and Bakulkatha". *Summerhill: IIAS Review*, 17.1 (Summer 2011): 37-48. Print.

Datta, Dipannita. *Ashapurna Devi and Feminist Consciousness in Bengal: A Biocritical Reading*. New Delhi: Oxford University Press, 2015. Print.

Debi, Ashapurna. *Matchbox*. Trans. Prasenjit Gupta. Haryana: Hachette India, 2015. Print.

Lahiri, Jhumpa. "Introduction." *Matchbox* by Ashapurna Debi. Trans. Prasenjit Gupta. Haryana: Hachette India, 2015. xi-xxxiii. Print.

Roy, Manisha. *Bengali Women*. Chicago: University of Chicago Press, 1972. Print.

Tharu, Susie and K. Lalitha, eds. *Women Writing in India*, Vol. 2. New Delhi: Oxford University Press, 1995. Print.

Chapter 3

The Age-old Relationship between Man and River: A Study of *Padma Nadir Majhi* and *The Hungry Tide*

Subhasnata Mohanta

Since man is a social animal, it is very much impossible for him to live in complete isolation from society. Art and literature, therefore, cannot escape the influence of social and physical backdrop in which it is produced. Throughout the ages, literature has captured the social scenario of contemporary time. In prose narratives, particularly in short stories and novels, socio-cultural descriptions have been treated in a very elaborate manner. A similar thing is noticed and portrayed in the river novels which are the area of discussion in this paper.

Novels characterized by river-narratives are based on one or the other river and communities inhabiting the banks and the adjacent areas of the rivers occupy the central position in the narratives. These communities are sometimes peripheral, sometimes made up of native fishermen—mostly they are illiterate. It is also to be noted that the society depicted in such novels is generally of the tropical area and their way of life is the subject of discussion in river-centric novels. The river which occupies the central place of the novel, on the one hand, plays an important role to shape all the frustrations, losses, and sufferings of the community and on the other hand, it nourishes their dreams. This paper, through a detailed study of Bengali modernist classic *Padma Nadir Majhi*, written in the mid-twentieth century, and *The Hungry Tide*, written at the beginning of the twenty-first century, searches the different aspects of the river centric community's life and culture that evolved along with the natural course of the river. With the fluctuating flow of the river, an unforeseen social change comes in inter-community culture and intra-culture among the communities living within its basin. By applying the "scope of ecology" as involving "not only human relations with all species of animals and plants but also those conditions of human society (material and intellectual) that influence our responses to the opportunities and challenges posed by nature" (xi)—according to Irfan Habib's Preface to *Man and Environment: The Ecological History of India*—this is an attempt to identify how these fictional narratives are shaped by this dynamic relationship between man and nature of the said locality surrounded by multiple water bodies.

Human life is always vibrated amidst two ever conflicting forces—rest and motion. The flow and pattern river are always identical to that of life. There are numerous novels in the world literature that talk about rivers. Some of them are—*Life on the Mississippi* (1883) by Mark Twain, *Old Man and the Sea* (1952) by Ernest Hemingway, *The Heart of Darkness* (1899) by Joseph Conrad. There are also a considerable number of river-centric novels in India written in regional languages—among them *Chemmeen* (1956) in Malayalam written by Thakazhi Shivashankar Pillai deserves to be mentioned. Keeping the pace with the literature around the globe, the novelists of Bengali literature has also produced many novels on the life-sustaining river like *Padma Nadir Majhi* (1936) by Manik Bandyopadhyay, *Titas Ekti Nodir Nam* (1956) by Adwaita Mallabarman, and *Ganga* (1957) by Samaresh Basu. In these novels, several aspects of human life and culture of the fishermen communities have captured that float with the natural currents of the river. In the lower part of Bengal, rivers are the most crucial geographical elements that determine the socio-political and economic organization along with shaping the psychology, culture and religious practices of its people. Radhakamal Mukerjee describes the Ganges plane as the "genus of life", and emphasizes the regional identity of this river-centric land; as a result, man and the environment that surrounds him evolve "through mutual influences" (13).

Manik Bandyopadhyay's *Padma Nadir Majhi* or *The Boatman of Padma* is depicted against a typical geographical as well as socio-economic background. The novelist portrays a picture of a relentlessly struggling community of fishermen living along the banks of the Padma, emphasizing the issues of hunger, poverty, and want that eventually engulf their lives. Manik deals with the pettiness and wretchedness of marginalized people in his other works. *Padma Nadir Majhi*, perhaps the most memorable one among all his works, is distinguished among those. Bangladeshi critic, Abu Hena Mustafa finds Manik as the second boatman of the Padma, the first boatman being Rabindranath Tagore who also wrote on the people and their lives revolving around the river Padma. While Tagore has written about the mystery of the inner world of human mind, Manik describes the reality of those people with close and intimate eyes.

The novel depicts the story of a poor fishermen community living on the banks of the Padma river in a fictitious village called Ketupur in present Bangladesh. The narratives revolve around a fisherman, Kuber who is the sole bread earner of his family. The Padma is not just a river here merely providing the background, rather it acts one of the central characters of the novel around whom the narrative progresses. It is both the preserver as well as the force of destruction in the lives of the fishermen. The novel in this way reminds us of the agony of the Aran island fishermen community depicted in J.M. Synge's tragedy *Riders to the Sea*.

Kuber and his community live in a grotesque, morbid, fatalistic, and dark world. Their struggle for existence keeps the narrative floating around the river. The novelist emphasizes how their life is cut across by the forces of poverty and exploitation, and how they constantly battle to resist the neo-capitalist forces like Hossain Mian who nurtures Robinson Crusoe like dream to create a utopian island of his own. He wants to use the fishermen as cheap human labours and therefore, he lures them with money and promises them a life of comfort and luxury. Kuber was among the many fishermen who engaged in a constant battle with the hostile river in order to earn bread for his family. Kuber is not an idealistic character, he has been defeated the battle of life. In the narrator's own words—"All the year-round he would have to depend solely on the fish from the Padma. Even this dependence was not too strong; he did not have the nets suitable for catching fish in the Padma" (5). Kuber, the protagonist of the novel, thus represents the struggle for existence of the whole working-class community that resides on the bank of the Padma.

It was almost impossible for Kuber to escape the grim monotony of life. He knew that he was destined to become prey of the whimsical attitude of the river and his oppression and exploitation at the hand of the society were somehow predestined. He knew that imperialist people like Hossain Mian preyed upon the uncertain insecure life of the poor and underprivileged fishermen like him and thereby gained absolute control over them. The novel describes the age-old struggle of the 'haves' and 'have-nots'. Through this novel, Manik describes the struggle of the fishermen of lower Bengal, their hopes and ambitions, despairs, grief and how in their longing for a better life they are forced to negotiate with capitalist people like Hussain Mian. In order to provide food and shelter for their family, they are tempted by the offers made by Mian, who deprives them and betrays them taking advantage of their empty stomachs. Hossain Mian has created the island of Moynadeep very cheaply by exploiting the fishermen who have come there with the dream of a better future. The innocent fishermen are lured away by the false promises for the island was wild and the fishermen are made to combat with hostile nature and its wild animal for survival. According to the few people, such as, Rasu and Aminuddin who has somehow managed to return from Moynadeep describe the horror of the land where Mian forces them to clear the jungle in order to cultivate. At Moynadeep fishermen live at the mercy of Mian who claims to have converted three fishermen families into land tillers on his island. In the narrator's own words, "Not that people of the fishermen's quarter were completely in the dark about the secret plans of Hossain Mian" but "They would continue to accept any help offered by Hussain Mian with their heads bowed down" (27-28). They are chained to a system that is beyond their control.

In the locality of Kuber, there is no struggle with religion. People from different religions lived together harmoniously. They can live happily only because religion is more aesthetic and less practical to them. God does not live in their society as the narrator says: "If you were looking for God, go there—the gentlemen's quarter" (13). When there is no food to eat, God betrays the poor, life remains the same, and at the end of the day, religion is just a mere regularity. They have only two primitive needs—hunger and lust, and these two are the root sources of their despair. Kuber understands it very well that Hossain Mian is very cunning and exploitative, but he remains with him because he has no other choice. He ultimately surrenders to him and agrees to go to Moynadeep. Kuber's journey to Moynadeep through the waterways somehow resembles the journey of Bengali working-class people. The poor have no choice of their own and they have to yield to human lord always. Fishermen need to learn to master the unpredictable waters on which they earn their livings. They must know about the habit of the different fishes and they must organize their lives according to the seasonal changes. For Bandyopadhyay, nature is a threat for both fishers and farmers and the author emphasizes its negative impact. For the author, fishers are caught between changing socio-economic forces on one hand and nature on the other. Flood is an age-old problem of the lower Bengal and those most affected are the poor people living in the coastal area. Although Bandyopadhyay's understanding of the natural world is somehow negative, in *Padma Nadir Majhi* there are some passages where the river is portrayed with a positive note. On his journey to Moynadeep, Kuber thinks about the river he loves and only floating on the river gives him immense pleasure. Kuber loves the river and believes, it is not the river but the society that causes him so much hardship.

Another text for examination is Amitabh Ghosh's *The Hungry Tide*. The narrative takes place in Sundarbans—a complex geographical location with tidal waterways flowing among thousands of tiny islands, creating the largest delta of the world. It is also one of the largest mangrove forests of the world covering about 2300 square miles in Bangladesh and the Indian state of West Bengal. But today, the lush groves of this island are at peril by the continuous rising of sea levels and the extinction of various wild species. On the wider level, *The Hungry Tide* is about the Sundarbans itself with its unique sensitive ecosystem, and also the crucial importance of the tide country's existence. The novel also talks about the environmental and social injustice in a postcolonial phase where people are forcefully evicted from their own land in the name of dubious environmental policy.

The story of the novel is woven through Kanai and Piyali—two outsiders' continuous interaction with local people and sometimes with each other. These interactions have their own importance in ecological, economic and also in cultural terms. The novel has two sections—"The Ebb: Bhata" and "The Flood: Jowar". Sundarbans is a place where man, rivers, sea, animals all co-exist. This co-existence is not always in harmony, as sometimes it is in competition. People from the underprivileged, marginalized community rushed there to establish their new identities. This land also provided shelters to the refugees of political persecutions. "Here there would be no Brahmins or untouchables, no Bengalis and no Oriyas. Everyone would live and work together" (51).

Kanai Dutta, a bachelor of forty-two, runs a business in Delhi. Piyali Roy, an NRI who came to Sundarbans to study a rare kind of dolphins. Kanai's uncle and aunt, late Nirmal and Nilima both were settled at Lusibari from years. These two outsiders' interaction with each other and with the local people provides the necessary link for the narrative. The water or the river plays an important role in the novel. Ghosh uses the river as the agent that always determines the social matrix of Sundarbans. Being the motif and agent, the river frames the narrative as well as the history and geography of the land. In Sundarbans, there are no permanent borders between sea and river, freshwater, and saltwater. Some of the islands have survived intact over the centuries, but on the other hand, there are also some others whose life expectancy can be measured in hours. Every single thing is uncertain here—islands here appear and disappear with the ebb and flow of the time, that too in the course of a single day. Apart from the continuous fear of the hungry tide, people are also not much safer on the land, as Ghosh in the novel points out—"Every year dozens of people perish in the embrace of that dense foliage, killed by tigers, snakes, and crocodiles." People are so scared of the tigers that they do not even utter its name, as they believe "to say it was to call it" (108). The fishermen who go out to the sea hardly return. The girls of the tidal country are growing up, believing they are destined to be widowed in their early twenties: "When the menfolk went fishing it was the custom for their wives to change into the garments of widowhood. So many perished in their youth, men especially that without exception the fate the girls have prepared themselves for did indeed befall them" (80-81). The novel ends with a devastating impact of the great storms of 1970—the result of which was in author's own words: "The water rose so high that they killed thousands of animals and carried them upriver and inland. The corpses of tiger and rhinoceros were found kilometres from the river, in rice-fields, and in village ponds. There were fields covered with the feathers of dead birds" (204).

Thus, in both cases, the river has become the central force controlling the course of the narratives. The river sustains the emotion of the people. Sometimes it causes their frustrations and despairs and often it nurtures their dreams. Here through the study of *Padma Nadir Majhi* and *The Hungry Tide*, the age-old relationship between man and river is relocated and established with new perspectives.

REFERENCES

Bandyopadhyay, Manik. *The Boatman of Padma*. Trans. Ratan K. Chattopadhyay. New Delhi: Orient Blackswan, 2012. Print.

Ghosh, Amitav. "The Folly in the Sundarbans." *Amitavghish.com*. Amitav Ghosh Essays, 2004. Web. 20 Jun. 2019. <http://www.amitavghosh.com/essays/essayfull.php?essayNo=57>

—. *The Hungry Tide*. Noida: HarperCollins Publishers India, 2016. Print.

Habib, Irfan. *Man and Environment: The Ecological History of India*. New Delhi: Tulika Books, 2012. Print.

Mukerjee, Radhakamal. *The Changing Face of Bengal: A Study in Riverine Economy*. Kolkata: The University of Calcutta, 1938. Print.

Chapter 4

Exploring Nirmal Bose's Diary as a Social Document in Amitav Ghosh's *The Hungry Tide*

Syed Foyez Ahmed

A diary usually records one's personal feelings like pleasure, sorrow, and experiences. Hence, a diary is simply a private document where one's thoughts are written. So, the diary is never subjected to public scrutiny or reading except in case of a great personality. The diaries of great personalities like Rabindranath Tagore, Jawaharlal Nehru are objects of great interest and curiosity. These diaries are of course preserved in an archive so that the future generation can also read their experiences. The diaries of the great persons are considered as important documents for both historical value and personal history. In this way, the private experiences and public events are reconstructed in case of a diary. Nowadays the diaries are published as books. Of course, a diary is not considered as a conventional source of history because there may be certain doubts about its authenticity and acceptance. In his novel *The Hungry Tide* (2004), through Nirmal Bose's diary Amitav Ghosh presents the Marichjhapi episode. Marichjhapi is an island in Sundarbans that has long been hidden from public knowledge. If the diary would not have been found by Nilima, wife of Nirmal Bose, the massacre of Marichjhapi would not have perhaps appeared in the novel. But here the diary of Nirmal was written keeping in mind specifically the incidents of Marichjhapi, as the diary was written in two days. In the diary, he wrote about the misery of the settlers who came to the camp risking everything. The massacre of Marichjhapi that took place in the year 1979 had long passed in oblivion but through the diary Amitav Ghosh has dug up the issue in people's memory. Thus, in a way, the diary supplements conventional knowledge sources. Nirmal has actually preserved the diary to leave a trace of the issue of the settlement problem and the injustice that had been met to the refugees to readers. The diary contains the extent of misery Nirmal went through during that period. It is a reflection of an individual's response to the event. Ghosh employs the diary to add a personal narrative of the incident because Nirmal had been a close witness of the happenings in Marichjhapi. Nirmal Bose had been a schoolmaster for thirty years in the island and when he came to know about the news of the settlers, he was at once drawn to the issue. Thus, being an educated, sensitive, intellectual person Nirmal gives a very personal narrative of the incident.

The novel starts with the character of Kanai Dutta, a famous translator based in Delhi and also the nephew of Nirmal Bose who comes to Lusibari on the invitation of Nilima because Nirmal had addressed the diary to him. The diary was confined to Nirmal's own self. It was kept outside the purview of the public till it was found and read by Kanai. Thus, the diary is intended to bring the hidden knowledge to the public domain. The diary had been addressed to him (Kanai) and his uncle had immense faith upon him. Nirmal says: "I will hand it [the diary] to Horen in the hope it finds its way to you, Kanai. I feel certain you will have a greater claim to the world's ear than I ever had. Maybe you will know what to do with it" (278). This remark of Nirmal is important because he thinks that Kanai can arrange something to get the diary published and let the world know about the incident. As a schoolmaster of a remote village he did not have the acceptance of a writer in the market. So, Kanai's job as a translator is very important. The word translation has derived from 'translatio' which means to carry over. In this context, it may mean to carry over the sufferings of the people of the island and disseminate their condition among a large section of people.

Nilima has a great deal of respect and curiosity for the literary abilities of her dead husband. The contents of the diary have been excavated/unearthed. The diary was written in the month of May 1979 and Kanai has started reading it in 2002.

Therefore, the diary had kept the Marichjhapi massacre which took place on 16 May 1979 hidden from public scrutiny. Amitav Ghosh has brought to light many facets of the incident. First, he brought the issue of the future of the displaced people who came to Marichjhapi in large numbers from a resettlement camp in Dandakaranya. Secondly, the play of power relations surrounding the illegal settlers is brought to light. Thirdly, there is an unmasking of power centres.

Ghosh chooses to focus on the Marichjhapi incident perhaps because of the gross injustice done to the poor, downtrodden people by the ruling class of society. It was because of the wrath and fear of the government that Nilima decides not to help Kusum in her cause. Nirmal's sensitive mindset gave voice to the pleas of the marginalised section of society. Nirmal puts forward the hapless condition of the refugees and settlers on the island. Ghosh has brought to light that the worth of human feelings, emotions, fate is of less importance than that of the protection of the tigers. The powerful class of society has demeaned the worth of human lives. Ghosh gave voice to the sufferings of the poor people who don't have voices of their own as they are 'subalterns'. News of the Marichjhapi massacre had though hit newspapers, but on a low scale. The predicament of the refugees is best expressed by Kusum as she said to Nirmal:

> The worst part was not the hunger or the thirst. It was to sit here, helpless, and listen to the policemen making their announcements, hearing them say that our lives, our existence, was worth less than dirt or dust. Every day, sitting here, with hunger gnawing at our bellies, we would listen to these words, over and over again. Who are these people, I wondered, who love animals so much that they are willing to kill us for them? Do they know what is being done in their names? Where do they live, these people, do they have children, do they have mothers, fathers? As I thought of these things it seemed to me that this whole world has become a place of animals, and our fault, our crime, was that we were just human beings, trying to live as human beings always have, from the water and the soil. No human being could think this a crime unless

> they have forgotten that this is how humans have always lived. (261-62)

Kusum's comments are tinged with irony and raise a pertinent question that in whose name the government is trying to drive away the refugees and whether they are aware of what is being done in their names. Ghosh has quite aptly spoken the sad reality of the marginalized class of people through the character of Kusum.

> Marichjhapi was a tide country island, a couple of hours from Lusibari by boat. It fell within a part of the Sundarbans reserved for tiger conservation but unlike many such islands, it was relatively easily accessible from the mainland. In 1978 it happened that a great number of people suddenly appeared in Marichjhapi. In this place where there had been no inhabitants before they were now thousands, almost overnight [...]. But in time it came to be learnt that they were refugees, originally from Bangladesh. Some had come to India after Partition, while others had trickled over later [...]. But it was not from Bangladesh that these refugees were fleeing when they came to this place; it was from a government resettlement camp in central India. In the years after Partition the authorities had removed the refugees to a place called Dandakaranya, deep in the forests of Madhya Pradesh, hundred of kilometres from Bengal. (118)

The settlers who had taken shelter in the island had been promised earlier that they would be allowed to stay in the place permanently, but the government turned against them using its full force to evict them. The already displaced were again on the verge of displacement. After leaving their camps they staked everything to settle in the island. The government, in the name of protecting the environment, was hell-bent in driving away the illegal settlers. The role of the government was very important on this issue. The political party which was at the helm of affairs earlier promised to the settlers that they would be given shelter in West Bengal when they would be voted to power. But the party backtracked on its promise and stood up against the settlers' tooth and nail. The refugees had perhaps assumed that they would not face much opposition from the government's end, but this was a miscalculation. The government seemed absolutely oblivious of its earlier promise. The government was fighting for the cause of tigers, but they did not have greater concern for the tigers than the lives of human beings. They had clearly indulged in making false promises to the refugees who were then staying in a resettlement camp in central India. The political party played with the feelings, emotions of the refugees. If the party had not promised the refugees in the first place, they would not have been attracted towards this island and come all the way from central India risking everything.

Deep Halder in his book *Blood Island: An Oral History of the Marichjhapi Massacre* has interviewed some of the victims in the government-sponsored killing in Marichjhapi. Most of the respondents are severely critical of the Left Front government which backtracked in its promise. One of the biggest allegations against it is that the East Pakistani refugees were targeted because most of them were low caste Namasudras. It is assumed because of their low caste identity; no mercy was shown to them. In fact, this incident did not even shake the conscience of the society except that of a few people. One of the respondents, Mr. Sakya Sen, an advocate who fought for the refugees in Marichjhapi, says: "Although I have to admit that even when the issue came to light, there wasn't an outpouring of support from the general public. It was a failure, not only of the legal system but of a generation—my generation—then in their twenties and thirties. We lacked collective conscience. We destroyed Marichjhapi—all of us" (115). Hence, in this book, we hear an echo of Nirmal's account about the Marichjhapi massacre.

Various issues that played a major role in making Nirmal interested in the cause of Marichjhapi. The first motivation was, of course, Raina Maria Rilke, a German poet who kept coming in throughout the diary. When Nirmal first quoted from Rilke, it was very evident that Rilke is a big influence upon him. As he can think only of Rilke's words when he saw the situation in Marichjhapi for the first time:

> beauty is nothing
> but the start of terror we can hardly bear,
> and we adore it because of the serene scorn
> it could kill us both [...]. (*The Hungry Tide*, 69: emphasis added)

One of the reasons why Nirmal wrote the diary as he says: "perhaps I can make sure at least that what happened here leaves some trace, some hold upon the memory of the world". It may be that he wants to archive the incidents. In this case, the role of memory is very important. Kusum, Kanai's childhood friend, is an inspiration for Nirmal to engage himself in this settlement problem. Nirmal was closely attached to Kusum as it becomes evident when he describes Kusum as his 'muse'.

The diary of Nirmal Bose is undoubtedly at the centre of the novel, because if Nirmal had not left the diary for him, perhaps Kanai would not have come down to Lusibari, a place where his aunt Nilima lives. Before knowing the contents of the diary Nilima had already begun to believe that her husband's literary reputation would be posthumously restored by the contents of the packet she had found. When Kanai was reading the diary, he was reliving the terrifying incidents that took place in an island called Marichjhapi. Through Kanai, Nirmal has actually tried to preserve the incident and not letting it pass into oblivion. The diary is actually based on Rilke's *Duino Elegies*. Rilke worked as an inspiration for him. He writes, "as for Marichjhapi, Rilke himself had shown me what I could do. It remained only for the time to come when I would receive a sign and then I would know what I had to do". Then he quotes Rilke's lines:

> This is the time for what can be said. Here
> is its country. Speak and testify. (275)

Nirmal's diary was written keeping in mind the feelings and sensitivities of Kusum in particular. Being inspired by Rilke, he sings in praise of the lower strata of people:

> some simple thing shaped for generation after generation
> Until it lives in our hands and in our eyes, and it's ours. (193)

At the end of the diary, he writes about the faces in the candlelight and their smiles. Then he sees Rilke's lines:

> Look, I'm alive. On what? Neither childhood nor
> the future grows less [...] More being than I'll ever
> need springs up in my heart. (278)

Thus, Rilke is very important in dairy. Rilke is like a constant companion to Nirmal. If Rilke's inspiration had not been there, Nirmal would not have the ideals before him.

The pitiable and helpless situation of the *baastuhara*, i.e. the refugees is best highlighted by Kusum, one of the faces of the resistance put up by the settlers. The settlers like Kusum are already marginalized by the social system before taking shelter in Marichjhapi. In the years after partition, the refugees are removed to a place, namely Dandakaranya, a place in the deep forest of Madhya Pradesh. The authorities did this. The refugees were not allowed to leave that place and so many were killed because few tried to getaway. The security forces had surrounded the refugees. But according to Nilima they called it "resettlement" and people see it as a concentration camp or a prison. Hence, the situation in the resettlement camp is worthy enough for the refugees to escape to somewhere else. Thus, Kusum had also decided to accompany the refugees to Bengal.

The character of Nirmal Bose must be analysed to get to the depth of the contents of the diary. Nirmal always thought about revolutionary ideas. Thus, Nirmal has been a communist throughout his life. He strongly hates the idea of being an egalitarian. When he comes to know about the settlement problem in Marichjhapi, he instantly reacts against the ruling class and joins the resistance put up by the refugees. He sees the image of thousands of people, who want nothing more than to plunge their hands once again in their (our) soft, yielding tide country mud (165). Then the lines of Rilke come to his mind:

> Each slow turn of the world carries such disinherited
> Ones to whom neither the past nor the future belongs. (165)

The incidents of Marichjhapi can be read in history books. All such accounts lack the passions, feelings of a person allowed in real-life situations. Nirmal is an intellectual and sensitive human being who strongly believes in human values, equality and internationalism. Otherwise, he would not have been able to quote a European poet like Rilke and relate to the poet's ideas. Nirmal's diary gives a vivid description of the contemporary situation in Marichjhapi and anguish, humiliation of the refugees. The diary truly conveys anxiety of a person. In the diary, we can sense the throbbing of a heart. It immediately communicates anger, joy, and lamentation of a person. It can safely be said that the diary has an affective quality to transform one into a new being. The public knowledge almost supplements any other conventional source of information of a historical event. Through this diary, the true colour of the political leaders is unmasked and it has been shown that in their hunger of 'power' they can make false promises to get votes to reach to the power throne and when in power, they can betray the same people whom they have promised. In this diary, the refugees who are always regarded as the 'subalterns' also get their voices to protest against the injustice against the powerful forces. The historical aspect of the diary on the Marichjhapi incident is true and accurate. There was indeed a confrontation in 1979 between the refugees who had escaped from a resettlement camp in central India to Marichjhapi and the state government in West Bengal. After the publication of the novel, there has been a great deal of consciousness about the Marichjhapi episode among the people. Thus, the diary can be regarded as a social document without any doubt.

REFERENCES

Bandyopadhay, Biswajit. "The Tale of Marichjhapi: Review of the book *Marichjhapi chhinna desh, chhinna itihaash*." radicalsocialist.in. *Radical Socialist*, 19 Feb. 2012. Web. 28 May 2019.

<http://www.radicalsocialist.in/articles/socialist-peoples-history/454-the-tale-of-marichjhapi-review-of-the-book-marichjhapi-chhinna-desh-chhinna-itihaash>

Ghosh, Amitav. *The Hungry Tide*. Noida: HarperCollins Publishers, 2004. Print.

Halder, Deep. *Blood Island: An Oral History of the Marichjhapi Massacre*. Noida: HarperCollins Publishers, 2019. Print.

Mondol, Chandra Jagadish. *Marichjhapi: Naishabder Antaraley*. Calcutta: Sujan Publications, 2009. Print.

Pal, Madhumoy, ed. *Marichjhapi: Chinna Desh, Chinna Etihas*. Kolkata: Gangchil Publishers, 2009. Print.

Rai, Alok. "Sage of Marichjhapi." Outlookindia.com. *Outlook: The Fully Loaded Magazine*, 12 July 2014. Web. 28 May 2019. <https://www.outlookindia.com/magazine/story/saga-of-marichjhapi/224432>

Randolph, Eric. "The Marichjhapi Massacre and the End of the Left." Palashupdates.blogspot.com. Palash Updates, 16 May 2011. Web. 28 May 2019. <http://palashupdates.blogspot.com/2013/07/the-marichjhapi-massacre-end-of-left.html>

Sengupta, Sukharanja. *Marichjhapi Beyond and Within*. London: Gardener Books, 2010. Print.

Chapter 5

The Prism of Paranoia: A Kaleidoscopic Representation of the Cultural Schizophrenia and Rhizomatic Dialectical Materialism in Orijit Sen's Graphic Narrative *The River of Stories*

Ramprasad Dutta

The 'graphic novel', rather the 'graphic narrative' is an experimental genre in World Literature today as it manifests visual-verbal literacy and upholds the absurdity of the fluid (meta)-narrative storytelling pattern and addresses myriads of serious socio-religious and political issues of the postmodern world. Through the amalgamation of images and words, graphic narratives demonstrate several burning issues like the dissemination of cultural hybridity, the insalubrious existence of the fragmented urbanity, the ubiquitous presence of trauma in the posthuman psyche, the vulnerability of camouflaged human identity, etc. Now, let's try to clear the notion regarding the definitional problems in 'comics', 'graphic novel', and 'graphic narrative'. One of the great icons of Comics, Will Eisner imagined both graphic novels and comics to be sequential art as he said that it is, "a means of creative expression, a distinct discipline, an art and literary form that deals with the arrangement of pictures or images and words to narrate a story or dramatize an idea" (11). Chute proposed the notion of "graphic narrative" instead of the graphic novel, as many "graphic novels" are non-fiction and she depicts graphic narrative as, "a book-length work in the medium of comics" (453). In *Understanding Comics*, Scott McCloud opines comics as: "Juxtaposed pictorial and other images in deliberate sequence, intended to convey information and/or to produce an aesthetic response in the viewer" (20). Since the time of prehistoric man, people have been narrating tales with the aid of pictures instead of prose. In India, the actual presence of a proper full-length graphic novel came to the existence with the publication of Orijit Sen's magnum opus *The River of Stories* (1994). Like Art Spiegelman's *Maus* (1986; 1991), Sen's *The River of Stories* studies discourses related to historical events. It demonstrates the meta-historic "performative memorialization" (a term given by Lisa A. Costello while talking about the retrospective aspect of Spiegelman's *Maus*) by putting the Narmada Dam issue into a different allegorical 'chronotope' in his graphic novel *The River of Stories*.

Figure 1: The definition of 'comics' by Scott McCloud in his *Understanding Comics* (p. 20)

Orijit Sen's *The River of Stories* is a magnificent, succinct, and visually sumptuous tale woven around the Narmada Bachao Andolan. It begins with a dream sequence set in the room of the protagonist, Vishnu, who is a journalist working on the Rewa Sagar Andolan, which, according to him, has a great impact on the question of human existence and the proliferation of power through some 'repressive apparatuses' as they 'destroy' the idyllic, cool sequestered domain of the 'subalterns' to 'create', rather, establish their own territories. Apart from Vishnu's narrative, there is another parallel narrative which introduces Malgu Gayan, who is telling a tale which reverberates the tale of Vishnu. Again, within the narrative of Vishnu lurks a very distinct voice of a timid subaltern called Relku who can be seen as a victim of radical political vandalism implemented by the capitalists and feudal landlords (fundamentally by Rathore in the novel). So, the novel is highly experimental in its own way. It's more like a dream sequence; a 'dream-within-a-dream'—kind of technique as conspicuous from the following comic-strips:

Figure 2: Malgu Gayan's narrative (p. 9)

Figure 3: Relku's narrative (p. 13)

It's a real fact that comic books become extremely useful when it discusses history and memory. Marianne Hirsch in her article "Collateral Damage" refers to Roland Barthes's notion that images "have an intensified power to move an audience"; if "seeing is a form of wounding and being wounded, a 'shot of the eye,' then to see, to be a spectator, is to respond through body and affect, as well as through the intellect" (1212). Consequently, readers, thinkers, and audiences are more prominently influenced when they observe. Undoubtedly, a graphic-novel reader can feel the excruciating pain of the victims more deeply and can understand the psycho-somatic trauma felt by the victims than any other narrative readers. Besides, as Hilary Chute elaborates, "it is through the flexible architecture of their pages, with their stitching of absence and presence that graphic narratives comment powerfully on the efficacy and the limitations of narrativizing history" (270). Now, if we read Sen's novel very diligently, we will be able to understand how beautifully this novel has demonstrated the issues related to the very experience of trauma and its repercussions as well. The issue of trauma is primarily exhibited through the character of Relku: she had tasted the very acerbic flavour of life in her past days, and now she is ruminating about those esoteric images of her past days in a totally different 'space'. Though she has quite 'adopted' the new culture of the city, she has not totally become an 'adept' of this new culture and at the very corner of her mind she has stored the very exuberance as well as the very trauma of her past life. In this context, we can say that the room where Vishnu and Relku are sharing their thoughts (basically Relku is narrating to him her story) becomes the real 'contact zone' as Mary Louise Pratt has conceptualized the term in her epoch-making book *Imperial Eyes: Travel Writing and Transculturation* (1992) by saying: "I use the term (i.e. 'contact zone') to refer to social spaces where cultures meet, clash and grapple with each other, often in contexts of highly asymmetrical relations of power, such as colonialism, slavery, or their aftermaths as they lived out in many parts of the world today" (4).

It goes without saying that through this book Sen wants to explore the traumatic experiences of a tribal community in the village of Jamli which is near the river of Narmada. It shows how this particular tribal community is caged into a crystalline grand menagerie created by the so-called elite groups of the society filled with hypocrisy, corruption, and falsehood with a complete totalitarian approach. It is a place (rather 'space') which is created especially for the 'proletariats' and the 'subalterns' by the representatives of the upper-class society to establish panoptic surveillance from outside the menagerie upon the creatures living within the space. For we all know that surveillance establishes the autocratic power and destabilizes the very normative normalcy of that particular space and turn the very structure of that space upside down. Now, this particular idea gets manifested more beautifully in the second part of the novel where Sen shows cameramen filming the tribals, almost weaving the camera into the narrative of the Rewa dam. Unanimously, this scene projects the issue of 'double colonization'. It shows how they are maligned, oppressed, and marketed in a twofold way both by the eyes of the cameramen and by the eyes of the viewers of the media. P.K. Nayar in his critical book *The Indian Graphic Novel: Nation, History and Critique* has rightly pointed out that:

> [...] Sen calls attention to Rewa as a *media* story, the displacement and suffering of the tribals as a mediated story. The camera is the symbol of the media, but it is also something more in the tale. I propose that it is *the camera that makes things happen* in Sen. The enactment of suffering is possible because the cameraman and his device sets out to record this suffering. In other words, the historical events of displacement are 'arranged' based on *a priori* assumptions of suffering that are to be recorded by the media. (116)

Figure 4: *The River of Stories* (p. 48)

If we look at the issue of 'dislocation', we would certainly be able to understand the imposition of 'cultural hegemony' on the proletariat group and the inherent shrewd power politics behind the apparent goodness of the representatives of the 'civilized class'. This issue of dislocation of the tribal community can be interpreted as the dislocation of the 'center' to the 'periphery' (rather, decentering the center), because, to the so-called civilized upper-class community, the culture of the tribal community appears quite inferior compared to their (superior) culture, which, needless to say, manifests the 'Manichean binary' and creates an invisible wall between them.

Sen's magnum opus *The River of Stories* projects the dissemination of rhizomatic dialectical materialism in an innovative as well as a prismatic way. Needless to say, this entire process grows haphazardly in the socio-political domain of a community violating the specific, traditional hierarchical order of society what Gilles Deleuze and Felix Guattari termed as 'rhizomatic' in their epoch-making work *Capitalism and Schizophrenia* (1972-80). Sen has encapsulated this particular issue in his text beautifully. He also envisages the ubiquitous presence of an 'interpellated' and 'hegemonized' identity through the portrayal of Somariyo, who, unlike Antriyo, is quite happy with the present critical condition and doesn't want to bring any change. That's why he says: "I don't know about right or wrong. All that I know is that if we stay in their good books, we at least have food in our bellies. If we try to meddle with them...we're DEAD!" (26). Again, when Maaru, brother of Antriyo (who becomes a victim of political vandalism), is lynched pathetically by the goons of Rathore, and Antriyo goes to the police station for justice, they refuse to even write a complaint against Rathore; instead, they say: "now where did a jungli like you get the gall to come making complaints against civilized people?" (25). Needless to say, through this episode, Sen has magnificently captured the very poignant image of 'repressive state apparatus' and its workings in a society:

The novel is actually an amalgamation of myth and reality; it follows a highly experimental story-telling pattern by introducing two distinct separate narratives and ultimately uniting them into one. This avant-garde technique is not completely unprecedented, but Sen has used it in his novel River of Stories very uniquely. He questions the very development model that suggests the replacement of age-old tribal culture with large-scale modern innovations for agriculture and industrialization through the 'Narmada Bachao Anadolan' theme. Again, when Malgu Gayan

Figure 5: The projection of 'repressive state apparatus' in Sen's *The River of Stories* (p. 25)

of myth creeps into Vishnu's domain, the transition is entirely incoherent not only because of Sen's expertise of his genre but also because the Adivasis of the Narmada valley seem acutely similar in every sense. Significantly, Maglu Gayan's song is used as a symbol to show unity and also to tell the tale of the creation of Rewa. The epilogue of the novel is highly satirical as it enunciates the utter absurdity of life and an anti-materialistic approach of Malgu Gayan:

Figure 6: *The River of Stories* (p. 58)

Unanimously, Sen's graphic narrative challenges the traditional outlook of postmodern readers and invites them to come out of the camouflaged whitewashed garb of the dilapidated past by breaking the stereotypes; rather, it is the past which detects and encounters a new attribute in the present world through the non-linear, multi-layered language of the graphic narrative of Orijit Sen. While talking about the experimental narrative of the graphic novels, Orijit Sen says:

> the tension between image and text provides one of the primary dynamics of the language of comics, image and text are like the wrap and weft on which the narrative is woven. The patterns emerge when these threads interplay in various ways: through convergence, divergence, contradiction, intersection, etc. In some ways, image and text must remain incomplete within themselves, each finding its resolution finally in conjunction with the other. (8)

As Amruta Patil's *Kari* (2008) exercises the belief in 'lesbian continuum' and questions the receptacle of traditional hetero-normativity, and as Sarnath Banerjee's *Corridor* (2004) explores the 'layers' of people replete with idiosyncrasies and enigmatic eccentricities, Orijit Sen's *River of Stories* demonstrates as well as contradicts, valorizes as well as satirizes, narrates as well as questions, the very historical document which bring the present narrative quite closer to the "palimpsests on which the scrambled game of identity and relations is ceaselessly rewritten" (Schaberg, 79).

REFERENCES

Chute, Hilary. "Ragtime, Kavalier & Clay, and the Framing of Comics." *MFS Modern Fiction Studies*, 54:2. (2008): 286-301. Web. 21 June 2019. <http://muse.jhu.edu/article/240720/pdf>

Eisner, Will. *Comics and Sequential Art: Principles and Practices from the Legendary Cartoonist*. New York: W.W. Norton, 2008. Print.

Hirsch, M. "Editor's Column: Collateral Damage." *Modern Language Association*, 119:5 (2004): 1209-15. Web. 25 June 2019. <https://www.mlajournals.org/doi/abs/10.1632/003081204X17798>

McCloud, Scott. *Understanding Comics: The Invisible Art*. New York: Harper Perennial, 1994. Print.

Nayar, P.K. *The Indian Graphic Novel: Nation, History and Critique*. London: Routledge, 2016. Print.

Pratt, Mary Louise. *Imperial Eyes: Travel Writing and Transculturation*. London: Routledge, 1992. Print.

Sabhaney, V. and O. Sen. *First Hand Graphic Non-fiction from India*. Vol. I. New Delhi: Yoda Press, 2016. Print.

Schaberg, Christopher. *The Textual Life of Airports*. London: Continuum, 2012. Print.

Sen, Orijit. *The River of Stories*. New Delhi: Kalpavriksha, 1994. Print.

Chapter 6

A Narratological Study of K.V. Dominic's "Burn Your Horoscope"

S. Barathi

Application of critical theories to the works of art always helps in better comprehension than when reading individually. In this regard, taking a short story and applying a narratological model will help the learners, readers as well as the aspiring writers to note how the story has evolved and what decides the success of a story, etc. In this regard, the short story titled "Burn Your Horoscope" was selected from the anthology *Sanchita Karma and Other Tales of Ethics and Choice from India* by K.V. Dominic.

K.V. Dominic's short stories, as well as his poems, are a 'concretization' of his creative impulse. In a traditional country like India, people are exploited in the name of religion. The short story "Burn Your Horoscope" highlights this issue. The present paper is an attempt to analyze the story from narratological perspective. For this, Labov's narrative structure containing six aspects are used and it tries to highlight the effectiveness of narration in making the story a successful one. Readers often expect a written narrative to have some kind of structure like that of oral narratives. The pattern of narrative (i.e.), a narrative in a fixed model or framework could make the story interesting to readers. This probably involves detailed storytelling or writing, as in the case of written form of stories.

Labov, a sociolinguist has modelled a six-aspect framework predominantly consisting of the elements such as abstract, coda, complicating action, evaluation, resolution, and orientation. So far, these aspects are applied only to oral narratives. The main focus is on the plot and structure and how it is told and not on who said the tale. Labov had observed that personal experience narratives minimize "the effects of observation" (2001). After this, it has been found that "such narratives are delivered in a similar fashion" in various societies with different cultures (Maranhão, 1984). The analysis of oral narratives and their efficiency began with "the initial analysis of Labov and Waletzky 1967", which was further developed, where Labov's model serves as the foundation on which other narratives were modelled. The narrative is structured in such a way to include six vital aspects. The first being "reportability or tellability" (Norrick, 2005), which relates the situation narrated by narrator to the audience. This is an aspect which Labov discusses in his model. The story selected comprises a social issue and a reviewer about the collection remarks: "Clearly, the aim of the author as a 'social critic' has always been the betterment of his society, state and nation" (129). Thus, the book reflects the society and tries to make it a better place for the impoverished people in society.

Dominic's "Burn Your Horoscope"

The story begins with the description of the protagonist Praveen, a young and dynamic bachelor. The complication in the story is his horoscope. Due to the horoscopic prediction that his wife will die after one year of their marriage, none of the prospective brides and their parents was ready to take him as their groom. Praveen has liberal thoughts and tries to locate a girl with liberal and rational views like him. Finally, he decides to give an advertisement in the matrimonial column. It is where he locates his life partner Parvati, who had a similar horoscope, which read that husband would die after six months of their marriage. Praveen decides to marry Parvati, but their parents hesitate due to Parvati's horoscope. But Praveen convinces both of them and they get married. To the relief of both the families nothing serious occurs in their life. Only they come across happy events, they celebrate their wedding anniversary by burning their horoscope. The story ends with Praveen and Parvati celebrating their silver jubilee wedding specially arranged by their children.

Labov's model is basically applied to oral narrative but could be applied for written narratives such as short stories. Based on the inferences from the fieldwork he conducted, he listed six narrative categories, viz. Abstract, Orientation, Complicating Action, Resolution, Evaluation, and Coda. Abstract indicates that a story is about to begin and catches the reader's attention. The title "Burn Your Horoscope" gives a clue to the plot of the story. Here, the problem arises due to the horoscope. Thus, the title relates to the central issue in the story. Hence, the title like the majority of short stories serves the purpose of the abstract. For a narrative to be successful, it should contain an abstract. In the case of this story, as the title suggests, it is the Abstract which catches the attention of the readers. The speciality of the story is, it gets its title both from the plot of the story, which is spun upon the belief in horoscope and the conclusive part of the story, where the protagonist addresses the audience on his 25th wedding anniversary and suggest them to burn their horoscope in order to succeed in life.

Orientation refers to the place of action and the reason for the particular action in the story. In the story, the place of action is Praveen's house and the temple, where Praveen and Parvati got married. This is evident in the lines, "The marriage date was fixed. 10th November at the nearby temple" (67) and "their son Prasanth and daughter Pallavi have arranged a feat in their house" (68) provides ample evidence that most of the story takes place in their home. In this story, further details by the narrator are provided towards the end after the wedding of Praveen and Parvati, which leads to a series of events. There are many complicating events in the story. The first one is the horoscope of both Praveen and Parvati, which read, "Horoscope predicts wife's death within a year" and "Horoscopic alert: husband may die within six months" (66) as well as "Praveen's villain is his horoscope" (65). All these mark the beginning of a complication in the story. It was a sheer coincidence that both Praveen and Parvati had similar horoscopic predictions.

The resolution marks the conclusion of the story, in other words, it sums up the events that happened in the narrative. In this story, the couple "celebrated their first wedding anniversary by burning their horoscopes papers like a campfire" (67) proves that the horoscopic prediction had gone wrong in their case and the couple continue to live a happy life together celebrating their silver jubilee, which marks the end of the story. In addition to the plot, there are some elements that catch the attention of the readers at some vital moments. Everyone in the couple's family was worried about their horoscope, but to their surprise there was a sudden turn of events that not only surprises the protagonists but also the readers. "To the amazement of all, gift raffle ticket which Parvati got from the jewellery shop [...] won first prize of one kilogram of gold" (67) and Parvati securing a permanent position in a government college as lecturer, Praveen too promoted as an executive engineer, all add to the surprise of the readers. Further, they were happy to beget two children a male and a female, thus continuing their family line. Finally, coda signals the completion of the story. Praveen's speech at their silver jubilee marks the end of the story. In his speech, he insists on the audience as well as the readers not to trust their horoscope and indeed should "burn your horoscope. Then success is yours" (68). Thus, Praveen justifies setting down his life as an example for others.

The study showcases the writer's use of words that helps in the evaluation of the story. Besides the six elements analyzed, the use of adjectives like "very handsome", "highly orthodox" (65) demonstrate this fact. Further, from the evaluation part, it appears that a series of positive events ultimately lead the couple to ditch their horoscope and thereby set an example for others. Despite the fear of parents, Praveen marries Parvati, the only daughter of affluent parents and their life moves without the turn as expected from their horoscope. Thus, the story serves as moral to others who blindly believe in such things. It is also worthwhile to note that the analysis foregrounds the writer as a realist and an idealist.

REFERENCES

Dominic, K.V. *Sanchita Karma and Other Tales of Ethics and Choice from India*. Ann Arbor: Modern History Press, 2018. Print.

Labov, William. *The Social Stratification of English in New York City*. 2nd Ed. Cambridge: Cambridge University Press, 2001. Print.

—. "Uncovering the event structure of narrative." Georgetown University Round Table, 2001. 1-23. Web. 17 Feb. 2019. <https://www.ling.upenn.edu/~wlabov/uesn.pdf>

Labov, William and Joshua Waletzky. "Narrative analysis." *Essays on the Verbal and Visual Arts*. Ed. J. Helm. Seattle: University of Washington Press, 1967. 12-44. Print. Reprinted in *Journal of Narrative and Life History*, 7 (1997): 3-38. Print.

Maranhão, Tulio. "The force of reportive narratives." *Papers in Linguistics International Journal of Human Communication*, 17.3 (1984): 235-65. Print.

Norrick, Neal R. "The dark side of tellability." *Narrative Inquiry*, 15.2 (2005): 323-44. Print.

Chapter 7

Ashapurna Debi and her Literary Contribution to Feminism in India

Juhi Gupta

The calendar date 8th of January 1909 saw the birth of Ashapurna Debi in the divided province of Bengal of an India that was still serving the British. She was born in a conservative Hindu family that was rooted in superstitions and conventional belief system. Her father was an artist, and her mother was a literature-loving homemaker. The thirst for knowledge in Ashapurna Debi was visible from her early childhood, but the superstitious belief system of her grandmother that, "literate women are widowed early on in their lives", kept Debi away from receiving much education in her early childhood.

Ashapurna Debi's mother, Sarala Sundari was a literate lady with a penchant for reading, which she transmitted into the soul of her daughter, Ashapurna. Later in Ashapurna Debi's childhood, her immediate family shifted their home from Vrindaban Basu, Kolkata Lane to Acharya Prafulla Chandra Road, Kolkata. This gave Sarala Sundari the opportunity to quench her thirst for reading and allowed little Ashapurna to get herself educated. During the years when Ashapurna Debi was growing up, what India saw was perhaps the most tumultuous phase in its fight for Independence. Ashapurna Debi was a sensitive child, and she observed that—while the entire nation is engaged in the fight for freedom, not much is said and done for half of its population that comprised of the Women of India. They were denied the right to have their individualities, were expected to follow the sayings of men and act subservient at all times. The mentality of the entire Hindu society back in the days of Ashapurna Debi was extremely prejudiced. It laid down stringent gender roles, which required women to play submissive, and men to be authoritative. Some women took this practice as 'God's will', while others loathed this system, but all had to follow it under the fear of ostracisation.

Women in those days became preys to several vices of society. They had little knowledge of the outside world, were kept illiterate and were married off early in their childhood. Ashapurna Debi was a novelist and a short story writer, who wrote in Bengali. Being a woman with an empathetic soul, she felt their helpless plight and heard the voices that were muffed by the unjust and adamantine norms of the society. Debi felt them—their cries, their pleadings, uncared for wishes and their desires to possess free souls within their bodies. She saw it all, she heard it all and then she picked up her pen, to depict it all, through characters she would shape with her pen.

The central characters of her novels are mostly women, around whose life the plot of the novel revolves. Her stories follow a course which unfailingly shows gender discrimination in the middle-class Bengali family in vivid terms. Her works depict women's desires, their mistreatment, and their fight to break free from the constraints laid down by the patriarchal belief-system. Ashapurna Debi was a staunch feminist at heart, and so she sketched heroines who were iconoclasts, who dared to defy the society and raised their voices against the injustice prevalent in it. Ashapurna Debi was fifteen when she was married off. She observed all the rampant injustices going on around her, though in her personal life, she was a contented figure. Debi had no formal education but was self-educated. She was a figure who lived within the four walls of her household. She said that her husband encouraged her to write, and so she did, she depicted the family life of the women in Bengal using her mother tongue, Bengali.

Prothom Protishruti (The First Promise)

The trilogy of *Prothom Protishruti* is Ashapurna Debi's magnum opus. The first part "Prothom Protishruti" is a facsimile of Debi's life. Debi once stated—"Over the years, great clouds of protest have accumulated, unexpressed in my mind, and Satyabati, the heroine of my novel is the expression of that protest". The novel *Prothom Protishruti* centres around Satyabati, a girl in whom the seed to disregard unjust expectations germinated. She received values and education from her father before getting married at the age of eight. Her married life with Nabakumar was comprised of harrowing experiences that were brought upon her mostly by her in-laws. She had immense dedication towards her husband but there was boredom that was felt by the flame in her soul with each ticking of the clock.

The novel in one of its sections depicts a gruesome incident, where a 10-year-old bride faces death at the hands of her in-laws as she has refused to let her husband touch her out of fear and Satyabati's attempt to attain justice for her. In another section of the novel, Debi addresses the issue of colonialism when Satyabati is seen responding to the call of humanity over conventional femininity. She brings into her house a British doctor to cure the pneumonia of her bedridden husband. An act that held her guilty, by the then caste-based society, which had its mind bent upon the idea that the touch of a British (a person who did not belong to their caste) was abominable and inauspicious.

However, Satyabati's hopes are seen to be centred on one person, her daughter, Subarnalata, in whom she sees her own reflection. She voices her ideas against child marriage and subdues any voice in her household that favours the vice. But her wishes are thwarted when her mother-in-law Elokeshi, a believer in child marriage secretly marries Subarna off behind her mother's back. Satyabati arrives late on the spot to see her dreams of raising her daughter in shambles. Unable to do anything about the situation, a heart-broken Satyabati leaves for a pilgrimage on a bullock cart, never to return. Ashapurna Debi addresses the issue of women being women's enemy. In this novel, the greatest of hardships that Satyabati faces are thrown on her path by women, who could not tolerate her assertive individuality and her upright nature. Debi lays bare for us to see that, if women support each other by rising above the pettiness and insecurities, they can make life easier and more meaningful.

Satyabati is Ashapurna Debi's mouthpiece, through whom she claims a woman's need for space in the household and society.

Debi says—"Women need a special kind of self-sufficiency [and this] can come only with the consolidation of female power". However, as far as the feminist perspective is concerned, the character of Satyabati, though a dynamic character, had her limitations. This spirited woman had a firm conviction that "husband is God" (translated), and she (Satyabati) also takes a stance against widow remarriage. In *Prothom Protishruti*, the Jnanpith Award winner addresses in a restrained manner, various social vices that restrain the growth of a woman as a person. She draws mind-numbing scenarios of women who are left with no choice but to succumb to the social pressures. She talks of superstitions and irrational mindsets that are responsible for brainwashing the younger generation girls into thinking that they are lesser human beings and belong either in the kitchen or in the bedroom. She upholds for the middle-class *bhadralok* society to see the plight of their neglected wives, mothers, and sisters who suffer in silence.

Subarnalata

Subarnalata picks up the story where *Prothom Protishruti* left. The newly wedded child-bride Subarnalata, the daughter of Satyabati, is without much education when she is married off. As a child, she is very much unlike her mother; she is a meek and tame character. She is often burdened with a heap of duties and responsibilities that are too much for her age. As the course of the novel proceeds, we see that Subarna has inherited the same spirited flame from her mother. Subarnalata is the story of a woman in quest of her own identity amidst stagnating mind-sets. This feminist novel by Ashapurna Debi is set against a backdrop of India's fight for independence. Subarna, who is married at the age of nine gradually, grows up with the consciousness of her surroundings. Her upright morality propels her to desire the same rights that are given to her male counterpart. Subarna is a lady who is moral, indomitable and is not daunted to do or say the right things. Society and social conventions are seen to impede her path but the headstrong of her does not let restrictions hinder her path. Most of the novel shows Subarna's lonely battle against social evils and inflexible relatives who humiliate and mortify her. Probodh, her husband is of a suspicious character who adds to her agony in more ways than one throughout the course of the novel.

Much to her in-laws' dismay, Subarna grows up to be an avid reader. Her quest for her own identity is coupled with her desire for freedom which has been masterfully represented by a motif—the south-facing balcony, which Subarna wants her husband to build in her new house. She realizes that for a woman to be genuinely emancipated, knowledge of the outer world is imperative, and therefore, she wants a south-facing balcony, to have a glimpse of the outside world. But her desires are thwarted as her husband forgets to build the balcony, the only thing she asked for!

Subarna's hopes and dreams are harped on her daughter Bakul, whom she wants to educate. She fights the society, her in-laws and her own sons who advocate child marriage, to save her daughter from the hands of this social evil that she firmly believes should be eradicated. Subarnalata's dynamic nature, her ideas, her quests, and her fearless activities are not perceived well by society and much less by her in-laws. Subarnalata was a ground-breaking and a radical character to the Bengali readers in 1967. Subarnalata remains to be the character that created tremors in the established hegemony of the Bengali society, as it unmasked society's ugly face and blatantly pointed out all that was wrong in the established order.

Bakul Katha

Bakul is the third of Debi's women in the trilogy. Bakul is the youngest daughter of Subarnalata and Probodh. She grows up to be an observer. She sees, observes, and pens everything down under the pen-name of Anamika Debi. Bakul is the model of the emancipated woman, who does not need to put up a fight to pursue her ideas and goals. Though a writer, she is utterly unable to convey to her children, the sufferings of her mother and grandmother. Bakul shows remarkable objectivity in her writing. She addresses not just the woman's issues but various other social concerns that haunted mankind of India that had attained freedom.

The repertoire of Ashapurna Debi (1909 to 1995) consists of 242 novels and novelettes, 37 collections of short stories and many children's books. Debi remained the voice of Bengal's awakening to the social concerns that concerned women. The prolific writer has the Lila Prize (1954), The Bhutan Mohini Dasi Gold Medal (1966), the prestigious Jnanpith Award (1976 for *Prothom Protishruti*), and several other accolades to her credit.

Debi used her pen as a weapon to bring to society's notice the agony and disdain of women in Bengal and India. She voiced women's frustrations as they thrived to break free from a system that stunted their growth, by keeping them within the four walls of their households, by forbidding them even a glimpse of the outside world and by pressurizing them to live a life shrouded by dark clouds of injustice.

Ashapurna Debi is one of the first names in Bengali Literature who sought to change the prevalent scenario in India by championing women's cause. She compelled people who were engrossed with only the war-torn world of the outside, to think about the inside world too as there resided half the nation, who were often beaten, who were never given the right to have a voice, who were prisoners in their own bodies. She became the voice of those who were destined to die unheard because they committed the sin of being born as women!

REFERENCES

Debi, Ashapurna. *First Promise*. Trans. Indira Chowdhury. New Delhi: Orient Longman, 2004. Print.

—. *Subarnalata*. Trans. Gopa Majumdar. Chennai: Macmillan, 1997. Print.

—. *Bakul Katha*. Trans. Prof. P. Madhavan Pillai. Thrissur: Current Books, 1988. Print.

—. "Indian Women." *Indian Women: Myth and Reality*. Ed. Jasodhara Bagchi. Hyderabad: Sangam, 1995. 19-23. Print.

Chapter 8

A Comparative Perspective: A Case Study of Bengali and English Novels of Indian Writers

Debajit Paul

Comparison is, in fact, an instinct of man. It is a man, who becomes able to show different devices of comparison in accordance with various objects. On behalf of man, it is only possible for being the possessor of rationality. Comparison between two things or objects different in kind is called simile and metaphor as for the figurative aspect. Comparisons are closely connected with the attitude of man. In the terrain of literature, various forms of comparisons are found, and these forms are made with, in the main natural objects.

Be that as it may, the comparison is the soul of comparative literature. In comparative literature, comparison and contrast are possible between two more kinds of literature. Especially giving emphasis upon common and unique quality, the comparatists with sincerity and seriousness, elicit comparative elements, from literary pieces, though there are some technicalities of comparison of literature that are theme and genre. Based on various angles of vision, comparatists travel in the gold mine of literature to gather gems and jewels, that are skillfully and artistically placed in the heart of comparative literature to shed light on the quality of uniqueness, which is as equivalent as ambrosia. The ambrosial aroma with sweet savour and flavour make such a world for the comparatists, who look out similarity and dissimilarity among literary genres. As a matter of fact, there is a subtle standpoint of comparatists in this case. Thematically, a common point assists to clear and expand the way of comparative circle. It can be grasped through the diagram given below:

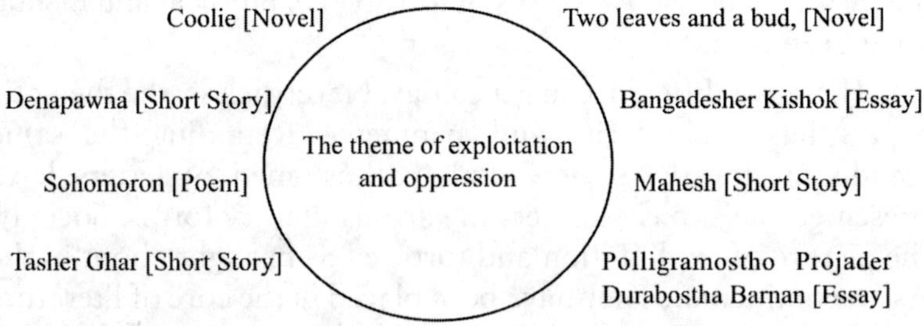

The theme of exploitation and oppression has, in a word, been reflected like water in these major genres of literature.

The pivot [theme of exploitation and torture] is like a piece of magnet that has attracted iron like literary genres such as novels, essays, short story, and poem. These have been composed according to various local colours and points of view of men of letters, though there is the ceaseless flow of pathos [Karuna Rasa] and awful sentiment [Bhoyanaka Rasa] in these literary pieces. Needless to say, the entity of comparative literature has been self here in this comparative study keeping the harmony, symphony, and symmetry with Indian culture and literature, an aspect of humanism has been hidden in the core of these literary pieces.

To make a comparative level in literary world, the texts which are chosen are—*Two Leaves and a Bud* and *Coolie* by Mulk Raj Anand, *Bag Desher Kishok* [Farmers of Bengal] by Bankim Chandra Chattopadhyay, *Polli gramosta Projader dur obostha Barnan* [Description of the barnan by predicament of tenants in villages] by Akshay Kumar Dutta, *Mahesh* by Sarat Chandra Chattopadhyay, *Denapowna* [Debt and Due] by Rabindranath Tagore, *Sohomoran* by Satyendranath Dutta and *Taser Ghar* [House of Cards] by Tarsankar Bandopadhyay. Sohomorn means voluntary burning of a widow on the funeral pyre of her dead husband. From the literary angle of vision, it is clear that there are various genres in the above-mentioned texts. In general, a comparative aspect is automatically made here centring around two novels by the Indian novelist, Mulk Raj Anand. Exploitation, oppression, humiliation torture and so on are the main themes of this comparative subject. These have the gentle touch in the above texts, though two types of torture, i.e. physical and mental have been found there.

There is a difference in genealogy. Nevertheless, the thematic aspect has a similarity and symmetry. Retaining the same standpoint for the society with pathos, men of letters have presented the subject matters in various literary forms. Socially, the picture of exploitation and torture has brought about in the Asian continental. They have been placed in the core of literature through realism. In accordance with idealism, a sorrowful feeling, sentiment, and emotion have been nested in the heart of the above-mentioned literary texts.

In Mulk Raj Anand's novel *Coolie*, he has related an exploiting life of Munoo, who has been tortured everywhere. Being a poverty-stricken person, he has been harassed and tortured very much. At last, he is attacked with tuberculosis and leaves their mortal earth. The Indian novelist next has dealt with the picture of ruthlessness in his novel *Two Leaves and a Bud*. Here, in this novel, there is a gruesome picture of the torture and the exploitation of the natives by the white-skinned person (the British rules).

Gangu is a Punjabi farmer, who as labour, works in the tea plantations of Assam. Reggie Hunt is the owner of a similar plantation. His daughter, Laila works there like Gangu. The wife of Gangu has passed away. Whatever, seeing the youthful beauty of Laila, Reggie Hunt has become bewitched one day. He does not hesitate to pursue her. She, realising the situation, starts to run to her hut to save herself from him. Gangu, under these circumstances, tries heart and soul to retrieve his daughters from this demon, who like a stormy-hearted person shot him point-blank to slay him. Later, Reggie Hunt is exempted from the legal punishment in spite of killing such an innocent person. In the short story, *Denapawna*, Tagore has presented as a cruel picture of Nirupama, who is mentally tortured by her mother-in-law, as her father has failed in giving enough dowry to her father-in-law. This mental torture has compelled her to leave this world forever.

On the basis of the incident of suttee custom in the society, the poet, Satendranath Dutta has recounted it in the form of a poem in *Sohomoron*. The social superstition has made this net so that after the death of husband, the young wife has been kept on the burning pyre. The youthful wife, according to the account of the poet, jumps into a river to save herself from their inhuman torture. She has later expressed it to a person, who rescues her from the water of river. In Bankim Chandra's essay, *Bangodesher Kishok*, the event of torture and exploitation for the poor peasants in the village by the Zamindars has been printed clearly and directly. The Zamindars' cruelty for them has no bound. Showing the bloody eyes for them, they try to collect the tax from them.

Sarat Chandra's *Mahesh* as a short story has drawn out the horrible picture of the society consisting of humiliation, torture, insult, and exploitation. The Zamindar in the village is at the root of humiliation, torture, insult, and exploitation. Gafoor, a poor Muslim farmer has often been insulted and humiliated mentally and physically he has been tortured as his cow, Mahesh has fled from the cowshed for hungry. It, entering into the garden of the Zamindar, damages the flower plants. Shutting the mouth, he bears with all kinds of insult. At last, he kills his innocent cow. He, of course, has to put up with the mental pain. Through starvation, he spends the days with his motherless daughter, Amina. Akshay Kumar Dutta, a Bengali essayist, has placed the predicament and privation of the poor peasants in his essay *Polligramshoto Projader Durabostha Barnon*. The Zamindar and the landlords have a cruel philosophy on the poor villagers, whose lives basically depend upon the cultivation. But they demand lion's share of the cultivation from the poor cultivators, with the extra tax and cess. They are overhead and ears in debt, as they lend money from the moneylenders, who taking the scope of penury, misbehave with them in a ruthless manner. As a spy of the landlords, they show the bloody eyes upon them. Shila's mental torture by her mother-in-law for breaking one cup has been pointed in Tarashankar's short story *Tasher Ghar* (House of Cards). An angry feeling has grown in the heart of mother-in-law of Shila after hearing that she (Shila) has broken one of the cups among five cups.

In the above-mentioned texts, there is a relation between exploiters and exploitation. The exploiters heroically and awfully have treated with exploitations, whose lives are replete with pathos. That is to say, there is an association of various emotions or sentiments, i.e. Pathos (Karuna Rasa), Roudhara (Sentiment of Horror), Bhibatsha Rasa (Sentiment of Repulsion), and Bhoyanaka Rasa (Awful Sentiment). These are grown in the mind of the exploiters and exploitations. Torture is involved in these sentiments or emotions.

As a matter of fact, in spite of being a common thematic aspect with these emotions or sentiments, they have a comparative form belonging to various local colours and the characters. The life of Munoo, Gangu, and Laila can be compared with the poor farmers, Satti girl, Nirupama, and Gafoor from the pathetic points of view. But the attitudes of the exploiters have been reviewed persons like Hitler, Shylock, and Draco. Conflict and tension have been brought forth in those characters of Indian literature for exploitation. Naturally, conflict, tension, and oppression have loomed over the shadow of tragic flaw in their lives. Indian men of letters have elucidated them in a literary while a comparatist has set froth it in a thematically way with uniqueness.

REFERENCES

Anand, Mulk Raj. *Coolie*. New Delhi: Penguin, 2000. Print.

—. *Two Leaves and a Bud*. United States: Liberty Press, 1954. Print.

Banerjee, Asutosh. *Essay on Comparative Literature*. Kolkata: Progressive Publishers, 2007. Print.

Chattopadhyay, Sarat Chandra. *Sarat Rachana Samagra*. Kolkata: Ashok Book Agency, 2019. Print.

Chattopadhyay, Bankim Chandra. *Bankim Rachanaboli: Upannash Samagra*. Kolkata: Ashok Book Agency, 2017. Print.

Naik, M.K. *A History of Indian English Literature*. New Delhi: Sahitya Akademi, 1982. Print.

Paniker, K. Ayyappa. *Spotlight on Comparative Indian Literature. Calcutta:* Papyrus, 1992. Print.

Pollack, Sheldon, trans. and ed. *A Rasa Reader: Class Indian Aesthetics*. New York: Columbia University Press, 2016. Print.

Shastri, Asokenath. *Rasa and Bhaba*. Kolkata: Sanskrit Pustak Bhandar, 1980. Print.

Chapter 9

Asif Currimbhoy and the Question of Representing Authenticity

Indrani Chakraborty

> Others may have followed, but Currimbhoy is India's first authentic voice in the theatre. He has written that country's first plays of dissent. He presents life as it is, not as something it should be, the age-old curse of India's classical theatre. (qtd. in Currimbhoy, *The Doldrummers*, viii)

One of the most striking features of *Goa* is the relationship between the Goan Nationalist and the Portuguese Administrator. The Goan Nationalist actively participated in the movement when the Indian troops marched into Goa to liberate it, ending 400 years of Portuguese rule. However, Currimbhoy adds more dimensions to the entire liberation movement to give the text the multitude of palimpsest, the nationalist says that he colluded "with the liberator to free my people from the yoke [...] a yoke which many did not seem to mind" (*Goa*, 79), he further ponders over the prospect of a new liberated Goa:

> Tourists will come and industries will develop and this pleasant sleepy town with the languid Portuguese atmosphere will develop into an Indian metropolis, giving opportunities to all. But I sometimes wonder [...] I sometimes wonder [...] what will become of that stranger, that invader, that "liberator", who will now have to find his own peace, within himself. (*Goa*, 80)

These words imply the fact that in spite of being a nationalist himself, he missed his "old friend" (Currimbhoy, 80), the Portuguese Administrator:

> I said "hello" to him countless times and enjoyed the glass of beer together and had our occasional tiffs too, but we enjoyed our little quarrels. It was good fun and games and we never really intended to be serious till [...] they wanted the invasion. And we found we wanted it too. (80)

The monologues of the Goan Nationalist, thus, unravel certain exceptionally sensitive realms of the human psyche, notwithstanding with the common exploitation of the theme of colonizer/colonized binary. It is, therefore, quite unfortunate that the playwright does not offer a more intensive perspective to these two multilayered characters. He, rather, opts to explain the human condition by exploiting a crude and contrived plot structure to create a political allegory with three symbolic characters—Senhora Miranda, Rose, and Krishna.

The first appearance of Rose is strikingly romantic. She is seen to be sitting on the balcony and when she speaks, "Her voice comes like a single silvery shaft of moonlight" (15); her words quaver with lyrical grace and poised poetry. She is a "dark-looking girl and about fourteen with a beautiful innocent face and a strange voice" (15), and most importantly, as Alphonso declares: "Rose is Goa. Goa is Rose" (37). Rose, the epitome of Goa, gets raped by a foreigner, Krishna, in the second Act; the date is 18 December 1961, the day on which Goa was invaded. Evidently, the scene bears a symbolic significance. Nevertheless, on the realistic plane, the scene becomes unbearably horrible when we come to know that Senhora Miranda had been raped by a foreigner and therefore, she wanted Rose, the child of violence and oppression to have the same destiny. The proposition, however, in spite of being strongly effective as a political observation and commentary on the role of India in the liberation movement of Goa, does not quite conform to the basic requirement of dramatic credibility. Dramatically, the scene evades the logical progression of reason and action when Krishna explains the reason behind Senhora Miranda's agency to get Rose brutally raped:

> So you, Maria, not I, started the game. Dangled Rose before us, not through competition for you, but for her [...] Used us, not to rape one who had already been raped, but to rape one who had not been raped! [...] Who constantly reminded you of your former self. Whom you wanted also on your point of equalization. (77)

Finally, when Krishna commands Maria to hold Rose by her black hair so that she could be raped by Krishna, Maria rises to his command and the horrible act is done. As the second scene in the second Act begins, "A few weeks or months later" (79), we find that Rose has become a prostitute. Krishna visits her place once again which follows the climax of the play. In the scene, we find Rose emerging from her room, "[...] still with blind over her face, the negligee torn and blood-stained, to her mother's arms, crying" (92). The last line of the play is a piece of stage direction:

> With trembling hands, the mother removes the blind. Slowly, Rose disengages herself from her mother's arms, walks back to the room, shifts aside the curtain, as KRISHNA's nude body falls out, with a dagger in his heart. (92)

The play is generally considered as a discourse concerning the political situation of contemporary Goa. The devastating impact of colonization, invasion, and domination encountered by a geo-space is represented by Rose. Krishna represents the ruthless forces of capitalism that first allure the victim by pretending to be its benefactor and finally brutally attacks its innocence to satisfy his hunger. The mother represents the once-colonized nation that still bears the bruises of the experience. The terrible memory of those experiences is embodied in her present through her daughter; she is dazed and bewildered by violence to the point of insanity, the insanity explained by the Goan Nationalist:

> After the invasion there was the occasional case of rape but on the whole the troops were very well behaved [...] the troops have withdrawn now, and we have civil administration and the freedom of choice. (*Goa*, 79, emphasis added)

Krishna represents the binary opposition that Colonialism invariably carries, except some "the occasional case of rape"; the troops were "well behaved":

> SENHORA MIRANDA: You are not soft, Krishna; you're hard.
>
> KRISHNA: Soft...to Rose.
>
> SENHORA MIRANDA: You don't have love, Krishna. You have hate.
>
> KRISHNA: Love...for Rose.
>
> SENHORA MIRANDA: You're not peaceful Krishna; you're violent.
>
> KRISHNA: Peaceful...to Rose.
>
> SENHORA MIRANDA: (Pause) Is that...how Rose sees you, Krishna?
>
> KRISHNA: Yes. (61)

By murdering Krishna, her violator, Rose finally makes her choice, the choice implied by the Goan Nationalist. Undoubtedly, the allegory is crafted very well and bears an authentic testimony to the political repression, economic mismanagement and above all, institutionalized violence. Nevertheless, there is no way to escape the fact that the plot of *Goa* is extremely artificial and crude for a symbolic play. The playwright chooses to depict violence and injustice by literally *showing* violence and injustice, which destabilizes both the symbolic undertone and the realistic overtone, disturbing the verisimilitude of the plot.

The Doldrummers (1961) opens with Tony singing a current film hit tune with his guitar, Rita is described as "a young thing", leaning barefooted on the tree and fondling Tony's hair; sitting at the foot of the opposite tree "ogling Rita's legs and thighs", is Joe, with "ratty intelligent eyes" (*The Doldrummers*, 10). As the play advances, certain basic characteristics of the principal characters are chiselled out. For example, Tony loves luxuries:

> I like the feel of a fancy silk shirt, or a sporty tie, or [...] or [...] one of those nice pointed shoes for dancing that I can polish and see my face in. Same way as a woman likes a bunch of flowers or a diamond bracelet. (30)

At the same time, he listens to the world of ideas from Joe:

> […] "Tony, reach out to ideas", he says, Joe does. He talks to me about Plato sometimes. He says that somewhere there exists a perfect world of ideas. It gives me gooseflesh just thinking about it. (31)

Thus, Tony is presented before us as a character standing on the verge of consummation and contemplation. Joe is presented as a sharp and practical man, with a perception of something deep and vulnerable living within the human body:

> […] They say that matter is indestructible. You burn up refuse, and it goes into smoke. But you collect all that smoke and you'll get back the same weight as that dirty refuse […] Everything reincarnates, except what lives within us, which alone is completely destructible. (27)

Rita, described by the playwright as "fully physical" (*The Doldrummers*, 10) acts as a kind of bond between these two apparently opposite characters, however, for the two of the friends, Rita's role is quite uncanny:

> Rita: […] Tony, there's nothing at all you have in common with Joe.
> Tony: I know it. But it doesn't matter.
> Rita: Friends should have something in common.
> Tony: Joe once told me we had you in common. (32)

This poignant conversation loses its sharpness once the readers comprehend that by that apparently intriguing statement Joe simply meant their mutual perspective to Rita, both of them share the playwright's observation that she is a "young thing" (10), with a slight difference concerning the implication. Rita finds that Tony would never restrain from taking gifts from others ignoring the fact that Rita would leave him for that. She speaks with Joe to find a solution. The conversation, however, leads her to a grim prospect:

> Joe: Liza […] has many rich friends […] admirers as she calls them.
> Rita: She's a slut.
> […]

> Rita: You are suggesting that I change and become like Liza so that I may be able to afford to give presents to Tony and keep him to myself.
> [...]
> Joe: I know a rich friend [...] I *can introduce him to you.* (39-40)

Thus, apparently, it's Joe whose advice makes Rita choose the way of prostitution in order to buy expensive gifts for Tony. Joe's agency becomes even more shocking when Joe rapes Rita, and it is exactly the point when the play loses its quotient of a basic structural coherence between the plot structure and the causality of its movement. It is important to note that the playwright never attempts to explain either covertly or overtly what he intends to mean by "Doldrums" in this context—if all these three characters are explained under the blanket term "Doldrummers", then it becomes thoroughly necessary to understand what does he precisely mean by *Doldrums* in the first place. The play does not specify any socio-political time (except the opening song which contains an oblique reference to "Satyagraha" (11) to infer the basic reason behind the alienation of the three characters that makes them commit feverish activities. It is clear from the title that the playwright intended the characters to live in certain *Doldrums* (Joe declares the fact as well in one of his dialogues (50)—indicating the playwright's intention that he wants the readers to think that the driving force of the play is the socio-political destabilization that misleads the youth of contemporary times towards consumerism, prostitution, moral transgression and so on. Nevertheless, instead of viewing the situation to be the driving force behind their activities, we find that all the three characters are themselves responsible for what happens to them. Tony could escape his doom either by accepting Rita's degradation or by rejecting it—but he chooses not to see it at all. Rita could resist nurturing her deep hatred for Tony, which was the inescapable outcome of thwarted expectations by simply admitting the fact that he knows about her profession, which he evidently does. However, instead of registering the fact that Tony is a useless, pampered fellow who is too much addicted to his luxurious lifestyle to admit the fact that Rita brings those commodities by commodifying herself, Rita keeps on thinking that Tony did not strike Rita's customer who asked Tony whether or not Tony helps Rita in procuring "friends" like him, doing nothing " [...] while I begged him...to kill the man. [...] But he just stood there" (61), simply because Tony was "completely dazed" (61) at the situation. Rita, as well as Tony, understands that admitting the fact would demand either his revolt or his acquiescence, both of which means an agency, which Tony chooses not to have. The most disturbing character of the play is Joe; not a single action of Joe is justified throughout the play. We are not given a clue why he chooses to spend his time with Tony and Rita, without having a little speck of affection towards any of them. He betrays Tony, assaults Rita and disappears from the scenario. Unlike Tony, Joe is shown to be a prompt, strategist who knows what he is doing. However, his knowledge of his own self does not any way enlighten the readers. He remains a *doldrummer*, who is an achiever-lost-track. He also *chooses* to be so. We are not shown any external circumstances that compelled them to be what they are. Joe is a usurper, but he is no way responsible for Rita's moral degradation. Not every woman chooses prostitution as her first resort to give expensive gifts to her boyfriend simply because one of a friend of her boyfriend suggested her to do so. It was Rita's choice. She is not a victim of circumstances, no character in the play is. And it is a fact that breaks the causality. If the principal characters of a play choose to be the victim of their own choices and continuously struggle to believe that they are victims of circumstances, the plot becomes paralyzed. In spite of the supreme craftsmanship visible through the brilliant dialogues and impeccable stage directions, the play cannot escape losing its authenticity and becoming rather vapid, leading us to downplay the superb mastery of the playwright while depicting the scene when Tony softly hums the song:

> Let's go my friend,
> We'll go together, my friend,
> To where the doldrums end.
> [...]
> So hold my hand,

'Cause I understand,
'Cause I understand [...] (92)

This is the only moment of transcendence for Tony as he, for the first time, identifies himself with Joe. This realization could help him to see the true nature of the *doldrums*—it is nothing external, therefore, it would never pass as a course of nature or chapter of social turbulence. They will be forever in the *doldrums*, whatever the circumstances are, because it is their choice, and it is a reason that there is nothing tragic in it. Far from presenting a realistic picture of India (the setting of the play is Juhu Beach, in the suburbs of metropolitan Bombay), it presents random images of some decadent youth whose alienation is not from the world but from themselves—and it is what they wanted for them in the first place. As a result, the movement of the play becomes redundant, its climax mere moral rhetoric, the characters wooden, and the plot contrived. It is true that "He presents life as it is, not as something it should be" (qtd. in Currimbhoy, *The Doldrummers*, viii), but at the same time we must take into account the remaining part of Bower's observation, "I am not necessarily saying that Currimbhoy is a great dramatist" (qtd. in Currimbhoy, *The Doldrummers*, viii).

Finally, I would like to point out one of the fundamental reasons behind the surprising observation made by Bowers. He considered Currimbhoy's voice to be India's first authentic one, not because he believed him to be a great dramatist, as he himself says that he believes quite the contrary. The reason behind this declaration is simply a lack of translation. Asif Currimbhoy remains the first authentic Indian voice in theatre because Madhusudan Dutt, Rabindranath Tagore, Dinabandhu Mitra, Utpal Dutt, Badal Sarkar did not write in English. Taking translation projects under sincere consideration remains to be the only avenue to assist India's authentic voices receives a wider readership.

REFERENCES

Bowers, Faubion. See Currimbhoy, *The Doldrummers*. Kolkata: Writers' Workshop, 1992. Print.

Currimbhoy, Asif. *Goa*. Kolkata: Writers' Workshop, 1993. Print.

—. *The Doldrummers*. Kolkata: Writers' Workshop, 1992. Print.

Chapter 10

Tracing Man-Woman Relationship of the Victorian Era: A Study of Kamala Markandaya's *A Silence of Desire*

Durga Patva

> Man for the field and woman for the hearth:
> Man for the sword and for the needle she:
> Man with the head and woman with the heart:
> Man to command and woman to obey.
>
> (Tennyson, *The Princess* n. page)

Society is governed by the mutual understanding or human relationship either it is social or personal. Society is a mesh up of human collaboration where interactions with one another make this world a better and healthier place to live in. As it is said that man is a social being by nature and he cannot remain as an individual, untouched from his surroundings. People remain connected with other members of society for the completion of their social, political, personal, and economic purposes and needs. All the people of the society are interconnected with one another intellectually, morally, spiritually, and religiously, and this connectivity helps them to survive smoothly. Human qualities like kindness, love, compassion, rationality, and mutual affection create a feeling of oneness among them. Hence, it strengthens their bonds and relationship. In short, it can be said that human relationship brings people close to the fulfilment of their social needs and humanitarian deliberations. This human relationship is enhanced by the combination of human sympathy, trust, camaraderie, co-operation, truthfulness, and devoutness.

The term relationship can be defined as a close attachment or bond between two persons, especially one involving romantic or sexual feelings. The human relationship can be categorized into two types external and internal. Friendship and neighbourhood come under the external kind of relationship while the internal relationship is genetic, which includes family members, and children and parents. This relationship can be named as the relationship between father and son, mother and son, father and daughter, mother and daughter, brother and sister, friends and neighbour and so on. All humans are given a particular role in the society to be performed and so is the case with man and woman. Man and woman are given their places in a society based on their gender. Gender-based discrimination gives women fewer human rights compared to men. Women are restricted in many ways while men always remain free of doing anything. Among all human relationships, the relationship between man and woman plays a significant role in a smoothly running society. Marriage is one of the social customs which allows a unique relationship between a man and a woman. However, internal relations like blood relations are also worthy enough to bind persons with profound reciprocal care, love, and affection.

Kamala Markandaya is such a novelist who finds literature as a suitable medium for the delineation of the man-woman relationship and gender-based discrimination. In her narratives, she records the happenings of Indian society and relates them in a very realistic way. On account of her narrative skill, she secures an important place among the novelists, namely Mulk Raj Anand, R.K. Narayan, Raja Rao, Babhani Bhattacharya, Nayantara Sehgal, Anita Desai, Arundhati Roy, Shobhaa De, Bharati Mukherjee, Mahasweta Devi, and Manju Kapoor. She is one of the earliest Indian women novelists writing in English for whom William Walsh stated that she was "the most gifted" novelist. In her novel *A Silence of Desire*, Kamala Markandaya explores man-woman relationship from varied perspectives. She describes that the relationship between man and woman has not only been strong-minded and swayed by mutual understanding and devotion to each other, but it is also influenced and determined by the family status and socio-cultural principles, customs, norms, beliefs, and values. The representation of the man-woman relationship in her novel shows that the gender-based discrimination between man and woman is still applicable in Indian families in such a way as it was in the Victorian era.

Different Realms of Men and Women during the Victorian Era

The span from 1837 to 1901 is known as the Victorian era in English literature. This was the era of Queen Victoria's reign. In this age, the role of man and woman is more intensely demarcated than any other literary period. The men of the Victorian era used to work in places like the factory, shop or office, etc. It shows that all the financial authority and superiority in the family were reserved for men. Women were left at home for performing domestic duties. Ironically, the exact reason for this situation was the strict control of Victorian society on women. During the Victorian era, women were domesticized. An ideal woman was the one who preferred to stay at home and managed all the tasks of a good wife and mother. Society pressed for women to be the angel of the house; they were responsible to foster children, manage their home and satisfy their husbands. Many Indian novelists expressed their ideas regarding man-woman relationship and their role in society, Kamala Markandaya is one of them. Her novel *A Silence of Desire* implies that the Victorian concept regarding man and woman's role in Indian society is still the same as it was in the Victorian age. Presenting man-woman relationship, Markandaya also throws light on human emotions like love, hate, and sympathy and she describes how these emotions affect a person's life. Markandaya gives a realistic portrayal of the female character, she invents in this novel. She expresses the sufferings of a poor Indian woman. Some significant pieces of information regarding woman can be found in the novel that are similar to those of the nineteenth-century woman.

Indian social system becomes problematic for Indian women as they face discrimination, exploitation, subjugation and they get very little opportunity to uplift them. They get fewer opportunities to empower themselves within their home and society. Indian women get their proper place within the title of wifehood and motherhood because Indian patriarchy believes in the ideology of manuscript, according to which, "A faithful wife, who desires to dwell (after death) with her husband, must never do anything that might displease him who took her hand, whether he be alive or dead" (156). In *A Silence of Desire*, Markandaya lays emphasis how women in Indian families are deprived of their freedom and real human rights. Like the women of the Victorian era, they occupied a limited place which was confined to domestic duties. A fine blend of Victorian compromise can be seen in *A Silence of Desire* in which man stands for the office work and woman stands for the household work. Dandekar, the protagonist is represented in the novel as a dominant man who wants his wife to be confined within the four walls of the house. He expects her to remain in the house as a perfect wife by performing domestic duties. "It was the wife who made the home, who cared for her children within it, who brought her husband back to it when work was done, who provided the hot dinners and created the atmosphere of comfort and protection" (Calder in Danielova, 2009: 8). Markandaya describes the psychology of Dandekar as, "One evening, her absence for the first time itself, creates uneasiness, showing signs of suspicion. Sarojini, from the horse mouth [...] a good wife [...] good with children, an excellent, and efficient" (*A Silence of Desire*, 204). Further, she writes: "Manager of his household, a woman who still gave pleasure after fifteen years of marriage, less from the warmth of her response than from her unfailing acquiescence to his demands" (204). It shows that like Victorian men Dandekar finds peace, joy, and strength when he sees his wife waiting for him when he returns from office. He is the male bigot for whom a wife is a robot or a well-crafted mechanical device for the fulfilment of his desires. For instance, on Dandekar's return from office, his wife starts working when, "she heard his step in the country yard, and she would be putting the potatoes into fry. The agreeable hiss would last until he has washed and changed and by them, she would be ready for him and so would be evening meal (*A Silence of Desire*, 47). It shows that both, the husband and his wife have to enjoy limited right from the inception of their marital life. Both Sarojini and Dandekar have some limited right and they perform their duties well just as a couple of the Victorian era used to do.

Clash of Scientific and Religious Views

The Victorian era was marked by the ceaseless conflict between science and religion which represents a clash between head and heart. W.H. Hudson once remarked regarding it that "the Victorian age was marked throughout by the prominence of the spirit of inquiry and criticism, by scepticism and religious uncertainty, and by spiritual struggle and unrest, and these are among the most persistent and characteristic notes of its higher literature" (450). In Markandaya's *A Silence of Desire*, the clash between the faith and reason is quite implicit in the behaviour of Dandekar and his wife Sarojini. His wife has faith in God, and she believes that her illness must be cured by the grace of God, so she worships Tulsi plant while Dandekar has a different view regarding the Tulsi plant. He calls Sarojini superstitious and a fool because of her faith in the Tulsi plant. Markandaya shows how a wife's spiritual faith and a husband's scientific reason create a clash and unravels the fact that faith and reason do not have a confluence. But, when Dandekar comes to know about the tumour of his wife, he feels extremely sympathetic. Dandekar repents saying, "I left her to sleep on the floor, he said to himself. She was ill and I let her lie on the floor while I slept in comfort" (101). He advises her to go to the hospital, but Sarojini has lost her faith in hospitals because it is a place where her mother and grandmother died. Sarojini is afraid of medical intervention because her mother and grandmother died after surgery. Hence, the spirituality and faith of the traditional Indian housewife collide with the scientific and rational mindset of her husband. Through the character of Sarojini and Dandekar, Markandaya draws attention that how religious faith comes to believe in all kinds of miracle, superstitions, ritual, and traditions which cannot be explained, proved or tested by science or reason or logic.

Love, Sex, and Marriage

The Victorians were not opposed to the indulgence in love and sex, but it was delimited its region to mere conjugal status. Lovemaking was not prohibited but it must remain holy and unpolluted and must culminate into wedlock. In the Victorian era, marital love was given preference. In the novel, *A Silence of Desire*, Markandaya delineates that women are always bound with the circle of chastity even after marriage. They should not look at the other men except their husbands. On the other hand, men are always free to do what they want without any restriction. Just as Dandekar in the novel, believes that a married woman should not talk with a stranger. Dandekar thinks "a married woman didn't have male friends who were not known to the husband of the family" (*A Silence of Desire*, 5). On the contrary, he goes to prostitutes to satisfy his carnal desire. Hence, it seems that Markandaya satirises patriarchal biasedness towards men of the society through the character of Dandekar who has failed to maintain a balance in his relationship with his wife. Sarojini, on the other hand, is represented as a pure, innocent, and loyal woman like that of a woman of the Victorian era where a woman is expected to remain devoted to her husband. There is a lack of love and trust in their relationship which is the plinth of a happy conjugal relationship. Focusing on the issues of marital life of Indian culture, Markandaya appealingly represents the most poignant man-woman relationship that is determined, influenced, and regulated by customs, traditions, faith, beliefs, and suspicion. The foundation for a man-woman relation is trust and love which is lacking in Dandekar and Sarojini's relationship. Though he wishes for the changes, but when he finds that his wife and children are becoming affected by the scientific changes, he becomes furious. He says: "Yet times were changing but not so fast," he cried furiously. "Not so far as to touch the old generation like me, my wife, we are stable" (*A Silence of Desire*, 54). One day on his returning from office, when Dandekar finds his wife missing in the house, he inquires of it and finds that his wife was following the instructions of a Swami. He suspects his wife of betrayal but he does not ask her directly, instead, to know the truth that where she goes, he follows her and finds that she was suffering from womb disease and to cure this illness she follows the Swami's instruction. She does not disclose her activities to her husband, not because she is doing anything immoral or unethical but simply because her husband would not permit her to go ahead with what she contemplates faith. Sarojini's talking with the Swami compels Dandekar to suspect his wife. Kamala Markandaya exposes hypocrisy in the name of morality which is one for the woman and other for the man. This is because in Indian society, like the concept of the Victorian era, there is a prescribed code of conduct for women which require them to be dedicated to their husbands.

Markandaya's novel *A Silence of Desire* seems to hold a mirror to the society which has been dominated for ages together by the blatant and dominant nature of man, with the strong support from the patriarchal culture. Kamala Markandaya prefers home with its inmates to focus on human relations. She represents the authentic picture of marital life living in contemporary India. Through the relationship between Dandekar and his wife Markandaya also delineates the class of people who have been tremendously influenced by science and faith which causes a clash between the religious and reasonable ideas. Dandekar represents the class of people who have been tremendously influenced by science and modern developments. But it hurts his ego when his wife does something secretively. Through the character of Dandekar, Markandaya unravels the fact that mostly Indian husbands still want their wives to follow the law propounded in *Manusmriti*, "though destitute of virtue, or seeking pleasure (elsewhere), or devoid of good qualities, (yet) a husband must be constantly worshipped as a god by a faithful wife" (154). In the novel, Dandekar is represented as a modernist. He thinks like a modernist when it concerns himself and when he finds it concerning his wife, he rejects to accept it. It shows that men cannot bear a woman to be independent. They like to change but only when it is related to their will. They don't want changes which are related to their wives' 'freedom'. They always want to keep their wives in their grip and their possession. They always want women to act according to their will. Hence, it is not easy for a woman to break the concept, "Man for the field and woman for the hearth." Today most of the people talk about women's empowerment and women are getting empowered but it is also the reality of a patriarchal society where they are given a secondary role in their family.

REFERENCES

Angom, R. *Kamala Markandaya's Novels*. New Delhi: Akansha Publishing House, 2012. Print.

Bhatnagar, Manmohan. *Kamala Markandaya: A Critical Spectrum*. New Delhi: Atlantic Publishers & Distributors, 2000. Print.

David, Lodge. *The Modes of Modern Writing: Metaphor, Metonymy and the Typology of Modern Literature*. London: Edward Arnold, 1977. Print.

Elena, J. Kalinnikova. *Indian-English Literature: A Perspective*. Ghaziabad: Vimal Prakashan, 1982. Print.

Henna, Papanek. *Separate Worlds: Studies of Purdah in South Asia*. New Delhi: Chanakya Publications, 1982. Print.

Hudson, W.H. *An Outline History of English Literature*. New Delhi: New Delhi: Atlantic Publishers & Distributors, 2008. Print.

Jha, Gauri Shankar. *Multiculturalism and Diasporic Dilemmas: The Fiction of Kamala Markandaya*. New Delhi: Adhyayan Publishers & Distributors, 2012. Print.

Krishnaswamy, S. *The Woman in Indian Fiction in English*. New Delhi: Ashish Publishing House, 1984. Print.

Markandaya, Kamala. *A Silence of Desire*. New Delhi: Penguin, 2019. Print.

Misra, Pravati. *Class Consciousness in the Novels of Kamala Markandaya*. New Delhi: Atlantic Publishers & Distributors, 2001. Print.

Pattanaik, A. *Kamala Markandaya: A Critical Study*. New Delhi: Omega Publications, 2011. Print.

Tennyson, Alfred Lord. "The Princess." *The Norton Anthology of English Literature*. Web. 25 Mar. 2019.

<https://www.norton.com/college/english/nael/victorian/topic_2/nature.htm>

Trodd, Anthea. *Domestic Crime in the Victorian Novel*. New York: St Martin's Press, 1989. Print.

CHAPTER V. *Manusmriti*. Web. 8 May 2019. <http://www.sacred-texts.com/hin/manu/manu05.htm.>

Chapter 11

Breaking the Barriers: Space and Time in Badal Sircar's *Basi Khabar* (*The Stale News*, 1979)

Subhankar Dutta

The throbs of the anguished heart have different languages of articulating protest. Some pick up a gun, some rely on the sword, arrow, and some believe that "the pen can be mightier than the sword". But all of these stem out of a condition of unrest and exploitation: conspicuous or surreptitious. In the mid-nineteenth century, the Santhal Rebellion (1855-56) was one significant testimony of social unrest and exploitation in India. Not only the historian or scholar of that time but later scholars also engaged in a critical and creative endeavour to find out an idiom that can question the very relationship between oppressed and oppressor; colonized and colonizer; victim and victimizer. Theatre as a socio-cultural space brings forth several points of contestation that compels us to rethink, re-examine, and reconfigure our social understanding both analytically and conceptually. Theatre has always been considered as a means of propagating ideas—both political and philosophical (Sarkar, *Theatre's Audience*, 1). Badal Sircar's *Basi Khabar* (*Stale News*) is one such theatrical piece that re-engages us in a critical account about our present society, looking through the mirror of the past. Sircar (1925-2011), initially an engineer by profession, is an influential Indian dramatist and theatre director who pioneered an egalitarian theatre known as 'Third Theatre'. Sircar has established the theatre company "Shatabdi" and wrote more than fifty plays of which *Evam Indrajit* (*And Indrajit*, 1963), *Michhil* (*Procession*, 1974), *Pagla Ghora* (*Mad Horse*, 1967), *Basi Khabar* (*Stale

News, 1979) are significant pieces. In this paper, I explore how Badal Sircar's *Stale News* presents the idea of space and time in theatre and, in the life of Santhals. My focus is on Sircar's life like theatre pursuit and engagement with "third theatre". The paper analyzes the ways in which Sircar changed the earlier 'grammar' of theatre and presented public arena as a theatrical space. It also highlights how the issue of Santhal Rebellion, along with the description of *Damin-i-ko* brings conceptual tools of looking at the idea of time differently. The first part of my paper examines Sircar's association with theatrical thoughts and his dynamism in using space for theatrical presentation. In the second part, I have looked into the issue of situating a nineteenth-century rebellion to a late twentieth-century play. How this positioning of the movement impels us to re-imagine time in a new way? The primitiveness of the cult, the 'timelessness' of Santhals, Sircar's theatre and the post-colonial history formation, are contesting with each other in the matter of relocating Santhal Rebellion within the mainstream time frame. I argue in this paper that Sircar's play *Stale News* is relocating Santhal tribe and Santhal Rebellion from their 'primitiveness' to a historical understanding which is not static, rather continuous.

Stale News was a joint venture by Badal Sircar and Shatabdi group, first staged in 1979. Shatabdi was a non-paid theatre group who used to assemble on spare time of their work for this theatre endeavour (Sircar, *A Letter*, 53). The Theosophical Society of College Square in Kolkata was the space where *Stale News* was first performed. As Sircar mentioned in a letter to Richard Schechner: "An old building in the congested College Square area, occupied by the Theosophical Society of India for more than ninety years. The lecture hall on the second story, 58 feet long and 24 feet wide, with its old dusty cupboards full of books on Theosophy and faded oil paintings of potentates of Theosophy, was given to Shatabdi on rent every Friday after much persuasion. The first performance of *Basi Khabar* was a culmination of a year-long process. The first experience of Shatabdi of creating a play collectively" (Sircar, *A Letter*, 52). However, while looking at the play, it is essential to look at Sircar's understanding of theatre. Theatre for Sircar was much more than artistic pursuit. Theatre, coming from the Greek word *theatron* (behold), for him, was a tool for social awareness and reformation. As he says: "Only those who feel the urge to change and want to use theatre to contribute to the forces of change, can be in this theatre" (Sircar, *A Letter*, 57). Born and raised in a "monster city that grew by sucking the blood of a vast rural hinterland which perhaps is the true India" (Sircar, *A Letter*, 51), Sircar felt the genuine need for a theatre that speak to all, "understood equally by the educated of the city and the illiterate of the village" (Sircar, *A Letter*, 52). This was the reason Sircar engaged his group to prepare theatre that can talk about the oppressed: the village people who are struggling with issues of land and cultivation under the domination of Zamindars, landowners, and the British. For him, theatre should speak for itself not only for others. For this, he used to do workshops in villages to make the villagers perform their own struggle stories as theatre form. Taking the theatre away from the monopoly of 'educated' he looked forward to a mass theatre: 'theatre of the people, by the people and for the people'.

I

Sircar's vision for a 'Third Theatre' stems out of creative and reformist zeal that become prominent in the latter half of his life: from the 1970s-90s (Joshi, 156). However, to him, the folk theatre, as well as, the West borrowed proscenium theatres are confined to a city-based intelligentsia which is hardly accessible to the 'common' gentry (Sircar, *A Letter*, 56). We need to move from the 'First Theatre' (Folk Theatre) and 'Second Theatre' (Proscenium Theatre) to a more 'flexible', 'portable', and 'free' form that can make theatre a movement in itself. So, Sircar felt the emergence of 'Third Theatre' as a social need. Under this sort of socio-cultural condition, the play *Stale News* stands as an emblem to Sircar's understandings. The first part of the play concerned with the Santhals' Rebellion, who settled near the Bengal-Bihar border (Sircar, *A Letter*, 53). It was a massive rebellion by the Santhals where "The hungry, the half-naked Santhals took up their primitive arms, spear, axe, bow and arrow and fought against the trained, well-fed troops with guns, cannons, horses and elephants, liberating village after village in Bihar and Bengal, not giving up until twenty-five thousand were killed after nine long months of heroic struggle" (qtd. in Bhattacharya, 204). However, the oppression on the Santhal is not only the prime focus of the play. Instead, it concentrates on different forms of socio-cultural oppression and deprivation that the Santhal Rebellion can point. Sircar wants to look at the plot of the play from the perspective of contemporary youth who "[...] is confused by this bombardment of a barrage of information, quite often contradictory, full of contrasts and perhaps even the most shattering bits of information come as stale news" (Dutta, 8). The play stems out of a fundamental question that Sircar posited—what will be the reaction of a young man at the account of Santhal Rebellion? (Sircar, *A Letter*, 55). The play starts with a chorus of eight who gradually give descriptions of Damin-i-ko ("later described as Santhal Parganas"—Sircar, *Basi Khabar*, 125). Followed by the accounts of upper-middle-class gentry of society, different offices of British ruler, and the money-based economy that they introduced: as the second chorus cried out "the barter-based economy and social life of the Santhals began to crumble under the impact of the exploitation and the money economy they introduced [...]" (Sircar, *Basi Khabar*, 160).

While talking about colonialism and the ways it is being contested by the anti-colonial endeavour, Sircar in the play speaks about the association of Bengali middle class in the entire gamut of things. It is a time when a whole class of Bhadrolok was emerging as an urban professional class. Under the British advocacy and Zamindars' help, they are creating a subject formation hostile to the rural land and land-workers. Apart from Santhal Rebellion, few years after, the massive Indigo Rebellion (1859) is a testimony to the sheer oppression and manipulation of land in favour of British which is articulated by both British and native lords (Wadikar, 1). To Sircar, these people are working as a collaborator to the colonial cultural legacy, which is still prevalent. The latter part of the play talks about the emergence of the Bengali Renaissance. "Zamindars, traders, professors, teachers, clerks, caste Hindu, the lackeys of the British and contractors" (Sircar, *Basi Khabar*, 135) who participated in the 'movement' to emphasize that "without the support of the English, there's no way to revive the eternal religion", and "The English are friendly rulers" (Sircar, *Basi Khabar*, 138). The subsequent section of the play gives descriptions of several social injustices of the twentieth century onwards. The oppression and torture were not confined to the Santhal only. Many poor tribes, Harijans become the victim of inhuman torture: "In the first nine months of 1978, 3019 cases of atrocities on the Harijans. One hundred and seventy-five Harijans killed, 129 Harijans women raped, 289 cases of arson [...]" (Sircar, *Basi Khabar*, 160). The continuity of similar events across decades is suggested at the end of the play when the chorus said "the nineteenth century [...] the twentieth century [...] the fifties [...] the seventies [...] British India [...] Independent India" (Sircar, *Basi Khabar*, 163).

To delineate all these events of torture, oppression, and revolt in theatre performance one needs sheer involvement. As Sircar said: "It is not a theatre one can perform by 'enacting'. It can only be performed by 'state of being'. The performer acts out his own feelings, his own concerns, contradictions and guilt" (*A Letter*, 55). To have his reformist zeal at the place, the theatre performer has to have close and impactful connectivity with the audience. The earlier proscenium theatre and the folk theatre were dependent on-stage system having aesthetic distance between the performer and audience, and the performers are fixed in a place where the audience used to come. Sircar wants to change the whole dynamics in the reverse order and wants to make theatre portable and mobile. As Suvendu Sarkar mentioned: "[...] by dispensing with the entire paraphernalia of the naturalistic theatre—props, costume, make-up, spotlights, and artificial sound system—Sircar's theatre turned portable as it could be carried anywhere with ease" (*Bikolpo Thiyetarer*, 210). Communication was the key intention here. So breaking away the barrier between audience and performers is necessary. They started "performing in public parks, slums, factories, villages, wherever the people are" (Sircar, *A Letter*, 56). They "stopped using sets, spotlights, costly costumes, make-up-not as a matter of principle, but because we realized that they are not essentials, even if sometimes necessary". They "concentrated on the essentials—the human body and the human mind" (Sircar, *A Letter*, 56). However, by moving away from the earlier construction of the theatre, they also faced constraints of money and very little advocacy from the economic strata of the society. This is also one reason behind experimenting with the earlier forms. In fact, what Sircar propounded is quite similar to the Western notion of avant-garde theatre which engaged in experimenting with theatre form and theatre space. Sircar's association with Richard Schechner, a theatre director, and performance studies professor is already being mentioned. There have been several other associations with experimental theatre persona of the West, which I discussed later in the article. However, I am looking at Sircar's alternative theatre space creation, which is free and much democratic. It is a sort of 'third space' creation where the concern is community, not a single individual; seeking social change rather than individual growth. For an example, we can look at the Sundarbans (Southern Bengal) theatre group consisting illiterate and landless agricultural workers who presented their life's problem and demand through theatre immediately after the workshop of 'Shatabdi' group (Sircar, *A Letter*, 58).

As the theatre space is becoming portable and connective, the impact also travels beyond the confinement of situational. So, under Sircar's endeavour, the theatre space becomes more of a 'think tank' where new ideas and notions are nurtured. This 'massification' of theatre also brings a considerable youth engagement into it. Quite in a similar fashion, Etheridge Woodson said: "ensemble theatre and performance uniquely engage the web of relations and therefore, the space of being human" (181). Woodson took the term 'third space' to describe a non-hierarchical theatre space where there is significant youth engagement. Sircar also looking for similar space creation, in theatre and society, where there will be no hierarchy between the performer and audience, and the high culture and low culture. However, "the demand of the spectator in the new theatre is not an illusion of reality, but of reality itself, the reality of the presence of the performer" (Sircar, *The Changing Language*, 26). Thus, in the hand of Sircar, theatre made a journey from the Proscenium theatre to *Anganmancha* (close indoor) and

Muktamancha (open outdoor) (Borthakur, 152; Mitra, 65). In both the techniques, there is no proscenium stage, and there is minimal alienation between the performer and the audience. In *Anganmancha*, the audience sits or stands in close proximity to the performers sharing the same light and platform. As Anjum Katyal said: "The actors can be behind or beside the spectators, look into their eyes and communicate with them individually. The audience can be touched and felt" (23). *Muktamancha* aims at performing in open spaces like market, school ground, etc. Rather than *Anganmancha*, this is more of a travelling theatre which "goes to the audience by themselves and performs before them" (Borthakur, 152). As Sircar himself said: "Theatre can show very little, but whatever it can show is here, now. The performers and the spectators come to the same place, on the same day, at the same time; otherwise, the event of theatre will not happen. [...] That is the strength. That should be emphasized" (*Voyages*, 8). The rural landscape, which is often being romanticized in theatre presentation, for Sircar, is "a vast rural hinterland which perhaps is the true India" (Sircar, *A Letter*, 51). Because of this Sircar tried to expand the theatre space to the rural land through *gram parikrama* or village tour conducting theatre presentations and workshops. As Sircar himself said: "We were having workshops, relating sometimes to the cruel absurdities we live in. Enormous wealth and immeasurable poverty. A devastating flood ruining hundreds of thousands in the villages. [...] Democracy and police brutality. The stupidity of man, the cruelty of man, the achievements of man, the callousness of man—not just in this country, but in the whole world" (*A Letter*, 53). *Stale News* was first performed in *Anganmancha* (Mitra, 63). Later on, it was also presented in open spaces. Innovatively, Sircar used interchanging characters and situations which have maximum impact on the audience. He used different newspapers to connect all the events of oppression and exploitation that have occurred through the pages of history. The eight characters without any name created an impact which is beyond any particular situation or a specific event. The anonymity of the names creates the impact universal. The dead man becomes very important as an emblem of 'dead' humanity, holding in the right hand, the contemporary news and on the other, the accounts of Santhal revolt (Sircar, *Basi Khabar*, 124). The members of the chorus move in a particular order and shout to portray the agony of the Santhal. The flexibility of 'Third Theatre' enables Sircar to change the action of the play frequently from birth of man, civilization, colonialism, Bengal renaissance to Santhal revolt. The gestures, the changing characters throughout the play (139), the movement from the centre to the corner of the theatre space (148, 159), the division of the eight characters to form specific situation (151, 155), and the different signals of the dead man—are profound use of space with subtle technicalities. Along with this, "The repeated expressions lend a musical pattern to the play. There is the use of both the verbal and non-verbal expressions throughout the action of the play, and this has given a distinctive sound pattern to *Basi Khabar*" (Venkateswarlu, 216). Thus, Sircar's experimentation with the form and content of theatre brings a new idiom for theatrical pursuit.

Sircar's engagement with the experimentation of theatrical forms also has several links with the Western theatre of the same time. In some fashion, Sircar's theatre has similarity with Jerzy Grotowski's Poor Theatre: theatre which can be "performed without make-up, costumes or any other supports, but it could not be performed without the resemblance between actors and spectators" (Borthakur, 153). Though Grotowski's theatre was not an open theatre, in the matter of bodily performance it has resemblances with 'Third Theatre'. Sircar's theatre does have some formal characteristics of Richard Schechner's Environmental Theatre. Along with using non-proscenium stage (Mitra, 63) Schchnner's focus on the bodily expressions of the performers could be seen in Sircar's works also (Borthakur, 153). The Brazilian theatre of August Bowel, namely the Theatre of the Oppressed, is also significant in this respect. In matters of creating spectators socially conscious, and in the case of communication between the audience and performer, there are similarities (Clark, 52). In the case of dialogue in the play *Stale News*, we find similarities with absurd dramatist like Samuel Beckett. In the approach towards life, Sircar's play also looked at the absurdities of life as we can see in absurd dramatists. Sircar himself said: "We were having workshops, relating sometimes to the cruel absurdities we live in" (Sircar, *A Letter*, 53). So there is no doubt about the Western influence on Sircar's approach to theatre space. But they cannot be put on the same line as the context of their theatre pursuit is quite different. For example, Sayoni Mitra quoted words of Sircar's interview, "Influences will always be there. The question is whether you are copying something exactly or whether you are assimilating things and doing your own thing, I mean fulfilling your own needs" (qtd. in Mitra, 67). There are subtle differences between the forms they used and that of Sircar himself (Mitra, 67). This association, as well as assimilation of different theatre forms of different places, brings the peculiarity in Sircar's concept of theatre and in his art of using theatrical space. Thus, *Stale News* in particular and 'Third Theatre', in general, shows Sircar's innovative and profound use of theatre space which has aesthetic and social significances.

II

Stale News starts with mentioning the very birth of man and then continues to the human civilization, industrialization, and colonization to the twentieth-century atomic age. The play covered almost a thousand years of history in the plot. In the total time frame of the play, the Santhal revolt has a central importance in theatrical development. Damin-i-ko and Bhagnadihi become significant space formations in the play, which portrays the spatial dimension. On the other, several historical moves bring forth the temporal dimension to it. However, the reason behind associating an old movement to a twentieth century play significantly can be traced from Sircar's own words which engage us in re-examining the idea of time concerning Santhal revolt or the Santhal *Hool*. Sircar said: "The aboriginals are always subjected to the worst kind of exploitation and injustice. Pushed beyond limits, they have often burst out in spontaneous revolts. But the accounts of such revolts do not find any place in the history textbooks" (Sircar, *A Letter*, 53). This loophole in between historical knowledge and historical practices brings conflict between "time as a mode of succession to the past and time as a practice for the future" (Banerjee, 209). In the mid-nineteenth century, Colonial India was engaging in the process of historical sensibility along with the endeavour of history-making. Historical imagination has been presented as a counter to 'primitive past' (Banerjee, 209). The chronological pursuit of history-making has negotiated with the presence of the primitive events of Santhal Rebellion. It put the rebellion in the framework of chronological understanding, which gives it a temporal existence. And in this process, the multiple temporalities of the uprising are lost, and Sircar's play is obliquely pointing towards that. As Banerjee said: "In other words, by making the rebellion into an event, chronology—as a purely formal succession—was made to overdetermine and defuse what were clearly temporal contradictions between Santhal practices and the colonial modern teleology" (210). There is no doubt that the Santhal rebellion has a significant impact on the national freedom struggle. Just two years after the rebellion, Sepoy Revolt took place: the first 'popular' freedom struggle. But, whether the revolution of Santhal was for a nationalistic identity creation or it is the perpetual revolt in search of a better life, this needs to be looked. More importantly, the inclusion of Santhal rebellion under the nation struggle movement might give access to the citizen subject, but at the same time, it will devoid it from other situationality that it revolted against. In the words of Banerjee, "The *hool* seems to propose an alteréd everyday which was irreconcilable with the continuum of numerically overdetermined eventualities that historiography admitted as chronological" (211). The problem is not in associating temporal understanding to it, but the very representation of the revolt as a single temporal continuous event has blurred the multiple temporalities that the revolt ascribes to. As Sugandhi said: "This effort was fraught with difficulties and contradictions—not only in terms of rationalizing the disruption of the causal everyday through the processes of colonization, but also in the expression of an acute anxiety stemming from the simultaneous dependence on, and requisite distancing from the encounter between the *anarya* primitive and *arya* historical subject" (906). On the one hand, the historiographic narrative looked at the *hool* as an act of temporal contestation, which requires casual representation as an even in the chronological history. On the other, for the Santhals, the *hool* is a critical act against the "transformed nature of everyday time, marked by the written order and disciplined by chronology [...]" (Sugandhi, 907).

While we are looking at the events in the past with a sense of temporality, and at history-making as an assimilating work, Sircar's play *Stale News* also posit into that sort of endeavour. The methodology that Sircar used for bringing temporal events into a spatial dimension shows his inclination towards a process of history-making which doesn't adhere to chronological restrictions. In the play, we can see the different locations where the Santhal revolt was taking place. Bhagnadihi becomes one central place where the Santhal assimilated: "Ten thousand Santhals representing 400 villages assembled at Bhagnadihi" (Sircar, *Basi Khabar*, 146). Also, the different events related to revolt are happening at a different time. The dis-association of the Santhals from the history is mentioned several times in the play when the characters speak out "In the distant past, in nearly prehistoric times [...]" (Sircar, *Basi Khabar*, 118). The play refers to the temporal association of Santhal *Hool* and the manipulative absence of their long history: "For thousands of years, their drums, beaten to the same rhythms [...] almost without any change until the eighteenth century" (Sircar, *Basi Khabar*, 119). All these snippets are pointing towards a lost past in narrative. Sircar is trying to reconfigure this lost past and reconnect it to the present as a continuous process of history. The connectivity is being established in the play when the characters start giving descriptions of the events of atrocities from the twentieth century onwards (Sircar, *Basi Khabar*, 162). Thus, by connecting a past event to contemporary situations, the play wants to show the continuity of similar narrative of oppression through ages. Though the spatial dimensions are different according to different temporalities, it does refer to several other temporal events of 'prehistoric' time, which is lost in the process of history-making. So the Santhal Rebellion should be kept away from the singular causality of anti-colonial nationalistic struggle movement, and also from a singular temporality of event. Rather it should point at the continuity of similar events happening in multiple temporalities. Sircar in his *Stale News* is trying to portray Santhal Rebellion as an epoch time in Indian history having multiple temporal imperatives that are still working in today's socio-political scenario. To quote Sircar: "Through research we became more and more confirmed in the belief we already had—that conditions have not changed fundamentally even today" (Sircar, *A Letter*, 54).

Thus, Sircar is also trying to put this Santhal Rebellion beyond any chronological history-making and trying to portray it as a mouthpiece of oppression and deprivation which worked in different temporalities of time. Rather than the limited time frame of the rebellion, the acts and its association with the more immense humanity become much more critical segment. From the Santhal Rebellion to the killing of Harijans (1978), the continuation of exploitation—suggest the ever-going process of oppression that the lower sections of the society are subjected to. Taking it away from the mere chronological understanding, Sircar tried to represent Santhal Rebellion in relation to other contemporary events which will save it from being historically constrained. The Santhals exist today; the poor 'Harijans' exist, so do exist the exploitation and oppression. So, restricting Santhal revolt to a chronological time will be a historical misrepresentation. Instead, it points at the "death, blood and fear" that "rule over this land" and also points to the situation that "will happen behind the prison walls" (Sircar, *Basi Khabar*, 163). In fact, time no longer remains the same because of the changed temporalities of the Santhal lives before and after the *hool*. So, bracketing this rebellion within a formal duration without enough focus to the pre- and post-rebellion situations will constitute a historical time which doesn't give holistic understanding. The Santhal Rebellion is more of a response to everyday reality rather than to any historical event. That is why Banerjee also said: Santhal Rebellion "[...] had to be contrasted to and casually predicted upon the 'normal' everyday of Santhals" (215). And taking these issues related to 'normal' everyday life out of the components of historical events is the problem with the historical narrative of Santhal Rebellion. Sircar's play refashioned the limited presence and constricted representation of Santhal Rebellion, as a token, that can be relocated within the frame of historical events as well as beyond it.

Thus, the dimension of space and time are dealt with precision and innovative theatrical technicalities in *Stale News*. The move from the earlier notion to a more flexible form of theatre enables Sircar to make theatre more inclusive. Though critics question about Sircar being politically inclined towards leftist ideologies, restricting him to merely political understanding will be a limited expression to the enormity of his contribution. As Banfield and Crow said: "In his writing Sircar is not explicitly politically partisan, insofar as he refuses to align himself with any one political party, preferring instead to preserve the integrity that this independence has afforded him. His motivation for writing has, however, become characterized by a passionate personal response to the injustices and oppressions endured in the lives of the poor and dis-enfranchised, both of his own country and beyond" (117). The play in particular and the associated issues that it brings forth compels us to relocate the play in today's socio-political scenario. The play has been written and performed, almost forty years before describing the continuity of the tyrannous social power struggle and the unspoken sentiments of the Santhals, but the "conditions have not changed fundamentally even today" (Sircar, *A Letter*, 54). There are numerous accounts of social oppression along the line of the socio-political power equation. Hansda, a Santhal himself, gives an engaging account of oppression on Santhal which is post 2013: "We are like toys—someone presses our 'ON' button, or turns a key in our backsides, and we Santhals start beating rhythms on our tamak and tumdak, or start blowing tunes on our tiriyo while someone snatches away our very dancing grounds" (Hansda, 170). However, in *Stale News*, the concern is not only the Santhal per se, but it aims at all such social construction of manipulative power equation. It is more concerned with a humanistic approach of Sircar, which attempts at sensitizing people of the society. I would like to quote Tripathi's observation that echoes similar purport as of Sircar's *Stale News*: "On the surface [it] may appear to be a riveting tale of the face-off between the tribals and the state, but a layered interpretation of the stories may read it to be a confrontation of the hierarchies of the society—the powerful and the powerless, the rich and the poor" (195). To conclude, taking art, aesthetics, and socio-political issues together, Sircar is trying to look forward to a society which is much more egalitarian in thought and action. In the contemporary situation when we are looking at the ideas of liberation in thought and action, plays like *Stale News* re-engages us with the fundamental issues of equality, freedom, and compels us to re-examine the earlier dictum again and again: "Eh aazaadi juta hain" (this Independence is a lie).

REFERENCES

Banerjee, Prathama. "Historical Act? Santhal Rebellion and the Temporality of Practice." *Studies in History*, 15.2 (1999): 209-46. Print.

Banfield, Chris and Brian Crow. "Badal Sircar's Third Theatre of Kolkata." *An Introduction to Post-Colonial Theatre*. Cambridge: Cambridge University Press, 1996. Print.

Bhattacharjee, Shampa. "*Badal Sircar's Street Plays: A Thematic Study.*" M.Phil. Dissertation. Warangal: Kaktiya University, 1994. Print.

Clark, Jude. "Acting up and speaking out: Using theatre of the oppressed and collective memory work as alternative research methods and empowerment tools in work with girls." *Agenda: Empowering Women for Gender Equity*, 79 (2009): 49-64. Print.

Dutta, Ella. "Introduction." *Three Plays*. Badal Sircar. Kolkata: Seagull Books, 2009. Print.

Hansda, Sowvendra Shekhar. *The Adivasi will not Dance: Stories*. New Delhi: Speaking Tiger Private Ltd., 2017. Print.

Joshi, Swati Sureshrao. *A Critical Study of Badal Sircar's Selected Plays in English Translation*. Ph.D. Dissertation. Swami Ramanand Teerth Marathwada University, 2017. Web. 21 May 2019. <shodhganga.inflibnet.ac.in/handle/10603/192721>

Katyal, Anjum. *Badal Sircar: Towards a Theatre of Conscience*. 1sted. New Delhi: SAGE India, 2015. Print.

Mitra, Shayoni. "Badal Sircar: Scripting a Movement." *The Drama Review*, 48.3 (2004): 59-78. Print.

Phukon, Pranab, and Satyakam Borthakur. "Third Theatre: A Media Closer to the Folk."*Asian Journal of Research in Social Sciences and Humanities*, 5.2 (2015): 148-57. Print.

Sarkar, Subhendu. "Theatre's Audience: Audience's Theatre." *Journal of Humanities and Social Sciences*, 2 (2005): 286-305. Print.

—. "Badal Sarkar: Bikolpo Thiyetarer Khnoje (Badal Sircar: In search of Alternative Theatre)." *Korok* Sep-Dec 2013: n.p. Web. 14 May 2019.

Sircar, Badal. "A Letter from Badal Sircar." *The Drama Review*, 26.2 (1981): 51-58. Print.

—. *The Changing Language of the Theatre*. New Delhi: Indian Council for Cultural Relations, 1982. Print.

—. *Basi Khabar*. Trans. Samik Bandhopadhay, *Stale News*. Kolkata: Seagull Books, 1985. Print.

—. *Shri Ram Memorial Lectures IV: Voyages in the Theatre*. Delhi: Shri Ram Centre for Performing Art, 1993. Print.

—. *Beyond the Land of Hattainala and Scandal in Fairyland*. 1994. Trans. Suchanda Sarkar. Calcutta: Seagull Books, 2003. Print.

Sugandhi, Namita Sanjay. "Rev. of *Politics of Time: 'Primitives' and History-Writing in a Colonial Society* by Prathama Banerjee." *Anthropological Quarterly,* 80.3 (2007): 905-10. Print.

Tripathi, Priyanka. "Rev. of *The Adivasi Will Not Dance: Stories* by Sowvendra Shekhar Hansda." *Rupkatha Journal on Interdisciplinary Studies in Humanities,* 9.4 (2017): 193-96. Print.

Wadikar, Shailaja. B. "Spirit for Revolution in Badal Sircar's *Stale News.*" *Pune Research,* 2.3 (2016): 1-10. Print.

Woodson, Stephani Etheridge. *Theatre for Youth Third Space: Performance, Democracy, and Community Cultural Development*. Bristol: Intellect Ltd., 2015. Print.

Venkateswarlu, K. *Badal Sircar's Third Theatre with Special Reference to Procession, Bhoma, and Stale News.* M.Phil. Dissertation. Sri Krishnadevaraya University, 1993. Web. 17 May 2019. <shodhganga.inflibnet.ac.in/handle/10603/85828>

Chapter 12

Motherhood and Profession: A Comparative Study of Mahasweta Devi's *Breast-Giver* and Vijay Tendulkar's *Silence! The Court is in Session*

Anirban Kahali

In India, there is "a Sanskrit proverb *Janani janmabhumischa svargadapi gariyasi*", which according to Mr. Kashikar means, "Mother and/ The Motherland,/ Both are even/ Higher than heaven" (30). This is the most common notion that the Indian mass believes by their heart and soul, but unfortunately, this is just the tip of the iceberg. While we praise motherhood and equate mothers with gods, at the same time we have a contrapuntal notion regarding this issue where class, social norms, tradition, and occupation legitimate the biological act of giving birth to a child. Motherhood is considered to be sacred and it is the only thing that makes a woman "complete", but we have a different attitude when it comes to the professional sphere. Where in some cases, motherhood turns out to be a woman's profession; in other cases, it causes a great threat to a woman's profession. As we can find in Mahasweta Devi's *Breast-Giver*, Jashoda's motherhood becomes her identity and when her husband becomes incapable to earn them two square meals; her motherhood becomes their source of income. She becomes a wet nurse and thus turns into the universal mother. On the contrary, in Vijay Tendulkar's *Silence! The Court is in Session*, motherhood becomes a curse for Benare and is forced to commit an act of "infanticide".

Both these writers are sympathetic towards the social issues and have addressed several of them in many of their literary works. Mahasweta Devi (1926-2016), who was one of the leading Bengali writers, was committed to social and political issues and criticized them from a leftist perspective. In her works, she mainly focused on the plights of the peasants, outcasts, women, and the tribal people. She was also one of the major feminist writers of our country and through her works; she raised voice against various oppression against women. Vijay Tendulkar (1928-2008), a major contemporary Indian playwright along with Badal Sircar, Girish Karnad and others, was also a sympathetic commentator who pointed towards various social and political issues in his Marathi dramas, though it's true that he was not a feminist conventionally, yet he depicts how this society witnesses the exploitation, subjugation, domestication, and sufferings of women.

In her story "Breast-Giver" ("Stanadayini", 1980), Mahasweta Devi deals with the theme of exploitation of a working-class woman. The protagonist of this story is a woman, Jashoda, who unlike the other protagonists of Devi's story, belongs from the higher strata of the Hindu caste system, Brahmin, whose husband Kangalicharan is a helpless victim of the rich patriarch Haldarbabu's clan, whose "new son-in-law's Studebaker and the sudden desire of the youngest son of the Haldar-house to be a driver" (1069) brought havoc to her life. As her husband loses his ability to earn for his family, Jashoda accepts the job of a wage earner of the household as her children "Gopal, Nepal, and Radharani whine interminably for food and abused their mother" (1073). Until she becomes useless to the Haldar family, they keep her as a wet-nurse. Here the dynamics of a woman exploiting another woman is portrayed in a vivid manner, where the women of the upper-class Haldar family exploit the poor Jashoda and pay her with food and shelter instead of money. The relentless collusion of patriarchal and capitalist ideologies in the exploitation of the disadvantaged are shown vividly by Mahasweta Devi. In this story, Mahasweta Devi points out how the women of the Haldar household, who are themselves, victims, are the chief exploiters of Jashoda and "the status of wage earner not only fails to release Jashoda from the expectation of wifehood and motherhood but saddles her with the untimely self-destructive task of being mother of the world." Nevertheless, neither victimization nor its awareness fully robs Jashoda and Kangalicharan of their sense of agency and power" (1068).

In this story, Mahasweta Devi reveals how society uses certain parameters to distinguish between the different sexes. In order to do so, they assign different roles to them. These culturally accepted roles or practices turn a 'male' into a 'man' or a 'female' into a 'woman'. Such practices had basically originated from the "reproductive system of men and women which are biological, but under the social context, they are invested with particular meanings" (89). For example, women are biologically capable of bearing children. This biological activity has certain values associated with it. Thus, the feminists argue that these social values attributed to nothing but some biological acts. This means that the woman's biology and biological functions are evaluated, determined and governed not merely as biology but from social values attributed to them" (90). Motherhood is one such important social value, which makes a woman "complete" in her life. The Sanskrit proverb, which says "*Janmi janmabhumishcha svargadapi gariyasi*", which means that mother and motherland, both are even higher than heaven. This clearly indicates the importance we give to the act of motherhood. In India, motherhood is considered sacred and a mother is worshipped in our society. Often it is noticed that a woman who has given birth to a child is considered holy and is asked to perform different rites in many auspicious occasions, whereas, those women who have not received the 'blessing of motherhood' is often barred from entering many occasions. While reading *Silence!* we find that people criticise and gossip about Mrs. Kashikar, who does not have an issue. Even in our mythologies, we have high regards for motherhood. We can see those images of motherhood being related to Jashoda in this story. Not only does the protagonist, but Jashoda's name also symbolises the name of the mythical character Yashoda, the mother of the beloved child-god Lord Krishna. Furthermore, the readers witness how the professional mother merges with other Indian icons of motherhood, namely sacred cows, the lion-seated goddess, and "mother India" herself.

From the feminist perspective, this theme of motherhood has been used to provide a glitter wrapping to the inhuman exploitation of the protagonist. The working-class protagonist, Jashoda had to become a "professional mother" (1069) because she had the responsibility to provide food for her family. Exploitation appears in many different forms. According to the Marxist feminists' perspective, patriarchy had "risen from the capitalist economic system: it requires, and benefits from women's unpaid labour at home" (94). Even in this story, Jashoda does not get her payment in cash but is provided with food, clothes, and shelter as her payment. She is oppressed not only by the men but also by the women, who themselves are oppressed by their husbands. The women who had employed Jashoda oppressed her economically and psychologically. They treat her as a commodity rather than an actual human being. She is used by her employers and also by her husband. She had fed the children of the Halder household with her own milk, but when she grew old; her employers fired her from her job. Even her husband, whom she provided with food and clothes, disowns her when she was admitted to the hospital, counting her last few days. Thus, the commodification of Jashoda by the patriarchy shows us the dynamics in which exploitation takes place. Sarah Grimke in her work *Letters on the Equality of the Sexes and the Conditions of Woman* points out: "All history asserts that man has subjected woman to his will, used her as a means to promote his selfish gratification, to minister to his sensual pleasures, to be instrumental in promoting his comfort; but never has desired to elevate her to the rank she was created to fill" (11).

Finally, we can say that the story is a representative of Mahasweta Devi's fiction, in which mythic and satirical inflexions create an impact on the deceptive surface of a seemingly realistic narratives of linear plots. While the many layers of meaning in "Breast-Giver" are accessible even in translation, much of the power of the original derives from Mahasweta Devi's distinctive style and voice. In this story, as in the author's other works, classical Hindu myths connect with quotations from Shakespeare and Marx. Different kinds of slang, dialect—literary Bengali and English blend together to create a powerful language that in many respect resembles modern Bengali usage, yet remains a unique creation of Mahasweta Devi.

Tendulkar has produced some excellent Marathi plays, which contains twenty-eight full-length plays, eleven children's plays and around twenty-four one-act plays. Among all these plays, *Silence! The Court is in Session* (1967) won him immediate success and brought him into the limelight. The play revolves around an amateur theatre group which visits a village to perform a play. Due to the absence of one important member of the group, they decide to train a local boy who can play that role. To do this, they start playing a sadistic game of a mock trial within themselves, where they trap and torture the protagonist of the play Miss Leela. The play is in the form of a play-within-the-play, which depicts the plight of a young woman, who is betrayed by the patriarchal society.

The protagonist of the play, Miss Leela Benare, an independent woman of thirties, teaches in a school. She is proud of her profession and in an introductory conversation with Samant, a local man, she proudly says: "I haven't heard a single reproach for not being on time these past eight years. Not about my teaching. I'm never behind with my lessons! Exercises corrected on time, too! Not a bit of room for disapproval—I don't give an inch of it to anyone!" (4). Being an independent woman, she challenges various social norms and thus in a planned manner, the male lawmakers of the society corner her and punishes her for her independent nature. To sideline Benare, the male members of the group use illegitimate affair against her and shame her for becoming a mother without getting married. Here, interestingly enough, another noteworthy thing is the fact that Mrs. Kashikar's, an important member of the group, secret agreement in attack on Benare symbolises women's internalization of the dominance of men over themselves and this is shown as a natural phenomenon and all these turn against other independent women and frame then as "others".

Here motherhood becomes a weapon, which is used against progressive-minded Benare in order to subdue her. One can also understand that motherhood is not only a biological phenomenon; it is also a social institution, which can only be accepted by our society if one adheres to some of the socially accepted parameters regarding motherhood. Benare clearly belongs to the economically middle-class section of the society, the most complex section whose mentality is reserved and conservative. The middle-class people cannot accept the fact that one can become a mother without getting married. Such an act not only brings serious social stigma but also it carries a serious economic threat to a woman. In our country, there are many jobs, which strictly prohibit motherhood even today. Thus, Arundhati Banerjee says: "the accusation brought against Benare at the beginning of the trial turns into the verdict because contemporary society cannot allow the birth of child out of wedlock" (VIII).

Amazingly enough, the male partner, who was a middle-aged professor, prof. Damle was not blamed for the deed. In her article "*Silence! The Court is in Session*—A Strong Social Commentary", Subha Tiwari said: "The whole responsibility of morally upright behaviour is bulldozed on women. Men are by nature considered to be wilful, wild, childish, innocent, and mischievous. Their sins are no sins at all. The society has a very light parental and pampering sort of attitude when it comes to sexual offences of men. In case of women, the iron rod gets hot and hotter. No punishment is actually enough for such a woman. There is no respite, no shade and no soothing cushion for a sinning woman. She must be stained and abandoned. Her femininity, her needs, her very existence must be ignored or rather destroyed. She must be concerned and brutally killed both in physical and psychological senses. This play is about the pathetic position of women in the male-dominated Indian world." Even Mahasweta Devi points out to this aspect of the society in "Breast-Giver" where she says that "Such is the power of the Indian soil that all women turn into mothers here and all men remain immersed in the spirit of holy childhood. Each man the Holy Child and each woman the Divine Mother" (1074). Thus, to every man, a woman is just a commodity to satisfy his sexual needs. This is why Benare is cheated twice in love, once by her uncle and once by Damle, and our other protagonist Jashoda is abandoned by her husband when she becomes old and cannot bear any more children. The plight of Benare intensifies when the mock-court held her guilty of her sin and punishes her in an inhuman way. In the play, finally the judge Mr. Kashikar says: "The time is up. The accused has no statement to make. In any case, it would be of no use. The cup of her crime is now full. Now—the judgement [...]. The crimes you have committed are most terrible. There is no forgiveness for them. Your sin must be expiated. Irresponsibility must be chained down [...]. Therefore, this court hereby sentences that you shall live. But the child in your womb shall be destroyed" (76).

Thus, to conclude, we can easily witness the difference between the two different ladies, who belong to two different socio-economic classes but are exploited on the basis of motherhood. On one hand, motherhood in the case of Jashoda becomes a way to earn her living; on the other hand, it becomes a curse for Benare as her professional life comes under trouble. Along with the social stigma, she also faces an economic threat as her motherhood does not satisfy the social norms and tradition as Mr. Kashikar said: "Social customs, after all are of supreme importance. Marriage is the very foundation of our society's stability. Motherhood must be sacred and pure" (75). Even today in our day-to-day life, in a middle-class society, any woman who is a single mother becomes a topic of gossip and is avoided by others. The worst part of politics becomes evident, as the play proceeds. The initial charge that was labelled against Benare was that of infanticide, but surprisingly in the judgement, all agree that the child should be killed. Thus, the duality of society with regard to motherhood is evident in these two representative texts.

REFERENCES

Banerjee, Arundhuti. "Introduction". *Five Plays*, New Delhi: Oxford India Paperbacks, 1995, Eight Impression, 2006. VIII. Print.

Chhabra, Shailja. "Exploitation of Women and Patriarchal Domination in Vijay Tendulkar's *Silence! The Court is in Session.*" *American International Journal of Research in Humanities, Arts and Social Sciences*, 13.3 (February 2015): 207-10. Print.

Devi, Mahasweta. "Breast-Giver". *The Norton Anthology of World Literature*. Vol. 2. Ed. Peter Simon. Trans. Gayatri Spivak. New York: W.W. Norton & Company, 2009. 1067-88. Print.

Grimke, Sarah M. *Letters on the Equality of the Sexes and the Condition of Women*. Boston: Isaac Knapp, 1838. 11. Print.

Nayar, Pramod K. *Contemporary Literary and Cultural Theory*. New Delhi: Pearson India, 2010. 82-120. Print.

Pilcher, Jane and Imelda Whelehan. *50 Key Concepts in Gender Studies*. New Delhi: Sage Publication Limited, 2004. Print.

Tendulkar, Vijay. *Silence! The Court is in Session*. New Delhi: Oxford University Press, 2011. Print.

Chapter 13

Who Wants Murder?: Solving Mystery to Confront Nostalgia in Kaye's *Death in the Andamans*

K.B.S. Krishna

Nostalgia is a key characteristic in diasporic writing (Huyssen, 149), as the craving for home or a homeland is inextricably associated with migrants (Nadarajah, 19). This desire for home, however, does not result in picturing a tangible place—as the home that they had left is located in the past, and thus, unattainable, but in imagining a space or an activity that they associate with home or homeland (Lagoumitzi, 27). Hence, nostalgia can be set off by various things, perhaps hardly pertinent in themselves, but significant nevertheless to individuals who associate it with a secure homestead in their memories—which may or may not be shared collectively (Halbwachs, 59). Flowers, toys, songs, colours, food, etc., therefore, can cause nostalgia. But can death cause nostalgia? Or, in fact, is it possible to be nostalgic for death—and that too not natural, but murder? This paper is an attempt to look at how even murder can set off a diasporic community on a nostalgic trip by a study of M.M. Kaye's (1908-2004) *Death in the Andamans* (1985), and thereon show how such nostalgia—and nostalgia generally, can be addressed to find and create a secure home without craving for something that is past and/or lost.

Kaye is a diasporic novelist who was born in pre-independent India in a British family but soon left for England for her schooling. While she spent most of her childhood and youth in England, she hardly had a place to call 'home' as due to her husband's profession she was translocated twenty-seven times in nineteen years (Horwell). Although she settled down in England in her final years, her desire for home, and mainly a desire for a place where she could feel secure is apparent in her writings. In *Death in the Andamans*, written in 1944 with the title *Strange Island* and published originally in 1960 as *Death on the Island*, this nostalgia is palpable.

The novel set in pre-Independent India begins with Caroline Olivia Phoebe Elizabeth aka Copper's visit to the Andamans on the invitation of her friend Valerie Masson, the daughter of Sir Lionel—the Chief Commissioner. When a couple of murders happen, Copper along with her friends (Valerie and her boyfriend Charles, and Nicholas Tarrent) decide to turn into an amateur detective and solve the mystery.

Copper's decision to turn detective, while seemingly foolhardy, is in keeping with the characteristics of country house mystery—which, according to Thomas Godfrey, is an intrinsically British tradition (xv). He goes on to state that this is because while writers of other nationalities had attempted to copy and write similar works, for the British it is home-grown as it had developed out of the Romantic literature of the late nineteenth century (xiv). Hence, the sub-genre is as British as late afternoon tea comprising brewed Earl Grey and scones (Godfrey, xx).

All country house mysteries share certain distinctive characteristics such as situated in a closed society, the presence of numerous suspects and a conceited villain, and an ethical amateur detective (Auden, 149-56). Moreover, the story needs to be a puzzle with a focus on the aspect of fair play so that the readers feel that they can compete with the amateur detective in solving the crime (Krishna, 53). However, the most significant aspect of the Country House Mystery is the implicit notion that crime is a disease and that the criminal is in some manner a diseased being, and hence, by finding a solution to the crime and punishing the criminal, the ills of world are once and for all eradicated, and the world again becomes a safe haven (Krishna, 65). Prominent examples of this sub-genre of detective fiction include *The Red House Mystery* (1922) by A.A. Milne (1882-1956), *Some Must Watch* (1933) by Ethel Lina White (1876-1944), and *An*

English Murder (1951) by Cyril Hare (1900-58). The sub-genre flourished mainly during the first half of the twentieth century, which is termed as the Golden Age of Detective Fiction, and Agatha Christie (1890-1976) was its chief practitioner, with both her first and last published novels belonging to this genre—*The Mysterious Affair at Styles* (1920) and *Curtain* (1975).

Kaye's *Death in the Andamans*, superficially, displays most of the characteristics of Country House Mystery novels. The detectives are amateurs for whom the whole issue of solving the mystery is a source of fun (Kaye, 444), which could hardly result in "much harm" (422)—as they are just indulging in, as one of the characters points out in a "three-ring circus" (466). The absence of the police force (422), due to inclement weather, is another feature of the sub-genre. There are multiple suspects who are enumerated (Kaye, 450), akin to Christie's *Peril at End House* (1932). This is followed to the extent that even the designation of an unknown entity by an alphabet by Hercule Poirot in the Christie novel (*Peril at End House*, 100) is copied religiously by the play-acting detectives (Kaye, 425). Such oblique, albeit unspecified, references to other mystery novels abound in the book.

In fact, when Valerie and Copper decide to turn amateur detectives and solve the crime, Valerie comes up with a suggestion referring to the *modus operandi* of detectives in mystery novels of that ilk: "If we both write down every single thing that's happened during the last two or three days, we may spot something that will give us a lead. It always seems to work in books" (Kaye, 423). Valerie by referring to how it happens in fiction might as well have been referring directly to mystery novels such as Mavis Doriel Hay's (1894-1979) *The Santa Klaus Murder* (1936)—in which this is the method adopted to figure out the killer.

On a similar note, even the setting of the crime, an island in the Andamans, suggests Christie's *And Then There were None* (1939). Both crimes take place on islands, and though Christie's novel is set on an uninhabited island (*And Then There were None*, 79), Kaye circumvents it by stating that the number of suspects is restricted as the native population is summarily discounted as being capable or culpable of murder by the amateurs (423-24). Another novel by Christie too finds a reference: *The Murder on the Orient Express* (1934). After jocularly deciding that six of the suspects had a reason, however absurd, to murder the victim, one of the characters comments: "Oh well, we might as well make a good job of it and prove that they all did it" (Kaye, 469). In Christie's novel, this is exactly what happens as all the characters gang up on the victim and stab him one after the other as an act of vengeance (*The Murder on the Orient Express*, 238-39).

However, such similarities cannot deny the fact that Kaye's novel is not a typical Country House Mystery but a clever subversion of the sub-genre. The main issue here is that the amateur detective in the novel is neither courageous nor is she intelligent or even intuitive—although that is never really a criterion for a country house detective. Even when at the end of the novel Copper divines the murderer, it is more of a fluky exclamation on her part that results in the villain coming out into the open rather than any canny interpretation of clues (Kaye, 525). The protagonist, herself, confesses as much early on in the novel, when she says that clues make sense "only when there is a private detective with a brain like a buzz-saw to spot the clue" (423), whereas Copper would not be able to recognise one even if she saw one (422). The difficulty of detecting leads Nicholas, who is an accomplice in this game of detection, to fervently pray:

> God forbid that I should ever meddle with a job like this again! What we need is Scotland Yard and the Ten Best Brains of Britain to cope with this bloody jig-saw puzzle. And I—heaven forgive me!—had an idea that if we dug about we might with luck come across something that would give us a lead. But I didn't bargain for half a hundred separate leads. (Kaye, 466)

This inability or incompetence of the detective is brought to the fore when after the second murder, Copper is shown as being terrified and with a wild desire to flee the scene (Kaye, 482). This is in stark contrast to the amateur detectives in country house mysteries. In the sub-genre, while the detectives are amateurish, they still display courage (oftentimes stubbornly), are resolute, have resilience, and are savvy judges of men and means.

Kaye's amateur detectives, on the contrary, behave no different from a minor character in the very novel—who is shown to be frightened at the prospect of a murderer in the midst. As Copper remarks, "[Rosamund Purvis] keeps looking at everyone in turn as if she was trying to work something out. It's—it's almost as though she were playing 'Is it you? [...] Is it you? [...] Is it you?'" (Kaye, 355).

While the amateur detectives are parodies of their counterparts in Country House Mystery novels, the reason for the game of detection, the murders, is revealed as much by coincidence as providence. The first murder occurs at sea and should have resulted in the body being lost at sea, but it is swept to the shore almost immediately—without any damage by fish or reefs (Kaye, 437). This occurrence enables the detectives to undertake the investigation. The second body, which is put in a sack to dump in a coffin, is unexpectedly opened by the native servants and is thus discovered (431).

Such depiction of the fortunate recoveries of the bodies which leads the characters in the novel to realise that murders have occurred, which otherwise they would have written off as rather inopportune accidents, is significant in this context as it fulfils the desire of the protagonist and her friends to put into practice their clumsy theories on crime and detection. Their filling "in the time by playing detectives" (Kaye, 422) is pointless, and the whole mystery gives a feeling of a rigmarole drummed up to satisfy a bizarre yearning for mystery.

Such an inference, while seemingly weird, is much less so, when revisited after a perusal of Kaye's statements in the "Author's note" at the beginning of the novel. Kaye writes that when she visited the Andamans soon after the publication and success of her first crime thriller, she was struck by the fact that the setting seemed ideal for a murder mystery (Kaye, 279). She writes:

> No doctor on the island, no police, only a handful of the detachment of British troops, no telephone lines operating and no link at all with the main island, and despite the gale, the temperature and humidity so high that any

> corpse would have to be buried in double-quick time—and probably without a coffin at that! (279)

All these characteristics are woven into her novel, with the lone exception that there is murder—in fact, three of them. The novel, thus, satisfies Kaye's own desire for murder and mystery in a setting, though apparently romantic, was in reality mundane. This same craving for mystery comes through in the behaviour of the amateur detectives in the novel as well. They too are fed up with a mundane world and decide whimsically to investigate the murders. As one of them points out: "At least it would give us something better to do than sitting around twiddling our thumbs and cursing" (Kaye, 421).

However, along with this desire to indulge in an activity as a diversion and to combat boredom is also a desire to escape the feeling of insecurity caused by supernatural fears. At the very beginning of the novel, the female protagonist has a nightmare followed by the vision of a supernatural being (Kaye, 284). The being haunts the building they live in and is seen by Copper along with her friends later on in the novel (376). Inexplicable incidents such as the being stepping into water and managing to not leave wet footprints are depicted in the novel and are explained by the Indian guard in the story as the ghost of "One who returns, seeking vengeance". The terror inspired by such visions causes anxiety amongst the characters leading them to term the island as "Devil's Island" (Kaye, 286) and a desire to return home, which would be a safe haven. Kaye, in essence, was drawing upon her own experiences while writing these incidents in the novel, as she dwells on the "creepy" (278) nature of the island in her introduction to the book.

The only way in which to overcome this feeling of insecurity is by the use of logic. As Copper says: "But couldn't we try and see if there isn't something, we could do about it? Then we could at least think of it as a sort of cold-blooded problem, like a crossword puzzle or a cypher" (415). While she is mainly speaking about the uncertainty caused by the murders, it could as well be applied to the general feeling of strangeness that they were trying to thwart. This desire to create a rational world in a place infested by supernatural beings and incidents that they can hardly understand is a symptom of their nostalgic craving for a safe home, or a place where they were secure—in this case, England. Hence, the play-acting of amateur detectives in a Country House Mystery can be said to have resulted from a forlorn hope to recreate England in the Andamans.

Such nostalgic craving is not just limited to role-playing in the novel but is also evident in the innumerable references to Christmas in England accompanied by its festivities in sharp contrast to the depiction of the futile attempts at celebrating the same in the Andamans (Kaye, 291, 395, 479). Indeed, as the omniscient narrator, presumably Kaye herself, states:

> The conversation turned naturally to Home—for this was Christmas Eve and the acute nostalgia of the Exile for familiar scenes and the years that have been and will return no more, seized achingly on the little group under the frangipani trees. Memories of other Christmases. Of holly and mistletoe, mince pies and carol singers. Even Copper was conscious of a brief pang of homesickness. (330)

This rendering of Christmas Eve in the Andamans brings to the fore the longing for home and England.

For the characters, while their efforts at celebrating Christmas in the Andamans is foiled, they still seek to prevail over such nostalgic longing for home by going on picnics (Kaye, 295, 537) and reading old British magazines (Kaye, 479, 492, 498). However, all such attempts are still ways to mask their desires or relive past experiences which resonated with security in an insecure alien land. There is nary an effort to create a new home in the land that they had been either posted to or had shifted willingly.

The characters in the novel when they come up with the Country House Mystery pantomime show the first attempt to understand the world that they inhabited. This is an inevitable outcome of an endeavour to solve the murder mystery, as it leads to a better understanding of the characters of the island than they had earlier. This is evident when, at the end of the novel, as they discuss the mystery, the characters acknowledge that not all mysteries of the island are solved. It is, of course, in reference to the supernatural events in the island—which gave birth to the initial sense of discomfort among the characters. However, they no longer are bothered by this. As one of the characters remarks:

> [...] after a brief stay in these islands I'm prepared to believe almost anything. And then of course there is always that time-worn remark of the late William Shakespeare's: "*There are more things in heaven and earth, Horatio, Than are dreamt of in your philosophy*"—and that goes for Copper's nightmares too! (547-78)

The allusion to Shakespeare is important as it shows that while earlier the characters had looked at the supernatural events on the island with askance wondering what kind of strange world they had wandered into, now the peculiarity just reminds them of England—not in contrast to, but as being similar. Once the characters are able to view such incongruities without feeling insecure, the new place that they inhabit becomes a home—resulting in the end of nostalgia.

Thus, while the solution of the mystery is circumstantial, the characters' play-acting of Country House Mystery gives them a feeling of security as they are now able to revisit earlier threatening incidents from a rational standpoint and scoff at their own fears (Kaye, 539). This is evident in Copper's statement at the far end of the novel that the various incidents that had been depicted in the earlier pages of the book seem to be as ridiculous to be frightened of as Halloween (540). While such a reference to an English festival might seem like a harkening back to a gone world, it is not the case as all the characters pair off with their respective romantic partners (570)—suggestive of a desire to settle down and build homes for themselves, rather than reverting to or recollecting a shared and lost past.

Thus, nostalgia can be cured if there is a desire to confront problems rather than escape them, as it gives an understanding of the new place that they are in, and this understanding helps in creating security—and thus home. Thence, diasporic immigrants can circumvent feelings of nostalgia for a lost/past home.

REFERENCES

Auden, W.H. *The Dyer's Hand and Other Essays*. 1948. New York: Random House, 1962. Print.

Christie, Agatha. *And Then There were None*. 1939. New York: Berkeley, 1991. Print.

—. *Curtain: Poirot's Last Case*. 1975. New York: William Morrow, 2011. Print.

—. *The Murder on the Orient Express*. 1934. New York: Berkeley, 2000. Print.

—. *Peril at End House*. 1932. New York: Fontana, 1961. Print.

—. The Mysterious Affair at Styles. 1920. New York: HarperCollins, 1997. Print.

Godfrey, Thomas. "Introduction." *English Country House Murders: Classic Crime Fiction of Britain's Upper Crust*. Ed. Thomas Godfrey. New York: Mysterious Press, 1989. xiii-xx. Print.

Halbwachs, Maurice. *The Collective Memory*. Trans. Francis, J. Ditter and Viza Yazdi Ditter. New York: Harper and Row, 1980. Print.

Hare, Cyril. *An English Murder*. 1951. London: Faber, 2008. Print.

Hay, Mavis Doriel. *The Santa Klaus Murder*. 1936. London: The British Library Publishing Division, 2013. AZW File.

Horwell, Veronica. "Obituary: MM Kaye." theguardian.com. The Guardian News and Media, 4 Feb. 2004. Web. 18 Mar. 2019. <https://www.theguardian.com/news/2004/feb/04/guardianobituaries.india>

Huyssen, A. "Diaspora and Nation: Migration into Other Pasts." *New German Critique*, 88 (2003):149. Print.

Lagoumitzi, Georgia. "The Uses of Nostalgia in the 'Imagination' of Diaspora: The Case of the New Pontic Greek Refugees." *Defining and Re-Defining Diaspora : From Theory to Reality*. Eds. Marianne David and Javier Muñoz-Basols. Oxford: Inter-Disciplinary Press, 2011. 25-40. Print.

Kaye, M.M. "Death in the Andamans" (1985) in *House of Shade*. London: Penguin, 1993. 271-570. Print.

Krishna, K.B.S. *The City as a Nightmare: A Study of Hard Boiled Detective Fiction*. 2009.

Hyderabad: The English and Foreign Languages University. PhD dissertation.

Milne, A.A. *The Red House Mystery*. 1922. New York: Vintage, 2009. Print.

Nadarajah, M. "Diaspora and Nostalgia: Towards a Cultural Theory of Indian Diaspora." *The International Conference on the Indian Diaspora*, 2 November 1994, University Grants Commission and Rajiv Gandhi Foundation, University of Hyderabad, Hyderabad. Presentation.

White, Ethel Lina. *Some Must Watch*. 1933. Montana: Kessinger, 2004. Print.

Chapter 14

Marginalised Victimhood: Doubly Subjugated and Triply Marginalised with a Detached Subhuman Existence by Hegemonic Caste System: A Case Study of Select Dalit Autobiographies

Anindita Chowdhury

Even instead of appreciating the artwork of a Dalit artist, they are labelled as 'activists' in the present social scenario. Dalit writers like Urmila Pawar, Baby Kamble, and Bama Faustina produce their narratives of a life full of pang, agony, humiliation, subjugation, and torment to express themselves through their autobiographies. Although they were written in regional languages first, yet they arrived its pinnacle of popularity with the movements led by Dr. B.R. Ambedkar and Jyotiba Phule. Autobiography can be well defined as the story of one's unique self. A Dalit woman is a Dalit amongst the Dalits. They are oppressed doubly by a patriarchal and tyrannical caste-oriented society. They are deprived of their human rights, marginalised and subjugated in every possible way by society. They are taken to be detached set of low casts who are victims of the hegemonic caste system. Deep-rooted caste prejudices in their sub-conscious Dalit mind would not allow them to have a real sense of equality, freedom and citizenship rights. Thus, this research paper will deal with the vivid picture of violation of human rights found in the famous translated

Dalit women autobiographies of Bama Faustina's *Karukku* and Urmila Pawar's *The Weave of My Life* and Baby Kamble's *The Prisons We Broke* and *Viramma.*

In the practical social scenario, the Dalit female plight is pitiful. While in field they have to put up with molestation by upper cast male counterpart, at church they have to be priest's slave licking his shoes getting threatened with tales of God, Heaven, and Hell and finally at home in spite of performing all the household chores they have to yield themselves to their husband's torture. Although the Dalit men writers tried to represent the Dalit female lives, yet that focused more to sympathise them rather than projecting the reality. The naked portrayal of Dalit's lives were not at all going to help them in getting their human rights back from marginality to identity and finally, women came out with their stories in front of the whole world with the truthful illustration of their everyday struggle through their personal narratives. People with traditional mindset didn't accept the path shown by Ambedkar. The state of being impure and unequal lower order of social strata has brainwashed their psychology. But few who revolted among them fought for their equal rights following the path of Ambedkar by showing resistance against subjugation, oppression, social hegemony and putting their tales in pen and paper. As writing promises worldwide support, these deprived women took writing as their medium of expression. But in a society where cast prevails as prior identity, it is really tough to write an autobiography about them who are silenced because of their cast-based identity. Still, the Dalit women took this drastic step of choosing this daring genre to expose worldwide their stories of getting marginalised. They vent out their voice narrating their agonized tales. Urmila Pawar, Santabai Kamble, Bama Faustina, Baby Kamble, Viramma are renowned Dalit women writers whose works got translated from regional languages.

Urmila Pawar was the iconoclast to break all the traditional shackles by expressing her views with the help of her writings. In her *Aaidan* meaning weaving of Bamboo translated as *A Weave of My Life*, she compares her mother's weaving of bamboo baskets with her writing. She describes how the weaving of bamboo is seen as a cast-based occupation in Konkan region of Maharashtra. She narrates the prevailing gender-based discrimination, labour, untouchability, sexual torments in female lives. She gives a vivid picture of everyday humiliation that Dalit women face while selling their products in marketplaces. They take a long journey barefooted heavily burdened with products on their shoulder eating a very scanty amount of dry food and finally after taking the same long sojourn to come back home, they get engaged in household chores, looking after children, feeding them and finally to satisfy their husband's sexual demands. And again they will wake up early hours of the next day to finish cooking and all major domestic activities before starting for the laborious sweaty journey for the market. Life has transformed them into lifeless feeling-less machines. They keep on begetting children until they give birth to a male child. Education is a daydream to them. They are taught since they are born that their qualification will make them widows. They have a deprived childhood. Being the poorest and untouchable caste, they are forced to all the unsanitary duties of society. Still, now manual scavenging is done by Dalits only. They are considered as racially inferior, impure pollutant members of society. Consequently, they are forced to live as an isolated community. Following the path of Ambedkar, Dalit women who took the initiative of sharing their opinion, get brutally criticised. Consequently, very few of them participate in meetings to raise their voice. The pressure of discrimination is so high that Dalit family sometimes hiding their identities pretending to belong to the higher segment of society.

Baby Kamble in her *Jeena Amucha* translated as *The Prisons We Broke*, talks about her village people who were considered as dirt by upper-class Hindus pretending themselves as pious as God. This autobiography narrates the niche of women imprisoned by patriarchy and cast. They are victims of starvation as well as ignorance system as well. She gives the vivid record of her misery and the struggle for resistance against age-long traditions of oppression and subjugation.

Karukku, written in the Tamil language by Bama, was translated in English by Lakshmi Holmstrom. *Karukku* and *Sangati* are her best works. Through her autobiography, she tells her story as Dalit Christian women. In spite of being well-educated, she was also marginalised and suppressed because of her Dalit origin. *Karukku* tells about the duality of the Christian religion with hypocritical tactics, i.e. one hand it says about equality before God, on the other practically it is indulging the cast system by not letting Dalits come inside the temple and treating the Dalit women as slaves. Through *Karukku,* Bama wanted to interrupt the slumber of the Christian Dalit Women and let them go beyond the limits of managing household and kids, having higher qualification, doing meetings, writing books and so on. She is hinting at looking at a woman as an individual without any prejudices. She scaled a new pinnacle of success by introducing them to a new globe with education and this help to express the outlook with utmost pride.

Shantabai Kamble's autobiography *Majhya Jalmachi Chittarkatha*, is translated as *The Kaleidoscopic Story of My Life.* She tells how Dalit women are Dalit among Dalits, being marginalised by both upper classes as well as by Dalit families. Her protagonist character is triply marginalised by class, caste, and gender. She narrates how it feels in a caste-prejudiced patriarchal society to struggle as poverty-stricken Dalit women. Being a follower of Ambedkar, she believes education is the strongest medium of preserving Dalit women rights. Ambedkar in one of his speeches to the Dalit Mahila Federation in 1942 said:

> I am conscious of the fact that if women are conscientious the untouchable community will progress. I believe that women should organize, and this will play a major role in bringing an end to social evils.... The progress of the Dalit community should be measured in terms of the progress made by its womenfolk. Every woman should stand by her husband, not as his slave but as his contemporary, as his friend. (47)

In *Viramma: Life of an Untouchable*, we can see her father's head in his hands which was enough to guess the sex of the newly born child. The voice from inside the house shouting "Here's another little bitch been born!" (3) was loud enough to proof the female niche in the social order. Birth of a girl in the family, irrespective of caste hierarchy, has never been an occasion for celebration. This occasion is seen as the onset of misery. Pariah girls were exposed to fieldwork at a very young age so that after marriage they could work in the fields along with their husbands to earn money. Thus, they were groomed to contribute to the family earnings along with household work. It is shown: "Listen little girls, life is not just songs. You can't play like that forever. You must learn to use your hands. One day you'll go and make your life elsewhere and people must be able to say, Here's a good worker! Here's a pair of hands that'll bring in money and not just another mouth to feed!" (*Viramma*, 9).

Pariah girls' childhood, unlike other children, was spent in learning the skills for earning a livelihood and the value of hard work. They were deprived of the freedom to have fun with other children. "In my day we did our education in the fields" (*Viramma*, 12). Viramma's childhood was a little short as she was only eleven when it was decided to get her married. In Hindu society, a boy is precious, an asset but in the matter of marriage even he succumbs to his parent's wishes. Parents want to get rid of daughters at the earliest and majority of the girls, deprived of decision making, are unable to resist compulsive marriage. the girl is always presented as a decorative object by her family before the people from the groom's side who like buyers after proper assessment of the qualities of a good daughter-in-law in the girl give their consent or refusal for marriage. Here endurance, meekness, and submissiveness are the parameters that decide the final consent. Patriarchy prevails at large here.

Moreover, in addition to virtues, a girl has to provide a dowry to gain acceptability in her in-laws' family. Because it is well accepted in society that insufficient dowry means excessive domestic violence. Commonly referred to as victims of dowry deaths become statistics only. She underwent different ceremonies at the onset of puberty. Her puberty was the 'sign' for what everybody in the family was waiting eagerly. A 'sign' that gave her new identity and she enters in her womanhood turning her known world upside down. The irony here is the 'sign' that becomes the reason for celebration, gives the stigma of 'uncleanliness' to women. This is the sole reason that women are still not allowed to go inside Sabarimala temple being filthy and impure. Menstruation establishes a girl's identity as a woman which also signals the change in the attitude of people towards her. The solitary confinement of Viramma during menstruation was pathetic. At her in-laws' house, she discovered that women are defined and restrained by male boundaries. They are just vaginas to be ruled and dominated by male laws. Initially, unaware of her obligation to satiate her husband's sexual desire, Viramma resisted Manikkam's moves to come closer to her. However, after a few days of the severe beating, she finally surrendered before him: "The man came in last. I shut my eyes straightaway. I was curled up like a shrimp, my head in my hands [...]. I was as still as a corpse [...]. I was suffocating under his weight. I was trembling. I was terribly wet as if I'd pissed [...]. It felt like he was tearing me. He roared like a lion, giving great thrusts and for once, I suffered in silence" (43).

The enforced sex without her consent and the colonization of her body make sex synonymous with domination and violence. In this patriarchal society, sex is coercive and degrading to women and sexual penetration demands domination and submission. This was exhibited by Viramma's husband when he forced himself on her without her consent and without making her comfortable. Manikkam did not see her as an individual. He saw her as a wife, a subdued woman, on whom the patriarchal social structure bestowed him the right of coercion in intimate marital space.

When a woman resists the patriarchal tradition, her act is seen as bringing disgrace to her family. Anban, her son behaved in a conservative manner towards his sister. But Viramma sided with her daughter to resist the forced codes and patriarchal restriction to assert individual choice and decision making. She strongly felt that women should articulate their choice in marriage and sexual matters. Viramma had a traumatic experience of sexual violence during the consummation of her marriage. She did not want the same for her daughter. She in her life narrative asserts that man-woman/husband-wife relationship should be based on mutual understanding besides in conjugal love both should agree. By supporting her daughter, Viramma resisted the cultural and patriarchal norms which reduce Pariah women to sexual commodities in marriage without considering their emotions. The second type of resistance exhibited is against the caste system where she talks about that of Pariah woman as a labourer and as an untouchable. As Viramma grew up, she realized her low status as Pariah and understood that she had to behave and work according to the prescribed caste code.

Statistics on rapes committed against Dalit women are unreliable and are based on Brahmin patriarchal culture that believes that Dalit women are available to get exploited all the time. Sexual harassment or rape of Dalit women by the upper caste men is not taken as a crime. Pariah women's breastfeeding is supposed to have good nutrient value. Therefore, Pariah women's breastfeeding is on demand for the children of the upper caste in spite of facade of rituals of pollution. Ignorance, illiteracy injustices, and discrimination thwart Pariah women from visiting dispensary during pregnancy and delivery. Due to ignorance, Pariah women are bewildered and often laughed at by nurses. Women's sexual harassment is a common occurrence in hospitals. Like a Brahmin nurse who was molested by a sweeper during duty hours in the hospital.

The people from high castes who have money exchange their girls with the Pariah boys with the help of nurses. Thus, the incidents of baby swapping in the hospitals prevent these Pariah women to avail medical facilities. While swapping the babies the upper-caste people overlook the Pariah boy's caste which exposes their pretence. The root cause of women being more superstitious lies in the circumstances and society in which she lives. She is ignorant about the ways to escape these situations. She faces failures, frustrations, grieves in her life. Patriarchy in our society doesn't allow her to find the out of this maze of blind faiths. The status and space allotted to women bend them towards superstitions. Through superstitions and rituals, women try to give meaning to their lives and see them as the ways to escape their predicament. The situation of Pariah women becomes more difficult as it is much more a question of daily experience, of struggle. These women worship a whole lot of village deities in order to be saved from disease, bareness, and other externally induced misfortunes. They believed if not the doctor then God or spirits or sorcery would heal them and take care of their children. Viramma gave birth to twelve children but only three survived. Her children died because of lack of medical treatment and malnutrition. However, in her life narrative, she calls diseases like cholera and chickenpox as goddesses who kill people to maintain balance in the world.

For centuries, the untouchables of India were denied the benefit of education. They were even subjected to harsh punishments if they dared to read or write the Hindu scriptures. Even hearing of religious scriptures was out of bounds for them. Pariah women received fewer wages as compared to men. She exposes the duplicity of the social workers who provoked the Pariahs against landlords. Viramma is critical of the double standards adopted by the social workers who claim to work for the upliftment of Dalits but create hierarchies between Dalit men and women, thus pushing these women towards further oppression and suffering, and thereby thwarting their move towards freedom. Pariah women toil along with their men in the fields, but it is only man's work, which is recognized. Regular hard labour in the fields and home along with frequent pregnancies make Pariah women prematurely old. In addition to this, frequent pregnancies and abortions have further made them very weak. It is shown here:

> What would it be like if we were as civilized as you, always clean and beautiful? But don't worry we can't stay beautiful as long as you. Young, yes, we're as strong as tamarind seeds, but after children start coming, it's all over. We lose blood with each child and, on top of that, there's all the work we get through planting out, weeding, harvesting, looking after the cattle, collecting cow dung, carrying eight jars of water [...]. A Pariah woman loses her strength and beauty very early [...]. We come home in the evening exhausted, covered in sweat. We don't take the time to wash, we go to bed as we are. (*Viramma*, 52)

Viramma in her life narrative also talks about the dress code, a potent sign to differentiate Pariah women from the upper-caste women. Pariah women were strictly prohibited to cover the upper part of the body. Dalit women were forced to uncover their breasts. In order to keep the tradition intact, strict laws were imposed. However, Dalit women were not mute acceptors. *Viramma: Life of an Untouchable* establishes Viramma's identity as a dignified Pariah woman. She is conscious that as a Pariah, she is at the margin but, at the same time, she is aware that it is because of the margin, the centre exists. Hence, Viramma never displaces the centre from its space but brings the margin in focus and compels her readers to recognize the margin as a distinctive space and to appreciate the differences. She opined: "you just had to raise your voice" to move from resistance to resurrection.

Violence done to these Dalit women is evident enough to prove the level of exploitation. Thus, they need the encouragement to fight against suppression, discrimination, and deprivation. B.R. Ambedkar and Jyotiba Phule Movement gave them a beginning to fight for equal rights. Being deprived of the accessing knowledge of English language, Dalit women writers started writing in regional languages to express their painful, agonized lives through their autobiographies. Later their works were translated into the English language during British rule and thus their voice reached globally.

REFERENCES

Ambedkar, B.R. *Annihilation of Caste with a Reply to Mahatma Gandhi.* New Delhi: Samyak Prakashan, 2013. Print.

Ananthamurthy, U.R. *Samskara: A Rite for a Dead Man.* Trans. A.K. Ramanujan. New Delhi: Oxford University Press, 1976. Print.

Faustina, Bama. *Karukku.* Trans. Lakshmi Holmstrom. New Delhi: Oxford University Press, 2012. Print.

—. *Vanmam: Vendetta.* Trans. Malini Seshadri. New Delhi: Oxford University Press, 2008. Print.

Hartmann, Eva-Maria. *The Dalit Movements in India: Local Practices, Global Connections.* New Delhi: Oxford University Press, 2009. Print.

Jaffrelot, Christophe. *Dr. Ambedkar and Untouchability: Analysing and Fighting Caste.* Delhi: Permanent Black, 2005. Print.

Kamble, Baby. *The Prisons We Broke.* Trans. Maya Pandit. Hyderabad: Orient Blackswan Private Limited, 2008. Print.

Kandasamy, Meena. *The Gypsy Goddess.* Noida: HarperCollins Publication, 2014. Print.

Kumar, Raj. *Dalit Literature and Criticism*. Hyderabad: Orient Blackswan, 2019. Print.

Limbade, S. *The Outcaste*. Trans. Sharankumar Bhoomkar. New Delhi: Oxford University Press, 2003. Print.

Omvedt, Gail. *Understanding Caste: From Buddha to Ambedkar and Beyond*. New Delhi: Orient Blackswan, 2011. Print.

Pawar, J.V. *Dalit Panthers: An Authoritative History*. Tran. Rakshit Sonawane. New Delhi: The Marginalised Publication, 2017. Print.

Pawar, Urmila. *The Weave of My Life*. Trans. Maya Pandit. Kolkata: Stree, 2015. Print.

Satyanarayana, K. and Tharu, Susie. *From the Stubs, Steel Nibs are Sprouting: New Dalit Writing from South India*. Noida: HarperCollins Publication, 2013. Print.

—. *The Exercise of Freedom: An Introduction to Dalit Writing*. New Delhi: Navayana Publishers, 2013. Print.

Still, Clarinda. *Dalit Women: Honour and Patriarchy in South India*. Oxon: Routledge, 2017. Print.

Viramma, Josiane Racine and Jan Luc Racine. *Viramma: Life of an Untouchable*. Trans. Will Hobson. London: Verso, 1997. Print.

Chapter 15

A Representation of Unexplored Existential Consciousness in Namita Gokhale's *The Book of Shadows*

Pratibha Patel

Indian women writings seek to glorify the female individuality in the present scenario. Women writers indulged at large to bring forward the female autonomy to create the room of their own for equal acknowledgement in every sphere of society. Women writers of post-nineties have taken a proper step to peep into the deft at every corner of women's soul. Writers like Shashi Deshpande, Anita Desai, Manju Kapur, Shobhaa De, Chitra Banerjee Divakaruni have presented the lives of Indian women not as the shadow of men but as a subject who dares to occupy the centre for their own being as an individual. According to Uma Nayantara, "Third world feminism is not a mindless mimicking of Western Agenda in one clear and simple sense. Indian feminist is clearly a response to the issues related to Indian women" (243).

Born in 1956 in Lucknow, Namita Gokhale spent most of her childhood in New Delhi and Nainital. Namita Gokhale is the novelist who is known for the bold portrayal of woman like Paro. Her female characters are the symbol of the quest towards their passion, individuality, consciousness, and the assertion at large. She is a writer who redefined the role played by women through her very first novel, *Paro: Dreams of Passion* (1984) which was contemptuously applauded because of its impish voluptuous humour. Later came her novels *Gods, Graves and Grandmother* (1991), *A Himalayan Love Story* (1996), *The Book of Shadows* (1999), and *Shakuntala: The Play of Memory* (2005). In all her novels, there is an intense concern for the well-being of women as a subject. Namita Gokhale is a writer of great repute for bringing the close aspects of women not only to increase the impartial cognizance of emotional situations, but they focus their aspirations to test the restrictions and obstructions of social taboo. Namita Gokhale in her article, "Women's Writes" says:

> Ever since the first sari-rippers tore off the veil of discreet silence which swathed the Indian literary establishment, books for, about and by women continue to proliferate [...]. There is, however, in real life, an ongoing conflict between biological imperatives and habituated role-playing in all gender attitudes. (40)

The present paper is the close introspection about the existential dilemma of a woman who decides to search her identity amid the range of Himalaya. *The Book of Shadows* is a novel in which Namita Gokhale tries to uncover the difficult moments of an acid victim. The novel portrays the life event of a female character Rachita Tiwari, who was an English Literature teacher at Jesus and Mary College. She always tries to explain the concept of alienation to her students. She says: "Alienation is a device to make the unfamiliar familiar, I said, addressing a sea of guileless faces, or to render the familiar unfamiliar" (*The Book of Shadows*, 4).

The present novel revolves around the very traumatic incident in the life of Rachita, who tries to escape from the painful surrounding in order to attain mental peace. When she was teaching in college, her fiancé commits suicide thinking that she has betrayed him, "There was a long suicide note, written in Anand's sloping italic hand, which went something like this: 'Goodbye, cruel world! I bid thee farewell! You have tried me sorely; you have abused my trust! My tryst with time is over! Tell the faithless one, the Delilah, that her betrayal will cost her dear [...]' And so on" (5). Her fiancé's sister who taught chemistry at the same college, pours a beaker of acid on Rachita's face, the day just after Anand's death to take a revenge of her brother's suicide, "my fiancé's sister, as unstable a specimen as her sibling, had thrown a beakerful of acid on my face the day after the inquest" (5). Rachita describes the whole incident pathetically:

> I had encountered her as I was re-contouring the shadow on my eye in the misty mirror in the bogs next to the cafeteria. There's a separate dressing room for staff and faculty upstairs, but I didn't want to face the other teachers. This was my first day in college after Anand's death. I saw her in the mirror, her face almost at my shoulder, and turned around in a vague panic. And then it happened. As my vision blurred, as my consciousness dissolved in a river of searing pain, I could hear the tinkle of her bangles, glass against gold, and the swish of her starched cotton sari as she walked, but leaving me alone in the toilet block. I tried to reach for the water tap, I realized it was the thing to do, but even as I dragged myself across the smooth mosaic floor, I knew that although the first monsoon clouds had gathered themselves around Delhi the taps would inevitably be dry [...]. The pain, the unbearable pain. (5-6)

This distressing incident had changed Rachita's whole life in a second. She became restless in her own city where she used to hold a dignified position as an English Literature teacher. She tries to hide herself to overcome the feeling of being disfigured. She began to ask herself the philosophical question and questions her own existential identity. She thinks:

> Who am I? This essentially philosophical question has suddenly assumed a tangible immediacy. We define ourselves by the people that we know, by the face we see in the mirror. In my case, all the parameters have changed. I can feel the doors to self-knowledge banging shut upon me. Even the face I might meet in the mirror is no longer mine. (3)

The acid attack had left the indelible imprint on her life and caused unbearable pain. Despite surgeons tried to restore her face, it became disfigured and left her heart-broken to ponder on how she used to look earlier. She narrates:

> The acid had worked on the bone cartilage, and the surgeon has been cautious in his restorations. I have not looked into

> a mirror for months now, and my face, that familiar index of my being, has dissolved into absurdity and abstraction. Even my fingers do not recognize the changed contours of my cheeks, of the injured flesh. The avengers of my vanity have broken me, humbled me with these small depredations of skin and bone and tissue, leaving me less than I was. (7)

Again, she contemplates over the incident that made her feel to question her existential state of being. She says:

> My face had been banished from memory. Even in the bathroom, they had taped up the mirror so that all I could see when I brushed my teeth in the mornings was a white sheet of paper that flapped faintly when the exhaust fan near the window (the barred window) was switched on. This was a fancy hospital, a plush and expensive one, where the staff were full of care and concern and new-fangled ideas about the psychology of the patient. I did not see my face there. I have not seen it since [...]. After great pain, a formal feeling comes—The Nerves sit ceremonious, like Tombs—The stiff Heart questions was it He, that bore, And Yesterday, or Centuries before? (21)

Rachita, after being flawed, decides to fight the battle of her life. She used to cover her face with *Muslin Chunni* to hide it which was now full of scares. She decides to go amid the beauty of Himalayan hills to sustain her life in Ranikhet, "I have come to the hills to heal, to hide, to forget. To forgive, to be forgiven [...]. I needed solitude and soliloquy to come to term with what had happened" (6-7). She took a decision to go to her the place where she had spent her childhood days and says:

> I already belong to it. It has taken me in, enveloped my hurt. It soothes my hatred, hushes my sorrow [...]. This old and gentle house, built by a missionary a hundred years ago, was the repository of my youth, the custodian of my dreams [...]. I am determined to be that again; to forget Anand's indulgent and wanton act of self-destruction, ignore his stupidity, and restore my life to its own course once again. You see, I have all the right intentions. (6-7)

Ruchita tries to seek shelter in the lap of nature which is considered as a great source of peace from the hurdles of a tiresome life. She thinks of the nature around her to get rid of the memories of the hospital room, the shock of Anand's suicide and the hideous moment when Anand's sister splashed the burning mess of hate and pain and unappeasable anger upon her face and changed her life forever. Nature seems to become a stemming force for Rachita towards self-realization. She tries to find the solace and joy in natural surroundings. Nature helps her to come out of the rigorous past life incident. She describes the beauty of nature:

> The deodar tree, a sort of Himalayan cedar, is considered by the hill people to be a living divinity (45). […] I remember looking out of the window at the Himalayan ranges, the joy and abandon of discovery in my eyes. It was a clear day, and the afternoon snows shimmered golden yellow as the dawn through my prism. The mountains seemed to be thrusting up, to be breaking and breaching the boundaries of their mountain-ness and becoming part sky, part valley. Then I lost the prism, it just disappeared, it was not there in the desk or the drawer or anywhere in the house, although Lohaniju and I searched for it everywhere. (75)

We can assume how sometimes mother nature becomes a great source of inspiration as well as a divine healer of our pains and shadows of life. Rachita feels the same divine presence amid nature. She sits down in her room and feels the breeze that comes from the hill. She illustrates:

> Sometimes, silence is the greatest blessing in all the worlds. I sat down in my room and savoured the sounds of sunlight and breeze. I could hear the rustle of pine needles, and I could feel the shadowed presence of a tree outside the window. The tree presence filled the room with pine scent and cedar-sighs. Something gentle, something redeeming and forgiving, overflowed from the window into the room. It relaxed the tight muscles of my back; it loosened the iron crunch of the rubber band that held my hair tied back in a punitive loop. It massaged my cratered skin, my ravished

> eyebrows, my dry lips, until they forgot their conditioning of stealth and despair. It made me want to smile. (211)

In the middle section of the novel, there is the description, how Rachita seeks to consolation in books, "The past few days have gone in a haze. My only consolation is an old school arithmetic book. I spent hours and hours completing the simplest sums, taking delight in the certainty and predictability of the answers" (65). Apart from this, there is the description of books and their writers about whom Rachita's discusses at large to forget her state of existential struggle. Being a teacher of English Literature, there was a great critical efficiency in Rachita that made her feel the state of self-realization and helped her to distract herself from the haunting memories of the hospital room where she had to live with the darkness.

> I went to the bookcase by the stairs to look for something new to read. I needed to distract myself, to slide into this altered mode obliquely, as it were. I found an old volume of Mahadevi Verma's poems [...]. It was only now, many years later, that I actually read her poetry [...]. Her poetry is beautiful, mystical, though perhaps a little abstruse. The Chhayavadis—Sumitra Nandan Pant, Nirala, Jayshankar Prasad, and of course Mahadevi herself, were self-acclaimed poets of the shadows. They recoiled from the new realities of modern India and retreated into a regressive post-Romantic swoon [...]. I'm not comfortable with Hindi, with the Devanagari script, and yet I am compelled to read these poems [...]. In spite of Chaucer and Spenser and all the alien metatext that has been rammed down my throat by nuns and missionaries and well-meaning academics, Professors and Doctors of Literature who dream of Keats and poesy [...] the tyranny of the English tongue, in spite of all these factors I find that I do at last recognize and understand Mahadevi's poetry. I understand it, I respond to it. (71-73)

She further critically examines the poetic world of Mahadevi in such way:

> Mahadevi's totally metaphorical activities exclude any hint of the real. The completely subjective play is peopled

> with elusive symbolic figures—the Woman, the Widow, the Beloved—depicted weeping, waiting, strumming the vina. This extended metaphysical conceit co-opts the private universe of abstracted emotions until [...] until [...] until I tear up these lying words, repudiate this nonsense, paint my nails a blazing scarlet. (71-73)

With the habit of reading books and spending quality time in the lap of nature, Rachita started feeling healed, "This is the most beautiful time of the year in our hills. The leaves begin to change colour, and a shadow of red sits upon the hillside [...]. It is a time to harvest, to conserve, to await a trial of strength with the elements. It is a time of joy and resolution" (218-19). She had developed the analytical quality to see the deeper side of things. This was the turning phase of her life which built-in her the philosophical awakening to see herself from a new perspective, "Today I distinctly heard an inner voice speak. It whispered from the debris of clamorous emptiness that is my centre. It said to me, 'Hang on. Just hang on, okay?'" (212). She further explains it in detail how she got a sudden insight and felt all right to exist as a part of God's creation.

> When dawn broke, I felt all right. I felt as though I had the right to exist, as though I was a part of creation, of the dawn chorus, of the healing sunlight that was showing up in sky dappled patches in the garden. I was a glob of consciousness, of reactions and conditioning, enveloped in skin (damaged skin, but nevertheless). I was defined in time and space and dimension; I had the right to exist! That was the breakthrough, the sudden insight into my innocence, my lack of culpability, my exoneration. (213)

Towards the end of the novel, the writer has defined through the protagonist Rachita, that the hope of to sustain one's life with the self-realization of having equal existence on earth helps a lot in reviving life. Rachita Tiwari after having met the shocking experience of her life decides to retrieve her days to find herself again. She examines the whole things that happened to her in the last couple of days and thus finds herself there to fight back. She says:

> If you lose—if one loses one's sense of self, there is no remedy but proceed on a simulated model. All self-image is anyway a construct of circumstance. If you lose an arm or a leg, you cannot or get what you have lost, the phantom pain is there to remind you, but if you have lost your sense of selfhood things are quite different, for (this is the important part) you are no longer there to know it. Who will find you again? I felt be like asking somebody—anybody—if I was really meat all. I needed an impartial examination into the whole thing [...]. I looked at the mirror, and for the first time in months, I saw my face [...]. I looked just fine—quite nice really. I am thinner than I used to be, so the structure of my face showed better [...]. A little foundation, a slash of lipstick, and I could surely face the world again [...] the deep disturbances in my self-image, my body ego, the sense of depersonalization that was dogging me, simply vanished [...]. I looked in the mirror again, through a blur of tears, and thankfully, I was still there. (216-18)

Towards the conclusion, it has been made clear that if there is the sense or feeling to make or remake one's life to hold the precious moment, one needs to discard the harsh portion of life. Rachita did the same thing in order to change the outside world for her. She bid goodbye to all her haunting memories and achieved the state of existence and possessed herself again. Herewith the help of Rachita, Namita Gokhale had presented her views on re-creation of life with the applauded effort of encompassing vision of living with self-realization:

> To be ourselves we must remain in control of our scripts. We must make and remake ourselves, possess and repossess our world, cast and recast our lot in every precious moment. Above all, we must know what to hold on to, what to discard, in this radical flux which is life [...]. I felt disquietingly alive. My repertoire of memory had run out: I had bid farewell to the world of my confabulations. I had acquired, achieved, possessed myself again [...]. Pain is a habit; pain is an orientation. It can be repudiated. It can be left behind [...]. The world outside is full of change, and

> I do not know if these memories can endure. This hillside will remain, as will the snow mountains that watch over us, even if nothing else does [...]. I think I know that I will remain. (229-32)

In this way, we can say that the present novel is full of ecstasy of conscious understanding of one's existential survival to challenge the whole world to live on.

REFERENCES

Bhagdikar, Vandana. *Fiction of Namita Gokhale: A Critical Study*. New Delhi: Prestige Books International, 2015. Print.

Gokhale, Namita. "Women's Writes." *Indian Feminisms*. Eds. Jasbir Jain and Avadhesh Kumar Singh. New Delhi: Creative Books, 2001. Print.

—. *The Book of Shadows*. Haryana: Penguin, 2001. Print.

Nayantara, Uma. *Indian Women Writer's at the Cross Roads*. New Delhi: Pencraft, 1996. Print.

Chapter 16

Torn Apart and Tied Up in Relations: Exploration of the Theme of Motherhood and Daughterhood in Kamala Das and Eunice de Souza's Select Poems

Anamika Ghosh

Kamala Das and Eunice de Souza are prominent names among Indian women poets. Their poetic voices present "many aspects of being a woman in modern Indian society" (Naik, 184). They are also among the earliest female writers who explored the inner world of a woman's psychology. They are the storytellers of female physicality. Female sexuality, as well as women body, is no longer a taboo in their writings. Kamala Das, in a number of autobiographical poems like "An Introduction", "Composition", "Freaks", boldly asserts her sexuality and shares the secrets of her female body. In the poem "The Looking Glass", she writes:

> Gift him what makes you woman, the scent of
> Long hair, the musk of sweat between the breasts,
> The warm shock of menstrual blood, and all your
> Endless female hungers [...]. (15)

On the other hand, Eunice de Souza, who has a Catholic background, boldly writes in her poems about the patriarchal oppression of women in the Catholic Portuguese Society. In her poems like "Sweet Sixteen" and "Catholic Mother", she exposes the process of subjugation and control of women by different patriarchal institutions like religion and school, marriage, etc.

She writes how the female body becomes a means to control her mind. In "Sweet Sixteen", she writes:

> The preacher thundered:
> Never go with a man alone
> Never alone
> and even you are engaged only passionless kisses. (116)

Kamala Das (1934-2009) and Eunice de Souza (1940-2017) are contemporary poets. Their experiences as women and poets were shaped by the same socio-political and socio-cultural undercurrents. They grew up in a postcolonial nation where diverse and conflicting ideas and ideologies found their place. Though in post-independence India, patriarchy had the strongest voice, feminism and Women's Rights movements still started gathering momentum. The reflection of contemporary society is clearly visible in the works of these two women poets. Kamala Das and Eunice de Souza had the soul of a rebel, but they could not deny the reality; thus, they opted to write about the women question unbiasedly.

While discussing different layers of woman's existence, they explored the identity of a woman in different relations too: particularly woman as a wife and as a mother. The biological bond between mother and daughter was crucial for them to celebrate female bonding just like "the lesbian continuum" (coined by Adrienne Rich, 1986) or sisterhood. Where feminist ideas like "lesbian continuum" and sisterhood are deeply rooted in the Western and First World views, in the Third World nations like India, female bonding is not always celebrated. Sometimes a woman herself becomes an agent of the patriarchy. Different socio-political and socio-cultural institutions are at work to control and curb women solidarity. Das and de Souza were completely aware of this reality. Thus, they did not restrict the definitions of motherhood and daughterhood to their political association with feminism. Rather, their conception of motherhood and daughterhood reflect socio-political (feminist) and socio-cultural (patriarchal) notions equally.

Eunice de Souza, like Adrienne Rich, believes in the oneness of mother and daughter: both in body and mind. On the other hand, Kamala Das echoes Simone de Beauvoir in her views as she tried to expose the patriarchal attitude towards motherhood and daughterhood. Different patriarchal institutions like religion and the Indian family system celebrate the idea of motherhood, but they nurture a silence when it comes about daughters. Mothers are hailed when they give birth to a male child as in a patriarchal society the male child is considered as the legal successor. On the other hand, the daughters are neglected, and their voices are muted in the family as well as in society.

The celebration of motherhood in the socio-cultural domain is deeply rooted in history. In religions like Hinduism and Christianity, motherhood is a celebrated idea. A mother with her child is the symbol of divinity; where a mother transcends her physicality and metamorphoses herself into something divine, as Beauvoir puts it in the chapter "The Mother" of her book *The Second Sex* (1949):

> [T]he mother [...] is no longer an object subjugated by a subject [...] she is this ambivalent reality: life. Her body is finally her own since it is the child's that belongs to her. Society recognizes this possession in her and endows it with a sacred character. She can display her breast that was previously an erotic object, it is a source of life: to such an extent that pious paintings show the Virgin Mary uncovering her breast and begging her son to save humanity. (613)

The same notion is reflected in Kamala Das's poem "Seven Ages of Woman" (1990). She writes:

> A woman with her baby in her
> Arms becomes a divine, resembles
> Mary and the infant Christ, or
> Yasoda with her blue lotus
> of a son [...]. (28)

But this metamorphosis of the mother and the glory of her physicality is not her own. Beauvoir calls it 'illusion' as it belongs to the child and ends with the separation of the child from her mother's lap. Kamala Das writes, "yet a mother's glory has/ its waning phase, the children stalk out/ of their mother's arms, growing out of their need" (29). The patriarchal society endows a mother with divinity when she gives birth to a male child, but the birth of a girl child is a horror to an Indian mother: "Born squalling into sudden gloom/ The girl-child's first wail resembled/ A cry of distress" (27). The daughter from her birth is aware that she is unwelcomed here as "each cell within her did tell that she was unwanted there". The chord of love that links her to the mother is cut open by the man-made society: "the search for a love that was/ kith and kin to the celestial/ realms of the unborn" remained a life-long companion of the daughter as the quest continues till her death. Kamala Das's poem "Seven Ages of Woman" is a brilliant document of different phases of a woman's life. Issues like motherhood and daughterhood in relation to patriarchal social structure are explored to its core. The poem shows how the mother and daughter throughout their life searches for love in different relations. The mother never turns towards the daughter to share her love as the daughter can never give her a secured and respectable position within a male-centric family system and in a patriarchal society. On the other hand, the daughter learns to cope up with the reality from a tender age when the mother's body is substituted by the lullaby of the nursemaid:

> Milk has slight taste of rubber
> She learns and recoils from the perfumed
> arms that welcome her once a day
> or once a week; recoils to hide
> her face in the warm nest of her
> nursemaid's bosom. (27)

Again the journey from daughterhood to motherhood is a difficult one. In her youth, a woman passes different phases of her life in quick succession: from daughter to wife and then to a mother. The journey, according to Kamala Das, is a physical one as the woman started realising the earthliness of "mucky [...] marriage" (28). The glorified motherhood is also a surprise to her:

> Then
> in silence the woman conceived

not sure if she fancied that
celebrated motherhood at all. (28)

The biological process of motherhood is full of "savage pain" as "no leap in science could yet alter or mitigate" the pain of childbirth. If the mother gives birth to a boy, then her motherhood is celebrated. If the child is a girl, the same story repeats in every family. "Seven Ages of woman" is a universal tale.

This poem also explores the relationship between a mother and a boy child. The mother, according to Kamala Das, is a thing of necessity to the boy. There is no place for an emotional bond. When the boy becomes an adult he starts discovering "mother's newfound ugliness" as "the old have black-rimmed nails and scalps from which emanates sweet mouldy smell" (29). The mother found her place in an old age home with a promise of 'a long letter' and 'a phone call'. The final lines of this poem reveal the harsh reality of Indian motherhood:

Yes, mothers are merely
a displaced generation [...]
they seek their cheap analgesics,
bitter gourds, fruit salts, health foods and
misplaced ration cards, they seek that
long forgotten thing, the concept
of love [...]. (29)

As discussed earlier, both the poets were contemporaries and had souls of rebels but still, their personal experiences moulded their worldviews. Kamala Das was married to K. Madhav Das when she was barely fourteen. In her twenties, she was already a mother. Just like other Indian women, motherhood did not come as a choice to her. The reflections of her own life are everywhere in her works. On the other hand, Eunice de Souza, a professor and an independent woman, spoke for new women. Her privileged life did not turn her blind to the oppression of ordinary women. Her poem "Catholic Mother" is a striking example. In this poem the father "Francis X D'Souza, father of the year" boasts the birth of seven children (in seven years):

By the grace of God he says
we've had seven children
(in seven years)
we're One Big Happy Family. (39)

Ironically, the mother of this "Big Happy Family" is silent. The poet here criticises the concept of motherhood as celebrated by patriarchy. This poem also hints towards the process of commodification of women by religious institutions. The biological, as well as the psychological trauma of a mother who gave birth to seven children in seven years, is hinted in the poem through her silence.

Eunice de Souza explores different shapes and shades of motherhood and daughterhood. Sometimes mothers are agents of patriarchy, sometimes they are the saviours of the daughters. Even at times, she is merely a womb to carry the baby for nine months. In her poems the daughters are not always the victim; sometimes they are blind to the sufferings of the mothers like the son of "Seven Ages of Woman".

Eunice de Souza's "Forgive Me, Mother" is a confessional poem where a daughter engages herself in a conversation with her dead mother. This is a poem of guilt, shame, and struggle. The story of the struggle of a single mother: her loneliness, betrayal by her daughter is told by the guilty daughter within the frame of a tiny confessional poem. Here Arvind Krishna Mehrotra's commentary on de Souza's poetic-style needs mention. He writes: "Eunice de Souza's poems have the brevity, unexpectedness, and urgency of telegrams" (114). The struggle of a single mother is reflected here in this poem. Here the mother was "a life-long widow". The society was against her motherhood, but she managed to give birth to her child. The lines like "It was kill or die/ and you got me anyway" (118) are very significant to expose patriarchal society's attitude towards the single mother. As the mother was a widow, society tried to control her sexuality, body and even her identity as a mother. The phrase "life-long widow" is very suggestive. It indicates that the society became aware of her mother when she was already a widow. In a patriarchal society, a woman does not have her will to become a mother; the child must bear the father's name. Simone de Beauvoir in the sixth chapter—"The Mother" of her book *The Second Sex* writes that a number of First-World mothers feel hesitant to celebrate their motherhood, as she puts it, "until she decided to consider her husband as the newborn's father (611). These women want the sanction of the patriarchal society for the glorification of their motherhood. The mother of the girl in "Seven Ages of Woman" is no exception, but in Eunice de Souza's poem the mother went against the tide and gave birth to the girl child.

Feminism on a political praxis defines and discusses, even protests different hegemonic discourses about motherhood and daughterhood. For the feminists, the identity of a woman in different relations is a part of the hegemonic representation. Chandra Talpade Mohanty's discussion on the relation between 'woman' and 'women' is also crucial to understand the concepts of motherhood and daughterhood. Mohanty believes that the relation between 'woman' and 'women' is arbitrary in nature and culture specific. A 'woman' as a mother or daughter in Indian society is a part of representational game where different institutions and ideologies play crucial roles to assign a particular meaning to her. On the other hand, motherhood and daughterhood relate a realistic and collective history of Indian 'women' (Talpade, 53). The separation between the real and representation is impossible. The patriarchal definition of mother shapes the definition of motherhood. In the pages of history, when the voices of women were muted or inaudible, it was patriarchy that shaped the definition of motherhood. In recent times, when women boldly assert themselves, the real becomes audible. Eunice de Souza and Kamala Das belong to that group of poets who explore the relationship between reality and representation. They are aware that it is patriarchy which controls a woman's identity as mother and daughter. They do not allow them to perform beyond their decided role-playing game.

In Eunice de Souza's poem "Sweet Sixteen", 'mammas' and 'madams' are the agents of patriarchy. The voice of the Preacher is heard at the end of the poem; primarily it is mothers who cooperate with patriarchal forces to keep daughters ignorant of their own body and sexuality as "mamas never mentioned menses" (116). The tutelage to substitute 'brassieres' with 'bracelets' by the nun's hints towards the process of alienation of a woman from her body and her sexuality. The poem shows how mothers in a patriarchal society are the first oppressors of daughters. But the poem is a revolutionary one; the daughters belong to a different generation from their mother. They lack the knowledge of their body and sexuality, but still, they have the spirit of protest. Sex is no longer a taboo to them. When the mothers act as agents of patriarchy; the daughters help each other to break the shackle of oppression:

> At sixteen, Phoebe asked me:
> Can't it happen when you're in a dance hall
> I mean, you know what,
> getting preggers and all that, when
> you're dancing?
> I, sixteen, assured her
> you could. (116-17)

Interestingly, for these daughters' motherhood becomes a means of protest and a way to fight against the established norms. They are not like those mothers of Beauvoir's *The Second Sex*, who sought patriarchal sanction to celebrate their motherhood. The daughters of this poem usher the possibilities for the arrival of new mothers.

As already noted, different layers of women physicality and sexuality are explored dauntingly in Das's poems. The concept of motherhood, which is a crucial stage in a woman's life, for Kamala Das, is an unhappy surprise as we have seen in "Seven Ages of Woman". In her poems, the mother never cherishes her motherhood unless she gives birth to a boy child. It is a cyclic process where the mother and daughter exchange their role. There is no possibility of a new tale. There is no mother like Eunice de Souza's Rita, whom we meet in "For Rita's Daughter, Just Born". In the aforementioned poem, the mother prays to God for the safety and happiness of her newborn daughter. She does not mourn the birth of her daughter; rather she celebrates it. She addresses her daughter as "luminous new leaf" and she prays, "may the sunrise gently on your unfurling" (121).

So, it is clear that Kamala Das has viewed motherhood as an intuition which never allows a woman to transcendent her physicality. But for Eunice de Souza, the very same motherhood is integral to women identity and acts as the symbol of women power. Her reproductive power does not stoop a woman to the level of commodity; rather it is the symbol of her creative power. Here a woman transcends her body. So, the bond between the mother and the daughter is not only biological; it is also mental. Adrienne Rich in her famous book *Of Woman Born: Motherhood as Experience and Institution* (1986) has commented that a crucial part of a mother's existence is her oneness with the daughter: both physically and psychologically. This physical and psychic oneness is what she calls 'enwrapment of one female body with another' (219). She shares: "I start to write [...]. This the core of my book, and I enter it as a woman who, born between her mother's legs, has time after time and in different ways tried to return to her mother, to repossess her and be repossessed by her" (219). These words of Adrienne Rich speak for the universal mother-daughter relationship as Eunice de Souza's poem "Forgive Me Mother" echoes the same when the daughter of the poem says: "In Dreams/ I hack you" (118).

To conclude, we can say that Kamala Das and Eunice de Souza, the two contemporary poets, have brilliantly explored multifaceted motherhood and daughterhood. Their views of motherhood are entirely unique from each other. Where Kamala Das is a critic of motherhood as she believes it to be a patriarchal institution, on the other hand, de Souza celebrates motherhood as a symbol of women emancipation. But it is undeniable that a clear understanding of the mother-daughter relationship and different layers of motherhood and daughterhood in political as well as cultural context could be achieved through the pages of their poems.

REFERENCES

Baumeister, Roy F. and Jean M. Twenge. "Cultural Suppression of Female Sexuality." *Review of General Psychology*, 6.2 (2002): 166-203. Web. 4 May 2019. <https://pdfs.semanticscholar.org/26cf/592c500860d43ceab39d218166 54e53e9c6c.pdf>

Beauvoir, de Simone. *The Second Sex*. New York: Vintage Books, 2011. Print.

Das, Kamala. "Seven Ages of Woman." *Savvy*, (December 1990): 27-29. Print.

Das, Sanjukta. *Derozio to Dattani: Essays in Criticism*. Delhi: Worldview Publications, 2009. Print.

de Souza, Eunice, ed. *Nine Indian Women Poets: An Anthology*. New Delhi: Oxford University Press, 1997. Print.

Mehrotra, Arvind Krishna, ed. *Twelve Modern Indian Poets*. New Delhi: Oxford University Press, 2004. Print.

Mohanty, Chandra Talpade. "Under Western Eyes: Feminist Scholarship and Colonial Discourses." *Third World Women and the Politics of Feminism*. Eds. Chandra Talpade Mohanty et al. Bloomington: Indian University Press, 1991. Print.

Naik, M.K. *Indian English Literature 1980-2000: A Critical Survey*. New Delhi: Pencraft International, 2004. Print.

Rich, Adrienne. *Of Woman Born: Motherhood as Experience and Institution*. New York: Norton, 1986. Print.

Sarkar, Jaydip. *Kamala Das and Her Poetry*. Kolkata: Books Way, 2009. Print.

Chapter 17

Interrogating the Female Poetic Voice: A Comparative Study of Sylvia Plath and Kamala Das

Ritushree Sengupta

The concept of eulogizing oriental women by harping on their distinctive ability to blend tradition and modernity, a much-celebrated trope of identity formation in the name of nation and nationality, the late nineteenth century Indian society, specifically Bengal, emerged with the concept of the 'bhadra-mohila', a chastised-educated domestic figure that can be at par with her European counterparts. However, the idea of womanhood before independence and after the epoch is visibly different. But if traced intensely, significant trails of colonial hangover as well as anti-colonial, neo-liberal essence can be observed in the domains of literature and art. With the flush of nationalistic ideas the popular poetry written by both male and female poets, the genre itself became hyped with similar patterns of traditional outpourings. Bruce King aptly says: "Poetry of the pre-independence period was, the writers felt, a mass of sentiments, clichés, outdated language, and conventions, the ossified remains of a colonial tradition badly in need of a new start through grafting on a vital body of contemporary verse and contact with contemporary life and speech" (11).

The stark difference between the poetry of the pre-independent India and the post-independent jingoistic India was visible in the growing nouveau cultural space created by the poets, publishers, journalists, sponsors, and critics. The emergence of the new poetic culture grew on a parallel pace with theatre, painting, etc. which added to the value of the newly developing generic domain. Women's writing in this period had somehow moved beyond the logical consolations of contemporary clarity and kept on turning towards normative themes of rewriting the legendary narratives, praising the agrarian and the natural and fixed upon the marks of morality, ethics, and religiosity often diverting into ideas of romantic love, death, and personal grief. The idea of 'bhadra-mohila' had subsided down to a level of modern elite 'bhadra-mohila' whose former counter-European stance now needed to be replaced with a new image of modern Indian woman. King opines: "While outmoded diction and sentiments were at last overtaken in favour of a more contemporary and less artificial manner, the subject matter of the women poets was often limited to well-meaning platitudes about romantic love, which were treated without depth, complexity, interest or even the projection of much emotion" (147).

It was a serious blow to this settled placement of women's writing when in 1965 Kamala Das's *Summer in Calcutta* appeared. It was not only different from the nationalistic or moralistic, more widely accepted poetry in that time, but it was a strong counter wave of new feminist voice that ripped apart the dominant hetero-patriarchal social structure of the society through the poised yet unsettling rampage of her poems. Das's poetic adventure was a real break from the initial phase of Indo-Anglican poetry which had a considerable inclination towards the European literary culture and also towards traditional faith and customs. In a society not entirely introduced to the idea of modernism or modernity, Das brought along a revolution through her writings which were tremendously bold and dangerously blasphemous for the reigning patriarchal culture of that period in which she was writing. While the earlier poets mostly dealt with general ideas, Das and her contemporaries tried to pour out their internal torments, trauma, and experiences to let people know them and their ideas with every odd bit of imperfections, malice as well as beauty. One of the most transparent and powerful voices of postcolonial period, poems of Kamala Das display a wonderful exploration of feminine sensibility, its potential of being celebrated and the prevalent culture of ignoring and thus thwarting its possibilities in a pseudo-liberal patriarchal society. The confessional spirit of Das is prominent in most of her poems which are widely read and appreciated for their autobiographical elements and how they voice a rebellion against the waves of conventional conformism, severely political stances to dominate women from pursuing their aspirations. Playing on the tropes of personal, political, and universal, Kamala Das also lays threadbare through the realist vibes of her words how women are even denied gaining control of their body and mind and left helpless and trapped within the repressive constructs of patriarchy. The culture of eulogizing women or treating them as consumer products or mere commodities is still valid and through the webs of capitalism, it still keeps on compromising on the situation of women's liberty and formation of identity. Das counters these through her poems and reworks on the prevalent ideas of women's bodies, constructed ideas of female beauty, and figures of feminine charmer or Goddess or even mystique.

It is not an altogether impossible thing to have found images or themes of love, marriage, desires of sexual intimacy in Kamala Das's poems, but her idea of love as reflected in the poem is not an all-encompassing and blinding love. Rather it is a love of one's self, acknowledging the intensity of devotion towards the self that generates strange bravery to walk naked towards the truth, the only way through which one becomes capable of loving someone truly, casting away every kind of social and cultural facade. King says:

> [...] the poems of Kamala Das when focused on love treat it within a broader sense of themes, intensity of emotion and speech and a rich, full complexity of life. Das's themes go beyond stereotyped longings and complaints. Even her feelings of loneliness and disappointment are part of a larger-than-life personality, obsessive in its awareness of itself, yet creating a drama of selfhood. (147)

It is often unjust to categorise a poet's work strictly under certain fixed genres, but such a possibility at the same time eases the complexities involved in poetic endeavours for certain features associated in particular to certain genres brings forward various hints to interpret the poem with more clarity. Kamala Das as a poet is not much versatile, but what makes her exceptional, is her brave choice of baring her threadbare mind, relentlessly chaotic and fluttering in protest and excitement of life and the rapid transformations that it keeps on facing. Depending more on her instant creativity and less on technical editing, Das keeps alive the fascinating feistiness of her poems giving her the license to challenge the inner and the outer world at the same time. Remarkable for holding the status of one of the earliest Confessional poets of independent India, poetry was for Das a window that contributed towards her motive of relentless protest against patriarchal domination.

The genre of Confessional poetry emerged in America around the 1950s and 1960s. The movement was led by several American poets such as Anne Sexton, Sylvia Plath, Robert Lowell, W.D. Snodgrass and even certain prominent Beat poets like Allen Ginsberg was also often considered to be close to that school in his style of writing. For some of them, poetry was therapy, for them the agency of venting out the repressed emotions within, but what was most significant about this school was that they outgrew the socio-cultural inhibitions and imprinted on paper not just their social outlook but also their psychological growth, overgrowth or even undergrowth working behind their eccentricities and chaotic vision of life, far from the borders of normative monopolization of the capitalist society.

Robert Lowell had directly influenced Sylvia Plath and Anne Sexton which is much evident in their early works. Lowell's bold attitude towards dealing with personal or private experiences as he writes in his book *Life Studies* had been a milestone in the history of psychological literature and the canon of American literature at large. The genre of Confessional poetry heightened the gusto of dealing with rather discomforting topics or rather subject matters not previously discussed in the public literary domain. Experiences absolutely subjective and private were introduced in such poems such as sexual experiences, death, trauma, psychological depression, abandonment, homicide, etc. which were presented in an autobiographical manner. It is the close association of confessional poetry with psychological situations (especially Anne Sexton started writing poetry under the advice of her psychological therapist) that has given it also the status of therapeutic poetry. The first principle of Confessional poetry is its continuous focus on the 'I' or the self, where the subject becomes the main ideal, based on whom the poetic narrative unfolds to the reader gradually revealing the absolute truth that the poet wants to bring out, perfectly shaped in craftsmanship long practised or spontaneously created.

Sylvia Plath is considered to be one of the most significant Confessional poets since her works including the novel *Bell Jar* (1963) got published. Her troubled life full of anxieties and anticipations over relationships, career and even identity of her persona as a mother and as a writer is vividly reflected in her poems. A parallel of such anxiety can also be witnessed in Kamala Das's poems. It is still a matter of substantial significance that post-World War II, the space or attitude reserved for women in both creative or regular arena had transformed which amidst all the situational and social chaos finally gave rise to a firm voice of womanhood, a voice bold and brave enough to talk about among several other things, one's own sexuality. Considering the obvious differences between the two female poets, it is thus quite possible to find a similar rebellious nature venting out through the verses of both Das and Plath. Battling against the filial notions of shelter and protection which actually were shackles of disappointment and betrayal for both of them, they rose to their power by mastering the art of controlling and expressing their emotions, wounded but not exhausted and thus creating extremely powerful works. Kamala Das writes in her poem, "The Suicide":

> I must pose
> I must pretend,
> I must act the role
> Of happy woman
> Happy wife. (*Collected Poems,* 71)

It clearly echoes Das's battle against the long-kept ideals of patriarchy which propels the woman to conform to certain images and symbols loyal to societal norms and conventions. Sylvia Plath's poems also speak about giving away the agencies of patriarchy and also the doses of restrictive love, the kind which dominates the other and chokes them with malign and remorse in the name of marital and domestic bliss. Plath brings her personal suffering through her poems time and again. Her poem Daddy although apparently is about the loss that she suffers after her father's death also at the same time touches upon the situation of her own marriage with Ted Hughes. She writes:

> But no less a devil for that, no not
> Any less the black man who
> Bit my pretty heart in two. (*Poetry: An Introduction*, 260)

The agony of an individual woman trapped in a web of despairing grief intensified by the early loss of the father figure and then the loss of a lover turned into a failed figure of domestic disharmony and betrayal is poignantly evident in Plath's poetic works. Confessional poetry as an intriguing genre in itself brings out the darkest of one's individual secrets, fearlessly indulging into the cross-examination of one's close association with the family, society and life at large. The matter gets more intense when the issues of women's liberation in terms of her body and mind are delved upon. The parallel colours of Das and Plath as reflected in their respective poetic endeavours suggest certain obvious common points of reading them together for a clearer and ironically a fragmented picture of a woman trapped in a world shaped by the norms of patriarchal practices. It is the collective loss of personal and social space and severe anxiety and despair caused by it that marks the poems of both the Confessional poets concerned. The language or the poetic style differs to a large extent, but the themes latent or projected sharply calls for a closer look towards the immense suffering of women and their gradual cornering leading towards a violent outburst of protest that marks the ground of parallel reading in a more valid way. As Das writes, in "An Introduction":

> I don't know politics but I know the names
> Of those in power, and can repeat them like
> Days of Week, or names of months, beginning with
> Nehru. (*The Old Playhouse and Other Poems*, 26)

The subtle yet strong claim of not knowing politics, as something not at all important to be known with sincerity is at the same time a visible mockery of the political scenario of the country or conscious ignorance of it for there is no hope left in its carcass for a woman to have faith in it, for it really does not do anything but oppress her in every possible manner. The nation from which Kamala Das rises is not an equal society and thus when she writes in the poem named Krishna,

> Your body is my prison Krishna
> I cannot see beyond it.
> Your darkness blinds me
> Your love words shut out the wise world's din. (*Collected Poems*, 38)

We are made to realize that sexual relationships in the name of love does not liberate the woman but imprisons her more violently in the name of social norms and constraints which restricts her movements and aspirations and thus choking her to live in confinement. It is the patriarchal hegemony that also operates in the poems of Plath as she resists the traps set for women indomitable and oppressed as well with an equal amount of torment and pressure.

Born in rural south India, Das felt the pangs of living in a conservative society from her very early age. Although her mother Balamani Amma was a reputed writer in Malayalam, Das's aspirations were more vivid and ambitious and they become dangerously visible in her poems as well as her autobiography. Moving through structures of filial orthodoxy, her marriage apparently was a release from certain social agencies an unmarried girl must abide by. But soon it is affected by a sense of disillusionment for it fails to generate the kind of love that a woman, here Das desires and expects. Thus, her irresistible shriek breaks in resistance as her lovelock with the man traumatizes her entire existence as she realizes that this has been the accepted tradition all along and she must either bear with it or break away, for there is no scope of reconciliation or reconsideration within the frame of patriarchy. Thus, she writes:

When I asked for love, not knowing what else to ask
For, he drew a youth of sixteen into the
Bedroom and closed the door, He did not beat me
But my sad woman-body felt so beaten.
The weight of my breasts and womb crushed me.
I shrank pitifully. (*The Old Playhouse and Other Poems*, 26-27)

A similar theme is found in Plath whose love for Ted Hughes which brought her untimely suicide and abandoning of her most loved children. But it was her endless love for men in her life, first her father and then her husband that largely contributed to her poetic spree. After her father's death, she got accustomed to a sense of betrayal which only disappeared gradually when she met Hughes during her scholarship stay in the United Kingdom where they bonded over poetry and scholarly discussion. But her chronic depression and growing psychological disorders slowly destroyed her sanity and moreover, Hughes's betrayal of her totally brought her destruction. In "Ode for Ted", she writes:

From under crunch of my man's boot
green oat-sprouts jut;
he names a lapwing, starts rabbits in a rout
legging it most nimble
to sprigged hedge of bramble,
stalks red fox, shrewd stoat. (*Collected Poems: Sylvia Plath*, 29)

The fascination that Plath hoards in her heart for Hughes is a mixed desire for an individual with manly prowess and also the resistance towards that force for it shakes her from within. The conflict is slowly but strongly transformed into something that echoes nothing but the realization of a horrible loss, as she writes:

Now I am silent, hate
Up to my neck,
Thick, thick
I do not speak.
I am packing the hard potatoes like good clothes,
I am packing the babies,

I am packing the sick cats.
O vase of acid,
It is love you are full of. You know who you hate.
He is hugging his ball and chain down by the gate
That opens to the sea
Where he drives in, white and black,
Then spews it back.
Every day you fill him with soul-stuff, like a pitcher.
You are so exhausted.
Your voice my ear-ring,
Flapping and sucking, blood-loving bat.
That is that. That is that.
You peer from the door,
Sad hag. 'Every woman's a whore.
I can't communicate.' (229)

The transition of her mental and emotional condition is evident in her poems especially those published after her death. It is their valid tone of confession that allows us to have access to her personal life. The tragedies of one's lives are mostly personal, but when it reaches a larger audience, it reaches a different level altogether for it affects a number of individuals who suffer through similar situation. One of the best merits of confessional poetry is that allows a new space to the poets and also the readers to think out of the regular norms and bring out what is mostly left suppressed. Psychologically, it has been proved that emotions suppressed are the most dangerous things that can rule a human mind causing it tremendous loss and torment, and thus it is of utmost importance to vent out the unacknowledged or suppressed emotions. Both Kamala Das and Sylvia Plath successfully stand out as brilliant confessional poets because of their unorthodox and bold treatment of personal subjects which can be universalized across several generic, national and cultural boundaries. It is their collective celebration of the life, lived, and unlived that motivates the readers and even saves some of them from being lost in their own claustrophobic existence bereft of communication and connectivity. Thus, Das and Plath are continued to be read still today not only for they can be analysed in terms of their poetic creations, harping on their poetic quality, rhyme scheme or major themes but also as healing potions that are capable of curing gaps, silences, and isolations in lives of women trapped in patriarchal structures and thus motivating them to vent out their own lives to on pages or out of pages, battling and even battering against the wrecks caused in their lives, but never giving up. Life, as both Plath and Das celebrate is never to be given up even if death takes over, for life continues even after death, through words, metaphors, symbols and of course poetry. As Plath writes in "Kindness": "The Blood Jet is poetry/ There is no stopping it" (270).

REFERENCES

Agarwal, Suman. *Sylvia Plath*. New Delhi: Northern Book Centre, 2003. Print.

Das, Kamala. *Collected Poems*. Vol. I. Trivandrum: Kamala Das, 1984. Print.

—. *My Story*. Kottayam: DC Books, 2004. Print.

—. *The Old Playhouse and Other Poems*. Madras: Orient Longman, 1973. Print.

—. *Only the Soul Knows How to Sing*. Kottayam: DC Books, 1996. Print.

—. *Summer in Calcutta*. Kottayam: DC Books, 2004. Print.

Hughes, Ted, ed. *The Collected Poems*: Sylvia Plath. New York: Harper & Row Publishers, 1981. Print.

King, Bruce. *Modern Indian Poetry in English*. New Delhi: OUP, 2006. Print.

Rosenthal, M.L. and Sally, M. Gall. *The Modern Poetic Sequence: The Genesis of Modern Poetry*. New York: Oxford University Press, 1983. Print.

Ruth, Miller and Robert A. Greenberg. *Poetry: An Introduction*. London: Macmillan, 1981. Print.

Chapter 18

Gendered Logic of Indian Nationalism and the Voice of Toru Dutt

Deepayan Das

When it is said by Anderson in 1983 that 'the nation is home and home is mother', the maternalised loyalty is symbolized domestically (Sharma and Oomen, 116). Language is not just a composition of words, but it is taken to be a representation of a particular culture. Culture and language must have an area to which they represent, and the words used depict the particular representation. Women bounded in a particular arena of 'home', as the other spheres of society are dominated by the patriarchy. So, culture, language and women—when they come out of the bounded area are being considered impure and hybridized. Women involved in the ideological reproduction of the collectivism and transmission of culture, 'naturally' becoming a part of the discourse of 'national culture' (127). When women herself is the emblem then her coming out of the boundaries of the gendered cultural home puts her in the complexities of anti-national, alienated, and isolated identity in a colonized nation. In *Ramayana*, Sita has to prove to the public at large, and to her own husband Ram that she has remained faithful to him. To get rid of the charges of infidelity put on her, Sita cries out to the mythic earth and it splits open to receive her daughter. Every women writer, in the same way, had to call upon their roots to accept them, so that they can prove their authenticity and nationality. Sita came out of the boundaries and fall into the traps of Ravana but after she was freed and wanted to return, she had to undergo the Agnipariksha to prove her chastity and purity. Such is the case with Toru Dutt, who had to go through the 'Agnipariksha' on the measuring scale of colonized male culture to secure her identity as an Indian nationalist and culturally authentic. Here the oppressed became the oppressor themselves in front of whom she had to reform her fractured feminine identity. As she came out of the boundaries of her own culture and nation (not by her own choice), it was difficult for her to return and it was her works in the last years of her life, the translation of portions of mythological stories, a connection to her roots became her 'pariksha' taken by the culture—"Ram" (male), "society" (patriarchal). She says: "Like gold, we must be tried by fire;" (*Savitri*, part iv, 97-100).

The Bengali intelligentsia in colonial India always found its intellect and reason getting attracted towards the culture and nationalism of the West. The Dutt family's acceptance of the language and culture ('babu culture') brought an estrangement between them and the common mass as they do not share the belief that education in English means hurting or damaging the deep-rooted ancient faiths and the values treasured since a long time by the Indians. They saw in it the hope of a new intellectual life and uplifted nation. Being raised in the cultural and geographic complexities, Toru Dutt inherited the treasure of literary intellect and rationality from his ancestors. Thus, an imprint of colonial domination is detected in her language by the common mass and the ultimate result is a fracture of her sanctioned feminine identity and national identity. Toru was haunted by a sense of not belonging to any fixed place and she sometimes calls Indians as native, but later accepts her fault. What made her call so? Her love for her nation and culture can be found in her works like "Our Casuarina Tree", "The Lotus" and many more but that cannot shield her from falling into the difficulties of cultural displacement and brings forth Indian nationalist discourse and women question. It is a matter of discussion that either her use of different languages enriched those cultural languages or the Indian culture which got connected to so many nations through her; got portrayed to the whole world. If we talk about the Bengali culture, it is always receptive and never shows any kind of resistance, in fact, it keeps its culture intact and accepts the rational and logical parts of the other cultures. But one has to go through the fire-check to prove cultural intactness after the reception.

Women are always questioned for leaving its boundaries, in early and mid-18th century Bengal, the position of women was the central issue but with colonization and the politics of nationalism the question disappeared, and the society answered it in their own approved way. "Nationalists constructed "ghar" (home), "bahir" (the world) dichotomy which represents the inner and outer spheres of sovereignty respectively. The outer is the domain of political and material interest and inner is spiritual" (Mondal, 914). The Indian concept of nationalism is derivative but declares itself superior in terms of a spiritual realm. The patriarchal society which was working to free itself from the colonial rule physically connected women to the inner sphere because of physical weakness as compared to the men and also created an essence that women are the preservers of culture and tradition and through their reproductive feature, passes it on to the next generation. Women became cultural emblem, but the gender of culture is male as created by the patriarchy. Here comes the contradiction, which can be answered by the fact that the culture is a construction of the patriarchal society, formulated in a way, not to bound oneself to subaltern gender or class. In this culturally diverse society of India, community leaders (mostly male) actively defined the authentic culture which determines one's identity and finally nationality. The nationalistic discourse, which is an extension of the women question where nationalism is a 'sign' referring not to actual women but to the 'culture' of common people, the gendered culture. It can be seen that "the burden of representing the inner and authentic realm of the nation in nationalist discourse fell largely on the figure of the 'modern Indian woman', women writers to show the authentic 'Indianness' which should be anti-western" (Sinha, 624).

Toru Dutt, when put into the format of the 'authenticity', is found to be the first wave of modernization as a liberated feminist thinker, but with a tortured self-consciousness. Here Toru is not a traditionally sanctioned image of a woman. She fights colonialism in a way as she has to fight back the colonized culture which undergoes change and declares English as a part of accepted colonization. It is her maturity which could hold together some requirements of established beauty in her own chosen language. As she returned to India, she could feel the burning shame, the humiliation, the terrible sense of being an outcast and this sensation is the outcome of the burden of improvised nationalism upon her. Her identity is put into question because the authentic identity constitutes cultural tradition but in her case, it got hybridized due to mutation as in "The Lotus" where she gives out the colour of the lotus as a combination of the colonized and the colonizer either intentionally or unintentionally, but it is her own nature in reflection, and she could understand it and thus made an effort to learn Sanskrit, the dialect of Indian tradition because "anything could be built only on the edifice of tradition" (Azhar, 75).

Due to cultural colonization, there arises a strange position or dilemma while using the language and rationality of the culture of colonizers but being an intellectual they understand that culture can progress only when it shows adaptability. Although they are conscious of their own Indianness, they feel identity crisis as identity in a country like India after the nationalist movement depended upon one's ability to strengthen or preserve the Indian tradition—nationalism is traditionalism in this case. In spite of Toru's love for France and England, she chose mythology in the last phase of her life in the "Ancient Ballads and Legends of Hindustan". This choice was the result of her urgent need to overcome the crisis of identity caused by her exposure to the Western culture, literature, and religion. Her work came out as redefining mythology with Western outlook and boldness. It was the product of hybridized culture and showed post-colonial features which ultimately puts her in a false position and criticism. Indian society believes in materialism vs. spiritualism, tradition vs. modernity, nationalism vs. colonialism state, but it was Toru who brought tradition and modern outlook, a voice of nationality and language of colonizers together and gave the society, a liberal outlook from the feminist standpoint and paved the way for the next generation female writers.

Toru's *Ancient Ballads* is at the same time answer to the question of her identity and cross-cultural obscurities that appear in her letters, novels due to her blending of East and West. She exhilarated East with her own modernized and rational set of beliefs; her sense of honour and respect for the ancient faiths and culture can be seen in her choice of work as she understood the spiritual superiority of the Indian myths over anything and portrayed it to the world through her linguistic achievement. After a period of 'Tapasya' of learning the Sanskrit language, the stories from Hindu mythology—those of Savitri, Lakshman, Dhruva, Prahlad, Sindhu, Sita, and Bharat were taken up by her. Mondal aptly says: "Sati was a foundational moment in the wider discourse on social reform, which in turn was to be enveloped into nationalist discourse. Sati, functions, both as the act confirming the stoicism of women and as the practice that epitomizes their weakness" (916). So, feminity is the colonized sign but through 'Savitri' Toru modified or rationalized interpretations of the Hindu epics and Puranas. Her 'Savitri' gives an echo of the age where the social freedom of a woman is pressed. This was the period when womanhood is under the restrictions of gendered cultural bondage and the abolition of 'Sati-pratha' was the burning issue. It was Dutt's effort to bring out 'Sati' not as an image of love but also liberty. Savitri's interaction with Yama is like advocacy of women within her and the women in the society against oppression of any kind. She showed the victimized women of the age gaining superiority over 'Death' through her courage and if it is possible then one can free herself from anything on this world which is unfair. The translation gives a reflection of Toru's feminist ideas, which is far liberal than what the actual mythological stories.

In "Lakshman", we find Sita, not Lakshman as a dominating character, who is having her own voice for her own advocacy for her rights and the voice to fight verbally when needed. By bringing these two characters—Savitri and Sita to a position where the Indian colonial culture does not sanction their liberated dimension, Toru confirms to the Western impact on her thought. The war of words between Lakshman and Sita is a representation of the conflict between Eastern and the Western set of values and her postcolonial set of values moved the poet to utilize the superior language to express her own Indian tradition. She tried to reconstruct the gendered culture as it was creating a false notion for women which in a way making the society to indulge in it and judge others on the same criteria. Her tormented mind got relief when her poetic mind got connected to the native culture and religion. "Jogadhya Uma" is her connection to the Indian folklore and a representation of her imaginative eyes which always sees her country full of riches and at the same time, her use of English for the presentation of native beauty gives space to her work not only in India but worldwide.

In *Royal Ascetic and the Hind*, the story of King Bharat, where she declares vain the stage of 'vanaprastha' as forces one to shed off all the emotions and duties of one's life:

> [...] he had sinned in casting off all love
> By his retirement to the forest-shades;
> For that was to abandon duties high. (211)

In "The Legend of Dhruva", she favours the doctrine of Karma. The story of "Bharat" brings the Christian spirit but in "Dhruva" the Indian spirit. Thus, she cannot deny any of the influences. "Buttoo" brings the superior theme of the guru-shishya relationship, but also the evils of casteism and untouchability. Again in the poem "Sindhu", she shows aspects of Indian culture, the essence of a large family system and the role of *karma*. "Prahlad" is a portrayal of a child's faith in God. Finally, her most acknowledged work is "Sita", where we can find an outstanding poet rather than a translator. Toru wrote in one of her letters to her friend Mlle Clarisse Bader: "The heroine of 'our great epics are worthy of all honour and love. Can there be a more touching and loveable heroine than Sita? I do not think so" (Azhar, 74). Sita bears all the humiliation in an envious world around her and is exiled by her husband without any faults. She never did complain of it, and simply weeps at the undeserved treatment meted out to her. In fact, she is an embodiment of courage and self-restraint. Thus, her works cannot be called a mere translation but a translation of traditional into modern, a 'transcreation'.

Toru being a woman writer had to fight two wars—as a woman and as a writer and it has got verities of layers. She has got a voice and that voice has to undergo the filter of sexism and colonialism to bring liberal Indian feminism in the colonized world. She was not bounded by the geographical boundaries from her early life and this helped her to choose the superior. She decolonized herself by embracing the spiritual superiority of India over the materialism of the West and in a rationalized way she updated it, modernized it and presented to the whole world. Language has always and of course been an immensely controversial issue for Indian women writers from the nationalist perspective and Toru Dutt while refashioning it, secures a position by being a rebel to the sanctioned one. But even after years, we could find the burden of language in the words of Kamala Das, when she says: "Why not let me speak in any language I like?" (*The Old Playhouse and Other Poems*, 26).

REFERENCES

Azhar, Sheeba. *Toru Dutt*. Bhopal: Indra Publishing House, 2011. Print.

Das, Kamala. *The Old Playhouse and Other Poems*. Madras: Orient Longman, 1973. Print.

Dutt, Toru. "Royal Ascetic and the Hind." *The Calcutta Review*. Vol. LXIV. Ed. E. Lethbridge. Calcutta: City Press, 1978. Print.

Mondal, Anshuman. "The Emblematics of Gender and Sexuality in Indian Nationalist Discourse." *Modern Asian Studies*, 36.4 (2002): 913-36. Print.

Sharma, S.L. and T.K. Oommen. *Nation and National Identity in South Asia*. New Delhi: Orient Blackswan, 2000. Print.

Sinha, Mrinalini. "Refashioning Mother India: Feminism and Nationalism in Late Colonial India." *Feminist Studies*, 26.3 (2000): 623-44. Print.

Chapter 19

'The Triumph of Humanity': A Stylistic Appraisal of B.K.S. Ray's *Terror Must Die!*

Madhu Kamra

> The soul is progressive, it never quite repeats itself, but in every act attempts the production of a newer and fairer whole. (Emerson, qtd. in Deming, 53)

"The love of beauty is the love of splendour of society"—this may sound an adage if a survey of the creative contribution of B.K.S. Ray is put to a microscopic study. Shri Bijay Kishore Sunder Ray, a retiree from the post of Additional Chief Secretary (Home), Government of Chhattisgarh is in contemplation on Naxalism much widespread in Chhattisgarh. Writing against extremist violence is his hard-sworn conviction to save democracy and democratic institutions, though the might of pen and sacredness of ink. Naxalism is an instrument of terror out to destroy the development process with a mission to knock out terrorism, Ray upholds poetry to didacticism, for he writes: "Poetry is the most powerful weapon to defend humanity against the terrorist onslaught. [...] My poems are meant to mobilise the conscience of the masses to arrest the vicious trend" (Preface, *Terror Must Die!*).

Patriotic vein provides a sense of rapid reformation to check the bleeding hearts of the bereaved and the haunt of uncanny fear threatening life and thwarting solidarity. B.K.S. Ray paints the gory ugliness of blood, a driven fury of Naxalites in tragic and catastrophic images. The brutality of terror is here the first-hand impression and sketch-markings. Indiscriminate shootings, deep gashes, thrust of daggers, and knives, Naxalite tyranny are substances of sedate and serious readings. A reclining reader in a couch carries himself to be at his study table no sooner the lines seep into the blood of a ready-cautious reader. An attentive reading is not only a gesture in defence of life but a search for the measure to preserve humanity.

The collection embodies 26 poems, each depicting the ugly reality around. A glance at the index indicates the purposiveness of the poet. The collection begins with the titular poem "Terror Must Die!" where terror is defined with deft strokes through fertile epithets like "Inhuman Bloodthirsty" and "Butcher of Innocence"; "A Behind—The Scene Master"; and "A Round-the-Clock Slaughterhouse". With a story knit run-on-line structure, the poem details the brutal murder of poet's friend by a Naxalite, adding loud strokes of vividness to paint brutality—

> When my dearest friend died in Dantewada
> His throat was slit
> By the cruel hands of terror. (1)

Such details act fast on inoculating the neighbourhood and political interests to help the government agency to reintegrate such brutal criminals in the societies. They ousted willingly. Terrorism exists because of we the spectators who certainly can kill terrorism provided the 'will' takes the lead of 'the masses'. With equal ease and deftness, he paints the brutal murderer to analyse the psyche of terrorist at awe-inspiring cruelty.

> He drinks blood
> To quench his thirst
> He has built a slaughter-house
> In the name of liberation
> Killing of the innocents in
> His style of emancipation!
> On similar note of emphatic confrontation. (40)

B.K.S. Ray rhetorically questions the terrorists on perils of humanity—

Terrorists!
Knocking at the door of my motherland
How can I sleep? (3)

Seeing the "Enemies of humanity" choking throats via "Behind-the-scene" cowardice attacks, the poet's companion runs high to set his country free from fear and frenzy and highlight "Humanity's harmony" (3).

The ugly and fearful regime of terror is marked territory in "Democrats Can't Keep Quiet"—

All over the globe
Terror is on a murderous journey
Bomblasts in Baghdad
And blooming guns from
The caves of Afghanistan
The Chechan terror in Russia
Writing bloody chapters in Baster
The Dantewada bloodshed
Only show the Naxalite ugly face
Terror is ruling the roost
In its international supermarket. (5)
and
Sights of blood-shed,
Mutilated bloodies and wailing faces
Pierced my peace-loving nerves yet
I kept quiet
Shadows of tears choked me
suicide bombers
In the streets of Colombo
and Baghdad. (7)

Terrorism/Naxalism has its common axis of evil therefore the call of collectiveness as we feel to target it as a military strategy is the need of the day if humanity is to be preserved. Mere efforts to understand 'staircase to terrorism' as suggested by Moghaddam in *Understanding Terrorism*, 2006 and re-emphasised in 2007 is not more than a seductive idea. The efficacy needs more marrow to perform against 'malady of the conscience'.

In the following poem "Wither the Shining Path?", the poets stand perturbed at the sight of Peru "turned into a man graveyard" which was saved from further damage with the capture of Abimael Guzman. These "ideologies of homicidal maniacs are fond of bullets and make a terrifying terrorist territory"—"From Warangal to Bolivia/ From Dantewada to Chechnya" (11). Probing further into the diseased psyche of terrorists, he says—

> You can't treat life with contempt
> You must keep your hands-off humanity
> Your propaganda machine is fraud
> From all accounts a diabolical plot
> How can murderous be heroes!
> (*Writing Through Blood and Tears*, 25)

This resonates with the observation of the poet understudy the labelling of terrorists as 'Freedom Fighters'—a counterterrorism term has led to stray fundamental drives. The poet calls not for 'a saviour' but all gathering and compounding as muscle-brain power to save and rescue human life. Here his thoughts synchronize with another poet of long creative periods of Chhattisgarh origin named Nalini Sharma of loud sizeable acumen.

Nalini Sharma, a bilingual writer who hails from Chhattisgarh with a bulk of creative writing to her credit calls for patriotic enlightenment in her poem "Anger"—

> Anger on your skin, and fellow countrymen
> Is wrong and unjustified only selfish ends to gain
> For the right cause rise in genuine anger
> Burn to ashes, treacherous enemy and the traitor.
> ("Anger", 9)

With her cry of the mission, she says: "Poetry emanates when my heart is heavy. An intense urge drives me to express my thoughts. If suppressed I would suffocate. Clouds must pour" (*Rhythm*, Why I write Preface to the collection). Nalini Sharma defines in simple words who a terrorist is—

A pervert killer, an insult to human race
His blood grisly acts, a horrible menace. (19)

Her poem "The Terrorist" is loaded with ugly epithets to paint the ugliness of the 'mind' and false ideology as—'A live bomb', 'A handsome criminal', 'A pervert killer', 'An insult to human race', 'A horrible menace', 'A wicked creature', 'An elusive animal', 'An ill omen', A harbinger of death and destruction certain to bring annihilation—a gory game of death. The Naxalite barbarity and the spectre of violence put the poet on a warpath against this blood-freezing criminality. Masking off the brutalities in Chhattisgarh, he exposes the Machiavellian ways in *Dear Gadar! Where is Your Humanity?* "by emphatically confronting the deceptive daggers" as—

I see you as the enemy of a people's revolution
A hollow ideology hailing horror
Someone who rejects brightness
In favour of a dark, inhuman chapter
Where was your humanity?
When the relief camps in
Dantewada was set on fire (38-39)

The extremist tyranny of the Naxalite Beasts, the poet says with determination, will not end in a chapter of horror and hollowness. He even questions "the Sphinx-like silence" (46) of human rights groups. With intent to obliterate the obnoxious doctrine of destruction, the poet announces his heroic role against terrorism as—

I must be with the relief camps
Irrespective of the extremist bullets
For the sake of solidarity
For the sake of humanity. (43)

The newly achieved indomitable spirit in juxtaposed with heroic courage of jawans stationed against blood-stained boundaries—

I saw a couple of smiling jawans
Carrying AK 47 rifles
"What did you achieve?"

"Their attack was repulsed"
Its the beginning
For them dark days are coming. (42)

Optimistically, the poet visualizes blood-stinking territory changing into a smiling territory

"where the quest of happiness will
Perennially find home as a warm humanistic spring". (40)
and
Nevertheless, I am optimistic
The valiant tribal spirit is a flame of immortality
Gangsters, extortionists and killers
Operating behind a revolutionary ideology
Will face their graveyards
On the sail of Dantewada. (45)

B.K.S. Ray's strategy to eradicate terrorism is apparently visible even in-between lines. His call for common humanity and cultural bond seems to be sympathetically engaging. He does not detail the causes of terrorism which till date has mostly been seen through the political and economic lenses, through vague references to anti-state sentiment; romanticizing hero—identity and luxury rich life are sporadically made. Interestingly, he focuses much on disengaging from terrorism. By alluding off and on to actual violence than "Threat of Violence", he repeats the nature of terrorism. The objective of terrorism detailed in the collection embodies all the three traits of actual violence contributing to "definitional elements" (coined by Schmid and Jongman)—first, it spurs emotional reactions such as fear and panic to influence attitude and behaviour, secondly, its outburst is unpredictable and is aimed against no-one in specific and last of all it intends to gain social control through fear and threat. Hence, terrorism depicted and detailed here shows destruction of the non-combatants mentally as well as materially. Therefore, the clarion call should not fall on deaf ears as Nalini Sharma in "New Year Musings" writes—

Before you a brand new canvas lies
With the brush of hope a rosy vision you paint.

Far war-weary mankind, ere your tenure flies
Let not terrorism your reputation taint. (13)

And, finally, one cannot deny the sincere wisdom and concerted beliefs of 'the sages of the Puranas' that—

Hope fuels
Zest
For. (Haikus as Positive Thinking, *Rhythm*, 127)

REFERENCES

Deming, Richard. *Listening on All Sides: Toward an Emersonian Ethics of Reading*. California: Stanford University Press, 2017. Print.

Ray, B.K.S. *Terror Must Die!* Raipur: Samvad Publication, 2007. Print.

Sharma, Nalini. *Rhythm*. Raipur: Vaibhav Prakashan, 2005. Print.

Chapter 20

Hero in Transition: A Study of Dogra Peasant Hero in Ramnath Shastri's *Bawa Jitto*

Vishali Sharma

Legend in writing is viewed as an image choice; he shields the average people against abuse and debasement of the built-up control structures. At the point when the legend shows up the rising, it shows the defiant expectation in men when the author and the peruser pull back their regard from the heavenly to mortal men. Ihab Hassan in "The Pattern of Fictional Experience" remarks that legend is "an epic character, a figure someplace beneath the divine beings or more the regular runs of men" (326). Further, J.P. Clark (1978) characterizes protagonist as "a man of super-human characteristics supported by the divine beings, a demi-god. He is a distinguished warrior...a man appreciated for accomplishments and respectable characteristics" (2). Apparently, the hero speaks to his condition and his choice is centred on events. The legendary anecdote about protagonist is an old-style principle famously known in all societies of the universe and is seen as a reality by individuals in different occasions in various ways like in ceremonies, fantasy, sacred texts, and dreams and even ever. The knowledge about the legends of the various regions of the universe complements the significant penance of an unfortunate hero who has resolved to arrive at the piece of no arrival, to accomplish the objective of sparing his own kin reflects either the conciliatory enthusiasm of legendary protagonists, along these lines, making them *eironic* individual or their will to battle for a reason. The contention between his internal identity and that of the general public is viewed as the primary horrible part for him, be it traditional or present day. Be it Jesus Christ, Prometheus, Bawa Jitto, the prevalent Dogra legend in the province of Jammu and Kashmir or the Shakespearean saint, American, or African legend. In the Jammu slopes, the local heroes attempting to guard the coon enthusiasm of the average citizens have been treated as nearby gods from the early medieval periods. The primary explanation for the gigantic prominence was their caring battle that persuaded the local individuals to safeguard their enlivened the nearby individuals to battle for their financial rights. The nearby legends inspired the normal people to guard and represent the discouraged against the severe circumstance and the assessment authorities' exploitative strategies. The endeavours of these heroes are imbedded in their customary story. Some nearby legends, for example, Bawa Jitto, Mian Dido, and Data Ranpat have built up a considerable picture in the customary accounts of the district of Jammu. Discussing the hero's life, Erich Neumann in *The Origin and History of Consciousness* states:

> The hero is compelled to sacrifice normal living [...] the hero is conquering normal life which is the life of non-heroic always means sacrificing as his normal values and so coming into conflict with the collective. He sees things they do not see; does not fall for the things they fall for—but this means that he is a different type of human being and therefore necessarily alone. (378-79)

Thus, this study attempts to accentuate the transformation of the protagonist from *eiron* to *alazon* in Ramnath Shastri's *Bawa Jitto*. Accentuating the position of the protagonist, Ihab Hassan in "The Pattern of Fictional Experience" postulates that "Elements of the Greek *alazon*, impostor, compulsive rebel, or outside, the *eiron*, the humble, self-deprecating man, and the *pharmakos*, scapegoat and random victim, unite to form the tarnished halo weighing on his head" (327).

The hero under analysis in this paper is the Indian legendary hero from the Jammu region of Jammu and Kashmir popularly known as Bawa Jitto, the Dogra countryman hero who sacrificed his life for the rights of tillers against landlords, around 500 years ago. Jitto took birth in a remote village of Aghar situated near Katra Vaishno Devi and was brought up in very poor conditions. Jitto lived five hundred years ago in a feudal society when the relationship between the 'jaagirdaar' and the peasant was that of the oppressor and the oppressed. The cheating of the countrymen is not restricted to a little profit exploitation of the countrymen; it goes further to making them work as slaves. Ramnath Shastri's *Bawa Jitto* originally written in Dogri with an English translation by Dr. Vandhana Sharma is a touching depiction of the transition of Jitto from "the *eiron*, the humble, self-deprecating man" to the *alazon*—"the compulsive rebel" who in the end becomes the *pharmakos*, scapegoat, and random victim for the redemption of society. Describing the hero as rebel or victim, Ihab Hassan states, "Rebel or victim, the hero is at odds with his environment. He is at odds with himself. His energy is the energy of opposition, and his aggressions are either directed against himself (the victim) or against the world (the rebel). In either case, he remains an alien to society, a misfit" (329).

Bawa Jitto is initially the *eironic* figure but assumes *alazonic* position subsequent to experiencing the aches of foul play and henceforth prevails with regards to providing a voice to all those voiceless labourers by his act of fearlessness and penance. Jitto is resolved to bring another rent of life into society tormented by smothering superstitious practices and heartlessness of incredible rulers. In such an endeavour to revive the general public, the legend endures and forfeits himself as he has the fortitude to fight back against the abusive practices and question what is against the human law. Ihab Hassan in "The Pattern of Fictional Experience" observes:

> Courage, therefore, is the prime virtue because it is the virtue of self-sufficiency. It confers dignity on meaninglessness. The hero, as it is said, encounters nothingness, and his courage is the courage of simply being. For what is put on trial is the very existence of man, not his heritage or future, his property or beliefs. (32)

Jitto, a humble peasant possesses indefatigable courage to fight the evils of society, be it the evil tendencies of his cousins and aunt at the individual position or the atrocities of the jaagirdaar as a figure representing the central authority in feudal society. He is uprooted from his native place after the life-threatening attacks of his aunt and cousins and the unjust verdict of the village Panchayat favouring the wrongdoers. His disillusionment at being treated unjustly does not waver his faith on his own courage which is the outcome of his faith in the Almighty. He firmly believes that "Peasantry is not a mean job". When he is lured by the jaagirdaar to undertake lesser arduous occupation by sticking to the occupation suited to his caste which is that of a priest in a temple, he courageously says: "Only peasants eat fruits of their labour" (*Bawa Jitto*, 43).

Jitto's *eironic* position which makes him move from his nearby town, Aghar after the choice of town Panchayat begins his experience towards his *alazonic* position which is for significantly greater explanation. Consequent to arriving in Ghar Pinjor, the town of his partner Jitto is yielded a land package for developing by the jaagirdaar of the town relying upon the essential that he would give a fourth bit of the regard to Mehta. By toiling day and night, he makes the fruitless land arable and productive which bears superb yield. When Mehta, the jaagirdaar sees the idea of yield, he backtracks from his words and announces to have the half of the reaped. Jitto contends him and encourages him to recollect the deed which was settled at the time of allocation of land. By and by Jitto, the humble self-condemning specialist marshal's determination to talk all the more boisterously against the unfairness of the owner. When Mehta mentioned his men to finish off sacks without paying any respect to Jitto's supplication, Jitto possesses a particular articulation "fear that Almighty. This whole universe reels under His laws. Wilderness and confusion can deliver theft and plunders however not equity" (*Bawa Jitto*, 63).

Seeking justice from the unjust transforms Jitto from an *eironic* to *alazonic* and finally a *pharmakos* figure. When Jitto is convinced that his plea is unheard in front of Mehta, he sacrifices himself on the heap of grains by thrusting a dagger in his chest. While giving up his life he vehemently condemns the injustice of Mehta: "You have resorted to avaricious meanness again, Oh Mehta! Your demonic hunger will not be satiated by the dry grains [jumps and stands over the heap of grains]. I now intermix the yield of my land with my own flesh and blood. Jai Durga Maa! Jai Vaishno Maa!" (64).

Bawa Jitto killed himself with a dagger; his blood-soaked the corn of the heap. His alone daughter "*Bua Gauri*" accompanying him was stunned to see the situation and came forward and cursed the landlord and his courtiers for the accident which had taken away the life of a poor farmer having no fault of his. She also sacrificed herself cursing the whole family of the landlord. It is said that those families who shared blood-soaked grains were cursed. The dissidents of those families have to visit the *Samadhi* of Bawa Jitto every year at his death anniversary and pay homage to the deceased farmer. Nearby the place where Bawa Jitto sacrificed himself, the *Samadhi* has been erected along with the *Samadhi* of his daughter named as "Bua Gauri". In those times, Sati was thought to be an incarnation of the Goddess. This was the first instance of a young girl committing Sati. People started worshipping "Bua Gauri" as an incarnation of the Goddess. Bawa Jitto and Bua Gauri sacrificed their lives in the year 1482 and were immortalized in the annals of history. A critic, Professor Shiv Nirmohi, in his paper titled "Duggar Da Shaheed Devta: Bawa Jitto" describes Bawa Jitto as "a shaheed devta". According to him, the deification of a martyr has been a tradition in Duggar (another word for Dogra land) and a person sacrificing his life for his rights is deified and called a martyr deity in Duggar. Based on the life of Bawa Jitto, a film was made by the Doordarshan Kendra, Jammu. It was telecast in the famous annual fair of Jhiri in 1994. A three days festival with fun and fair is organized to pay homage to the departed souls.

The suffering of Jitto has a lot of more extensive measurements as it speaks to a social battle between an individual and the dictator rulers. Professor G.K. Das, a critic, interfaces the life of Bawa Jitto with the progressive figures of Abraham Lincoln, Mahatma Gandhi, and Martin Luther ruler who assaulted Man's viciousness against man. He calls Bawa Jitto "a protagonist and an all-inclusive saviour" as in battling for the reason to benefit the individuals, he surrendered his life to prepare the majority to challenge oppression than let it ruin their lives. Professor G.K. Das in the Foreword to *Bawa Jitto* writes:

> Bawa Jitto does not kill himself in desperation, but for a social and moral cause. We know of time immemorial practices of animal/human sacrifice for the regeneration of life and crop, and James Frazer's accounts of older community life and of fertility gods who were consigned to death for new and better yield. But those were cases of sacrifice of the other, not self-sacrifice. Bawa Jitto's action is unique in being performed not in self-interest, but indeed in the interest of the other. (viii)

The legend described in this paper is an exemplification of selflessness. Bawa Jitto penances his life and commits himself to crushing underhandedness irrespective of whether it requires generosity. Similarly, as Socrates needed to drink the hemlock, Christ to hold tight the cross, Joan to consume at the stake and Jitto's pushing a dagger in the chest symbolizes that the penance of respectable spirits may recuperate and recover a degenerate society. The legend later comes back to plan to reclaim the general public as has been brought up by Joseph Campbell in his observational investigation on hero in *The Hero with a Thousand Faces* that: "The hero has died as a modern man; both as an eternal man—perfected, unspecific, universal man—he has been reborn. His second solemn task and deed, therefore, is to return then to us, transfigured, and teach the lesson he has learned of life renewed" (20).

REFERENCES

Campbell, Joseph. *The Hero with a Thousand Faces.* New York: Bollingen Foundation, Inc. 1956. Print.

Dodds, E.R. *The Greeks and the Irrational.* London: University of California Press, 1957. Print.

Hassan, Ihab. "The Pattern of Fictional Experience." *Modern American Fiction: Essays in Criticism.* New York: Oxford University Press, 1963. Print.

Neumann, Erich. *The Origin and History of Consciousness.* Trans. R.F.C. Hull. Princeton: Princeton University Press, 1971. Print.

Shastri, Ram Nath. *Bawa Jitto.* Trans. Vandhana Sharma. Jammu: Saksham Books International, 2011. Print.

Chapter 21

The Reverberating Phonemes: A Poststructuralist Study of Rashid Jahan's Select Works

Guni Vats and V.P. Singh

> What poststructuralism offers is an opportunity and a cause for reflection…the language poststructuralism puts forward is more useful in prompting the uncertainty of questions than in delivering the finality of answers. (Belsey, 107)

Rashid Jahan, an iconoclast of her generation broke the ceiling of a colonized nation's attitude towards literature and the role that language plays with her unapologetic depiction of the vulgar reality in all its nakedness. The pioneer of the Progressive Writer's Association came under the scanner of the academic authorities with her collection of short stories *Angarey* in the second decade of the twentieth century. Many may argue that she was a feminist, many may call her the torchbearer of realism and modernism but this paper looks at her writings from a poststructuralist point of view which neither tends to seat her at a throne nor construct her as an icon but as Derrida would urge, look beyond the surface of meanings and try to read her words with the precision of a scientist dissecting every phoneme that she uses as the words could well be staged but the Freudian gaps is where the real play of signification takes place and it is here that we come across her writings in a refreshingly fresh context that might suggest what has been consciously overlooked. As Barthes would say, the task of the reader begins with the death of the author and thus the paper would not look at the writings from the purview of an emancipated educated woman but just as a collection of words assembled to mean something or even break the established meanings and the way we view the world as it presents itself.

"But, of course, these are modern times" (*Angarey*, 97) is how Aftab begum defines the twentieth-century India when she mourns and celebrates the time hidden behind the veils in the one-act play, *Behind the Veil*. Modernism, as one could argue, is a fairly relative term referring to the now and the difference today has engineered with respect to the yesterday. The play could plainly be read as a confession diary where two women gossip about their families, their medical conditions and the sexual appetites of their men or it could be challenged as a deliberate simplification of the 'reality' by two women who hold no real authorities and shatter many signifiers of the culture that had until now been carefully packaged with women and their issues precisely wrapped with the beautiful muslin clothes, bolsters, cloth fans, grand settings, and spittoons. Once every word is ordered to define its meaning or at least explain its signification, the wrappers unravel and we are transported behind the veil to a compartment where culture has been religiously obeyed to but is also questioned in the form that no one had ever till now expected, for the weaker sex to hold the position of authority in a text and to paint their side of the world. The title, *Behind the Veil* is poststructuralist enough in the sense that it urges the unconscious of the reader to scratch the surface a little more and not be sufficed with the women and their comfortable made beds. What women say is hiding as much in the gestures that have been neatly underlined throughout the text and the need is to probe a little too deep to realize the cracks of the culture that is but not said ever.

"A room with white flooring" (83) is precisely how the play begins, but why white, why specifically white? Does it intentionally steer you to the piety of the virgin that might have come to the home as a child bride or the purity of the *zenana* if we tend to respect the culturally accepted signification of white? but then the play carefully peels the signified 'white' of its every virtue with the mentions of sexual advancements of the husband and the conjugal ties that might scream marital rape for the 'modern woman'. The mattress in the center of the room established the position of the woman who has been placed on the central position giving an illusion of her being the subject whereas the story unfolds we soon realize she is anything but a subject, just a passive bystander of the household where the man decides who feeds the children because he can't risk the wife be more invested in her children rather than attending the lustful needs of her lord, the man of the house, the subject of the text. Betel nuts, *surahi*, spittoon have all but carefully constructed a domain for the reader to recognize the setting as the upper middle class or even rich Muslim household. These careful cultural constructions are meant to place the reader in the vicious cycle of precisely defined cultural signifiers that make the case even before the reading of text and thus only strengthen the stereotype, the myth of the *zenana*. The cloth fan with the pink frill is distinguishably interesting not because it is any less culturally coloured but if the reader of Barthes was to be summoned, he would immediately understand the contrast of the only other colour than the white of the flooring, the pink of the woman or the pink of the revolution, the frill that would play with wind to taunt the white flooring, but it is just placed there, it has no movement. All these props are carefully fixed in their positions just as these two women are fixed in their positions by the patriarch; they might enjoy the illusion of authority but can never actually have it.

Mohamaddi Begum begins the conversation by asserting how fed up is she of the world and if it were not for the children, she would have already ended her life. The characters are not greeted to better introductions, but they are reduced to mere references, references of how the world treats them and how would they react in such a culturally motivated society. Child marriage, frequent pregnancies, patriarchal authorities and their atrocities, medical conditions are ignored, lustful men, religion, hypocrisy and all the other filth of the society is unapologetically mentioned in the dialogue between the two women. The only question then is if the text drives towards sympathy or disgust or simply an objective portrayal because the women complaint and gossip and pray and curse and only establish what the culture has already strongly built. The begum during her conversation says: "Words have a strange way of changing track" (89) and indeed so is then the play jolting the reader out of the prescribed meaning and screaming to be understood otherwise because the phonemes have an accepted way of coming together to form a word and then the words have a scheme to come together to construct a meaning, but what actually becomes of this meaning when the words are but a subjective agency? Under the obvious shelter of the wronged women lies the sly construction of normalization of everything wrong that the subject of the text talks about. *Nanhi-bi's* doll and *Chote-mian's* ball—the vulgar books of the younger brother and his strong sexual innuendos when he cuts the girl's pyjamas are instances of only creating another generation of what is being openly condemned by the women. Is the text then discouraging the cultural evils or is it only helping in creating a vice and strengthening the meanings of the derogatory culture that exists? We may not jump to blame the author or question the culture in itself but rid the signification these signifiers from there accepted meaning because maybe that is the whole point of the text, to expose the filth under the veil and to separate the meanings from the words and force the reader to introspect and redefine the role and function of these words!

The culture is constructed with language, any and all knowledge we may possess is because of the language and thus all our understanding of the world relies on the language itself. Poststructuralism looks critically at language; it doesn't blindly accept it as the structural foundation but questions the very origin of how the culture and language depend on each other and how they together construct and normalize meanings. The basic understanding of the structure of a language might point us towards the existence of binaries and our ability to view the world in the context of only such binaries like old/young, black/white, woman/man, *zenana/mardana*, etc. All these sets of binaries have an inherent hierarchy; it's not innocently depicting the meanings but re-strengthening the stereotypes of where the power lies and who the subject is. Catherine Belsey states, "our ideas are not [...] the origin of the language we speak [...] ideas are the effect of the meanings we learn and reproduce" (*Poststructuralism*, 07) and what could be a better breeding ground for language and stereotypes than literature itself. Saussure has argued that the "Meaning resides in the sign and nowhere else" (10), whereas Kristeva urges to look "beyond the surface meanings" (16). Language is not only the written word but everything that happens around every day is but a form a language conveying the cultural stereotypes over and over again. To understand it better, let's read *Woh* by Jahan but again looking at it poststructurally.

The story opens with the very assertion that the narrator met the other, the third person in a hospital. I and the Other are clearly constructed in the very beginning and what will flow later would only be an assertion further of the thought in itself. *Who*, the third person is constructed carefully through not words but the disgust of everyone around her. She becomes a mere object when every bystander assumes the authoritative position of being a subject. In the very second paragraph, she is labelled *randi*, the derogative term used to assassinate character and also the punishment is announced right here where she is a disgusting woman whose flesh is rotting away and the author leaves no mercy to conceal the horror of her ugly. The venue of the encounter is carefully described and then the change is established as precisely, from a hospital to a school, the two apparatuses as necessary for a civilized society as is breathing to an individual. The 'I' is a faculty at a school and the 'her' goes to meet her there, no words are exchanged and thus defy any cultural falsity and stereotypes, she just offers a flower every day that the teacher accepts with confessed disgust. The reference to repeated disgust only portrays the hollow of cultural construction, but the stereotypes are strengthened and the falsity reaches its heights when the disgust is coated with a forced smile, the construction of the ideological apparatus of a woman who is an amateur in the actual world and thus is given little leeways because she is not yet a subject, she is still an 'organism' becoming a cultural subject. The story is not only about the hypocrisy of society or the filthy biased world we live in but how culture and nature interact and culturally we condition these amateurs. The setting of school is but a perfect example of this becoming, it is one of the most essential Ideological State Apparatus that constructs the very beliefs that society lives by.

The story also mentions a repetitive etiquette, *tashreef rakhiye*, something that the teacher always says to the other woman. The repetition could but be intentional, the unconscious fight between the natural and the cultural, the accepted behaviour and the rude, all a part of the process of becoming. No names have been used in the story except for the maid at the school, the constructed woman who at the end vehemently opposes the obscene act of the advances of the other woman trying to be a part of the culture. The two other women of the story only try to find their identity in the difference, of not who they are but who they are not, the prostitute who is rotting away who is not a part of the culture and the teacher who is not the object of disgust. They identify only as constructed objects, a play that takes away any authority from both the women and places it in the hands of the bystanders, the subjects of the culture that judge them and define them on the acts that either could be accepted or vehemently opposed by the 'civilized culture'. The referential identity could thus be the very motive of the texts, the submissiveness of the subjects only to carve a place in the ideologically constructed system. "Ideology secures the system by consent. It is not a conspiracy. Its reaffirmation is not deliberate" (36) and it is this consent that guides the behaviour of the object trying to become the subject.

REFERENCES

Belsey, Catherine. *Poststructuralism: A Very Short Introduction*. New York: Oxford. 2002. Print.

Cassirer, Ernest. *The Philosophy of Symbolic Forms: Volume One: Language*. Trans. Ralph Manheim. Virginia: Yale, 1980. Print.

Evans, Vyvyan. *The Language Myth: Why Language is not an Instinct*. UK: Cambridge, 2014. Print.

Jahan, Rashid. *Rashid Jahan ki Sampoorna Kahaaniyan*. Ed. and Trans. Shakil Siddiqui. Allahabad: Sahitya Bhandar, 2016. Print.

— *Angarey*. Trans. Vibha S. Chauhan and Khalid. New Delhi: Rupa. N.d. Print.

McAfee, Noelle. *Julia Kristeva*. New York: Routledge, 2004. Print.

Oliver, Kelly. *Reading Kristeva: Unraveling the Double-bind*. Bloomington: Indiana University Press, 1993. Print.

Chapter 22

Lack of 'musawa': The Issue of Gender Favouritism in Taslima Nasrin's *Lajja* and *French Lover*

Paulomi Banerjee and Sucheta Kapoor

As a strident critic of Islam, Taslima Nasrin considers it an utterly gender suppressive religion and thereby chooses to acquire a secular and Western feminist approach in all her writings. Though the fundamentals rejected her as anti-Islam, she continues attacking Islam and its cultural propaganda by influencing the feminist movement of her motherland, Bangladesh. When the other feminist critics of her country choose to be "conspicuously silent on the issue of sexuality", Taslima Nasrin becomes liberal enough to indulge in it fearlessly. Therefore, the exploitative agenda of Islamic patriarchy of Bangladesh blamed her for forcefully infusing the occidental ethos into oriental settings. But, being recognized as "female Salman Rushdie" or Bangladeshi Simon de Beauvoir the Islamic death threat "*fatwa*" couldn't create any hindrance in her free-speech agenda.

Strangely enough, the male counterparts of this androcentric set up are regarded as pragmatic, protective, and unassailable, whereas feminine beings are awfully deemed as unreasoned, submissive, and weak as well. Therefore, women being under the shadow of men mislay their socio-political identity due to the vehement patriarchal subjugation. This misogynistic perspective of Islam instigates her to opt for a neo-orientalist as well as a progressive feminist standpoint.

In her celebratory works like *Lajja* and *French Lover*, the author's sole intention is to denounce the traditional Islamic notion of gender roles prevalent in the socio-cultural set up of

Bangladesh. Nasrin's endeavour to expose the post-imperialist legacy of Bangladesh under the swathe of unidimensional theocracy becomes the recurrent motif of both the novels *Lajja* and *French Lover*. Centring "subjugation" as the theme, both the novels emphasize on the regressive religious agenda of the country. Some critics opine that due to the "geopolitical entity of the nation" women are tortured and dispossessed of their freedom of meeting individual desires. The androcentric notion of the novels would be rightly justified with French feminist Simone de Beauvoir's lines—"one is not born, rather becomes a woman", though the women of the novel strives hard to liberate themselves from the shackle of patriarchy and thereby create their own space, they are abominably hurled into subaltern spaces.

Semiotics of Subjugation in *Lajja*

Lajja, being a plot of anti-Islamic expression, was miserably banned in Bangladesh as a consequence of *fatwa*, issued by Islamic fundamentalists. But this dictatorship of Islam could not check Taslima Nasrin from raising her voice against patriarchal atrocities through her iconoclastic writings. The double alienation of women on the props of identity and religious ethos become the commanding theme of this novel.

As we perceive in her seminal work, *Lajja* which is set in the background of Babri Masjid annihilation, Maya, Kironmoyee, and Shammima Begum all are impelled to endure the patriarchal governance against their impulse. Behind the veil of motherhood and familial harmony, Kironmoyee is supposed to bear her husband's insatiable hunger, physical impotence, and the bodily ordeal silently. In every moment, she is relegated to the "subaltern status", be it her sexual craving, desire to settle in India or preserving her gold bangles. In the saga of being a puppet in the hand of patriarchy, she becomes a mere object free from physical and mental yearning. Under the pretext of family and society, how a woman falls victim to marginalization becomes the resonating essence of the novel. But instead of liberating herself from this eternal code of subjugation, she is seen to be a "patriarchal woman" and hence starts promoting the gender phenomenon with a pre-conceived notion of cultural and social superiority of men. In spite of being aware of the genital amputation of her husband she refrains from assessing him with a deformed and disabled identity. The tyrannical subjugation of a woman is again intensified on the ground of religious freedom. In that country only those who subscribe to Islamic values are granted as human and humane as well. Therefore, the Hindus, being in the minority at the core, are compelled to camouflage their religious identity. For instance, Kironmoyee strays from wearing 'sindur' and 'sankha' just as Subhamoy's wife strives to hide her religious identity out of the fear of socio-cultural rejection. Ironically enough, being in the "Republic of Bangladesh" women are deprived of their basic fundamental rights becoming the prey to religious orthodoxy. This novel deduces that as a bitter outcome of Babri Masjid wrecking how Hindu women are subjected to inhuman brutality of the Muslim fanatics of "Bangladesh". The heart-wrenching paradigm of women's subjugation gets an ideal culmination when the abduction of Hindu girls to douse the libido of Muslim men becomes a fearless practice. Be it Suranjan's unflinching desire to rape a Muslim woman in order to take revenge of her sister's rape and abduction or Muslim men's attempt to vilify and molest Hindu women it is a woman who becomes the receiving end of sexual violence. *Lajja* has been a story of persecution, protest, passion, and principle. Portraying the darker side of society of "Bangladesh" the novel criticizes the Islamic pride in torturing the 'other' in the name of religious ideologies. Sexual violence is seen to harm as much the physical and psychological flow of a woman so as the sexual deprivation does.

By classifying a woman as a 'good girl' or 'slut' is a part of politics of hegemony to maintain an utter culture of discrimination. Therefore, whereas, Kironmoyee's self-deprivation is rewarded as an "ideal wife" Shammima's breaching of patriarchal codes dismisses her as a "slut". As a part of Islamic mandation, the perseverance of virginity is wholeheartedly romanticized and, in that context, Shammima is woefully ostracized. From this aspect, depicting a narrative of gender "discrimination" the novel actually challenges the fundamentalist mindset to the core. Being recognized as "female Salman Rushdie" or Bangladeshi Simone de Beauvoir, the Islamic death threat "*fatwa*" couldn't create any hindrance in the free-speech agenda.

In spite of the fact that in the fragmented, "post-modern period" the voiceless entities are getting "voices" the suffocating societal norms of Bangladesh do not allow women to break their stereotypical silence. Now, this instance can be analysed through Western theoretical lenses. Dwelling into the psychoanalytic concept of "castration" we must expound that this "lack" actually symbolises the deprivation of social power. As Lacan asserts that the idea of phallus is more of social than biological, therefore in the realm of cultural hierarchy women are being dominantly silenced for lacking a penetrative organ. Using the Marxist approach of exploiter and exploited it must be assumed that the exploiter changes from time to time like religious masters, husband or son, whereas the exploited remains same. This religious nudity and the bleak aspect of fundamentalism have been echoed all throughout the work.

Colonization of the Female Body in *French Lover*

While talking of *French Lover*, it might be asserted that the novel is a burning plot of both Gender Studies and Psychoanalyses. Standing just at the crossroad of home-land and host-land, here Nilanjana, the protagonist makes unflinching endeavour to create her own identity. Nila, having a same-sex orientation fits into the word of black lesbian feminist writer, Audrey Lodre, who expounds that "whenever the bird with no feet flew/ she found tree with no limbs" (*Zami*, 43).

There is no room for her own, rather she always finds herself to be predestined to patriarchal restraints. In spite of being an intellectual entity with artistic zeal, she has to tolerate her husband's chauvinistic behaviour. In this regard, it is worth mentioning that Nila didn't possess an escapist approach, rather when her incessant effort to cope with her husband goes "futile" she out of her feminine sensibility chooses to leave him. Being exempted from "so many restraints and structure" (80), she wanted to possess a life full of intellectual liberty, be it self-destructive or not. In her novel, *No Country for Women* her expression would match the reality of Nila and her same-sex partner Danniele [...] girls become lesbians because men fail to make them contended. As Benoir, the man whom Nila clung on after leaving her husband, Kishanlal treated her as an object of sexual ramification, Kironmoyee in *Lajja* is also witnessed to be a commodity of her husband's will. Being the victim of "body politics" she experiences the mean phallocentric concern of her partners over her body instead of her intellectual possessions. Therefore, all throughout the novel, her body becomes the subject of patriarchal exploitation. From her husband Kishanlal, French lover Benoir to the so-called brother Sunil da, everyone treated her as a subject of fulfilling material lust, instead of caring for her emotions. Through this novel, Nasrin not only excavates the issue of enslavement of women but denounces the institution of marriage. Besides Nila, Danielle's inclination to homosexuality is nothing but a corollary of societal injustice she encountered from very childhood. When the society remains ignorant of the vulgarity and atrocity that she envisages, choosing the path of lesbianism might be treated as a form of revolt from her part. When the oriental tradition and culture engages to judge her actions, she is seen to make a frantic search of love and self-glorification as well. Having a cultural shock in Kolkata, when Nila shifts in Paris, she still failed to create a "realm of ecstasy" by proving that "subjugation" is neither regional nor national but global.

Though sometimes Taslima Nasrin holds accountable by critics for "artistically naive" due to her propagandist exuberance and blaring tone as well her carefully conceived plot and theme add magnetism to her novels. The critics of Islam expound that, though Islamic practices have always been very exploitative by nature, all oppressive cultures are not necessarily prevalent in Islam. Therefore, mere vilification of Islam would not help to mutilate gender discrimination. Instead of that, if she focuses on women education and empowerment like that of the other feminist of Bangladesh, Rokeya Begum, we must get a brave new world someday.

REFERENCES

Alam, S.M. Shamsul. "Islamic Governmentality? The Taslima Nasrin Case." *Governmentality and Counter-Hegemony in Bangladesh*. USA: Palgrave Macmillan, 2015. Print.

— "Women in the Era of Modernity and Islamic Fundamentalism: The Case of Taslima Nasrin of Bangladesh." *Signs*, 23.2 (1998): 429-61. Print.

Hasan, M.M. "Nasrin Gone Global: A Critique of Taslima Nasrin's Criticism of Islam and Her Feminist Strategy." *South Asia Research*, 36.2 (2016): 167-85. Print.

Lorde, Audre. *Zami: A New Spelling of My Name*. New York: Crossing Press, 1982. Print.

Nasreen, Taslima. *No Country for Women*. New Delhi: Vitasta, 2010. Print.

— *French Lover*. Trans. Sreejata Guha. New Delhi: Penguin Books, 2002. Print.

— *Lajja*. Trans. Tutul Gupta. New Delhi: Penguin Books, 1994. Print.

Chapter 23

"A Bit of Earth which had No Name, Lay Toba Tek Singh": A Critique of Individual's Identity in the No-Man's Land

Sayani Nayak

Prior to independence, geographical and political borders were neatly charted down which bifurcated the Indian subcontinent into three separate nations: India, Pakistan, and Bangladesh. The question that comes up immediately—what is the exact definition of a geopolitical border? Is such a border only the demarcation of national extent or it translates into other forms of metaphorical boundaries?

This machinery of construction of borders helped to consolidate a uniform national identity. As Meenakshi Mukherjee in her essay "The Anxiety of Indianness" points out how borders led to "an erasure of differences within the border and accentuating with what lies outside" (174). The difference that Mukherjee talks of is not only, as mentioned earlier geographical and political; but also, cultural, social, lingual, communal, and psychological. The intention, therefore, was to consolidate homogeneity in national and cultural identity. In the case of India, this country would be distinctive from its two neighbouring countries because of its unique cultural essence and also because of its inherent Indianness.

However, after the colonial invasion to expect homogeneity out of a colonized nation is ironical. Colonization inevitably leads to a hybrid and heterogeneous culture where the nation is akin to a receptacle of a myriad population. This, therefore, leads to Homi Bhabha's *The Location of Culture* wherein he leads the reader to ponder over the location of culture, where can culture be posited in a national context. Culture is a dynamic entity which is assimilated, adopted, transformed into something new after getting mingled with different strands of influence. He opposes the notion of cultural homogeneity and purity hitherto preached by the national leaders and contends to focus on the formation of cultural collage. Thus, the characteristics of culture are hybridity, flux, connectivity or interconnectedness and a gradual transformation or metamorphosis of different elements. This is termed as "cultural hybridity". He deliberately uses the word 'beyond' to justify his views. To quote Bhabha:

> It is the trope of our times to locate the question of culture in the realm of beyond [...]. The 'beyond' is neither a new horizon, nor a leaving behind of the past. [...]Beyond signifies spatial distance marks progress, promises the future, but our intimations of exceeding the barrier or boundary—the very act of going beyond—are unknowable, unpresentable without a return to the 'present' which, in the process of repetition, becomes disjunct and displaced. (1)

Salman Rushdie's *Imaginary Homelands* shows that displaced beings that are living the life of an exile not only temporally but also physically. Such a displaced being is devoid of his national identity because he then becomes the personification of a rich compensation of all cultures of the world, out of which he can fashion out his own cultural identity. The individual curbs out his cultural essence from the different cultural strands that the whole world offers him rather than just confining within the limitation of his own native cultural identity. As Bhabha opines, "The borderline work of culture demands an encounter with 'newness' that is not part of the continuum of past and present. It creates a sense of the new as an insurgent act cultural translation" (7). Bhabha and Rushdie foreground the idea of not an exclusively national identity which will be a signifier of a singular culture, but a cosmopolitan identity which will signify the gradual metamorphosis of cultures.

Rushdie in his "Introduction to *Imaginary Homelands*" refers to a picture of older times. The picture is reminiscent of the past which is not closer to the present wherein he lives. For him, "the present is 'foreign', but the past is home albeit a lost home in the lost city in the mists of lost time" (9). Rushdie asserts that a sense of alienation or loss of native land bothers the poets of diaspora who are actually displaced from their homelands and their roots. Such an individual is bound to adapt himself to a new being, who will have the hybrid culture—a mixture of both of his native culture which he has inherently acquired and the foreign culture which he gradually imbibes. What is more interesting is that this binary of native and foreign cultures renders the individual as a partial upholder of both the cultures—far removed from the native land thus native culture and simultaneously not actually located in the foreign nation or foreign culture. Rightly, he points out:

> It may be that writers in my position, exiles or emigrants or expatriates, are haunted by some sense of loss, some urge to reclaim, to look back, even at the risk of being mutated into pillars of salt. But if we do look back, we must also do so in the knowledge—which gives rise to profound uncertainties—that our physical alienation from India almost inevitably means that we will not be capable of reclaiming precisely the thing that was lost; that we will, in short, create fictions, not actual cities or villages but invisible ones, imaginary homelands, India's of the mind. (10)

Rushdie insists that an expatriate tries to cling to the past and 'reclaim it' back by his own memories of the past. These fragments of the memories of the past history are opposed to the nation's grand narrative of history allow them to recount a truer version of the narrative. The literature written by these poets does not need to be justified by the nation's history. Neither they unleash the story gradually, nor are they traumatized by threatening personal security; simply because the nation no longer considers them to have the right to speak at all, because of their contamination of the culture. In other words, their 'self' is demonized as 'other', "We are Hindus who have crossed the black water; we are Muslims who eat pork [...] my use of Christian notion of Fall indicates—we are now partly of the West. Our identity is at once plural and partial. Sometimes we feel that we straddle two cultures; at other times, that we fall between two stools" (15).

These, therefore, lead to a few questions that if an individual does not belong to any nation of the world, then what would be his national identity? Where will such an individual try to find his roots? However, Saadat Hasan Manto explores these issues of alienation, rootlessness, and feeling of otherness in one's own nation, communal disruption, partition, and political tensions in his short stories. The most exemplary story which critiques the concept of individual identity, nation's role in imposing the narrative and the ownership of a terrain of land which belongs to no man is blatantly critiqued in Manto's *Toba Tek Singh*. Manto is one of the Indian poets who was suffering from angst, depression, alienation, identity crisis during the post-partition era and was compelled to migrate to Pakistan because of boiling communal tensions.

Manto was one of the poets who would criticize societal problems and disregard excessive nationalistic zeal. However, after moving to Pakistan, he found himself unemployed, disjointed from the society, uprooted and traumatized by reminiscences of Bombay. Manto was like a tragic hero whose nuanced personality and hubris of explicitly criticizing the societal aberration led to a troubled personal life. He focuses on distress, destruction, madness, terrible shock, and anxiety were inseparable as the aftermaths of partition. As Ashis Nandy refers in *Map Making: Partition Stories from Two Bengals*:

> Partition, in fact, did not merely mean two new geographical dominions [...], it gives birth to a new psychic dominion as well [...]. The stories that have been written about the phenomenal event of the Partition and its causes and consequences are called Partition Stories. They reflect a strange world of human life. It is a different world of its own. The Partition stories are different from other stories in the fact that they are based on real events and incidents of unusual and eerie character. The horrors and experiences of the partition trauma left a deep and indelible mark on the Indian short story and brought into it the new elements of

> sorrow. Suffering, bitterness, pathos and compassion. The partition stories are powerful portrayals of the fragmented and wounded human society in the sub-continent. They can be used to reconstruct the relatively unknown dimensions of those tumultuous days when religious and communal feelings privileged over the secular and human feelings. (91)

Toba Tek Singh is an exemplary short story by Manto wherein he explores the themes of post-partition trauma, rootlessness, angst, cultural amnesia, and identity crisis. The setting of the story is a mental asylum in Lahore where there are both Indians (mainly Hindus and Sikhs) and Pakistan (Muslims) reside. The government of both the nations have called for an exchange of these lunatics after few years of partition. No sooner is the news of an exchange being circulated, it becomes the hot topic of discussion for them and they come up with umpteen numbers of questions for the officials. The question ranges from the reason behind the exchange, to the geographical and cartographical location of both India and Pakistan, and how can they live in Pakistan now because that part was India few days back. The madhouse is portrayed as a miniature sketch of the tumultuous socio-political background of the whole nation where the citizens have no more than a vague idea of the macrocosmic impact of partition. These apparently absurd queries problematize the role of the nation in demarcating geo-political border and thus foreground the futility of charting down cartographical boundaries. The absurd questions of the inmates of the madhouse critique the notion of sanity because the primary motive behind the exchange of lunatics was their religious affiliation which overpowered the "secular and human feelings".

Manto recounts the reaction of the inmates without judging the ethicality of the tale like an unbiased narrator. One of the inmates climbs the tree and declares: "I wish to live neither in India nor in Pakistan. I wish to live in this tree" (13). Thinking in the light of eco-criticism, we can understand that since the tree is a creation of nature, it is at par than the mere man-made boundaries and that a man hardly has a say on nature's creation. Thus, the tree neither belongs to any nation nor to any man. The other two European inmates were surprised after learning the news of exchange and were bothered about their food habits—that whether they will have to survive on 'bloody Indian chapattis'. The lunatics try to discursify their notion of strangeness about India when they called India as a land of devils, or as the place where razors are manufactured hints to their absurd notion of land that is beyond the border. This instance of a formation of discourse about the land beyond the border alludes to Amitav Ghosh's *The Shadow Lines* where the children invented stories about the other half to highlight the strangeness and absurdity of the inversion of normalcy. Ghosh intends to foreground the relation between nation and house when Tham'ma says of the post-partition discourse: "Everything's upside-down over there, I'd tell her; at their meals they start with their sweets and end with the dal, their books go backwards and end at the beginning, they sleep under their beds and eat on the sheets, they cook with jhatas and sweep with their ladles, they write with umbrellas and go walking with pencils [...] (125). This 'other' would, therefore, help to consolidate and strengthen the subjectivity of 'self' by distinguishing itself from the other. Similarly, the inmates of the madhouse unknowingly construct their nation to the imaginary strangeness of the other nation because as Tham'ma would affirm that "across the border there existed another reality" (219).

Bishan Singh or Toba Tek Singh, the protagonist of the eponymous short story *Toba Tek Singh*, is a Sikh man who has been imprisoned for the last fifteen years. He longed for his village named Toba Tek Singh enquires about the location of his village. This man was fairly old who hardly paid any attention to other matters except his occasional cries of gibberish chanting: "Uper the gur gur the annexe the bay dhayana the mung the dal of the laltain" (14). Not realizing the fuss about the partition, Bishan Singh sought refuge before one of the lunatics who called himself as 'God'. However, this demi-God proved himself impotent when he could not relieve Bishan Singh of his perplexity thereby failed to say his village's location.

Rather, the 'God' replied callously that he has not issued 'orders in this respect'. Bishan Singh angered by this apathetic statement remarks: "Uper the gur gur the annexe the mung the dal of Guruji da Khalsa and Guruji ki fateh [...] jo boley so nihal sat sri akal" (16). The statement probably meant that Bishan Singh accuses the 'God' of being partial of being a Muslim—had he been a Sikh God, he would have definitely been of some help. As a matter of fact; this ironical statement is inevitably directed to a man who considers himself to be the God having the potential of drawing borders, but then, end up being partial and unjust for someone or the other. His utterances reveal the hegemonic and oppressive nature of political stratagems and stupidity and absurdity of normal citizens waiting for justification of such a gruesome act. Manto herein ironically satirizes the sane minds and also highlights the hypocrisy that dwells within the minds of national leaders. Language as a means of communication becomes the conventionalized exchange of words and dialogues with repetitive phrases underlining the failure of communication to empathize at a post-partition era.

Eventually, the lunatics were taken to the Wagah border for exchange. Such a grave operation carried out by the state officials was tempered with shouts, abusive, cries, screams, songs, and also ambivalent reaction from the inmates who were giving out slogans of "Pakistan Zindabad" and "Pakistan Murdabad". Bishan Singh tried to make his final attempt for his quest and asked the official: "Where is Toba Tek Singh? In India or Pakistan?" (18). However, with sarcastic laughter, he got his answer that his village is now a part of Pakistan. He is shattered when he realises that not only, he lost his family, his relatives, but his last hope, his root that is his home. The notion of home as a place which provides with a sense of security, comfort, belonging, peace and where familial bonds are nurtured is vehemently challenged. His home constantly differs and defers unless he is transported to a barren strip of land which has no name. Manto exercises the psychological aspects because during the post-partition situation there was a plethora of psychological turbulence, confusion, conflict and the subordination of an individual's voice against the state's bureaucratic intervention. Although Bishan Singh's somewhat a legitimate question is repeated quite often, yet it is rendered ridiculous and farcical compelling him to be neurotic and reducing his queries to be mere babbling and screaming. When absurdities dominate the life of an individual, he gets trapped in a claustrophobic condition, a terrible state of despair from where he cannot escape. His sense of being has crippled thereby nullifying his existence and diminishing his identity to an uprooted individual.

Bishan Singh stands in-between the land of India and Pakistan. His misery reaches its climax before the sunrise when with an outcry, he collapses to death. The story ends: "There, behind barbed wire on one side, lay India and behind more barbed wire, on the other side, lay Pakistan. In between, on a bit of earth which had no name, lay Toba Tek Singh" (18). Manto intends a pun on Toba Tek Singh—which both the man Bishan Singh who was referred to as Toba Tek Singh by his inmates; and the piece of land from where he belongs named Toba Tek Singh lay there. Toba Tek Singh lies dead in the no man's land—a strip of terrain existing between two border posts serves as the exchange passage for migrants. As Tham'ma in *The Shadow Lines* would desire the in-between land, "[...] there's something—trenches perhaps, or soldiers, or guns pointing at each other, or even just barren strips of land. Don't they call it no-man's land?" (151).

Tham'ma is anxious about the nation's identity and by perpetrating national borders; she also perpetrates her own identity. Unlike Tham'ma who valorises the necessity of borders after bloodshed and war; Bishan Singh in his insanity opposes rationality, logicality behind the existence of tangible and tenuous borders. Manto undermines the jingoistic appeal and allows Bishan Singh to cross the borders only to die in a no-man's land.

The no-man's land is symbolic of the protagonist's willpower of not being subjugated by either Pakistan or India and to die where he has always wanted to live. The state's attempt to hegemonize the life and action of the individual is critiqued and satirized. What is more interesting is that the questions which Manto leaves unanswered for readers by the end of the story—what is the identity of an individual in such a blurred area or a common zone? Who controls and owns such unnamed territories? If all the institutions like nationality, religion, caste, creed, race, and language appear to be dysfunctional in at the no-man's land; then what factor other than his innate humaneness and his humanity would determine his identity? Hence, the only trait which would define the individual would be his humanity which surpasses and spills over everything else.

REFERENCES

Bhabha, Homi. "Introduction." *The Location of Culture. The Internet Archive.* New York: Routledge, 2017. Print.

Ghosh, Amitav. *The Shadow Lines.* New Delhi: Oxford University Press, 1995. Print.

Manto, Saadat Hasan. "Toba Tek Singh". *Kingdom's End and Other Stories.* Trans. Khalid Hasan. London: Verso, 1987. Print.

Manto. Dir. Nandita Das. Perf. Nawazuddin Siddiqui, Rasika Dugal, Rajshri Deshpande, Tahir Bhasin. Viacom 18 Motion Pictures, 2018. Film.

Mukherjee, Meenakshi. "The Anxiety of Indianness." *The Perishable Empire.* New Delhi: Oxford University Press, 2000. Print.

Nandy, Ashis. "Foreword." *Mapmaking: Partition Stories from Two Bengals.* Ed. Debjani Sengupta. Bhopal: Manjul Publishing House Pvt. Ltd., 2011. Print.

Rushdie, Salman. *The Imaginary Homelands: Essays and Criticism 1981-1991.* London: Penguin, 1992. Print.

Chapter 24

Burdened by Border: Mohsin Hamid's *Exit West*

Rimpa Roy

'War' and 'refugee' are the words which get connected to each other over and over again. Natural calamities, war and economic crisis are the consequences which made millions to migrate towards the West and the impact of relocation is not only physical but highly psychological. Every year millions and millions of people are forced to abandon their country, home, loved ones and everything. The migrants risk their lives to save themselves; some die on their way and some other way. The contemporary situation calls for a redefinition of inherited notion of identity burdened by the border. Immigration is always a concern for the natives of the country, where these helpless, homeless people seek rehabilitation. It often hampers the peace, prosperity and most importantly the security of a nation, including safety of the natives. The migrants belonging to a different nation, colour, caste and creed flooded the West. This made them implement strict rules against the intruders and borders were closed. Even if law in some countries entertained them, the natives think them as a threat to the well-being and economy of the nation and present scenario is the same.

Migration leads to human inequality; there comes a gap between migrants and non-migrants. People are burdened to dislocate; whereas it is a universal thing present in cultures old and new and central to those with the longest continuous histories. In spite of considering it as a boon to humanity, this process is restricted with a view of a threat to the set collective identities of national communities, as it may destroy the whole structure of community with a division. Border justifies the inequality within the whole community of human, hampers free market, encourages exploitation and oppression. The border creates identities and manages socio-economic peace and security agendas. The term refugee by UNHCR July 1951 is: "A person who is outside his/her country of nationality or habitual residence; has a well-founded fear of persecution because of his/her race, religion, nationality, membership of a particular social group or political opinion; and is unable or unwilling to avail himself/herself of the protection of that country, or to return there, for fear of persecution" (Whittaker, 2).

Mohsin Hamid criticizes the condition of closed borders and justifies how it hampers the identity of individuals when they are bound to deterritorialize. The closed and guarded borders are a threat to the diversity of the world. The novel *Exit West* by Mohsin Hamid is an eye-opener for those who follow anti-immigration views and develop negative thoughts. The story is about love, relationship, and sacrifice against the backdrop of a country met with war, youth fleeing for safety, elders staying back as part of roots and shows how people get the identity of the refugee. The novel has close resemblance to the contemporary situation as the protagonist can be seen as portraying the universal migrant figure and their belonging to an unnamed country makes the crisis both global and psychological, which both the natives and refugees could relate to. The citizens form a part of the nation and gain rights, identity and citizenship and they are granted the political, social, and economic right, which provides a layer of protection. But a sudden dislocation takes away all the above and makes them the 'other'. Getting access to cross the border easily doesn't help the migrants to be a part of other nation or gain citizenship. The condition becomes worse as they neither gain rights nor granted protection and facilities. The result is inhuman treatment, inequality, and oppression, lack of freedom to access the basic needs and finally life of a non-status resident. 'No border' politics rejects constructed identity and Hamid's text is a justification of this idea by showing dissatisfaction with border and migration control. The identities formed within border has been shown and the change outside has been manifested.

It is the love story of a man and a woman "in a city swollen by refugees but still mostly at peace, or at least not yet openly at war" (*EW*, 1). Saeed and Nadia are the protagonists who have been shown leading a normal life even in such state of crisis. Going for classes (preparing for the future), meeting at coffee shops are things of normal life, which they maintain, giving us an idea that daily errands cannot be stopped even in the face of death. A pale-skinned woman received mail from Saeed from far away in Australia. This shows how technology connects people, but men are still bound to be where they belong. This woman lives in a house which was once called 'home' by others. 'Home' is a very complicated matter for refugees. It is what holds back a person from being a global figure and gains world citizenship.

Nadia never prays but wears the black robe "so men don't fuck" (16). Her mother and sister are not like her. They live a life of women restricted within boundaries, but she, on the other hand, is of different identity and knows how to protect one and how to deal with police and aggressive men. The identity of a person seems to be very simple when one is with the same kind of people and consider himself one of them, as it is with Saeed. Nadia, on the other hand, tries to configure the edges of her identity with changing time and place. Both Nadia and Saeed dream of travelling to Latin America—Cuba and Chile respectively. Their psychology makes them shift every now and then, away from their own city. "Refugees had occupied many of the open places in the city, pitching tents in the green belts between roads, erecting lean-to next to the boundary walls of houses, sleeping rough on pavements and in the margins of streets" (*EW*, 23)—the picture of immigrants they saw in their own native homeland reflect their own picture and their identity afterwards. The social network is transnational and promotes migration. The superiority of the West always attracts attention of the East. "Nadia and Saeed always in possession of their phones [...] transporting them to places distant and near" (*EW*, 35) is the psychological journey which helps them free themselves from the burdens of the border.

Hamid's narratives and characters explore the impact of the border upon them and show how they are burdened. They show dissatisfaction with the contemporary border system and expresses that free human mobility is a utopia. His work is to bring an optimistic view of the narration. Even if one doesn't change one's home in one's whole life span, is a migrant, as said in the novel "everyone migrates, even if we stay in the same houses our whole lives, because we can't help it. We are all migrants through time" (*EW*, 209). The border brings the division—the insiders and the outsiders and thus they are made to characterize themselves as belonging to a particular group in the larger society.

The protagonists Nadia and Saeed fell in love in spite of their completely opposite views and accompany each other on the decision to leave the city and start a new life towards the West. They reached through magical doors, first to the Greek island of Mykonos, to London and then San Francisco. The doors have been used as part of magic realism to solve the situation but fail to bring solution. The author's idea of 'door' is a representation of the idea of power of free mobilization and open border. The doors substituting for border hides the element of trauma which the mass of uprooted humanity had to undergo while crossing the border. The traumatic experiences would have made the novel more aching rather than futuristic and optimistic. Here Saeed and Nadia survive the catastrophe and xenophobic resistance and Hamid's message is to think of the future rather than to hold on to the golden past and to construct the future not devoid of humanity.

The doors are not just black rectangles but also an image for the border which is connected to everyone. It is the border which makes us connect to a particular horizon and give ourselves an identity to differentiate it from those outside the horizon. One feels privileged to be within and a sudden intrusion is not accepted within that area except those who actually belong to it. Belief in a global nation is considered to be an act of modernity, but one is still polarized by the thoughts of insecurity from the immigrants. The door "felt equally like a beginning and an end"; the beginning of a new identity and the end of the old; the "passage was both like dying and like being born" (98). Both Nadia and Saeed begin a new journey accompanying each other with love, but it ends with their separation and change. They found better companions outside their psychological border. They fell in love in a situation of crisis and when it changed, their relationship too. The change which started in Mykonos, continued in London. Nadia "had never seen bitterness in him before.... It struck her that a bitter Saeed would not be Saeed at all" (*EW*, 102-03).

Both Saeed and Nadia had to leave their parents and they could never know whether they were alive or not. As it is said that "when we migrate, we murder from our lives those we leave behind" (94) has got multiple meanings. They not only murder the facts which were prominent for them as home, parents, identity, partner (love), but also the factors which determine these things for them. Saeed's parents saw innocence being taken away by war. His mother saw one of his students with a gun and his father witnessed how "teenagers, young men, and they were not playing with a ball but with the severed head of a goat, and he thought barbarians, but then it dawned upon him that this was the head not of a goat but of a human being, with hair and a beard, and he wanted to believe he was mistaken [...]" (*EW*, 82). The image reminds of Golding's Lord of the Flies, where the small boys lost their innocence while in a state of crisis, without any law and order. Such is the condition of a country struck with war.

The whole concept of crossing the border is being suppressed with the word 'door' but while passing through it, they felt frightened, threatened, relieved, and finally emerged the question of identity and nationhood. Saeed and Nadia felt the condition is same everywhere they stepped "faces and buildings had changed but the basic reality of their predicament had not" (156). The border creates an inability within a human to be a part of the larger view of the world. Saeed looked for empathy within the kind of people who are like him. The house "on Vicarage Gate, was a house known to be a house of people from his own country" (148). It is the familiarity of identity, language, and prayer that made him a part of them. Nadia, on the other hand, tries to be a part of the Nigerian group as for her everyone is a foreigner. Their journey from one place to another was a constant process of fear as the nativist threatens their existence. At one point "The mob looked at Nadia like a strange and violent tribe, intent on their destruction" (131). London has divided into dark and light London; dark London with locals who want wholesale slaughter of refugees, claiming Britain for Britain and light London with natives delivering food and medicine. The doors are considered to be a part of major global crisis by the leaders. The dichotomy between refugees and non-refugees is being clearly shown.

In London, there came a significant change in the two protagonists and in their relationship. Nadia is of independent opinion but, when burdened by the border, she had to restrict herself at time. When she came out of the native land, she felt much free and became reluctant to all the limitations. She spent her time showering and cleaning and when being disliked by Saeed, she expresses that these things are essential for human beings and she is ready to fight with Saeed to justify her point. Nadia speaks to him in a disgusting way "don't tell me what I can do" (123). Saeed is guilty and impatient about the fact that they are utilising the resources of others. Saeed felt the loss: "when the warmth between (Nadia and Saeed) seemed to lack, his sorrow was immense, so immense that he was uncertain whether all his losses had not combined into a core of loss, and in this core, the centre, the death of his mother and the death of his father and the possible death of his ideal self [...]" (*EW*, 188). Their relationship changed from a loving one to a protective one. Saeed and Nadia joined the worker camps and in exchange for their labour, they were assured of getting connection to modern utilities along with a house on forty square meters of land. Here these two protagonists are the migrant voices representing gender and identity crisis. Nadia struggles with her gender and Saeed with his identity. In California, they separated as a couple. Hamid gives an idea of nativeness through the place Marin where Saeed finds "almost no natives" (*EW*, 196). He tries to make the fact clear that 'nativeness' in the contemporary world is rare and Marin is a place, which can be considered as an example. Saeed here found people of his type and Nadia found a job to become independent again. They found people of their affection in Marin, where they were unburdened by their earlier identities and thus they were free to follow their own true self.

Although Hamid's purpose was to bring out the optimistic view behind the work, still the problem of refugee crisis in the contemporary situation can never be ignored. The flow is from developing nations towards the developed nations giving rise to transnational communities and identities. The name of the city is not given but some Middle Eastern city is being hinted at from where people exiting towards West. The image of the city is traumatic where "A window was the border through which death was possibly most likely to come" (68), funerals were much smaller affair, holding hand in public and listening to music was prohibited. The difference between East and West is created through the lines: "where on the Greek island of Mykonos, a great for tourists in the summer, and it seemed, a great draw for migrants this winter, and that the doors out which is to say the doors to richer destinations, we're heavily guarded, but the doors in, the doors from proper places, we're mostly left unsecured [...]" (*EW*, 101).

Mohsin Hamid spent thirty-eight years of his life shifting from Pakistan, UK and US and considers himself a mongrel and hybrid. Born in the East and grown up in the West, he offers a deep insight into the psychology of immigrants, defining their experience through obstacles and conflicts they encounter. The trauma of dislocation, an encounter with violence, communal clashes, refugees reminisce about their former home and many more. Our empathy for migrants is brought out in the novel so that we become more human towards them rather than being afraid and insecure. We can be one of them or on the other side, and both the sides should be taken care of. A sudden shift in the life of the characters brings a psychological shift within the readers which is unburdened by the border. Both the rectangles—books and mobiles make us cross the border easily as Nadia and Saeed did. Thus, we never cease to conjure new identities when it is a matter of survival above the very idea of the border.

REFERENCES

Bauder, Herald. "The Possibilities of Open and No Borders." *Geography Compass*, 9.7 (2015): 395-405. Print.

Hamid, Mohsin. *Exit West*. New Delhi: Penguin Books, 2017. Print.

Whittaker, David J. *Asylum Seekers and Refugees in the Contemporary World*. Oxon: Routledge, 2006. Print.

Chapter 25

Suggested Socio-Religious Reforms by Regional Sufi (Mystic) Poets: An Analysis of the Select Poets of Punjab, Sindh, Khyber Pakhtunkhwa, and Baluchistan

Shamaila Amir

The land, presently is titled as Pakistan, has produced a large number of saints and poets. These Sufis spent all of their lives in submission to Allah and to spread the message of humanity through peace, brotherhood, love, tolerance, and patience. Their poetry in the languages like Punjabi, Seraiki, Sindhi, Pushto, and Balochi has an essence of their soils in it, therefore, it attracts the hearts and minds as soon as one listens or reads these poets. They have rendered selfless services for socio-religious reforms which through their message which contains the basic elements of correcting the evils of the society such as spreading love, establishing peace, exercising tolerance, living a life of brotherhood, and practicing humanism within the society can be put across to the international community for the purpose of creating an image of Pakistan as a tolerant, moderate, progressive, and positive community especially in the present day when the country is facing the war on terrorism and having its adverse effects (*Rifat*).

The poetry of these Sufi poets has been translated into several languages other than Urdu and English. Still for the sake of real inspiration and to experience maximum enjoyment while reading the poetry, one needs to learn to read original languages of this poetry. It is also important because through these languages these Sufi poets have come to be known and respected by their readers and followers by becoming the lighthouse of peace and love apart from providing guidance for service to humanity and reaching God. All these Sufis appear to be reformists if deeply read and understood, well appreciated as peace activists and most importantly critical of those who create obstructions and miseries for the common people. These Sufis advise them to discover and take recourse to Almighty Allah. These Sufi poets since ages have also been inspiring the folk singers who ultimately have rendered their services by singing these poets and thus spreading their message among generations (*Rifat*). Sufi poets, which have been selected for this purposeful chapter to analyze their objective-oriented poetry, are Bulleh Shah from the land of Punjab, Bhitai from Sindh, Rahman Baba from Khyber Pakhtunkhwa and Mast Tawakkli from Baluchistan.

Socio-Religious Reforms of Baba Bulleh Shah (1680-1757)

Baba Bulleh Shah's most prominent feature as a socio-religious reformer is the support of human rights and religious tolerance against sectarianism and caste system (Anjum, 2011). His teachings are primarily based on the dignity of mankind and through his poetry he shows concerns about the honour of humans. He advises the man not to oppress or murder the weak and own brothers in lust of throne and property (Punjabi). He publicly criticizes the contemporary priests and is not in favour of violence in reply of violence. He propagates the teachings of religious tolerance and non-violence saying that even the slaves of Muslims and Hindus should not be harmed because both of these are children of God. The decision about them should be left to Him (Khokhar).

As a social and religious reformist, he opposes violence and extremism. He advises to give importance to the opinion of disbelievers and opposers and avoid quarrels with such person at every cost. He says that people may be forced to act upon helplessly on rites and rituals of society because they have weak beliefs and confidence or experience social pressure. People cannot survive against the criticism because of these factors and ultimately "roll away from true reality for fake ego" (Khokhar, 54).

Bulleh Shah calls such people flowing in the "awful social flood" of "counterfeit and spurious rituals" helplessly (Khokhar, 55). He advises people not to be afraid of these and live with strong will and determination. He advises standing against criticism of community even the society declares a person a "denier". In his opinion, "heart and intention" are what matter and that is it and pious heart and intention make it easy to eliminate the differences of Raam and Raheem (Khokhar, 55). Bulleh Shah is against intra-sectarianism also which according to him, is so useless a thing that no one can please God through sectarianism. It should be avoided, therefore. In one of his pieces of poetry, he writes that people are divided into sections just as some are differentiated with others because of having long hair or being clean-shaved. He, therefore, expresses his indifference to all this and for him the most important thing is that his sincere friend agrees to whatever he says. In present times, social disturbance is caused because of religions and sects because they are contrary and opposite to one another about the existence of God and His attributes. This disturbance is created because people are following opposite ways to get God's humans for themselves, although God exists nearer than their jugular vein. He is not far away and impossible to reach. He says that the division of names Raam Daas and Fateh Muhammad are not meant to create contradictions, but they have (Khokhar, 55). This is because everybody has "a thief" inside him and to end disputes it is necessary that this fact is known publicly. Purification of soul for that matter is necessary because without it and losing individual self, a person cannot be able to find the universal self. To understand this phenomenon in simple words, it can be said that this is the only way by which a human soul can communicate to God and become united with Him. This is the stage of ecstasy which is experienced only by a pure soul (Nicolson, 2007).

The aforementioned stage of ecstasy is only achieved through purification of soul and heart and to attain this stage, Sufis adopt different modes, physical and spiritual exercises.

Purification of heart and soul removes all grudges and lusts of the contemporary world. When the soul becomes pure, it seeks Allah's pleasure through various mysterious ways. This world seems of no importance "for a person whose soul is pure and refined. Bulleh Shah in a quatrain speaks of achieving Allah's pleasure" (Saifullah, 34). If a person acquires an abundance of knowledge and fights in the way of Allah visits the holy cities for performing pilgrimage and receives several titles of Qazi, Ghazi, and Haji but if he fails in achieving Allah's pleasure through all these religious experiences, this failure will be considered the major loss. The pleasure of Allah is what exactly all acts of worship are done for. This lesson of cleansing one's soul makes Bulleh Shah a big social and religious reformer of all times. He says that the ultimate humility is only possible when the "I" is removed, and the heart is free from any self-interest. Removing "I" means the removal of personal ego and dissolving it into an ocean of love and service of humanity (Qausain). A soul cannot even taste the grapes of Divine light without losing pride and ego.

In real sense, every human being has one colour and that is the colour of one Creator. This colour of God is reflected through His creations. It does not matter whether a person is Syrian, African, European, or Sikh. God is omnipresent so every colour represents Him. He reflects Himself through love and care and this makes Bulleh Shah follow the path of divine love, i.e. the love of God. Following this path, makes a human free from all restrictions that lie in his way to reach his beloved. He reaches his real destination that is of divine love. For Bulleh Shah, all those scholars are fraudulent and deceivers who involve humans in limitations and restrictions, as a result, people indulge in constraints of religion. These scholars are like hunters spreading their nets and giving importance to apparent actions and deeds. In actual, divine love is always free from all constraints of caste and religion. Bulleh Shah is a devotee of religion but his philosophy is to criticize and condemn all sorts of limitations that are created by sects, regions, favouritism, inequity, etc. He does not favour grouping and advertising of divisions. He sees divine love as an essential part of human life and preaches that love has no mental or geographical boundaries. Love for Bulleh

Shah is a matter of universality regardless of person, time, and place as he illustrates in one of his poems "Love is everywhere [...] love has its place on earth and heavens" (Saifullah, 34).

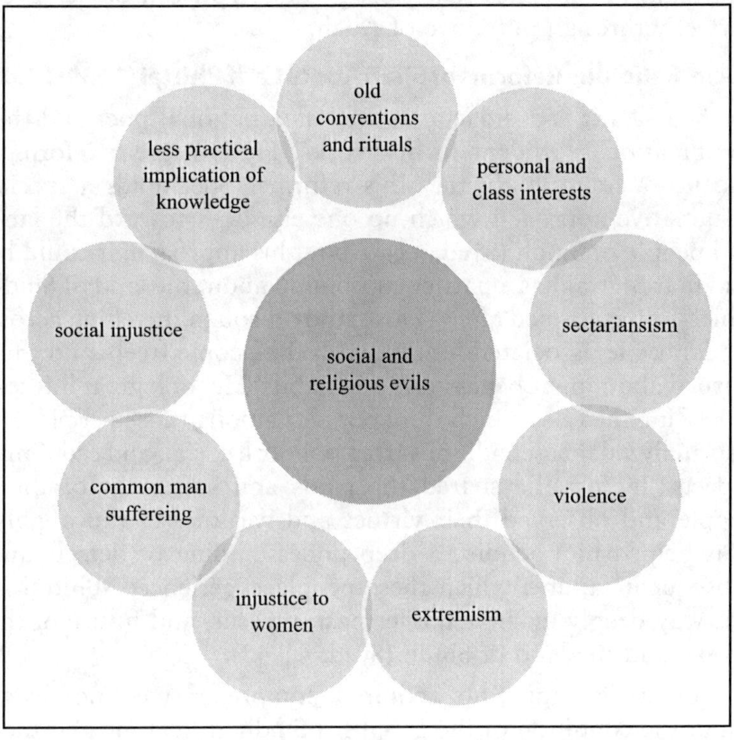

Fig. 1: Concerned socio-religious evils of Sufi poets

Mysticism is the only way if a person wants a garden which is full of spring of love and where peace and serenity prevails. To find the secret of mystic thinking means that a person will find the straight path which ultimately would help him lead a peaceful life. In that life, worldly troubles would not bother him anymore. In the path of Mysticism, equality exists and there is no discrimination or differences of any kind or sectarian differences. Love is a form of worship which shares equal value with other acts of worships. "Love is ever new and fresh" (Misali, 64) and it has no particular season. It is everlasting and all seasons are the season of love. The philosophy behind this concept of love is that the essence of all acts of worship is to bring man closer to God and to develop a constant relationship between Allah and man. He assumes that closeness of Allah can be achieved perfectly through pure love of Allah.

Socio-Religious Reforms of Shah Abdul Latif Bhittai (1689-1752)

Shah Latif is a didactic as well as a national poet and this combination is evident in his works. He is a great reformer, and no one can doubt that this reformer poet holds a special imaginative approach which no one else does toward the land and people of Sindh (Syed, 41). About his approach, it could be said that Bhittai has a particular opinion about the land of Sindh which he has formed after a close study through travelling across the land. He associated himself with the people freely and thus learned about their behaviours and habits. He took great interest in hearing the tales which were popular among those people. He also analyzed their conditions from political, social, and economic aspects. In fact, he shared the pains and sufferings of these people and observed their virtues and weaknesses thoroughly. This helped him acquire a deep understanding of defects and subsequent failures which these people experienced. Bhittai in this way deeply meditated over past, present, and future of the people and the land of Sindh (Syed, 41-42).

It was Bhittai who acquired comprehensive knowledge about the condition of the people of Sindh at his time and then developed consciousness for their well-being. When his poetry is analyzed, it can be observed that the following elements highlight his concerns for social and religious reforms in the people of Sindh: “Bhittai believes in the unity of religions and Pantheism which means that all religions are the same. They merely follow different paths but all these paths lead to one supreme goal” (Syed, 41-42), that is, God and “He tried to transform the theological concepts of pantheism into a political theory based on the spiritual unity of human beings” (Memon and Aman, 71-89). His political doctrine revolves around the creation of unity from diversity and he thinks that it is essential for the growth and development of Sindhi society. He wanted to construct a Sindhi society which should be based on of equality and social justice for humans, an economic system which is free of exploitation, where the dignity of labour and respect for women should exist and religious tolerance should be exercised. Peace and unity which should be the result of resolute struggle must prevail in this society. He is loud in expressing the doctrine of "unity in diversity" and states: "Diversity has emerged from unity. Hence diversity and unity are inseparable. The only truth is that the just path is the path of unity, not duality" (Memon, 71). This "unity in diversity" is explained in another line where he employs the echo as a metaphor: "What you call echo is, in fact, the reflection of the voice. Voice and echo are not two separate things, but they are one and the same" (Memon, 71).

According to Bhittai, the service of humanity is to be the real aim and significance of prayers. Bhittai showed his concern for the suffering class and he opposed to the ideas of the ruling class. He is a nationalist writer and he wanted to do some noble deeds the Sindhis. The Sayeds, the Pirs, the Pirzadas, the Qalandars, and the Sufis were icons of political power at that time. This made Sindh a region like none other than in Asia "so perfectly priest-ridden" (Memon, 71). He always urged people to develop the virtue of courage explaining that the nation, which becomes a prey to the evil of fear, would neither be able to achieve independence nor progress.

He believes that knowledge of the self or the self-realization is real knowledge and education. One of his services in this regard is the acknowledgement of Sindhi language at a time when the Persian language was considered the language of elite. He rejected that idea that the Persian language is supreme to any other regional language particularly Sindhi and equalled it to accepting the slavery. According to him, the proficiency in Persian language was not something that could make someone elite. He laid great stress on the self-knowledge aspect of mysticism because according to him "spiritual elevation and consciousness" (Majeed) are essentials of mysticism. "Your beloved is an integral part of yourself, and it is a futile exercise to search it beyond yourself" (Majeed). According to the poet, when someone is blessed with inner enlightenment, all he needs to do is look into his soul and then he would get the vision of beloved.

He believes that only through sacrifice and hard efforts is it possible to achieve the aim. He says that there is only one way to achieve this when every person in the land of Sindh learns how to sacrifice personal and class interests for the sake of the nation and the collective and common interests of Sindh (Majeed), and "if the sea is rough do not go to sleep. The shore is surf ridden like froth in a jar. Do not be sceptical but face the high tides, otherwise, there will be more pains for you" (Singh and Gaur, 137).

His most favourite heroine Sassue's sufferings and audacities to reach her beloved Punhoon are his role model for the people of Sindh. He argues that reaching to the destination is possible only with a strong will because hardships of this journey become insignificant if one has the willpower to do so. He represents these hardships as rough mountains, thorns that prick feet and the fingers that cannot bend anymore. The struggle must continue even barefooted if there are pointed stones injuring the feet (Majeed).

Socio-Cultural Reforms of Rehman Baba (1632-1706)

Rahman Baba is considered a great reformer of society. Throughout his life and through his teachings he had been providing guidance to human beings which could lead them in the right direction. Close studies of Rehman Baba's mysticism reveal that he as a mystic is the eternal beauty which according to him is none other than God Himself. He presents himself as a God-intoxicated individual. He believes that a lover of God follows the truth, and this makes his life full of hard work and extreme devotion. His principal aim is that the sinner should be saved from the fire in the hell. For this purpose, this poet that individual and society must go through a renovation. He hates sins but justifies his love for the sinners because the sinners are also the creatures of God. He, in fact, does not appreciate anything which he finds contrary to what God has commanded. He focuses on the character building because this makes individuals capable to face life's hardships with serenity (Khan, 42). According to him, an individual possesses many potentialities or capabilities which can be and should be used to serve human beings because only through service to humanity it is possible that the nearness and pleasure of God are achieved. He holds that man has evil lying inside him and through his courage to banish this evil he can be a winner and a successful person. Otherwise if he fails to do so and evil conquers him, he is simply a loser. According to Rehman Baba, God has made human beings superior to all other creations, but humans do not realize their supremacy and behave like animals (Khan, 274).

Tolerant in nature and kind to others are the best qualities according to Baba which can make a person near to God because it is in his nature to love God and to love God for Baba is to obey commands given by Him and service to humanity. In this service, one should not expect financial rewards because being rich means the richness of heart, and this richness is only achieved through the remembrance of the Lord. It should be realized that man is nothing but a humble slave of God. Man only makes himself slave of the slave when he stretches his hand before any other man. Baba is surprised at this act of human who makes themselves slaves of other human instead of being slaves of their real Creator and Master (Khan, 274). He strongly suggests that man should know his history of birth, growth, and development. For that matter, he advises that Ulama should become practical rather than having theoretical knowledge only because a practical scholar is a real scholar. Knowledge opens man's eyes and helps him to get introduced to God. This way, a person starts to obey commands given by God without any sort of hesitation.

Baba says that being a true human being is something becoming a rarity these days so a man should try to be a true human. His teachings are about numerous sides of life and are primarily based on "To enjoin Good and forbid Evil and eventually work for the establishment of a just socio-moral order in the world" (Khan, iv). He strongly recommends justice which according to him is essential to establish peace and unity in the society. The way he advocates his point of view make his courage and conviction exemplary and his concerns for humanity like no other poet. He has a great fear of God and he knows that the art of living in this universe is only being a true human being. Following his teachings purifies the heart from and helps to get rid of evil. It brings man close to God which provides him the requisite courage for fighting against all sorts of evils whether that is present in man or outside in the society. Conclusion of his teachings as a socio-religious reformer is that justice everywhere will bring harmony and peace and the society will turn into human society in true sense.

Socio-Cultural Reforms of Mast Tawakli (1825-96)

It is widely believed among Baloch folks that Mast lived near Kohlo and was a shepherd who happened to fall in love with Sammu who was already a married woman. Ishq is the instrument of his poetry, his philosophy, and his imagination through which he seems to find his poetry and perspective. He condemns violence through the gesture of love using the imperative form of communicating. Tawakli expresses his thirst for love and to spread love. As the Sufi tradition believes inequality of human beings despite their colours, race, and gender, Tawakli, through the lens of Sammu's love, addresses and discusses women in a very creative diction his poetry. Mast advocated the concept of women's creative aspect and condemns the then situation of women via his particular discourse in poetry wherein he addresses to all women condition through Sammu, his beloved, which women are not to be assigned the task of shepherding, rather much more creative work can be taken from them. Meanwhile, Mast portrays the picture of women in Baloch society of his era and seems unhappy to experience it.

Tawakli is much concerned with peace and emancipation of age-old rusting conventions. He uses poetry to create links with masses and form an identity which is religious in nature due to stress on equality and indiscrimination. Because of his experience of war, he wishes for peace. The common emerging patterns or notions in his poetry include truth-bearer, bravery, and resistance against the unjust social system. His themes chiefly fix themselves in discussing Sammu, ishq and love, through which he sheds light on lifestyles of tribal people and their thinking, their behaviour and treatment of women. Tawakli brings nature into life while portraying a bit of his thought and his specific discourse with much emphasis on softer expression. His poetry is closely attached to the sufferings of common men in the subcontinent. He was not only the harbinger of optimism in his time in Baluchistan but his work for the promotion of positive value and his inspiration is considered to be very effective and soothing even today, the aesthetical element is too innately ingrained in his poetry to be overlooked. There is a notable distinctive quality in his poetry that he showed the path of remedy to the oppressed and helpless women of his society. This aspect endows him a higher status than any other poet.

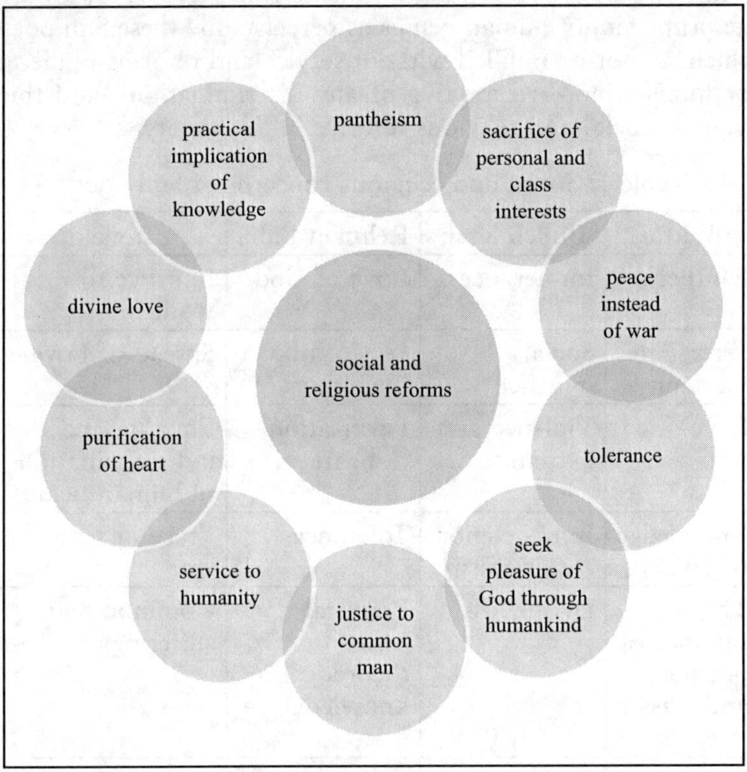

Fig. 2: Suggested socio-religious reforms by Sufi poets

If poetry and teachings of the Sufi poets are analyzed, few interesting facts are revealed. Each Sufi poet believes that the true destination of a human being is to seek God and His pleasure and mercy. For that matter, they stress on service to humanity and spread of love among human beings avoiding and elimination the evils that are present in self like social and class differences, extremism, and violence. They believe that society cannot be reformed until differences which are created on the basis of class, injustice, sectarianism, or even gender is present in it. They stress of purification of heart, the sacrifice of interests, practical knowledge, love, and knowledge of the self at an individual level and unity, justice, equality, and religious tolerance at societal level. It can be said that reaching and achieving pleasure of God is the prime aim of human beings as perceived by these Sufi poets which cannot be fulfilled without service and reforms rendered for humankind—irrespective of any discrimination—and thus bringing social and religious reforms in the society.

Table 1: Social and religious concerns of Sufi poets

Bhittai	Bulleh Shah	Rehman Baba	Tawakli
Pantheism	Intolerance	Love of God	Injustice to women
Service to humanity	Social injustice	Service of humanity	Spread of Love
Love	Violence and extremism	Purification of heart	Equality and indiscrimination of human beings
Knowledge of self	Intra-religion sectarianism	Tolerance	Peace instead of war
The sacrifice of personal and class interests	Divine love	Practical instead theoretical knowledge	Common man sufferings
Efforts of people against the supremacy	Purification of heart and soul	Following of truth	Resistance against social injustice
The pleasure of God	Old conventions and rituals	Peace, unity and justice	Old conventions and rituals

REFERENCES

Ali, Quasain. "Makkah Gaya Bulleh Shah." sufipoetry.wordpress.com. Sufi Poetry, 1 Nov. 2009. Web. 23 May 2019. <https://sufipoetry.wordpress.com/2009/11/01/makkeh-gaya-bulleh-shah>

Anjum, T. "Be Hell for Those Who Call me Saiyyid: Social Stratification among the South Asian Muslims and the Sufi Worldview." *Pakistan Journal of History and Culture*, 32.2 (2011): 43-64. Print.

Khan, H. Mysticism of Rehman Baba and its educational Implications. Pakistan: Qurtuba University of Science and Information Technology. Thesis. Web. 21 May 2019. <http://prr.hec.gov.pk/jspui/bitstream/123456789/3630/1/362S.pdf>

Khokhar, M.S., S. Ramzan and A. Munir. "Religious Tolerance in the Teachings of Baba Bullah Shah and Khawaja Ghulam Fareed; The Best Substitute of Current Situation of Terrorism." *Pakistan Journal of Islamic Research*, 10 (2012): 51-67. Web. 23 May 2019. <https://www.bzu.edu.pk/PJIR/vol10/eng%205%20Mahmood%20Sultanv10.pdf>

Majeed, S. "The everlasting story of Mast Tawkali and Sammo." Thebalochnews.com. The Baloch News, 15 Oct. 2017. Web. 3 Jun 2019. <http://www.thebalochnews.com/2017/10/15/mast-tawali-sammo/>

Marri, Y. "Mast Tawkali: The Great Baloch Poet." cssforum.com.pk. CSS Forum, 12 Dec. 2013. Web. 5 Jun. 2019. <http://www.cssforum.com.pk/css-optional-subjects/group-vii/balochi/88413-mastain-taukali-mast-o-samo.html>

Memon, A. and S. Aman. "Shah Latif's Poetry: An Alternative Source to Study the History of Sindh." *Pakistan Journal of History and Culture*, 32.1 (2011): 71-89. Web. 21 May 2019. <http://www.nihcr.edu.pk/Latest_English_Journal/4.pdf>

Misali, Y. *Kalam Baba Bulleh Shah*. Lahore: Mushtaq Book Corner, 2002. Print.

Nicholson, A.R. *The Mystics of Islam*. UK: Murine Press, 2007. Print.

Punjabi, Irshad Ahmad, *Thinking of Bullah Shah*. Lahore: Punjabi Literature, 1982. 25-28. Print.

Rifat, M.Z. "Paying tribute to popular Sufi poets." TheNation.com. *The Nation*, 3 Oct. 2011. Web. 15 Jun. 2019.

Saifullah, K. 2016. Discourse Analysis: Bulleh Shah's and Rumi's Poetry. *Linguistics & Literature Review (LLR)*, 2.1 (March 2016): 29-38. Print.

Shah, Baba Bulleh. "Selected Poems of Baba Bulleh Shah." scribd.com. *Scribd*. Web. 30 May. 2019. <https://www.scribd.com/document/102200884/Selected-Poems-of-Baba-Bulleh-Shah>

Sial, S.M. "Sufism and the Society of Sub Continent." End Term Paper. Pakistan: Quaid-e-Azam University. End Term Paper. Web. 10 Jun. 2019

Staff Reporter. "Anti-feudal voice—Mast Tawakali—remembered." Dawn.com. *Dawn*, 7 Oct. 2015. Web. 3 Jun. 2019. <https://www.dawn.com/news/1211444/anti-feudal-voice-mast-tawakali-remembered>

Surinder, Singh and I.D. Gaur, eds. *Popular Literature and Pre-modern Societies in South Asia: Alternative Voices from Sindh*. 2008. New Delhi: Pearson Education, 2008. Print.

Syed, G.M. Shah Latif and his message. Issue.com. *The Issue*, 10 Nov. 2011. Web. 17 May 2019. <https://issue.com/inayatkhoso/docs/shah_latif_and_his_message_-_g_m_syed>

Chapter 26

"Where are you going and where have you been?": A Reading of Adib Khan's *Seasonal Adjustments*

Malini Chongder

"Where do you think you belong? It teases and then bursts into a playful laughter as though hiding the answer is a game to be relished and played repeatedly" (*Seasonal Adjustments*, 9). Iqbal Chaudhary is "trapped between polarised worlds of disenchantment" (8). He has to remind himself constantly that he was born in Bangladesh and at the same time was reminded of his being "a foreigner who can afford the decorative luxury of a social conscience!" (136). Tim Winton believes that *Seasonal Adjustments* is a startling, heady novel about the sticky web of attachment and belonging. A very intense and inherent sense of emotional and physical dislocation undergoes throughout the chapters of the novel that is experienced by Iqbal Ahmed Chaudhary, who is "capable of overcoming the most serious of adversities" (161). Iqbal leaves the newly-born Bangladesh in the year 1973 and lands in Australia "with a huge dream full of sharply defined rainbows and realisable wishes" (32). The creator and the protagonist significantly share this move and it bares the ground for some relevant debates. Right from the very beginning of the narrative, there are references to pre-independence politics of Bangladesh and the war of liberation. And here memory plays a serious role in restructuring Iqbal's identity. Silent faces, distant places, snatches of happenings are embracing him, and he is unable to escape.

The main theme of *Seasonal Adjustments* as inscribed in its title is change and the ability of adjustment as represented by Iqbal, a displaced migrant deeply characterised by his ever-transforming identity. It depicts the existential journey of Iqbal, a teacher from Ballarat who goes back to his native country, Bangladesh after eighteen years which is "long enough to realise that for a migrant the word *home* is fraught with ambiguities" (61). But here Iqbal feels "an unfamiliarity about everything" (7) what he hears and sees. Iqbal's mid-life crisis as a burnt-out school teacher, complicated by the collapse of his marriage to his Christian wife Michelle concurs with the timing of his coming home, and by the poverty and squalor he experiences when reconnecting with his land, burdened by the aftershocks of the war with Pakistan. He is accompanied by his young daughter Nadine who will meet her paternal relatives for the first time. Her presence on this trip reminds him of the need to uphold the conviction of a possible world beyond the cruel demands of dominant cultures. For Iqbal, it is thus necessary that she also connects to her Bengali heritage so she can be enriched by it, adding new dimensions to her world in order to be "among a slowly growing minority which will learn how to combine traditions" (85) and also be capable of facing ridicule and the pains of non-acceptance that makes Iqbal "apprehensive about the exacting and sometimes cruel demands of cultural dualism" (161).

Adib Khan, a Bangladeshi diasporic writer based in Australia, propounds the possibility of adopting shared cultures on the basis of give and take principle. He is fortunate enough not to encounter any racial hatred and discrimination in his writing career in Australia and seems to be optimistic about dwelling in the space of in-betweenness or interstice while explaining the contributions of the dual cultures of East and West. In his words: "On the one side there were Homer, Virgil, Dante, Shakespeare and Milton. On the other, there were the influences of the Ramayana, Mahabharata, the Moghul poets, Iqbal and Tagore. The two sides met not in combat, but in a synthesis of ideas out of which I emerged considerably enriched in thought and feeling but without any clearly defined sense of belonging to a mono-cultural society" (qtd. in Alam, 197).

In a study entitled "Growing Up in Two Elsewheres", Ledgister explained 'home' as: "I found myself struggling to explain that where my parents live was not 'home', that where I was born was not 'home', that the places I had lived had never been 'home'. In clearer words, that home for me was wherever I happened to be [...]. Home is what I carry with me [...] elsewhere is everywhere" (Ledgister, n.pag). Iqbal endeavours "the pain of endless journeys" at first by leaving his country for Australia, that apparently appears to him "nearly perfect" and then returning after eighteen years to feel the sadness of a futile journey to a land that does not exist anymore. And throughout his journeys, the fundamental questions arise within—"Where am I from?", "Where do I belong?", "Where am I going?", "Where have I been?". He acknowledges that "Eighteen years is a very long time; Eighteen years. Close to half my life; and I haven't been back" (*Seasonal Adjustments*, 61).

Iqbal Chaudhary has endured "the lonely burden of a dissatisfaction that nobody else will understand" (296) but surely one can feel the change from his initial state of antipathy and disgust to a more disciplined and affirmed state. He is trapped in nothingness and often realised that "I have nowhere to go" (179). After his return to Bangladesh, Iqbal started finding meaning in cobwebbed memories: "The good things from the past can never be taken away. They are a part of you. Don't neglect them. Treat your memories well and they will work for you" (21). But, later on, Iqbal "wanted to erase the past and assume a more humane identity" (122) only to prove to himself that he could make it. Iqbal realizes that he cannot separate his life in Australia and Bangladesh and his experiences of past and present in clear section and the moment of epiphany occurs. He realised the calm within and the dullness of his surroundings as "a scintilla of nostalgia probes feebly" (104) into his mind "where the ruins of the past lie in scattered heaps". Though Iqbal decided to make his own home in Australia, but his deep affection for his homeland at Shopnogonj, Bangladesh appears to be deeply rooted in his memories that can never be taken away and "that is what gives reality the anxiety of uncertainty" (105).

Salman Rushdie asserts from his inherent experience—"Exiles or emigrants or expatriates are haunted by some sense of loss, some urge to reclaim, to look back, even at the risk of being mutated into pillars of salt" (*Imaginary Homelands*, 10). Bangladesh, the homeland of Iqbal produces a series of mental images for him. Iqbal says "My mind is a murky seabed where the ruins of the past lie in scattered heaps. A scintilla of nostalgia probes feebly among them. Briny ghosts dance nimbly around the remnants. They beckon me" (104). So, his return to Bangladesh brings forth the nook between his imagination and the visible reality, in which Iqbal felt the sadness of his journey, is thus producing an imperfect reality that is painfully difficult for Iqbal to acknowledge. He has to remind himself that he was born in Bangladesh. Life becomes "a raw, unhealed wound, painfully ugly" (101).

In the year 1995, *Seasonal Adjustments* (1994) won the Commonwealth Prize for the best first book and the narrative is set in Shopnogonj, Dhaka which is "a replica of the thousands of villages which confirm the rural primitivism of Bangladesh" (11). Khan shows how Iqbal faces bigotry, self-aggrandisement and racism from common Australians and "everything, from language to food, religion and accent, has been moulded into a composition to fit a uniform view" (147) is compared with the discernible presence of the same evils in Bangladesh and within Bengalis abroad. In a conversation with Michelle, Iqbal discloses his frustration of his "being treated as an oddity, a stray from the forbidding darkness of the world up there. I'm tired of misconceptions and assumptions, of being an object of curiosity!" (149).

Through the character of Nadine, Adib Khan highlights the cultural space of the second generation of diasporic Bengalis from their parents; this distance gets even more accentuated when the children come from mixed marriages, as in her case. Khan's view is that the second-generation migrant's cultural pulse is tuned to a different rhythm, where the original homeland appears more foreign than the actual "foreign" land. Khan's protagonists realise that things are not too good for the immigrant, that they have "sacrificed the right to belong" (117). So, finally Iqbal decides to return to Australia, despite his marginalised existence there, despite the fact that in Australia he has nothing he can really call his own. For, though it is not anything near perfect, it is still "a very liveable country"; and like any other Australian he too has been "seduced by the common dream of a brick-veneer house on a quarter of an acre of land" (122). In short, *Seasonal Adjustments* deals with Bengal and Bengalis both in the native land and in the diasporic situation, distance from exercising any simple parochial romanticisation or glorification of any particular land and human space. Through the following passage, Khan has depicted the feeling of being a migrant:

> Do you know what it means to be a migrant? A lost soul forever adrift in search of a tarnished dream? You live in a perpetual state of conflict, torn between what was and what should have been. There is a consciousness of a permanent loss. You get sick of wearing masks to hide your confused aloneness. You can never call anything your own. But out of this deprivation emerges an understanding of humanity unstifled by genetic barriers. No, I wouldn't have it any other way. I have had my prejudices trimmed to manageable proportions. You realise that behind the trappings of cultural differences human strengths and failures are global constants. That is a very precious knowledge. A Bengali can be as indifferent, mean, egotistical, loving, creative, heroic, generous, humane, cruel, and greedy as an Australian. It makes you appreciate the homogeneous blueprint of human life. It is this impossible mixture which binds humanity, and I am a part of it. No better or worse than anyone, but an equal. An equal because I know I am a composite of all those contradictory characteristics which are far stronger than any racial or religious differences. And that is worth celebrating. (143)

Far beyond inhabiting an exotic diasporic space, Iqbal strives to embrace difference by merging into a cosmopolitan consciousness, through which he can trim his ego and resist the essentialising labelling of dominator oppositional constructions (Western/Asian, national/ethnic, modern/traditional). What is of interest here is that Khan problematises Iqbal's migrant identity by constantly transcending his supposed hyphenated in-betweenness of here and there as his voice tells him "what it is like to be a stranger and yet to be at home, to live both inside and outside of one's immediate situation, to be permanently on the move, to think of one way return journeys but to realise at the same time the impossibility of doing so" (Khan, n.pag.). So, coming back to Bangladesh was not an easy decision to Iqbal as he had to readjust his perspectives and to go through the process of acclimatisation. Immigrants perpetually occupy the diasporic cultural space, since this reciprocation and assimilation is a continuous process and it will go on ever since. Iqbal's search for a sense of belonging is shaped by diverge vision and emotion that is sometimes enclosed or stretched. There has to be an ongoing engagement with multiple complex realities when one is living in a diasporic condition as Iqbal said that "he will never be able to close the sizeable hole at the centre of his life and shut out the view of that other world" (296). So, Iqbal tries to float with the tide and surrenders himself to life. Though there were multiple disadvantages of coming home to Bangladesh, "it was a great feeling to be in love with life again, to embrace it without the fear of rejection" (153).

This is also skilfully conveyed in the novel by Khan's frequent use of flashbacks, recalling specific events through which Iqbal strives to be simply human, himself and to tell his own unique story in order to comprehend how to live a life that "cannot be separated into their individual strands" but "must remain interwoven in a complex texture" (296). In his quest for self, Iqbal critically exposes the flaws of dominator configurations imposed and maintained by his family, education, religion, politics, and nationalism as global constants, from which the complicated entanglement of togetherness through the difference becomes a cosmopolitan forum of the human initiative for widening the horizons of mutual recognition and inclusion.

To conclude, characters like Iqbal, Nafisa or Nadine in *Seasonal Adjustments* are "caught in cultural and often contradictory crosscurrents of societal pressures, parental expectations and individual desires" which often result in alienation. But though Iqbal was torn apart "between the emotional claims of irreconcilable worlds", he never wishes to program Nadine's cultural pulse. Rather Iqbal is determined to preserve Nadine's cultural bond where she was born. Furthermore, one can see triple alienation of Khan's protagonist—from his motherland, from his adopted homeland, and finally from what he has become during the years of his displacement. Khan himself reveals:

> The notion of home for a migrant is a very peculiar one. Physically I am home. I have lived in the same house in Ballarat for twenty-three years, and yet in an emotional sense, as I grow older, I still look back to the house where I grew up—and it's not there anymore, and that's a traumatic experience [...] and people say if you are that bloody ungrateful, then why don't you go back. It's not as simple as that. [Broadcaster] Terry Lane keeps harping on how migrants should assimilate. I wish it were that simple. (82)

The protagonist in *Seasonal Adjustments* realises finally that he has "nowhere to go". His old friend Iftiqar had told the truth about his predicament: "As a first-generation migrant, you probably sacrificed the right to belong" (117). He finds the "lingering foreignness" about Australia really disturbing; in Australia and he feels that there is nothing to hang on to with conviction as he owns nothing. He does not feel passionately for anything that happens there. However, although he knows Australia is not anything nearly perfect, it is still "a very liveable country"; and like any other Australian, he too has been "seduced by the common dream of a brick-veneer house on a quarter of an acre of land" (122).

In the end, Iqbal's craving for "the security he once knew" in his ancestral village Shopnogonj, is lost permanently. So, he would tell his friend Claire, whom he addresses in the Prologue, that "the womb was there alright, but he could not fit into it anymore" (296). He decides to go back to Australia preparing to endure "the lonely burden" of a migrant's dissatisfaction. The stories that are composing Iqbal's life, the routes he decides to take, are the material out of which his identity is constructed. Not only his experiences at Ballarat and in Bangladesh influx into each other and contribute to new stories but those experiences which he does not understand often become living part of his life. These "are the catalysts of change which alter our personalities and people's perceptions of us" (273), Iqbal says to Shabana. While in one hand, he regrets his exposure to the diversity of cultural radiation, in another, he remains indifferent to cultural roles. Iqbal says: "I am a variable without a constant to measure myself against; a changing shadow whose exact composition cannot be determined" (9). So, it is impossible to bind him to a place. In the end, he says: "I shall never be able to close the sizeable hole at the centre of my life and shut out the view of that other world. I am destined to fret and pine and endure the lonely burden of dissatisfaction no one else will understand. I shall brood over what might have been. This is the way it must be. I have known too much to live contentedly" (296).

REFERENCES

Alam, Fakrul, ed. *Dictionary of Literary Biography: South Asian Writers in English*. Detroit: Thomson Gale, 2006. Print.

Boehmer, Elleke. *Colonial and Postcolonial Literature: Migrant Metaphors*. New York: Oxford University Press, 1995. Print.

Highland, J.M. *Asian Migrant Writers in Australia and the Negotiation of the Third Space*. Australia: Edith Cowan University, 2011. Web. 16 May 2019. <https://ro.ecu.edu.au/theses/156>

Khan, Adib. *Seasonal Adjustments*. Sydney: Allen and Unwin, 1994. Print.

—. "In Janus' Footsteps." *Australian Humanities Review*, 22 (June 2001): n.pag. Web. 19 May 2019. <http://australianhumanitiesreview.org/2001/06/01/in-janus-footsteps/>

Ledgister, F.S.J. "Growing Up in Two Elsewheres." *Jouvert*, 6.1 (2001): n.pag. Web. 19 May 2019. <https://legacy.chass.ncsu.edu/jouvert/v6i1-2/ledgis.htm#one>

Rushdie, Salman. *Imaginary Homelands: Essays and Criticism 1981-1991*. UK: Penguin, 1992. Print.

Sharad, P. "Seen through other eyes: Reconstructing Australian literature in India." *JASAL: Journal of the Association for the Study of Australian Literature*, 10 (2010): 1-15. Print.

Chapter 27

Cultivating Terror, Persecuting Humanity: The Fallacy of Insurgency and the Anxiety of Islam in Khaled Hosseini's Land of *Kite Runner*

Soma Mandal

While the world witness a huge exodus of refugees from Syria, Palestine, Yemen, Sudan, Rohingya, Iran, and Iraq, the most recent Israel-Palestinian conflict to the secessionist and insurgent uprisings, internal rebellions, religious fundamentalism, intolerance, hate crimes, and international issues of displacement, the stakes for humanitarian stability(-ies) is on the decline. The situation is beyond the control of international missionaries and organizations to provide constructive and futuristic hope on the current situation of several nations including Afghanistan undercut by extensive degrees of a humanitarian disaster. Given the scale of persecution and attack on the intrinsic and fundamental essence of humanity, human rights bodies across the world have become almost dysfunctional. Unable to address massive onslaughts of violence they have thus become mere tokenistic recipients of peace missions in war-torn regions and heavily militarized zones of the world.

Khaled Hosseini's *The Kite Runner* documents such changing landscapes of violence. It envisions a world of infancy, inarticulation and nostalgia which also parallel the lateral progress of adulthood, inhumanity and the failure of envisioning an immediate future. But the narrative reminds the readers of the importance of the thousand ways of restoring humanity in the wake of current persecution and death symbolized through Hassan's death. "There is a way to be good again" (1) as Amir looks up at the twin kites while sitting in San Francisco and remembers the chilling winter of 1975 in Kabul, Afghanistan, an episode which drastically transformed his life forever.

The numerous episodes of kite flying, the image of the kite as the connecting chord of hope, loss, despair and destruction resonate similar such kite-flying events which are not just conducted in Afghanistan but across many Middle-Eastern and Asian countries in particular. With the Taliban uprising, the ban on kite flying signals the curtailment of civil liberties that were to be imposed upon the Pashtun people of Afghanistan and across the Islamic countries in general. The paper, thus, intends to draw a (un)paralleled but the central image of the kite across numerous cultures, drawing from similar such occasions of kite-flying festivals that occur in Afghanistan towards a diversifying practice of celebration in Hinduism, where the kite is flown in Poush-Parbon beginning with the onset of the celebration in the month of December-January. The purpose to analyze and imagine how such a connection resembles similar cultural trope across nations and countries involve a general degree of acceptance and universal tolerance. The intention to draw a parallel is to analyze how kite-flying is an integral component of national celebration and unification of democratic spirit instrumental to the collective ethos of the community.

The kite also records the socio-political and historical trajectory of Afghanistan and the major changes that evolved during the period of Taliban uprising. The discontinuation of the kite-flying tradition as a criterion for an Afghan way of life enforced by Taliban rule meant a monochrome, numbing, pleasureless existence against a rich, kaleidoscopic mottled past which had its hovering, palpable presence over the present state of Afghanistan. The militarization of the Taliban movement and the recruit of thousands of new Afghan Pashtun boys and men into the military cadres like Assef, the boy who later becomes the Taliban leader and who rapes Hassan, tries to kill Amir and sexually harasses Sohrab (son of Hassan) signals the rise of extremist forces and political turmoil which forced many Afghans to flee Pakistan and the neighbouring countries during the 1980s.

In India, the festival of kites known as Uttarayan which also marks the international kite-flying festival takes place on Makar Sankranti or Maghi on 14 January every year. The day marks the end of the winter solstice when the sun makes transitions into the Makara (Capricorn) and celebrates the harvest season of the Indian agricultural sector. Ahmedabad hosts the international kite-flying festival, but the kite-flying tournament is noticeable in all the parts of India marked by Basant Panchami in Punjab and Pongal in South India. Usually, there are teams of two players, one flying the kite, while the other feeding the line of *manjha* (the string coated with a mixture of crushed glass and glue to cut the opponent team's kite). The *manjha* of the kite as the controlling mechanism for successive metaphorical 'flights' to make the kite soar in the air provides symbolic, liberatory and emancipatory modes of achieving independence. The soaring of the kite in the sky is emblematic of the high-tide of prosperity and the socio-economic elevation of the nation based on the auto-telic and the functional power of evolution of nation-states.

In Afghanistan, Persia, and the East Asian countries, kite-flying is observed as a national pastime. But in 1996, when the Taliban came to power in Afghanistan, it took away many of the freedoms that were existing in the country. The 'Sharia' as the central text of Islamic order, the outlaw and the ban on the kite-flying tradition implied that the succeeding decades of Afghanistan will witness would be tantamount to extreme degrees of violence, restrictions on freedom, and repression of basic fundamental rights of citizens. With unstable governments and sectarian disputes, political instability gave way to militaristic fissures and factions. The Soviet intervention of 1989 and successive kidnappings of political administrators made Afghanistan vulnerable to insurgency and internal attacks. The national interests of the country were taken over by the Wahabi(-ites) and extreme propagandism of individuals and militant terror outfits who tried to resist foreign intervention in Afghanistan.

The kite in Hosseini's narrative also symbolizes the Freudian apparatus for projecting repressed guilt and torturous impulses of childhood. Amir Sadiq whose memory retraces the narrative's journey to its past, through the meandering alleys of Kabul, the mountainous terrain of Kandahar and then to the present generational crossover to Pakistan and the United States indicated the kite's journey (embodied by the metaphoric journey of 'self') through the history of Afghanistan, thus becoming a historical entity and a document for capturing truth of an Afghan's way of coming to terms with new changes in the socio-political milieu of the nation fraught with displacement, destruction, and war crimes. The one stable entity in the life of Amir's family down the generations is the kite in which Hassan's memory is magnificently secured by the sanctity and victory of the kite's reiteration for Amir "for you a thousand times over" (Ch. 1).

The Persistence of the Religious Past

With the military invasion of Soviet Russia, the Afghan past is revived through the birth of the insurgent movement of Taliban and the ISIS which implemented the strict, conservative Islamic traditions of the Sharia in response to the non-Muslim external invasion from outside. There is also a marked difference between the Hazaras and the Pashtuns and the novel highlights the plight of Hazara Muslims who are not pure-blood Pashtuns and supposed to have descended from the Mongols. The characterization of Sanauber as a bad, dishonourable Muslim who was a Shi'a and a Hazara embodies the homogenizing ideology of the Sunni and Wahabi community and restricts inter-community mobilisation among the Shi'a and Sunni Muslims. Ali is constantly harassed and bullied by other children, "Hey, Bablu, who did you eat today? They barked to a chorus of laughter. Who did you eat, you flat-nosed Bablu?" (Ch. 2). The documentation of the history of the Hazaras provided by the Iranian historian Khorami in Hosseini's narrative makes the novel not only important from the historical point of view but also bears testimony to the historical process of marginalizing the minority, and the oppressed community of the Hazara as the Pashtuns "quelled them with unspeakable violence". The nurse, who fed Amir and Hassan, was also a blue-eyed Hazara woman who came from the land of the Bamiyan, the city of the giant Buddha statues. The Bamiyan Buddha as the site of historical importance which was destroyed by the Taliban Commander Mullah Mohammed Omar in March 2001 signals the unreasonable nature of violence and hate once war and insurgency become the norm. Amir's mother, who was one of Kabul's most respected and highly educated women, also becomes an important feminist figure in the narrative, whose feminist subjectivity provide subsequent context and contrast to the latter part of the narrative where the Taliban is responsible for the suppression of feminist liberation.

The strategic portrayal of Amir and Hassan's friendship as the backdrop for the loss of humanitarian principles in favour of radical elimination and extermination of civilians who are non-Sunnis as well as non-conformists helped in the justification of the militancy and *jihad* extremism. The cultivation of terror as a normalizing phenomenon for the administration of the political ideology of Islam quite reversely portrayed Islam of being anxious about its own existence since the logic of violence is foregrounded on the state of being either powerful or powerless. There is no denying of the fact that Islam by harbouring extremism has given birth to colossal shelters of *jihad* and savagery which can pre-empt the world of humanity on a demonic scale.

The Faultlines of Militarization, the Blame-Loop and the Indoctrination of Perennial Torture

The end of Baba Jan and Rahim Khan's Afghanistan and the ushering of a new era of existence is recorded by Amir when he says: "none of us had any notion that a way of life has ended. Our way of life. If not quite yet, then at least it was the beginning of the end. The end, the official end, would come first in April 1978 with the communist coup d'état, and then in December 1979, when Russian tanks would roll into the very same streets where Hassan and I played, bringing death of Afghanistan I knew and marking the start of a still ongoing era of bloodletting.... They weren't shooting ducks after all. As it turned out, they hadn't shot much of anything that night of July 17, 1973. Kabul awoke the next morning to find that the monarchy was a thing of the past. The king Zahir Shah was away in Italy. In his absence, his cousin Daoud Khan had ended the king's forty-year reign with a bloodless coup" (Ch. 5). The fear induced by the change in the political climate of the nation becomes the pretext on which the narrative contextualizes the interplay of the shifting nature of blame, a strategy that moves the onus of blame and the violence it produces to multiple locations and sources thereby blurring the lines of accountability. The *jihad* generates the popular mass sentiment and equips them with the only existing pedagogy of violence within the corpus of religion. The rhetoric of justified (holy) *jihad* or the liberalism of the military extravaganza of the West both targeted towards the expansion of the foundation and territorial acquisition are diversified, cross-sectional, and collateral forces of violence, hitting each other with equal intensity and power. The de-institutionalization of democracy as the culvert for the administration of epistemological and mechanized barbarism characterizes the pervasive nature of unobstructed violence.

"History isn't easy to overcome. Neither is religion" (Ch. 4). *The Kite Runner* critiques both, their embodiment represented by Soviet forces and the onslaught of the Talibs, the Al-Qaeda and the ISIS whose strategy to subject Afghanistan and Middle Eastern countries to an endless era of torture and political crimes raised questions of the futility of war, the nature of freedom, and captivity. The fallacy lies in the acceptance of religious indoctrination as a *jihadi* expression for liberation. The conception of insurgency to create separate hermeneutics of power which is premised on violence gets synonymously intertwined with the expression of torture and terror as both interpellate and co-habit each other. In the book *The Management of Savagery: The Most Critical Stage through which the Islamic Nation will Pass* by the Islamic political theorist Abu Bakr Naji, the justification for the persistence of terror induced by the administration of savagery through the political representation of the insurgents and militants is the necessary threshold for the creation of a universal Islamic regime. Historically, the cultural reductionism of the Third World into such categorization as the Arab world and the Ummah is resisted by Taliban, ISIS, and the extremist bodies. Their objective to create a universalizing archetype of authority and an archive of power originating from Islam provides the continuing inertia for their fundamentalist belief in religious extremism. *The Kite Runner* continues to haunt the horrors of inhumanity that characterizes contemporary society today. The necessity to restore to civilization, the doctrine of democracy and social equality that can minimize the tyranny of religion and maximize the secular agenda of pluralism is an important step for the eradication of repressive policies of politically organized systems of religion and nation-states in power.

REFERENCES

Devji, Faisal. "The Political Inheritance of ISIS." qatar.georgetown.edu. Georgetown University Qatar, 16 May 2016. Web. 26 Apr. 2019. <https://www.qatar.georgetown.edu/node/41201>

Hosseini, Khaled. *The Kite Runner*. New York: Riverhead Books, 2013. Print.

Naji, Abu Bakr. *The Management of Savagery: The Most Critical Stage through which the Umma will Pass*. Harvard: John M. Olin Institute for Strategic Studies, 2004. Print.

Chapter 28

Bacha Posh Tradition and Contradictions of Patriarchy in Nadia Hashimi's *The Pearl that Broke its Shell*

Mahamadul Hassan Dhabak

> I was a Little Girl and then I wasn't.
> I was a bacha posh and then I wasn't.
> I was a daughter and then I wasn't.
> I was a mother and then I wasn't.
> (*The Pearl that Broke its Shell*, Ch. 57).

"Since the dawn of humankind and throughout history, Afghanistan faced centuries of turmoil and strife. Only in recent years has the country been able to rebuild from the destructive and seemingly constant warfare that has plagued this land" (Runion, 1). In Afghanistan's history, the Taliban Regime is one of the notorious regimes which pushed the country backward. The Taliban enforced strictly the Sharia Law and revised the gendered structure of the country. The Taliban Regime (1992-2001) was "notorious in their treatment and policies toward women. As a result, women lost all sorts of freedom, including the ability to work and receive an education after the age of eight" (123). Modern Afghanistan was formed where new hopes and sound democracy were visible. By the democratic process, in October 2004 Afghanistan became the Islamic Republic.

Nadia Hashimi is a diasporic female voice exploring the issues of Afghanistan. In *The Pearl that Broke its Shell*, Nadia Hashimi demonstrates Rahima and Shekiba stories, two parallel stories of Bacha Posh (a girl dressed as a boy) in different times and location in Afghanistan. The novel consists of sixty-nine chapters. Out of sixty-nine chapters, thirty-eight chapters named 'Rahima' which give a detailed picture of Rahima and thirty-one chapters named 'Shekiba' represent the resistance of Shekiba. This paper unveils the bacha posh tradition, an ancient tradition and how it functions within the extremely patriarchal society. It also explores the gendered structure in Afghanistan and how Nadia Hashimi demonstrates the bacha posh tradition, gender performance and emotional turmoil during and after the gender transformation. This article examines the contradictions within patriarchy and how different type of patriarchies function in Afghan society.

The Tradition

The term "Bacha Posh" derived from the Dari language, a local language of Afghanistan means a "girl dressed like a boy". This is a hidden phenomenon practising for long ago. Nadia Hashimi describes "one Afghan solution for families with no heirs, although admittedly temporary, is to allow parents to convert a preadolescent daughter into a bacha posh by cutting her hair and dressing her in boy's clothing. She is assigned a boy's name" (Hashimi, n.pag). Nordberg argues 'Bacha Posh' is a very old cultural tradition of Afghanistan. It has a long history and has been practicing since the pre-Islamic era. So, it was 'before Islam had come to Afghanistan' and perhaps it is more than 1,400 years old tradition (114). Though the tradition has been practising since pre-Islamic era, yet the Islamic patriarchy helped to fuel up differently. "The practice of bacha posh in Afghanistan can be found across provinces, tribes, and socio-economic class. It is said that the tradition has been found in the country for centuries" (Sawitri, 14).

The religious fanaticism in the extremely patriarchal society of Afghanistan imposes restrictions on women and encourages gender segregation. The societal power structures depend on the gender separation where men always enjoy power and social privilege; and "women are 'second-class citizens' always beholden to and ruled by men" (Nordberg, 97). The Taliban regime imposed strict dress codes for women from early childhood stage and women must clearly signal her gender through their dress. Hashimi depicted "women looked differently now [in the Taliban regime] than they had a few years ago. Some wore long blue burqas and other long skirts and modest headscarves" (5). Nordberg aptly says: "In this society where being a girl means living as chattel and where families without boys are shamed, the bacha posh tradition arose" (5). Families without sons adopt this tradition of bacha posh and therefore, "every bacha posh has been the result of the parents' desire to have a son in the family" (13).

In *The Pearl that Broke its Shell*, Nadia Hashimi represented the bacha posh tradition interweaving the stories of Rahima and Shekiba. Rahima's story is depicted in the context of a specific historical trajectory of Afghanistan which witnessed several civil wars but the Taliban regime affects the civil life most; children are "pulled out of school, windows were blackened and music was banned" (27) and "with drug-addicted father and no brothers, Rahima and her sisters rarely leave the house" because of the societal gender segregation (Lisa, litandlife.blogspot.com, emphasis added). Therefore, the ancient tradition of bacha posh demands young Rahima to dress like a boy and then she can be treated as a son until her puberty. Being Rahim(a), she performed the masculine gender role and thereby, she challenged the conventional gender identity. Rahim is not alone who adopted "daughter-son" identity and before that, Rahima's great-great-grandmother Shekiba went through the same process along ago to save herself and thus, she built a new life. Shekiba's change helped her overcome her helplessness and neediness of life in a ruler village and she reached to the luxuriousness of a king's palace in Kabul.

Daughter-Son

Nadia Hashimi plays a very crucial role to demonstrate the gendered structure and the condition of women in Afghanistan. The narrator of the novel is Rahima, a nine-year-old girl describes how her elder sister Shahla became victim of eve-teasing. Women are treated as a commodity, therefore, any boy can claim "this is my girl" and "there is only room for one shadow here" (2). The girls are merely helpless, even the consequences force them not to protest against any type of sexual harassment. Nordberg examines the burden on women imposed by patriarchy, thus:

> The responsibility for men's behaviour, indeed for civilization itself, rests entirely with women here, and in how they dress they dress and behave. Men's animalistic impulses are presumed to be overwhelming and uncontrollable. And as men are brutal, brainless savages, women must hide their bodies to avoid being assaulted. (Nordberg, 101)

Rahima, the narrator has no brother and her father's physical condition has turned worse, therefore, the family needs a son who can perform the works of 'man'. Her khala (sister of the mother) Shaima convinced Rahima, as:

> It's simple and it's done all the time, Rahima-jan. Just think how happy that would make him! And you could do so many things that your sisters wouldn't able to do. (23)

The girl is encouraged to change her gender identity for her family. This is not a spontaneous act rather the gender manipulation is done out of the consequences of compulsion. Shamina's description of the positive aspects of the bacha posh convinced Rahima through the following argument:

> We could change your clothes and we'll give you a new name. You'll be able to run to the store any time we need anything. You could go to school without worrying about the boys bothering you. You could play games. How does that sound? (23)

Her family constructs the specific gender that works for it. It promotes the transformation from daughter to son (Rahima to Rahim) and encourages to work for the family. When the daughter-son reaches the age of puberty, the family again forces them to switch their 'gender' identity. Thereby, by this process of construction and reconstruction, the patriarchy within the family maintains its gendered balance.

When Rahim has become thirteen years old, the family suddenly became conscious about 'gender' and marriage. Rahim again is forced to change 'his' gender and the way of life. Rahim is in marriageable age and the patriarchy needs 'its' labour and reproduction as 'woman', so she was given a 'chador' to hide her boyish hair and instructed as:

> You are Rahima. You are a girl and you need to remember to carry yourself like one. Watch how you walk and how to sit. Don't look people, men, in the eye and keep your voice low. (138)

Generally, patriarchy subtly operates gender construction so that people hardly care about it. But in this specific bacha posh tradition, patriarchy roughly reconstructs the gender and it is more visible, more intentional. Patriarchy seldom cares for the consent of women and women are used as objects to draw structural gender pattern of the society. Therefore, the subjugations of bacha posh are seen at multiple levels.

On the other hand, Shekiba's burned face and other consequences forced her to work alone. After the death of her father, her uncles snatched all lands and enslaved her. When she was eleven, her uncle had offered her as a gift to General-sahib and said to him: "I hope you will accept my brother's gift to the amir-sahib. It is a small token" (145). In the king's palace, her life had been changed and she was appointed as a guard for King Habibullah's women. Shekiba's thick hair was cut and ordered to bathe and "given a set of clothing identical to what Ghafoor (a bacha posh) wore" (155). She was given the name "shekib", a man's name. She was not alone, "all of the guards in this house were actually women dressed in men's clothing" (155). All guards were forced to perform their duties because either they were bought or brought here as gifts.

Shekiba and Rahima both experienced the same patriarchal treatment. Like Rahima, Shekiba was also forced to alter her gender identity from the bacha posh to a woman. It led her towards the act of punishment and the king compelled her to marry with Agha Baraan without her consent. This imposition over Shekiba is being articulated as:

> She felt terribly out of place. And she was now a woman again. Her dress felt cumbersome and heavy. She had just

> about forgotten how to keep her headscarf in place [...]. She could not tolerate their jiggling, even though the corset chafed her raw wound. (361)

The patriarchy imposes gender segregation in a certain way where people take gender for granted. It constantly recognizes "a person as a man or woman, girl or boy. These gender arrangements are so familiar that they can seem part of the order of nature" (Connell, 5). Judith Butler advocates 'sex', 'gender', and 'desire' are the constructions of society and therefore, the notion of normalization or naturalization is being challenged. The gender is performed and the bacha posh performs their specific assigned gender. This assigned gender is reverse order of 'nature', yet it seems a normal tradition. So, "being a man or a woman, then, is not a pre-determined state. It is becoming, a condition actively under construction" (Connell, 5). The bacha posh are forced to embrace the specific identities from time to time. This is a type of gender violence because "the home and the family are particularly problematic sites for women as they may operate as a source of violence rather than protection from it" (Edward, 49). The pioneering French feminist Simone de Beauvoir states, "one is not born, but rather becomes, a woman". It can be seen in a slightly different perspective that is one is not born but rather becomes patriarchal. The bacha poshes are assigned the specific gender roles from time to time so that they can become a part of patriarchy and work for patriarchy.

Contradictions of Patriarchy

"The concept of patriarchy is widely used by feminists as both a description of the social position of women and as a theoretical explanation for the social position of women" (Best, 143). Heteronormativity is the backbone of patriarchy which exclusively encourages the heterosexuality, rigid binary gender division and defines the privilege of men. To understand the patriarchal pattern of Afghanistan, we need to fathom the social and the cultural structures of Afghanistan. Afghanistan has a much deeper and more remarkable cultural legacy as a seat of empires, a migratory crossroads, and a trading centre for more than 4000 years. This rich legacy existed before—and will extend beyond—any invasion. Patriarchy has full control on society in Afghanistan which presents constant and various threats to Afghan women, including domestic violence, honour killings and other malicious customs and practices. Customs including baad (giving away women to settle family or tribal feuds) and badal (families exchanging women and girls), as well as religiously imposed dress codes, sit alongside shortcomings "in access to education, financial independence, and political participation in shaping the heavily constrained lives of Afghan women" (Gereš, 21). Islamic cultural practice shapes the patriarchy in Afghanistan. Nordberg demonstrates in Afghanistan, the reference to Islam can be made by anyone, at any time, for any purpose. No matter the issue, a person may cite an appropriate vague hadith, said to represent the thousands of (often contradictory) opinions and life events of the prophet Muhammad, or a recollection of what a mullah has once said (Nordberg, 107). Religious norms and sometimes its misinterpretations shape the consciousness of the people which helps to the process of socialization of good Muslims. This concept of 'good Muslim' is exclusively a product of patriarchy which promotes only rigid binary gender divisions.

Muslim patriarchy does not allow the cross-dressing. A man is not permitted to wear a woman's dress and women are forced to wear dress according to religious instruction, sometimes even more. Therefore, Muslim patriarchy does not permit the bacha posh tradition. However, patriarchy is not a homogeneous concept or ideology, rather than there are multiple patriarchies exist in a society. Sometimes one type of patriarchy may be contradictory to another type of patriarchy. Therefore, there is no fixed notion of how patriarchy functions in a social system.

The bacha posh tradition is contradictory by nature with Islamic religious tradition but there is another patriarchy exists which promotes the bacha posh tradition since ancient time. This patriarchy of Afghanistan made spaces for the invisible tradition. It is acknowledged that "nobody knows the exact number of bacha posh in Afghanistan as becoming one is not something to be said aloud, although it is not entirely a secret. Because of social pressure and desperation, there are cases in which female infant is announced as son right after birth" (Sawitri, 14). Patriarchy devalues the women and therefore the birth of a girl child is not considered as blissful. On the other hand, patriarchy leaves space for the bacha posh tradition and gives them certain types of freedom. "Being a bacha posh might be empowering, but it is temporary. The girl and her parents know that one day she will have to go back and accept her nature" (Sawitri, 15).

The patriarchy normalized the gender segregation and made the binary gender division as only 'right' division. The patriarchy links 'sex' with 'gender', therefore, men and women are forced to perform their respective masculine and feminine gender functions. In the context of Afghanistan, gender performance defines a person whether he/she is a 'good' Muslim or a 'bad' Muslim.

On the other hand, when a family has no son, patriarchy encourages the bacha posh custom, where a girl dressed like a boy performs the masculine gender identity. Here, interestingly patriarchy excludes the link between sex and gender. If a girl works like a boy wearing specific girls' (women's) dress then it is a sin, a taboo. But if a girl wears boys' dress and performs masculine gender identity then it is a custom, a tradition. Therefore, gender never links with sex rather it has a very close connection with attire in the specific context of Afghanistan. People understand a bacha posh as a girl, but they pretend publicly about the bacha posh custom. In *The Pearl that Broke its Shell*, Rahima does not look like a boy but her mother said quietly, "this is how things are done. People will understand you" (36). Rahima narrates how people accept it:

> Everyone else—teachers, aunts, uncles, neighbours—they would accept my mother's new son without reservation. I wasn't the first bacha posh. This is a common tradition for families in want of a son. (36)

However, there are lots of internal contradictions of Muslim patriarchy in Afghanistan. The gender arrangement in the bacha posh tradition challenges the traditional patriarchal arrangements. Any type of gender segregation is artificial, manufactured, and arbitrary in nature.

The underground girls of Afghanistan resist in a different way. These bacha poshes are often termed as 'alakaana' in Pashto. This term indicates that these children are not unusual (Nordberg, 67). They are often termed as 'third gender' that is very problematic. The patriarchy shapes their specific roles for a certain time. They are not challenging the rigid binary gender segregation. This is not a spontaneous act to challenge the heteronormative structure of the society rather these children perform the bacha posh identity out of compulsion. Here, the patriarchy reverses the gender pattern for a small section to get their labours when it is essential to sustain. Therefore, the bach posh is used as a tool of patriarchy to create gender illusion and by default, these children become the victim of violence. Violence is one of the strongest weapons of patriarchy and by this it subjugates others and maintains the heteronormative pattern. In *The Pearl that Broke its Shell*, Nadia Hashimi examines the contradictions within patriarchy and how different type of patriarchies function in Afghan society.

REFERENCES

Connell, Raewyn. *Gender: In World Perspective*. Cambridge: Polity Press, 2009. Print.

Edwards, Tim. *Cultures of Masculinity*. New York: Routledge, 2006. Print.

Hashimi, Nadia. *The Pearl that Broke its Shell*. New York: William Morrow, 2014. Print.

Hashimi, Nadia. "Afghanistan's Female Sons: The Tradition of Bacha Posh". foreignaffairs.com. *Foreign Affairs*, 13 Apr. 2015. Web. 25 May 2019. <https://www.foreignaffairs.com/articles/afghanistan/2015-04-13/afghanistans-female-sons>

Gereš, N. et al. *Reflections on Gender, Patriarchy, and Peace: Results from the International Men and Gender Equality Survey (IMAGES) in Afghanistan*. Washington, DC: Promundo-US, UN Women, and Global Affairs Canada, 2018. Print.

Lisa. Review of Nadia Hashimi's *The Pearl that Broke its Shell*. http://litandlife.blogspot.com. *Lit and Life: For the Love of Books, Family and Life*, 8 May 2014. Web. 17 Mar. 2019. <http://litandlife.blogspot.com/2014/05/the-pearl-that-broke-its-shell-by-nadia.html?cv=1>

Nordberg, Jenny. *The Underground Girls of Kabul*. New York: Broadway Books, 2015. Print.

Reunion, Meredith L. *The History of Afghanistan*. London: Greenwood Press, 2007. Print.

Sawitri, Made Yaya. "Cultural and International Dissonance on Girls Empowerment: The Case of Afghanistan's Female Son." *AEGIS*, 2.1 (September 2017): 11-25. Print.

Chapter 29

The Application of Folklore Principle to Study Select Folktales of India and Bhutan

S. Chitra and Dechhen Dolma

Humans are not free agents but are subject to ideological control that the society creates for them and to have an individual identity, one must adhere to a set of rules or principles culturally practised from generation to generation. India, a pluralistic country is an amalgamation of different cultures and religious faith, which freely allows people to celebrate one's own tradition and culture. However, A.K. Ramanujan, the folklorist asserts "in cultures like India's, the context-sensitive kind of rule is the preferred formulation" (47). This statement affirms the close adherence of context-sensitive culture in the Indian ideology since the time of Manu, the Hindu law-giver. Thus, this principle formulates the identity of India. In the essay, *Is There an Indian Way of Thinking?*, A.K. Ramanujan deliberates the prevalence of two kinds of rules in cultural formulation, namely, the context-sensitive and the context-free. As a linguist himself, he has borrowed these terms from grammar to address the ways Indians and non-Indians, particularly the Westerners, lead their lives. He has foregrounded that, "sentences must have subjects and predicates in a certain relation [...]" (Ramanujan, 47). This organized linguistic idea shows the application of a prescribed rule to complete a grammatically correct sentence. In a similar context, he highlights the fixity in Indian culture where each object/thing is interconnected to one another. It is an ordered structure that holds Indian culture systematically.

In contrast to context-sensitive culture, context-free underscores the free will of an individual in carrying out any kind of activities in lives (Ramanujan, 47). The Westerners advocate a culture free from any kind of structure, with no fixed order to follow. Louden emphasizes Kant's philosophy on the human as, "chameleons-creatures with a self-transforming nature who, in virtue of their capacity of free choice, can fashion themselves in whatever shapes they prefer" (xxii). It shows the human capability in adopting and adapting to the ways of life as per one's own choice, with no boundaries to bar them. Louden also presents the view of Kant and Sartre on one's own capacity for free choice stating, "Man is nothing but that which makes of himself" (xix). Such thoughts of the philosophers highlight the freedom human need to have in their lives. Nonetheless, Ramanujan sets a debate around these two contradicting principles through certain traits such as the container-contained relation, the inability to distinguish self from non-self, the philosophy of Karma and the premise of universalism and particularism which govern the Indian thinking pattern.

Unlike the above theoretical principle, which largely governs the Indian way of thinking, Bhutan does not document any such specification in its cultural context. There are no such theories to label people's action as context sensitive. Neither, does it allow the will to self-fashion culture as one understands? Yet, it is true that culture is the binding force for the Bhutanese. Culture in the Bhutanese context as Evans points out is in the values which the country and its men follow. He states, "the desired cultural values reflect what participants believe to be important for the well-being of their nation" (Evans, 6). These values, as Evans mentions, are present in various fields such as in "education, freedom of speech, economic growth, social justice, environmental protection, continuous improvement, contentment and compassion in religion" (8). These values, however, are broader with no fixed or structured rules, unlike the Indian cultural context. Hence, this study attempts to analyse the folktales of India and Bhutan using the theoretical principles of Ramanujan to test their presence or absence in the select tales.

Analysis of the Tales: A Flowering Tree, Bum Dolay Penzom and Bo Serba Tung Tung using the Folk Essay on A Flowering Tree: A Woman's Tale

The woman-centred tale, *A Flowering Tree,* is about a young woman with a special gift. During her younger years, she takes the form of a flowering tree to help her poor mother. Later, knowing the secret of her gift, a prince marries her. Every night, she transforms herself into the flowering tree to fulfil her husband's desire. He yearns to sleep on the flowers produced from her body. Also, she obliges to fulfil her young sister-in-law's demand who wanted to show the flowers to her friends. The latter transformation makes her a 'thing': neither a tree nor a woman. This new form is due to her sister-in-law's negligence in carrying out the instruction to turn her into a human. Thus, the young woman lands up becoming a 'thing' for others. However, her husband who matures with time helps her come back into her human form after finding her in his eldest sister's house. Like most of the folktale endings, Ramanujan too attempts to take the readers into a happy ending.

The tale, "Bum Dolay Penzom and Bo Serba Tung Tung", one of the thirty-eight tales in Kunzang Choden's *Folktales of Bhutan* (1994) is a love story from Bhutan which portrays the heroic nature of the female protagonist. In this tale, Bum Dolay Penzom a rich girl falls in love with Bo Serba Tung Tung, a poor boy. Although the girl's family forbids them, the lovers meet secretly which ultimately leads to the death of the boy. The girl too burns herself in the pyre of her lover only to return to the human world as strangers. They take many rebirths in different forms, but they meet the same end every time. It is only at the end that the girl recognises the poor potter boy as her lover during their later lives as humans. Finally, they live with each other happily.

Classification of Tales

The Bhutanese tales are classified based on characters and themes as "characters and themes are two main criteria for this classification" (Penjore, 18). Characters in the Bhutanese tales are divided as humans, animals, spirits (srin mo and srin po), gods (lha) and inanimate objects. Each character is equated with another irrespective of size, class, caste, or any other distinguishing feature. The themes include morality, heroism, battle between good and evil embedded with Buddhist values. This classification advocates the way Bhutanese tale function in society. On the contrary, Ramanujan classifies Indian tales in the following categories, as male-centred and woman-centred tales. Despite variation in the categorization, the crux of the tales remains same.

To be precise, a woman-centred tale has a woman as the storyteller, with a woman leading the tale overshadowing the other characters. Ramanujan writes, "...in such tales, women predominate, and men are wimps, ruled by mothers, mistresses, or by wives" (xxvii). He clearly talks of a woman dominating and occupying the social space in these kinds of tales. Upon analysis, the study has identified the two-dimensional side of a woman such as a woman power and the role of a woman as a storyteller. Indian tales have characters like the princess in *Prince Sabar*, the poor girl in *A Flowering Tree*, and the king's daughter in *Dead Prince and Talking Doll* who resemble each other in their actions. All these women portray a strong sense of individuality to help their respective spouse or other characters in the tales. To cite an example, the girl in *Dead Prince and Talking Doll* nurses, the 'dead' prince for twelve long years in an isolated place. She bears the hardship all alone, but when he regains his senses, she loses her marital status to another girl. However, at the end she reclaims it. Through this tale, it is clear that the classification known as woman-centred depicts strong women characters who play the role of protagonist as well as antagonist. Similarly, the central women characters, in the other tales also act strong and brave to help their respective spouses. Women power is thus emphasized in a woman-centred tale.

The Bhutanese tales do not mention any such categories, but there are strong women characters such as *Bum* Dolay Penzom, *Bum* Sing Yangdonma, *Ashi* Dunglidolma, the Princess and Mekhay Doma to name a few in Choden's collection of folktales. All these female characters play similar roles in their own context; they overcome the problems that they encounter to lead a happy life. For instance, *Bum* Sing Yangdonma agrees to marry a beast for the crime committed by her father for stealing a fruit from his orchard. She uses her wits and runs away from his clutches fooling the beast's daughter. So, in a way, the other woman helps her overcome her problem. Resembling her actions are the other female characters in the Bhutanese context. Vladimir Popp underscores, "the vital components of a folktale are not its characters but certain actions of the characters, which are found to be constant in folktales of different places" (26-27). It shows that folktales need not replicate each other in the same form and content, but a certain feature will be consistently maintained. Action as an element of folktale accentuates the consistency of the above tales though they are categorized differently.

Discussion on Traits: Container-contained Relation

In order to find whether the Bhutanese folktales show the presence of context-sensitive principle in them, the following traits such as the container-contained relation, the philosophy of *karma*, the inability to distinguish self from non-self and the premise of universality and particularity will be analysed. The first trait known as container-contained relation shows the interdependent relation of things on earth based on the idea, one thing cannot exist without the other. The analysis of folktale scrutinizes this feature of 'interdependence' by means of nature-human and the parent-child relationship.

Nature-Human

The Indian folktale makes a metaphoric connection between women and nature. Especially, in terms of biological factors, a woman's life-stages are compared to a tree, along with the fact that both women and nature are susceptible to the mistreatment of society. Ramanujan, in his folklore essay on *A Flowering Tree: A Woman's Tale*, highlights:

> In Sanskrit, a menstruating woman is called a puspavati, a woman in flower, and in Tamil, puttal (flowering) means menstruation. Menstruation itself is a form and a metaphor for a woman's special creativity. Thus a woman's biological and other kinds of creativity are symbolized by flowering. (221)

Such a comparison of a woman's biological cycle to a flowering tree indicates special creativity that only a woman has in a society which is absent in men. Further, in the folk essay, Ramanujan mentions, "A tree that has come to flower or fruit will not be cut down; it is treated like a mother, a woman who has given birth" (Ramanujan, 221). Similar to the respectful manner in which motherhood and mothers are treated or supposed to be treated in a society, a flowering tree garners love and care from people around it. In both cases, the treatment is the same. Like a mother who assures her family's happiness, the tree in the folktale spreads happiness in the lives of people around it. These interpretations foreground the significance of women in creating a universe for her family; metaphorically nature acts as the provider for human needs and desires.

In a container-contained relation, one thing cannot be separated from another, instead one must depend on the other for existence. Ramanujan affirms the above statement saying, "Such container-contained relations are seen in many kinds of concepts and images: not only in culture-nature but God-world, king-kingdom, devotee-god, mother-child" (11). In such relation, there should be a balance between binary factors. For instance, men and nature should have a proper balance for co-existence, one should not try to dominate the other. In this folktale, the protagonist seeks the help of nature to help herself and her family. It is the flowers that are produced from the girl's body while she takes the tree form that helps her save some money. Understanding that she needs the tree to survive, she makes sure to protect every part of the tree. While directing her sister, she says: "then you pluck as many flowers as you want but do it without breaking a twig or tearing a leaf" (132); while instructing her husband, she tells him, "pour the water from this pitcher over me, and I'll become a tree. Wherever there is a broken branch, set it right. Wherever a leaf is torn, bind it together" (142). Through such phrases, Ramanujan highlights the significance of every small part of nature which needs proper care from the man to make it a whole. At the same time, it also intensifies the necessity of nature for man to survive. Thus, the tale propagates a biocentric view of our existence in the universe.

In a context-sensitive culture, Indian aesthetics advocate the people to live in union and harmony with nature, both externally and internally. If in case, such mandates are not followed, people must bear the ill consequences of their actions and thoughts, seem to be an inherent norm. In the folktale, the young sister-in-law of the protagonist shows irrational behaviour which ultimately leads to her death. As a daughter of the king, the sister-in-law uses her birthright and persuades the prince's wife (the protagonist) to change into a flowering tree, despite the protagonist's plea. The girl agrees after instructing her sister-in-law on the ways to change her back into human form. However, the negligence of the sister-in-law complicates the plot of the story. As a result, the protagonist remains as a 'tree', and her husband wanders in search of her. Ramanujan writes "what's happened to him? Has he become a wandering ascetic? Impossible [...]" (141). His parents, the king and the queen also worry about their son who acts differently; similarly, the eldest sister also tries her best to help her brother come back to his normal life. Had the youngest daughter been careful about taking care of the flowering tree, all these incidents would not have happened. The folktale mentions, "[...] after all, every wrong has its punishment" (422). The sister-in-law's undesirable thoughts of trying to claim the tree (nature) for herself leads to the sufferings of all her family members and her own end. While it is true that humans destroy nature, the fundamental truth is that human as a micro-cosmic organism lives with the macro-cosmic organism (nature). Thus, there should be a balance between nature and man is reinforced through this folktale.

On the other hand, the Bhutanese tale does not explicitly show the container-contained relation as a shared trait between nature and human. Nevertheless, this relationship is inherent traditional value. Dorji asserts that "local legends and myths help our people define their relationship with their natural environment on which they depend for their livelihood" (103). It implies that man-nature relationship in the Bhutanese tale is acknowledged through the myths and legends of the nation. Therefore, absenteeism of this relationship in the tale does not mean the absence of nature-human relationship. It is wise to state that the human is always a microcosm of nature. Therefore, analysis of tales affirms that the container-contained characteristic is very much prevalent in both the societies in the form of nature-human relation.

Parent-child Relationship

The container-contained relation is further extended to the human relationship in the folktale. From the beginning of the folktale, readers are presented with a family where the poor mother does some menial jobs to bring up her daughters. In order to ease her mother's labour and to supplement her mother's income, the younger daughter turns into a flowering tree. Here, Ramanujan foregrounds the way the relationship works in the context-sensitive culture of India. The daughter in the folktale takes the risk of turning into a flowering tree as her mother was doing all kinds of menial jobs to raise her daughters. For instance, the protagonist says to her sister, "[...] it's hard on mother to work all day for our sakes. I want to help her. I will turn myself into a flowering tree. You can take the flowers and sell them for good money" (Ramanujan, 132).

On the other hand, a mother is expected to provide everything for her children till they attain the age of maturity, and thus she works hard to fulfil her responsibility. Each character fulfils their respective roles as per social demands. Hence, the way mother-daughter relation is portrayed in the folktale underpins the fact that one thing would be incomplete without the other. As such, readers can see the way one depends on another in a context-sensitive society for survival. Children are the microcosm of a family, and their identity is established through their parents, the macrocosm. However, in the Bhutanese folktale, this relation is absent. The true feeling of Bum Dolay Penzom for her lover Bo Serba Tung Tung is disregarded by her rich parents and her brother even murders her lover so as to terminate their love affair. This can be reaffirmed through Choden's narration of the tale: "[...] two banana saplings grew on the spot of the cremation site, Bum Dolay Penzom's brother saw that and realizing that his sister and his lover were reborn in the form of these saplings, he promptly uprooted them" (60). The prompt action of the brother highlights his undue concern over his family reputation than his sister's happiness. Even after his sister's death, the brother fails to show any sign of remorse. Instead, readers see his thoughts centring around 'self' and not on other's happiness fulfilling the principle of context-free.

Nevertheless, the folktale takes its readers a step further and shows that the container-contained relation is present between the lovers when they try to establish a new identity in the society. In the folktale, the girl rebels against her parent's order and goes secretly to nurse her ill lover: "[...] she went secretly to nurse him every day" (Choden, 59). It indicates the need for a separate identity by Bum Dolay Penzom, apart from the identity given by her parents. The death of the lovers also shows that this trait is not only prevalent in living souls but will continue even after death until it finds the other part. For instance, Bo Serba Tung Tung's death impacts the girl so much that she forgets to distinguish between 'day and night'. It presents to its readers that the absence of one lead to a similar or worse condition of the other.

Moreover, the lover's rebirths in different forms such as a bull and a cow beside others also enhance the need for a container-contained relationship to attain completion. This is further exemplified when the girl jumps on the pyre of her lover to die alongside him. Choden writes, "[...] the blazing flames quickly engulfed her body and she too disappeared from this world" (60). The act heightens the possibility of the lovers trying to create the container-contained relation, through a different perspective. Even the ending of the story supports the fashioning of the container-contained relation when the two finally meet after many births in different forms.

As such, readers could perceive that even if the parental relationship is not maintained in this folktale, the container-contained relation is portrayed in Bhutanese culture through other means. Though the tale negates the presence of this relation through a parental view, it claims the possibility from the lover's point of view. This interpretation proves the prevalence of context-sensitivity in Bhutanese folktale.

Philosophy of Karma

The doctrine of *karma* is an equally important trait in the Indian and Bhutanese context. As a contentious philosophy, it is debatable through Eastern and Western perspectives. However, the study has attempted to analyse the presence or absence of this philosophy in folktales using Ramanujan's perspective of *karma*.

Ramanujan, in the folklore essay on *A Flowering Tree: A Woman's Tale,* states that "other kinds of women's tales counter various constructs and stereotypes (held both by men and women), like the passive female victim, conceptions of karma, or even chastity" (Ramanujan, 219), which assures the significant role of *karma* in the culture of context-sensitivity. Further, in the essay titled, *Is There an Indian Way of Thinking?* Ramanujan foregrounds, "karma implies the self's past determining the present, an iron chain of cause and consequence, an ethic of responsibility" (44). This statement foregrounds that the present lives of people are determined by the work and actions of their previous lives. The Bhutanese folktale evidently shows the presence of this philosophy in its context.

Unlike the westerner's dogmatic belief of *karma*, the eastern people believe that man and woman cannot escape from their karmic connection. Their existence as different people in the world cannot be rationalized. Bodhi (qtd. in Burley, 3) emphasizes about the doctrine of *karma* through the Buddhist scriptures, "by you [...] has the seed been sown; thus, you will experience the fruit" (3). It shows that a man must undergo the consequences of one's deeds of the past life which keeps on accumulating, whether positive or negative. For instance, in the folktale *Bum Dolay Penzom and Bo Serba Tung Tung,* the lovers die without getting to live together as they desired. Even after they die, they take rebirths in animal forms like cats, cattle, birds, and even as a banana plant, but they never meet. In fact, they are separated in all their rebirths. The idea of rebirth as male and female in all their different forms itself emphasizes the strong desire and longing to be together; their intense desire leads to more rebirths indicating the philosophical belief that karma is rooted in desires. Choden, has well incorporated the idea of *karma* in the folktale in the following words, "the lovers took on a series of rebirths and deaths. Their time together was always troubled and short. Their karma was still not cleansed enough, as we say in Bhutanese" (60). These sentences firmly assure the perception that until and unless a person comes clean from the desires of the past or the present, one cannot achieve the goal in life.

Burley also cites Edward's argument that belief in *karma* is "unbearably cruel even lacking in due humility" as the victim is blamed for any misfortune that happens in his/her life (qtd. in Burley, 16). Nonetheless, the same paper presents Lati Rinpoche's answer on suffering, "the individual victims must have done something very bad in earlier lives that led to their being treated in this way" (qtd. in Burley, 16). The two contrasting views of the West and the East respectively show the way people think of the doctrine *karma*. According to Western notion, to place the blame on one's *karma* is a blame game and escapism, while the East maintains the logical connection that it is the deed of the past which makes you suffer in this life. Akin to Ramanujan who expresses that every action has a reason, Lati Rinpoche also suggests that a person's karma can change if one adopts a pure attitude and practice with a pure heart (qtd. in Burley, 16). Thus, the Bhutanese folktale refutes the Western perception of *karma* as a mere theory. Instead, it presents the strong belief that the acts of present life do have relation to the next life of a person.

This doctrine, however, is absent in all the folktales that Ramanujan has collected and compiled. He writes about the philosophy of *karma* as "almost synonymous in some circles with whatever is Indian or Hindu" (44), yet, he also states, "[...] when I looked at hundreds of Kannada tales, I couldn't find a single that used karma as a motif or motive" (44). It maintains the absence of this philosophy in the Indian context. However, Ramanujan argues that *karma* in the Indian context is used in everyday language to scold oneself or as a synonym for self-pity. Tilak uses a Tibetan imagery of shadow to explain *karma* in the Indian context:

> A person walking along the road sees his/her accompanying shadow. A bird flying high also casts its shadow, but it

> cannot be seen. As it descends, however, the shadow begins to appear on the ground below looming over larger. Karma is the bird's shadow there, but not always apparent. (15)

This citation affirms *karma's* omnipresence in the lives of Indians like the shadow of the bird. In his essays, Ramanujan discusses *karma*, though it does not appear in the collection of folktales. As an argumentative philosophy, it is assumed that the dispute will be never-ending. Nevertheless, the trait of *karma* discussed with reference to the tales prove that the principle of context-sensitivity is strongly present in both the Indian and the Bhutanese folktales.

The Magic Bowls and The Phob that Provided Food using folk essay Some Folktales from India

In addition to many features, a folktale also encompasses supernatural elements (magic). Using such elements, the audience/reader comprehends the imagination and creative power of the storyteller who highlights the truth that cannot be revealed in direct words. Storytellers in the Indian and Bhutanese context reveal their imagination and creative power by the use of magical elements to add beauty to the tales without losing its cultural influence upon real-life events. The practice of class-conscious society has prevailed in India and Bhutan since its early days. Such practice deprives the weaker section in all fields of life. Therein, folktale acted as an agent through which the voices of the poor could be heard. To substantiate it: "folktales reveal man's attempts to escape from social repressions as well as from his geographical conditions and his own biological limitations" (Penjore, 26). It infers the functional ability of folktales to point out how society needs to function, free from any kind of oppression and repression. Ramanujan also says that folktales provide excellent 'corrective measures' to such stereotype. In fact, the inclusion of magical elements in tales helps people romanticize a society different from the oppressive reality.

In both the tales, the magical *phob* (a Bhutanese term for the bowl) is a common object. The *phob* stands equivalent to '*Atchyapathr*' in Tamil literature, which is attributed with the power to feed people endlessly (S. Chitra, 5th Himalayan International Seminar Paper, April 27, 2014). Besides sharing this similarity, tales highlight the presence of context-sensitivity that is analysed through the trait of universality-particularity and also the trait of self-non self.

A Brief Synopsis of Folktales

The Indian folktale has a poor couple; a lazy man and a nagging wife. The wife sends the husband away from home with only a bundle of stale rice instructing him not to return unless he earns something. The man reaches under a banyan tree where he decides to rest. The spirits that dwelt on the tree eat the stale rice and feels that they had tasted nectar and all the dishes of heaven. Pleased with the food, the spirits reward the man with four empty magic bowl, from which beautiful maidens appear bringing him and his wife with the finest dishes. However, a rich man in his village gets jealous and using a similar strategy he gets the magic bowl from the tree spirits. In place of beautiful maidens, from the rich man's bowl appear muscular men who punish the host and his guest at the end.

Similarly, in the Bhutanese folktale, a poor boy gets a *phob meaning a magic bowl* from a family of a sparrow in exchange for sparing the lives of six helpless chicks. He also gets a kid and then a stick from the sparrow later in the tale. The *mailiama*, the Bhutanese term for the matriarch of the rich household, was the poor boy's neighbour. Upon finding the poor boy's fortune, she succeeds in getting the *phob*, the kid and then the stick from him. Unlike, the first two magical objects the stick follows the boy's command, who had by then guessed the culprit and punishes the rich lady. The poor boy gets back all his objects and lives in happiness and prosperity.

Universality-Particularity

Ramanujan in his essay titled, *Is There an Indian Way of Thinking?* mentions about Immanuel Kant's proposal that law should be universal and all need to practise it to inculcate ethics in life (46). For Kant, everyone, disregard of class, caste, race, or gender, needs the same kind of treatment in all fields of life (universality), but at the same time, Ramanujan also emphasises Manu's perspective which differs from Kant's philosophy. The lawmaker strongly emphasises on following the law based on the distinction of class and caste as framed in the Indian context (particularity).

Through the treatment of people in the Indian context, the study intends to test the distinction between two principles; context-sensitivity and context-free. Ramanujan reiterates Manu's law, "each class (*jati*) of man has his own laws, his proper ethics, not to be universalised" (46). It highlights the law of the ancient Indian society which was based on the class and caste one belongs to. It suggests that there is no universal treatment of people in the Indian context and that they act according to the laws set by their lawmaker, Manu. The relevance of this culture had been disseminated through the folktale. As the poor man belonged to the low-class society, the perception of men about the class is highlighted through the way the villagers act and think in the tale. In the tale when the poor man invites all rich and poor to his house, "everyone was incredulous. Some laughed; others thought it a practical joke. There is a proverb: the guest of the poor come back home very soon [...] many of them have come fully fed as a precaution against a mean dinner" (Ramanujan, 360). Readers infer the inflexible notion people make of others based on the class one hails from. The people's perception of the poor man makes them laugh and come fully fed to the dinner from their respective houses. This does not happen while they go to the rich man's house. "Soon the people flocked to his dining halls, eager for unseen pleasure [...] many even fasted that day, intending to do full justice to his hospitality" (Ramanujan, 361). The paragraphs above establish the socially prejudiced notion of class and caste; the way villagers thought of the poor man's invitation differed from the rich man's invitation because of the ways they perceived them through their pre-conceived socio-cultural norms and practices.

However, this tale does not show the functionality of law in the Indian context as prescribed in *Manu Smriti*. Ramanujan writes, "to be moral, for Manu, is to particularise—to ask who did what, to whom and when" (46). In an Indian context, the law is fixed as per one's class and caste, rather than judging through the crime one has committed. In the folktale, the rich man is punished for his spirit of rivalry, but the tale does not show any distinction in punishment between the elite and the working class. So, the tale leaves its readers sceptical about the law. Nevertheless, Ramanujan foregrounds that the shift in the two principles is bound to happen due to the influence of modernity although the dictating principle remains the same.

In *The Phob that Provided Food*, readers do not find any distinction of caste. However, it does show the contradicting ideas between the high-class and the low-class people. Penjore explains, "[...] just as in the subaltern studies in South Asia, the study of selected Bhutanese folktales provides clues to social relations in rural societies—the relations of dominion and control, relations of power and authority [...]" (34). It helps readers understand the way society functioned in Bhutan in olden times, mainly based on power-structure. To validate, Sharma in his research asserts, "our folktales provide hints about our social structure [...] Bhutanese society, even in those times was divided into three classes," the royals, the rich, and the poor, "depending on privileges and economy" (98). Since the economy stabilises an authority over a weaker section, it leads to a division in class as presented in the folktale. For instance, the rich woman in the tale is the provider of food for the poor boy until he comes across the magical objects, however, she does not give it for free. She barters the food for the errands that he does for her. Had there been no such differentiation in class, the woman would have provided food freely as one human to another, which did not happen. Hence, it shows the hegemony of high-class people over the lower class.

Despite the tales agreeing on the class distinction in the society, the Bhutanese folktale does not show any distinction in following the laws of the country. Irrespective of class, it is presumed that the society progressed following one law for all people like that of what Kant proposes. A context-free society as Kant proposes, "acts as if the maxim of your action were to become through your will a Universal law of nature" (Ramanujan, 46). In this context, men irrespective of class, caste, gender, race, or any such things should be treated the same. Law should be one for everyone based on the degree of crime one commits, dissimilar to the specification done in the Indian context grounded in class and caste. The folktale showcases it through the punishment the rich lady receives in the end. A wrongdoer bears the ill-consequence for the action undertaken by him or her, regardless of one's class. There is no separate rule present in the tale. Had there been so, the rich lady by her social hierarchy would not have received the beatings from the magical stick. Thus, the tale undercuts the existence of class-specific rule and persuades readers to believe in the practice of 'one law for all'.

The above trait also supports the inclusion of context-sensitive culture in the Indian context, whereas the Bhutanese tale tries to balance between the context-sensitive and context-free culture. While the class-conscious system approves of Indian perspective, the egalitarian treatment of people through the law is justified in the Bhutanese context.

The Dichotomy between Self (Oneself) and Non-self (Other)

Dundes justifies the structuralist idea of binary to study the meanings of dichotomies such as 'self/other' and 'us/them'. He asserts that such studies affirm what one is in relation to and what one is not (qtd. in Bronner, 6). It alludes to placing one concept in the centre to understand the meaning of the other concept. However, Bronner argues by supplementing the post-structuralists view, "binary distinctions are necessarily motivated by a desire to dominate" (7). Here, the concepts do not have a position of its own. For instance, to understand about 'self,' the 'other' takes equal place to it. It is not positioned at the periphery or at the centre. Borrowing the idea of treating the binary factors as similar and not opposites, the folktale analyses the concept of self (oneself) and non-self (other) to test the presence of context-sensitivity.

The inability to distinguish self from non-self is one particular trait of context-sensitivity that Ramanujan portrays in the folktale. Ramanujan undercuts the structuralist view of binary opposition to understand one from the other. He underlines that there is no distinction between self and non-self in the Indian context, but they are the same. The underlying idea can be validated by means of the Vedanta philosophy (qtd. in Ims and Pedersen, 132) which states, "thou art that...Thou are one with universal being, and as such, every soul that exists in your soul and everybody that exists in your body". It explains the concept of 'Oneness' where there is no distinction between the 'I' and 'you' with an emphasis that everything around you is a part of you; it isn't different from self (oneself). This thought is presented in the folktale through the portrayal of the poor and the rich man. The poor man after getting the magic bowl, instead of hiding it from others for one's own purpose, decides to use it after offering public prayers to divinity and then for people through charity. Ramanujan describes, "[...] they decided that they should use their good fortune worshipfully, only after offering public prayers to the Almighty and charity to men" (360). These thoughts of sharing with the divinity and others would not have occurred in people who place importance on 'self'. As a culturally context-sensitive society, the poor couple, with nothing to their names, strictly adhere to their culture of positioning the 'others' and 'self' without differentiating between the two.

Paradoxically, the characters in *The Phob that Provided Food* do not treat the two (self and non-self) as one. The critics Ims and Pedersen state that, "the notion of selflessness or 'no-self' (*anatta*) is emphasized as central to Buddhist thinking" (131). Similar to the Indian's perspective, Bhutanese, as a Buddhist practitioner, high value, the concept of overcoming the 'self' or 'I' to attain *nirvana*. The poor boy and the rich lady both defy this concept to prove that Bhutanese do not follow the context-sensitive culture like India. Instead, it augments the concept of placing 'self' in the centre more than what the Indians preach and believe. Unlike the poor man in *The Magical Bowls*, the poor boy in this tale neither share the objects nor he talks of it with the rich lady from whom he begged food before. On the other hand, the rich lady also steals his objects for herself, demonstrating the significance she places on 'self' rather than 'Others'. The folktale verifies the woman's action in the following words, "the woman decided at once that she had to have the magical *phob*. She began to plan on how she could possibly get it from him" (Choden, 138) and illustrates to what extent people can go to fulfil their endless desire.

Even the way the poor boy treats the sparrow after losing his objects establishes his self-centred nature. The imprudent boy does not take responsibility for his own weakness, instead, he throws his tantrums in front of the sparrow. Upon losing his phob, the boy, in anger goes to the sparrow demandingly "to know why he had been cheated" (Choden, 138). It alludes that when self-centric, people forget to thank for good deeds done, but it becomes easier to blame someone for ones' own mistake. Therefore, the characters in *The Phob that Provided Food* dissuade the context-sensitive culture.

The above analyses of the tales lead to the understanding that the Indian folktale is strongly embedded in the context-sensitive culture as Ramanujan opines in his folk essays. The action of the Indians in the folktale demonstrates a 'selfless' nature, while, the acts in the Bhutanese folktale foregrounds 'self-centeredness'. Indeed, the folktale juxtaposes the context-sensitive culture through the action of the characters. It also highlights the distinct identity of Bhutanese society which follows neither Manu's concept of context-sensitivity nor Kant's philosophy of context-free culture.

The Outcome of the Discussion

The study hypothesised that Ramanujan's principles of context-sensitivity are applicable in the Indian and Bhutanese folktales. By means of close inter-textual reading and upon applying the following context-sensitive traits such as the *relation of container-contained, the principle of karma, universality-particularity, self and non-self* the hypothesis has been well supported. The study has thoroughly examined the select tales in relation to the specified traits and found that the Indian tales show the strong presence of the principle, unlike the Bhutanese tales which are positioned between the context-sensitive and context-free culture. The result authenticates the assumption that the theoretical approach provides intellectual insights to strengthen the awareness of indigenous materials. The presence of context-sensitivity in Indian culture as a structured order navigates the Indian way of thinking and their actions contrary to the Bhutanese tales which reveal the presence of unique culture distinct from the Indian and western perspective.

The Significance of the Findings

The close reading approach determines that the Indian folktales in accordance with Ramanujan's ideas on folklore are organized and governed by the principle of context-sensitivity. This assertion was further tested on Bhutanese tales through an inter-textual reading. The study highlights the cultural affinities between the nations not just in terms of thematic comparison but also in its theoretical approach. In this process, the study proves that the context-sensitive aspect of culture is prevalent in the chosen set of tales, despite their varied contexts. On the other hand, Bhutanese tales also show the presence of context-free aspect of the culture at a minimal level. As a result, tales relate and counter each other in certain ways. As a 'travelling metaphor', the study also proves that folktales are not immobile, but it keeps on moving with a clear motive of preserving it for the generation.

Unlike the old-fashioned way of perceiving folktales in isolation, this undertaken study is convinced about the application of folkloristic principles and their traits to understand the paradigmatic principles of folktales from Indian and Bhutan for the reconstruction of knowledge in its newer dimension.

REFERENCES

Bronner, Simon J. *The Meaning of Folklore: An Analytical Essays of Alan Dundes*. Logan: Utah State University Press, 2007. Print.

Burley, Mikel. "Karma, Morality, and Evil." *Philosophy Compass,* 9.6 (2014): 415-30. Print.

Chitra, S. "Cultural Insights in the Oral Narratives: Folktales of India and Bhutan." *The 5th International Seminar on the Cultural Traditions and Indigenous Knowledge of Himalayan Ethnic Groups: Issues & Challenges for Safeguarding,* Thimphu, 27-28 April 2014. Print.

Choden, K. *Folktales of Bhutan*. Thailand: White Lotus, 1994. Print.

Dorji, Tshering Cigay. "Preserving our Folktales, Myths and Legends in the Digital Era." *Journal of Bhutan Studies,* 20.1 (2009): 93-108. Print.

Evans, S. "The Impact of Cultural Folklore on National Values: A Preliminary Study with a Focus on Bhutan." *Journal of Bhutan Studies,* 20.1 (2009): 3-20. Print.

Ims, Knut J. and Lars Jacob Tynes Pedersen. *Business and the Greater Good: Rethinking Business Ethics in an Age of Crisis.* Cheltenham: Edward Elgar Publishing, 2015. Print.

Louden, Robert B. *Kant's Human Being: Essays on his Theory of Human Nature.* Oxford: OUP, 2011. Print.

Penjore, Dorji. "Dangphu Dingphu: The Origin of the Bhutanese Folktales." *Journal of Bhutan Studies,* 21.2 (2009): 7-42. Print.

—. "Oral Traditions as Alternative Literature: Voices of Dissent in Bhutanese Folktales." *Journal of Bhutan Studies*, 20.1 (2009): 21-36. Print.

Ramanujan, A.K. "Is There an Indian Way of Thinking? An Informal Essay." *Contributions to Indian Sociology,* 23.1 (1989): 41-58. Print.

—. *Folktales from India.* New Delhi: Penguin Books, 1991. Print.

—. "A Flowering Tree: A Woman's Tale." *Oral Tradition,* 12.1 (1997): 226-43. Print.

Sharma, Chandra Shekhar. "Bhutanese Folktales: Common Man's Media with Missions for Society." *Journal of Bhutan Studies* (2007): 82-112. Print.

Tilak, Shrinivas. *Understanding Karma: In Light of Paul Ricoeur's Philosophical Anthropology & Hermeneutics.* Mumbai: International Centre for Cultural Studies, 2006. Print.

Section II

Glimpses of South Asian Culture and Society

Chapter 30

The Innovation of the Sacred: The Movement of the "Sacredness" of Folk Religious Rituals and the Archaeological Process of Adaptation of Performances

Anna Lynn Tom and Hemanga Dutta

Durga Das Mukhopadhyay, in his book, *Folk Arts and Social Communication*, says that the performances of folk-art traditions evoke emotions of solidarity and 'identity' within their communities. Performative folk arts are therefore an approach to a unified sense of being of man within his closely-knit society and community. This also hints at the inherent origin of anthropological structures and feelings within the performative arts of social rituals—here, folk rituals (Mukhopadhyay, 1). Accordingly, the first part of the paper explores certain forms of performative folk arts and their significance as a sacred form of communion between man and the divine.

The Sacred Singularity of Folk Religious Rituals

One such religious ritual of the folk traditions of the *Bhuta* theatre in Kerala is that of the form and functions of *Teyyam*. The *Bhuta* theatre of *Teyyam* is one that believes in deities of spirits—of ancestors, heroes, tribal mother goddess, etc. (Varadpande, 57).

The *Teyyam* dancer is the performer of a sacred religious ritual—one that involves the venerable position of being able to summon God (*Varavili*) and is a vessel for the God who comes and leaves within the rhythmic beats of their movements. Such a position also involves a purification process of the self through the painted make-up, costumes and dance to the rhythms, for the performer through his act becomes the oracle who is the site for the visit of the deity (Balakrishnan and Raja). Thus, the site of the performance is the temple courtyard and the element of energy and veneration is the flames from the lantern that is considered a divine vessel, containing the powers of God. The performance thus employs a certain 'fear and awe' in the spectator devotees (Varadpande, 58). One of the underlying functions of such traditional folk arts is to also create the longevity and continuation of traditions and methods of the ways of life and being, through the generations. It is thus that these performances have more of a 'participatory' function rather than an 'economic' function (Subramaniam, 12).

One such art is the folk song tradition of the *Kamsale* artists. These artists are part of a rich tradition of believers of the Lord Mahadeshwara (an incarnation of Lord Shiva)—in South Karnataka. Their songs are part of a generative transfer—the oral narratives of worship towards this deity is passed down the family through the generations. Their songs contain long stories of faith traditions that narrate the promises that the Lord Mahadeshwara keeps with his people (Henry, 73). A folklore museum called Janapada Loka, in Ramanagara—off the outskirts of Bangalore—has a performance by a *Kamsale* artist by the name of Mallaiah. He performs the Janapada folk songs *Chellidaru Malligeya*, *Yaarige Oladhayya* and others, for the public visitors of the museum. Such an interaction is also indicative of the communicative bridge formed across people of different backgrounds, through an assertion of a natural art (Dyer, 57). On a visit to the museum, after the performance, when asked by a visitor—Mallaiah also mentioned wistfully that he would be able to teach it to his son as well, but if the learning process did not arise from the heart, it would never be a true performance. The underlying importance of such a statement lies within a certain perspective that oral narratives provide to the people of the community—a way through which poetry is a means of constructing their world through words (Finnegan, 127). When they are taken out of that world, the perspective lacks certain closeness to the heart. And although the performance evokes emotions in the listener—it is no longer from the same perspective of emotion.

However, the richness of his tradition does not fail to evoke a certain transcendental meditation of simplicity—*Chellidaru Malligeya* is the song of praise for the Jasmine flowers that fall to the earth—some that take root and some that don't. However, it is the symbol of the promise of the Lord Mahadeshwara. Similarly, *Yaarige Oladhayya* is a song that narrates through his multiple modulation of voice—the faith that is inherent within the devotee—that the Lord of the Lingam (*Lingaiah*) wove the world for the faithful devotees (*bhaktharige*) of his lands and the promise is written again—within the jasmine flowers (*Malligehoovu*). Another oral tradition that belongs to a certain community within the villages of Kerala is the *Pulluvan Paattu*. While the *Kamsale* artists of today—like Mallaiah can perform his oral narratives with simply the beats provided by a snap of the fingers, a clap of the hands or a hand-held drum, the *Pulluvan Paattu* is more intensive with respect to ritual performance. The folk songs indigenous to this community are sung by the men or the women, on an auspicious day to the snake god. True to the ritual of sanctity—the songs are sung to the accompaniment of the *Pulluvan veena*, after the distribution of the mixture of milk and lime to the snake god—in front of a Kolam drawing (Thiyyadi).

These nuances of symbols around which a performance is arranged are mentioned here in order to provide a framework that will enable us to see, how these very forms change in meaning when these sacred religious folk rituals are transposed into an arena of performative adaptation. The adaptation process not only involves the history of its sacredness but also of how malleable these moments of rituals are towards social and cultural influxes. It is this that we explore in the next section the method in which 'participatory' functions of sacred rituals also reflect the inter-cultural derivations of these performative arts as they grow through the ages and how they cross boundaries of performativity (Subramaniam, 182).

The Profane Performativity of Adaptation from Text to Performance

Richard Dyer in his book, *Only Entertainment* says of the folk form of art that the simplicity associated with it is long gone under the complex forms it takes in contemporary forms of performance (Dyer, 158). However, the meaning of 'simplicity' is to be examined in depth. According to the description of Mary Zimmerman, in her paper, "The Archaeology of Performance", the process of adaptation of the text into the performative art is an 'archaeological' process (Zimmerman, 25). With the examples we see within this section, it is often the case that the performative adaptation inculcates a simpler form of the folk art form, but it is the underlying web of meanings that have traversed through time—within the art of the folk tradition, combined with the significations of transformation from text to performance that offers the 'complexity' of multiplicities of meanings to the folk art and the new performative piece, together. The cultural influxes within this morphing are also of significance.

Now, one of the most crucial aspects of the transformation from text to performance is the story that connects the two. Consequently, it is with respect to this aspect that the paper will now examine the process of adaptation of Malayalam writer—O.V. Vijayan's novella, *Khasakkinte Ithihasam* (*The Legends of Khasak*) into a play by Deepan Sivaraman by the inclusive use of traditional folk rituals and performative art forms. The actors chosen for the performance are interestingly the local theatre group of Trikkaripur—a village within the heartlands of the performative tradition of the ritual of *Teyyam* (Lal).

Technical Aspects and Inherence

Although the open-air play involves the functioning of heavy technical equipment of light and sounds, the play and the essence of bringing out the story of the lands of Khasak, inculcates moments of senses jarred by the inherent movements and performative aspects within the adaptation (Ragesh).

Some of them are the harsh and painful exclamation of 'Allahu Akbar' that resounds through the quadrangle as the character of Nizam Ali undergoes a transformation of powerful emotion towards the old Mullah—his adopted father—Allah Pitcha. The character of Nizam Ali transforms through the play—from his moment of founding (by Allah Pitcha) to his antagonistic 'beedi selling' self towards Allah Pitcha and subsequent transformation as the Khazi—the self-appointed human vessel of the spirit of the founding father Sheikh Mian Sahib—through the elements of water, earth and fire. This is also one of the performative adaptations of the textual story within Vijayan's novella.

Fire—symbolises the inherent element of light within the play. It is evoked by the Islamic and the Hindu rituals within the play and the characters of Khasak. The presence of 'chootť'—a makeshift torch made of matted palm leaves and twigs also highlight many scenes of intercultural communication within the play's progression (Bhasthi).

In transposing the story of a fictional land within the play, the reality of this land's culture and traditions are reinforced by simple elements of sight, smell and taste. One of them would be the bicycle and manual loudspeaker that Nizam Ali drives around in order to 'advertise' his beedis—that are also blessed by the Sheikh Mian Sahib. Secondly, there are multiple instances of the use of talcum powder, Biriyani and Appam and stew—that spreads the smells and tastes of the village onto the senses of the spectator (Ragesh).

In certain moments of the play, the food is also distributed to the members of the audience—this transforming them into the "citizens of the land of Khasak". This moment signifies the true 'archaeological' grounds of adaptation—the moment of inclusion is not simply between the text, the story and the performance, but also towards the spectator of the adaptation. Within the performance of *Khasakkinte Ithihasam*, it is also the transformative allure of the mythical land of Khasak.

Transformative Moments from Text to Performance

The festival of the temple of the Bhagavati that the people of Khasak celebrates is depicted through an intensive use of fireworks, mats, Teyyam and moments that mimic Kalarippayattu (Varadpande, 59). Fire is also an element of power and fear—as employed by Nizam Ali as the Khazi—in his magic rituals of dark arts.

The depiction of the sexual encounters of the illicit relationships within the land of Khasak is portrayed with an intensity that connects the characters involved in the act to an outer element. For instance, between Maimoona and Nizam Ali, it is shown as a rigorous movement of play in the soil. At another point, between Ravi and his nurse, it is by the act of creating a pulp of tomatoes over the performers' bodies—without the characters touching each other at any point. In a later part, Ravi and Maimoona simply get wet under the rain, to denote the relationship between the two.

The land of Khasak in Vijayan's story is a microcosm of intercultural relations and syncretic ritualistic practices. The nuances of such a land and its characters' mental make-up transforms within little moments within the performance—for instance, when Allah Pitcha takes his role seriously—as the giver of mythical memories of the history of Khasak to the little children who come to the Mosque; he denotes such a moment simply by drawing the outline of a home with a dome and the Islamic symbol of the crescent moon and star at the top. The scene progresses to show the children, sitting within the box of the 'drawn mosque' (Ragesh).

"Teyyam" as a Performance

Likewise, there are obvious translations of attire and music to situate the Hindu traditions and characters of the play. But the defining transformation of the text into the performance is situated within the use of the performative tradition of *Teyyam* in the depiction of the festival of the goddess of the tamarind tree in Khasak (Vijayan, *The Legends of Khasak*). As mentioned earlier, the character of Kuttadan performs the ritual of *Teyyam* in the play. In it, the actor is not clad in the traditional attire—but he performs the dance to the beats of the music with the inclusion of the fire element—one that signifies purification and the divine element. At this point, it is important to mention, why *Teyyam* as an art form superseded others within the context of culture. Teyyam interestingly had Islamic folk influences within its tradition of divinity. In a certain village of Kasaragod, the myth of the Ali-bhuta—a Muslim man who becomes a spirit after he watches the Bhagavati in water and is killed by her—is transformed into the performance of the Ali-Teyyam. The latter is conducted with the attire of the performer in a Muslim dress, Turkish cap and a lungi (Varadpande, 58). This is interestingly the very characterisation of Nizam Ali—the man who becomes the Khazi (a human spirit blessed by the Sheikh) who also watched Maimoona wet by the Riverside (Vijayan, *The Legends of Khasak*). Thus, Deepan Sivaraman's inclusion of this folk art into the play has a deep-rooted archaeological significance—in the syncretic multicultural microcosm of the land of Khasak—one where the Hindus venerated the name of Sheikh Mian Sahib, even as the Muslims swore by the Bhagavati of the tamarind tree (Bhasthi).

The Use of Puppetry and Masks

Shadow Puppetry and its significances of colours, textures and the clothes of the characters is also a traditional art form used in the ritualistic practices of worshipping the Goddess Bhagavati during her festival (Helstien, 16). Very often, the use of puppetry within a performative genre was to indicate a movement away from the distinctions of ideology and into the free forms of natural sources of dance, music and ritual. In *The Sound of Music*—the performance of the "Lonely Goatherd" is seen as such a movement (Wise). Within a contemporary context, the emergence of Bread and Puppet theatre has been seen as a convergence of the forms of the old and of the new, with a view to reflect the contemporary situation (Bell, 62). Perhaps Deepan Sivaraman's use of huge masks and puppets within his performative adaptation can be studied as an amalgamation of the two aspects of puppetry within performative adaption. His use of the puppet in order to demonstrate Ravi's troublesome relationship with his stepmother is indicative of his search for peace—inside and outside himself. However, the use of the masked women of Appukili's four mothers denotes the lament of Appukili's mental condition, even as it commands the future innocence and earthy connection that Appukili has towards nature—in his eternal chasing of the butterflies and spiders. On the other hand, the use of puppetry to stand for the Goddesses' crown amalgamates the spiritual and natural character of Khasak even as it suggests the importance and the possibility of peaceful coexistence and flourishing of the intercultural relations of India's religious communities (Bhasthi). In our exploration of the journey of the sacred folk ritual, it is important to trace the form of the ritual of Kathakali. The latter ritual art form is an amalgamation of many ritualistic folk practices—including Teyyam—adapted in itself into a Brahmanical form of ritual performance and worship (Emigh, 174). Very often the inclusion of this art practice within performative adaptation is with a view to invoke the national culture of performativity.

However, as Arundhati Roy's description of the Kathakali practice in her novel *The God of Small Things* shows it is not the sacredness of the Indian culture that is so much important as the Indian story that the performative tradition of Kathakali narrates. Every little gesture is also a part of the narrative of the "great story" (Roy, 229-32). Therefore, it is the story—with all its histories and myths woven together into all its roots—that is the key archaeological aspect within the movement of adaptation from text to performance (Sivaraman). Thus, language expands within this arena of cultural adaptation into the realm of performativity within linguistic markers as well. The foregrounding of the story also functions in a way to assert that in the Indian context of adaptation, the process is the creation of a painting that moves temporally to describe the many nuances of faith and belief systems—all of which are enabled through the meanings added to them through the adaptation from text to performance.

Multiplicities of the Meaning of the "Sacred" Social Ritual

Victor Turner in his book, *From Ritual to Theatre*, speaks of social drama as a movement that functions to contain any breach of crisis within the linear "norm governed" functioning of the society (Turner, 92). Within this purview, the paper will consider Albert Camus' novel *The Stranger* and the character of Meursault. When this character is condemned for the crime a performance ritual condemns him because he refuses to take part in it. It is simply because he does not think that way. Or he is incapable of thinking that way. When Camus says that he was killed for “refusing to lie” what actually happened was that he refused to perform and he did not know how to lie or perform according to social dictates or social drama of justice in this case (Camus). The performance of absurdity tries to point out this schism, between the self and all that interacts with it outside the self by means of getting the self to respond through the social drama aspect. It is thus that, the sacred ritual of ‘Transitus’—a performance by Franciscan monks on the eve of the death of their patron is done with the intention of evoking the experience of pain, suffering and sacredness of Francis’ life and philosophy. However, many find this ritual ‘weird’ or ‘absurd’ (Chin). The reason for including this bit in the paper is to show the significance of what Mary Zimmerman speaks about in her essay the archaeology of performance. She says that it is pointless to try and publish her adaptation of certain text because “[...] their meaning the way in which they produced meaning is utterly dependent on all the original theatrical elements working in concert” (Zimmerman, 32).

This simply points to the fact that very often the adapted performance contains certain meanings that will appear completely observed to the text itself. But then, this is also the very moment in which the *multiplicities of meanings* are ascribed to the profane methods in which the sacred rituals of traditions are transposed into the performative adaptation. Thus, it is that *a new sacred* is created out of the very fabric of the multiple significations of the tapestry of performance in its entirety of adaptation from the experience of the text into the production of the sounds and actions of performance.

REFERENCES

Bell, John. “The End of Our Domestic Resurrection Circus: Bread and Puppet Theater and Counterculture Performance in the 1990s.” *TDR*, 43.3 (Autumn 1999): 62-80. Print.

Bhasthi, Deepa. “OV Vijayan: Return to Khasak.” *Openthemagazine.com*. Open: The Magazine, 20 May 2016. Web. 23 Oct. 2018. <https://openthemagazine.com/art-culture/ov-vijayan-return-to-khasak/>

Camus, Albert. *The Stranger*. New York: Cambridge University Press, 1988. Print.

Chin, Brandon. "Francis's Dignified Death." *thebvnewspaper.com. The Bona Venture*, 8 Oct. 2015. Web. 23 Oct. 2018. <https://www.thebvnewspaper.com/2015/10/08/franciss-dignified-death/>

Dyer, Richard. *Only Entertainment*. London: Routledge, 2002. Print.

Emigh, John. "Review: Beyond the Kathakali Mystique." *TDR*, 30.2 (Summer 1986): 172-75. Print.

Finnegan, Ruth. *Oral Traditions and The Verbal Arts: A Guide to Research Practices*. London: Routledge, 1992. Print.

Helstien, Mel. "Shadow Puppets and their Iconography." *Our Cultural Fabric: Puppet Theatre in India*. New Delhi: Ministry of Education and Culture, 1982. 23-32. Print.

Henry, Edward O. "Folk Song Genres and Their Melodies in India: Music Use and Genre Process." *Asian Music*, 31.2 (2000): 71-106. Print.

Lal, Amrith. "It Takes a Village." *Indianexpress.com. The Indian Express*, 17 Apr. 2016. 23 Oct. 2018. <https://indianexpress.com/article/lifestyle/art-and-culture/it-takes-a-village-2756713/>

Mukhopadhyay, Durga Das. *Folk Arts and Social Communication*. New Delhi: Publications Division, Ministry of Information and Broadcasting, 1994. Print.

Ragesh, G. "Staging 'Khasak', the Protagonist." *english.manoramaonline.com. Onmanorama*, 4 Apr. 2016. Web. 23 Oct. 2018.

<https://english.manoramaonline.com/entertainment/art-and-culture/khasakinte-ithihasam-play-by-deepan-sivaraman-review.html>

Roy, Arundhati. *The God of Small Things*. New Delhi: Penguin Books, 1997. Print.

Sound of Music. Dir. Robert Wise. Perf. Julie Andrews and Christopher Plummer, 1965.

Subramaniam, V. ed. *The Sacred and the Secular in India's Performing Arts*. New Delhi: Ashish Publishing House, 1980. Print.

Theyyam. Perf. Balakrishnan and E.K. Govindavarma Raja. *Thenga Productions*. 14 Apr. 2018. Web. 27 Oct. 2018. <https://youtu.be/vrBXizUR47M>.

Thiyyadi, Sreevalsan. "When Men and Women Sing for Nagas and Slither like Snakes." *outlookindia.com. Outlook* the fully loaded magazine, 22 Aug. 2017. Web. 23 Oct. 2018. <https://www.outlookindia.com/website/story/when-men-and-women-sing-for-nagas-and-slither-like-snakes/300648>

Turner, Victor. *From Ritual to Theatre*. New York: PAJ Publications, 1982. Print.

Varadpande, M.L. *History of Indian Theatre: Loka Ranga—Panorama of Indian Folk Theatre*. New Delhi: Abhinav Publications, 1992. Print.

Vijayan, O.V. *The Legends of Khasak*. New Delhi: Penguin Books, 1999. Print.

Zimmerman, Mary. "The Archeology of Performance." *Theatre Topics*, 15.1 (2005): 25-35. Print.

Chapter 31

River Tunga—The Mother of Malenadu: An Ecological Perspective

Prakash C. Balikai

"Naa Ninage Nee Nanage, Jenaguva" means I for you, you for me; come let's make the life full of honey and surrender our self to Lord. Through these words, Kuvempu's poetry leads from Physicality to Spirituality and rests at devotionality. Kuvempu says "The Land of Tunga is his Motherland and it is God's Land". Along with the banks of Tunga the places and temples bring the message to human life by uplifting human values through Spirituality. The great places and temples namely, Sharada Peetham (Established by Aadi Shankaracharya), Mantralayam Shree Raghavendra Swamy Mutt (Dakshina Kashi), Shringeri, The Saiva Cults and Clusters of Nava Brahma Temple constructed by the Chalukyas make the river rich with spirituality.

River Tunga rises at Gangamoola in the Varaha Parvata, accompanying with another river Bhadra, she takes a journey of 147 km. and 171 km. respectively, later travelling through Karnataka and Andhra Pradesh both together join the Arabian Sea near Mangalore. It is the same river by the name Pampa, which appears in the Epic *Ramayana* (there is another river Pampa by the same name in Kerala). The belief "Ganga Snana Tunga Paana", means we ought to take bath in the river Ganga and should drink the water of river Tunga, fascinates us to move towards the western Ghats, near Gangamoola. Along with the rise of the river Kuvempu's Place Shiva-Mukha, place of Lord Shiva that is Shivamogga, bring the spirituality in its name itself. After the ancient poet, Pampa in Kannada literature it is Kuvempu, the nature poet of Navodaya Janra who breaks the silence of greenery in celebrating Sahyadri and the river Tunga. He deconstructs the artificiality and constructs naturality in his poetry.

Nature is not celebrated individually; rather it is celebrated through all human senses in order to surrender the soul to Lord. With spirituality the poetry of Kuvempu makes us rethink over the scientific and commercial development which increased the desirableness of man through the intervention into the ecology. Kuvempu breaks the notion of the fall, i.e. ecology is subordinate to man so as G.S. Shivarudrappa, another National poet of Karnataka, calls him Kadina Kavi, i.e. afforest poet. The paper discusses "Water and Spirituality" focusing on the river Tunga in Kuvempu's poetry in a broader sense how the river and water source in Sahyadri brought meaning, faith and love for mankind by forgetting the Geographical sufferings of Malenadu such as Malaria, Diseases and Deaths, etc. Kuvempu brings the importance of spirituality, his poetry consists of human sufferings, hungriness, diseases, the death which make us rethink over the consequences of modern society's so-called growth. Kuvempu neither opposes science nor dismisses ancient Myths but through spirituality, he tries to find out the meaning for human life w.r.t. Water. Kuvempu gives anthropocentric and anthropomorphic views for the image of water in his poetry. He considers Ecology as his mate and Water (river) as a living being; personifying River as a mother. Kuvempu narrates Biocentric aspects of Ecology giving equal importance for plants, insects, Water and other Ecological Elements. We never find the human environment separated from Ecology in Kuvempu poetry. Nature is not celebrated individually; rather it is celebrated through all human senses in order to surrender the soul to Lord. With spirituality the poetry of Kuvempu makes us rethink over the scientific and commercial development which increased the desirableness of man through the intervention into the ecology. Kuvempu breaks the notion of the fall, i.e. ecology is subordinate to man so as G.S. Shivarudrappa, another National poet of Karnataka, calls him as Kadina Kavi, i.e. afforest poet.

In the poem "To Tunga", Kuvempu brings out his interaction, relationship and feelings with Tunga in his childhood, adolescence age and in his post-adolescence age. Mother Tunga gives a philosophical sense with spirituality to his life, i.e. how to build intervention and develop the strength of the Soul. He finds the truth that worshipping Nature is Worshipping God, i.e. 'Prakrutiya Aaradhaneye Parama (Shivana) Aaradhane'. The first half of the poem describes how the river is full of silence and also with revolution. The river leads towards internal transformation and revolution in us. In the later part of the poem we find, Tunga becoming the goddess of spirituality by constructing our internal stability, confidence, mastery. Kuvempu tries to find meaning for life through river Tunga. Kuvempu's lines cast-up the spirituality of the river Tunga in our mind to forget the sufferings and pains by loving nature which leads to love for mankind by bringing the message of truth, peace and harmony in us and these lines show this: "The Night of Full Moon/ [...] As the Gage of Moon Light/ Descends from the Sky/ River Tunga dazzles/ At a distance as if painted [...]" (Javare, 21). The image of the flow of Ganga's water from Lord Shiva's head itself brings Bhakti-rasa in us. Kuvempu compares the flow of Ganga's Water from the sky with Tunga's Water flowing in Malenadu as if it is the painting by God. Bhakti leads us to peace and enlightenment. The Melodious Singing of the Nightingales on the Banks of the river Tunga enriches the grandureness of the heavenly beauty of Sahyadri makes the whole universe Fashionable which is described in the poem "To Malenadu". Kuvempu takes back us to Malenadu to love human life by loving nature on the banks of Tunga. Imagery poems are found in the poetry where the writings appeal to our senses, thus Kuvempu successfully uses imagery, simile, metaphor and personification in his poetry to celebrate river Tunga.

In the poem "Anirvachaneeya", Kuvempu successfully tries to find out the magic of spirituality which is brought by the endless waves of Tunga. Poet says: O, Soul come let us dip in the Jalanidhi, i.e. the source of water, often we tried to find the secrets of the universe but as long as we travel we could not find the end, where is the end for God's Magic of creation? No, not possible to understand; we are defeated with fear to understand it. Now no need to think let us dip into the womb of mother Tunga and understand what life is! Kuvempu tries to find the remedy for the sorrows of life through the spiritual meaning of the running waves. In describing 'Karunadu' in the 'Naadageete' of Karnataka Kuvempu brings how spirituality is spread by the rivers Krishna, Sharavati, Tunga which became boon for Karunadu and are symbols of spirituality over the land.

The two poems with the same title "Art of Poet (Kavishaila)", appeared in the collection *Images of Malenadu,* describe how Kuvempu is blessed with mother Tunga standing on the banks and enjoying the beauty of Jog Falls, Agumbe, Shringeri, etc. where Kuvempu admits there is no greater beauty than mother Tunga who spreads spirituality to understand the meaning of life. The same meaning is conveyed in another poem *God's Signature* where Kuvempu describes how he became a Nature poet by borrowing the spirituality from mother Tunga and what she contributed to human society. Poet says the garden of Sahyadri was Amazed; sky above the Tunga was smiling with joy, to see the waterfall of the river Tunga. The beauty of Tunga brings the feeling of honey in the poet's heart; this experience is God's boon which made him a Poet becoming one with mother Tunga. God has put the signature for our Fate but in the Poem "God's Signature", Kuvempu brings the message of aesthetic pleasure which appears in the line of flying cranes ensures us that fate changes by the beauty of nature. Love for Nature lifts us from individuality to universality; This is the message Kuvempu brings in this poem, i.e. "Vyakti Nele Enda Vishwa Manava Neleyedege".

Kuvempu explores the whole Sahyadri in his poems. In his poetry, we find the breaking up of artificiality and building up of naturality. His poetry does not stable at physical level, but it leads us towards the spiritual word. Education works for the betterment of man and helps a man to turn into the original "universal man", which is possible by understanding the Nature and helped through spirituality. Kuvempu writes:

> The Religion of Humanity, the Universal Path, the Welfare of All Reconciliation, the Integral Vision—these five mantras should become view of the future. In other words, what we want henceforth is not this religion or that religion, but then Religion of Humanity; not this path or that path

but then Universal Path; not the wellbeing of this individual or that individual, but the Welfare of All; not turning away and breaking off from one another, but reconciling and uniting in concord and harmony; and above all, not the partial view of narrow creed, not the dual outlook of the material and the spiritual, but the Integral Vision of seeing all the things with the eye of the Divine. (Depalan)

REFERENCES

Depalan, Saju. "Trees are dear but Shama is dearer..." *iseeebirds.blogspot.com*. Iseebirds, 25 Mar. 2010. Web. 18 May 2019. <http://iseeebirds.blogspot.com/2010/03/trees-are-dear-but-shama-is-dearer.html?cv=1>

Javare, Gowda D, ed. *Selected Poems of Kuvempu*. Hampi: Prasaranga Kannada University, 2011. Print.

Kuvempu. *Kuvempu Samagra Kavya*. Vol. 1. Hampi: Prasaranga Kannada University, 2000. Print.

—. *Kuvempu Samagra Kavya*. Vol. 2. Hampi: Prasaranga Kannada University, 2000. Print.

Nangali, V. Chandrashekhar. *Kuvempi Kadambarigalalli Jaivika Jala*. Hampi: Prasaranga Kannada University, 2001. Print.

Chapter 32

The Oneness in the Other: Re-evaluating the Role of Sister Nivedita

Subhajeet Singha

The identity of a nation feeds on different and diverse minuscule morsels to a large chunk of historical progression, sociological evolution, cultural expansion and others. If we assemble them together, then a series of axiomatic cultural contraptions are brought together and be named as nationalism. It is the base upon which the foundational structure of ethnic identity or a nation is founded. It may fluctuate from one code of culture to another but one thing is always steadfast in their dogmatic approach or in their participation of national integrity, which is the construction of a superior "Self" against an oddball "Other".

Homi K. Bhabha keeps a valuable proposition for us in his essay, "Dissemination: Time, Narrative and the Margins of the Modern Nation". For Bhabha, the entry of the Europeans in the empire-building competition in Indian peninsula is somewhat different than the mighty Mughals or other preceding empires before the White domination. Bhabha indebts his notion of historicism to Anthony Giddens, who describes it as a long line of traditional, epistemological sources which supplies a certain cultural definition of a race upon its claim of nationalism. It is like a moment, a tremendous moment in the history of a nation or nationalists, marked as if like a founding moment, such as the arrival of the Normans in England after Norman Conquest in 1066 A.D. or the arrival of the Hispanic Conquistadors in Latin America, or the Robert Clive's fortunate victory in a skirmish outside Plassey, Murshidabad in 1757.

The racial insult that the British threw at the Indians, proved to be the founding stone of Indian nationalism later on. Female iconoclast has always been revered as sacred throughout many religions in the world, but in India, it is the synthesis of motherly grace of Virgin Mary with the decisiveness and precision of a Warrior-god like Lord Shiva that created the figure of the mother goddess. That is the idol the armed revolutionaries of Indian Nationalistic movement worshipped as their nation. The idea of "Bharat Mata" or the divine mother became a force, so impregnable, that it was pitted against the mighty lions of the British coat-of-arms. Indian independence was achieved through the figuratively dismantling of the chains around her, put by the British. The Nationalistic thoughts which flickered through the subconscious of the Indians were not only lit by the wretched condition of the native Indians, but their European masters or better to say a small contingent of it came forward to help Indians to liberate themselves. And Sister Nivedita, about whom I am going to discuss at length in the second section of this essay, was a member of that illustrious contingent.

Nivedita breathed her last at a premature age of 44. Even after Vivekananda's death in 1902, she made two visits to West, one in 1907 and the other in 1910, and this is to show that her unflinching love for her adopted country brought her back to India not once but twice. Being an Irish, she knew what it like was to be governed by an atrocious foreign rule. The famous revolutionary leader Rashbehari Ghosh, who founded I.N.A. and helped Netaji Subhas Chandra Bose to raise the army to fight against the British, eulogized Nivedita after her death. The national entity of India or the idea of India, therefore, lied dormant within the sub-continental subconscious. All it needed was a spur of radical intent and Nivedita brought the fire into the dried leaves of nationalism. She might not be a Pritilata Waddar or Matangini Hazra who came into the forefront as revolutionary women freedom fighter, but it is true that she was an inspirational figure for the youth of Bengal and probably out of the ineffaceable mark that she left on the history of this country, Rabindranath Tagore appraised her with the sobriquet, "Lokmata".

Swami Vivekananda bestowed that mantle of responsibility upon the competent shoulders of Sister Nivedita. In his poem, "Kali, the Mother", Swami Vivekananda envisages the deity of Goddess Kali, elsewhere Ma Kali or Adyashakti, as the allusion of death and violent and tremendous energy of cosmic kind. The death which he associates with Kali is not the literal death of us, the mortals. Swamiji somehow understood that the British dominion over India will not come to an end, until the force, the sleeping, unheeded, nascent force of thousands and thousands of souls, Indian souls, come to full awakening. The death Vivekananda, so keenly worships here, is the death of gross ignorance. In Hindu myths and scriptures, there we may find the custom of sacrifice before Goddess Kali. She is dark-skinned and looking like a wraith, menacing and vengeful. She remembers us of the fiery Maenad of P.B. Shelley:

> Of some fierce Maenad, even from the dim verge
> Of the horizon to the zenith's height,
> The locks of the approaching storm [...]. (298)

As Shelley found the spirit of destruction latent in the rise of West Wind, Swamiji found quite the same in his manifestation of the image of Kali. But both of them were not glorifying the apocalyptical visions of doom, rather they were apostrophizing the unbridled, unheralded and unforeseen forces of change.

But where does Sister Nivedita fit into this scheme of awakening the ignorant mass of Indians? She possessed the knowledge and the enlightenment principles of the West. But unlike the other capitalist agents of the West, she did not come to visit India in order to exploit the native indigenous naivety of the country, she was herself an Irish, subjected to British dominion for over centuries. When she came to India, she gradually understood that beside her religious quest, as ordered by her Guru, she also had other destinies to follow. She was not only the Colonial 'Other' to the Indian 'Self'. She made a journey from being the 'Self' and the 'Other' in one. The "Advaita Vedanta" philosophy assures us the synthesis of many, fusing into one, one in many and many in one. Nivedita metamorphosed into a true world citizen from a European by birth. The second section of this essay is a modest enquiry into her position as a being at the crossroads of culture.

II

India, the crown jewel in the crown of an oriental section of global British trade and commerce, was the nefarious "Other" in the eyes of the white empire. As Edward Said famously mentioned in his "Orientalism" that orient is weak, effeminate and fragile, it is once again established that the occidental "Self" will always eradicate the inadequate "Other". Said was a part of a relatively decisive academic conjuncture around the turn of the 1980s, drawing on theoretical progress in deconstruction, feminism and neo-Marxism. As Rudyard Kipling in his "The Ballad of East and West" wrote: "Oh, East is East, and West is West, and never the twain shall meet" (Kipling, 174), the Orient has been Europe's cultural competitor and, hence, one of the most significant images of the "Other".

During the length of the 19th century, throughout India, a strange confluence of crosscurrents was observed. There was embroidered veneration for the British epitasis in India as well as a self-same abomination for the British bureaucracy which was gnawing away the soul of India. The protest became more and more substantial after the Great Rebellion of 1857 and the divergent minds came together in search of creating an ideal, a nation for our own. India was always a 'she' against the three-lions emblem of British masculine state. But now it was the time to proclaim that India is the mother, the almighty 'Adyashakti' or the eternal strength of a mother-goddess who can alone destroy the enemies of the sovereignty of her children as well as capable protector of the realm too. The notion of "Bharatmata" was probably reinforced once Bankim Chandra Chattopadhayay's "Anandamath" was published in 1882 and "Vandemataram" or 'I bow to none but to the mother' gained popularity as the national symbol of unanimity among crores of Indians.

Does this call of the 'mother' only beckon her children of this country? There were Europeans too who did not come here to spread coercion but to share the pains of the obnoxious British atrocities upon the native Indians. There were Alexander Duff,

John Drinkwater Bethune, William Carey, David Hare, Henry Derozio, William Adam, Leonard Elmhirst and about whom we are discussing today, Margaret Elizabeth Noble or Sister Nivedita of Ramkrishna and Vivekananda who attended the cause of India against the British. They came from the domineering world of the "Self", embraced the world of the "Other" and became the one in the others.

In a tiny town in long away Ireland, the devout wife of a Christian priest became very worried at the time when she was about to give birth to her first child—will the child arrive safely? She took an oath to God that she would proffer her child to better service of mankind if her child is born safely. The child who was thus blessed at her being while still in her mother's womb, later became Sister Nivedita—the spiritual daughter of the world-renowned Guru, Swami Vivekananda. She was a cynic, a dissident at the beginning but this meeting of the disciple with her master was the destiny. She wrote, "As a religious teacher, I saw that although he had a system of thought to offer, nothing in that system would claim him for a moment, if he found that truth led elsewhere. And to the extent that this recognition implies, I became his disciple" (Atmaprana, 14-16).

She came into this 'system of thought', into this oriental paradigm of spiritual awakening along with her occidental belief, value system and education. Ireland, she came from, was under the British subjugation for so many years. Coming from such a colonially embittered racist background, it is quite certain for us, that Miss Margaret Noble must have the knowledge of the condition of the Indians under the British Raj. Well, that will be a gross misapprehension if we think so beforehand. Pravrajika Atmaprana, in her book, "*Sister Nivedita of Ramkrishna and Vivekananda*", cites: "Nivedita was not aware of the wrongs that the English as the dominant power had done to India. So, when the Swami openly and vigorously attacked the English in his morning talks, she stood for their defence. As in the London classes, she was the one who argued and protested, and always tried to protect her own judgements and assert her views" (45-46). It was only after her sojourn into the heart of India, then only she came to the understanding of the common fate of the people of her native land and the land she adopted as her spiritual destination. What Nivedita could have brought in the milieu of Indian philosophy and freedom struggle, was foreseen by Swami Vivekananda, when he wrote in a letter to Sister Nivedita (July 29, 1897): "India cannot yet produce great women. She must borrow them from other nations. Your education, sincerity, purity, immense love, determination and above all, the Celtic blood make you just the woman wanted [...]" (363). Now, that 'Celtic blood' is not Anglo-Saxon, rather belonging to the land of Britain even before the settlers invaded there. Vivekananda understood that Nivedita possessed the immaculate and efficient synthesis of the East and the West, the confluence of minds.

The idea of Western nation and the creation of the history of the nation are no doubt masculine. Ernest Renan in his essay "What is Nation?" writes: "Man, Gentleman does not improvise. The nation, like the individual, is the culmination of long past of endeavours, sacrifices and devotion" (Dasgupta, 20). The same idea is propounded by Nivedita, when she writes: "Such organization is obviously easy to gain by the conquest of the sea, where captain, first mate and second mate will be a father, with his eldest son and second son [...] and the love of hearthside and brood becomes exalted into that civic passion which can offer up its seven sons and yet say with firm voice, 'Sweet and seemly is it to die for one's country'" (Nivedita, *Footfalls of Indian History,* 2). The soul of all Western Empires taken together is axiomatically masculine. As she further cites: "[...] and he to the Norman, is to be regarded as the father of the feudal system and immediate ancestor of all modern European Empire" (2).

That is where Vivekananda and Indian philosophy reinstated the role of women in Nivedita. She writes in a letter: "India was absorbed in the study; a gang of robbers came upon her and destroyed her land.... Can the robbers teach her anything? No, she has to turn them out and go back to where she was before. Something like that, I fancy, is the true programme for India" (*Letters,* 34-36). She wrote in the same vein as Rabindranath Tagore revealed the nexus of deception that British brought to our shore. They came here to tread and trade, not to mingle and merge. In a poem, "The Footfalls", Sister Nivedita describes,

> We hear them, O Mother!
> Thy footfalls,
> Soft, soft, through the ages
> Touching earth here and there,
> And the lotuses left on Thy footprints
> And cities historic. (*Footfalls of Indian History*, 41)

The poem shows her metamorphosis from a Western sceptic to an Eastern mystic. She understood the role of women as the pioneer of education, as the machination behind the oriental "Other", which is not 'effeminate' but strongly boasts of feminine might, the strength of mother-goddess. But she was not a blind advocate of feminism. Vivekananda knew that astute feminism is as inferior as the absolute masculinity. If the West worshipped the unbridled masculinity, then he wanted India to be governed by a synthesis of masculine prowess with feminine responsibility and charm. Once he said that man making is his mission. His 'man' in question is not male but every 'human being.' Nivedita too understood the role her master wanted her to play dexterously. She writes to Mrs. MacLoed (July 24, 1902):

> We talk of 'women-making'. But the great stream of the Oriental Women's life flows on—who am I that I should seek in any way to change it? [...] It is it not rather by taking the national consciousness of the women like that of the men, and getting it towards greater problems and responsibilities, that one can help? [...] I don't know! [...] Only I think my task is to awake a nation, not to influence a few women. (Basu, 482)

That was the synthesis Sister Nivedita wanted to achieve, nationalism should not be gender biased but should be gender neutral. We all have to come through to unite under one identity.

It would be a severe foul, if I fail to mention her role in the armed revolution of the Indians against the British Raj. Her constant correspondence with leaders like Chittaranjan Das, Surendranath Banerjee, Lala Lajpat Rai held her position as a unique European among the ranks of her peers. The other Europeans I have mentioned before, likes of Bethune and Carrey, they were sympathetic to the conditions of Indians, and contributed in philanthropic works to make conditions better for them, but none of them took a plunge into Freedom Movement of India as Nivedita did. The Indian National Congress was going to be divided into sects of radicals and moderate and their difference of opinion was clearly visible through the fissures at the surface. But she understood that independence will not come at the expense of these factions among us. She worked hard to unite all the revolutionaries under one banner, and she came under the surveillance of the British police soon.

Thus, I may conclude that confluence of myriad historical thoughts met in her and cut a niche of her own in the history of Indian patriotism. Her indelible role as a white "Self" standing for the rights of brown "Other" is a true example of the synthesis of Eastern philosophy and Western metaphysics. The combining strength of becoming one with the "Other" gives her "Self" a new identity.

REFERENCES

Atmaprana, Pravrajika. *Sister Nivedita of Ramkrishna and Vivekananda.* Kolkata: Sister Nivedita Girls' School, 2017. Print.

Basu, Sankari Prasad, ed. *Letters of Sister Nivedita.* Vol. I. Calcutta: Ramkrishna Mission, 1982. Print.

Bhabha, Homi K. *Location of Culture.* London: Routledge, 2004. Print.

Dasgupta, Sayantan, ed. *A South Asian Nationalism Reader.* New Delhi: Worldview Publications. 2007. Print.

Dasgupta, Udit Bhanu. *Nivedita: The Queen of Indian Freedom Movement.* Kolkata: Bulletin of the Ramakrishna Mission Institute of Culture, 2016. Print.

Girvin, Brian. "National Identity and Conflict in Northern Ireland." *Politics and Society in Contemporary Ireland.* Eds. B. Girvin and R. Strum. Michigan: The University of Michigan Press, 1986. Print.

Kipling, Rudyard. *Selected Poems.* London: Penguin, 2001. Print.

Macleod, John. *Beginning Postcolonialism.* UK: Manchester University Press, 2010. Print.

Nivedita, Sister. *Footfalls in Indian History.* Kolkata: Advaita Ashram, 2016. Print.

—. *Hints on National Education in India.* Kolkata: Advaita Ashram, 2015. Print.

—. *Letters.* Vol. I. Ed. S.P. Basu. Calcutta: Nababharat, 1972. Print.

—. *The Complete Works of Sister Nivedita*. Calcutta: Advaita Ashram, 1972. Print.

Pintér, Márta. "English or Irish? Cultural Nationalist Ideology in Late 19th Century Ireland." *Bulletin of the Transilvania University of Brasov,* 3.52 (2010): 233-42. Print.

Said, Edward. *Culture and Imperialism*. London: Vintage, 1994. Print.

—. *Orientalism*. New Delhi: Penguin, 2001. Print.

Shelley, Percy Bysshe. *Selected Poems and Prose*. New Delhi: Penguin, 2017. Print.

Vivekananda, Swami. *Letters of Swami Vivekananda*. Calcutta: Ramkrishna Mission, 1970. Print.

Young, Robert. *White Mythologies*. London: Routledge, 1994. Print.

Chapter 33

Childhood Obesity in South Asia

Chaitali Bose and Alak Kumar Syamal

Obesity rate has increased globally over the past few decades. It poses a significant threat to public health as it incurs non-communicable diseases like Type 2 diabetes mellitus, hypertension, cardiovascular disorders, different cancers, liver diseases, gout and osteoarthritis.[1-3] The World Health Organization (WHO, 2018) in 2016, reported that almost 1.9 billion young adults (aged 18 years and older) were overweight and identified 650 million of them as obese. Among children and adolescents (aged 5-19 years) more than 340 million were overweight or obese and pre-schooler aged below five years also were not free from this adiposity, as 41 million of them were either overweight or obese.[4] Previously obesity was a matter of concern only in the economically enriched developed countries but over the past few decades due to socio-economic and nutritional transition, the wave of obesity has hit the economically backward developing countries as well. Undernutrition and infectious diseases which were predominant in the past now co-exist with 'excess fat' in those developing countries.

Obesity is considered as an accumulation of 'abnormal' or 'excess fat' that causes a risk to health. When the fat mass is stored excessively all over the body leading to more than 20% of the desirable body weight for height is called obesity. Childhood obesity becomes a health challenge for the policymakers in the 21st century. The WHO published a report on 'World Obesity Day' in 2017 which showed a tenfold rise in the number of obesity affected children and adolescents from the year 1975 (11 million obese) to 2016 (124 million obese) and estimated number of overweight children was 213 million.[5]

Obesity in childhood thrusts the children to become obese in later years and incurs life-threatening diseases in their early lives. Childhood obesity significantly affects a child's all-round development including physical, social, emotional and mental health. It also profoundly influences his or her academic outcome and self-esteem. An obese child has to go through a low-spirited life. Children who suffer from obesity may also experience glucose intolerance, insulin resistance, Type II diabetes mellitus, cardiovascular diseases, dyslipidemia, cholesterolemia, hypertension, obstructive sleep apnea, asthma, non-alcoholic fatty liver disease, cholelithiasis, cancer, improper balance and other orthopaedic problems.[6]

It is well-known that excess 'adiposity' is termed as obesity but there is no such agreement on the cut-off point for determining overweight or obesity in children and adolescents. U.S. Centres for Disease Control and Prevention (CDC) marks children or adolescents as 'overweight' or 'obese', whose Body Mass Index or BMI [weight (kg)/height (m^2)] are at 85th percentile - < 95th percentile or ≥ 95th percentile respectively for the same age and sex.[7] On the other hand, the WHO compares BMI to its growth standard median and measures the deviation to define overweight or obesity for varied age groups. From birth to 5 years BMI >2 SD and >3 SD above who growth standard median are considered as overweight and obesity respectively and for the age group 5-19 years, whose BMI >1 SD are grouped in overweight and those with BMI >2 SD are termed obese.[8] The International Obesity Task Force (IOTF) has also set an international cut point according to age and sex for determining adiposity in children belonging to the age group of 2 to 18 years.[9] Through this review, the author tried to emerge the present scenario of South Asian countries regarding obesity among children and adolescents and to highlight some corrective measures that can be adopted in time to intervene this health problem.

The Scenario in South Asia

The World Health Organization has declared that recently most of the overweight or obese children are living in developing countries and the obesity prevalence rate is also increasing there at a high pace. The WHO report (WHO, 2016) also claimed that the total number of overweight children below 5 years, living in Asian countries is actually the half of all under 5 overweight pre-schoolers in the world.[4] Not only the pre-school children but also the adolescents of Asian countries are suffering the most from the adiposity and it is varied from 24.5% in eastern Asian countries to 11.9% in western Asian regions. Data from different countries in Asia indicated diverse range of obesity, like 3.5% in rural Bangladesh to over 65% in the Maldives. Again 12.5% prevalence has been noticed among Chinese children to 30% was seen in countries like Iran or Saudi Arabia.[10]

Here among the south Asian countries, the author included countries like India, Bangladesh, Sri Lanka, Pakistan, Nepal and Bhutan under Indian subcontinent.

The Prevalence of Childhood Obesity among Different South Asian Countries

India: In our country obesity coexists with the curse of undernutrition and has become a leading health problem. In the following chart, the prevalence of obesity in different parts of the country and the studied population with the different cut off used has been presented.

Sl. No.	Author	Year	Region	Sample size	Age group	Method	Overweight prevalence	Obesity prevalence
1	Khadilkar et al.[11]	2011	DELHI, Chandigarh (North India), Kolkata (East India)	20243	2-17 yrs	IOTF-Cole et al.	14.9	4.70%
						WHO	11.1	15.9
2	Nayak et al.[12]	2011	Karnataka (South India)	2938	10-16 yrs.	WHO	7	5
3	Jagadesan et al.[13]	2014	Chennai (South India)	18955 (4703 Govt. school and 14252 private)	6-17 yrs.	IOTF	3% Govt. school, 17% private school	0.5% Govt. school, 4.4% private
						Khadilkar	6% Govt. school, 24% private	1.5% Govt. school, 12% private
4	Ghonge et al.[14]	2015	Pune (West India)	1281	10-15 yrs.	IOTF	9.99%	5.62%
5	Ahmed et al.[15]	2016	Maharashtra (West India)	360 (181 Urban & 179 Rural)	10-14 yrs.	Agarwal, K.N. et al.	Urban - 6.6%, Rural 3.4%	Urban - 2.2%, Rural 0.6%

6	Alok et al.[11]	2012	Surat (West India)	213 (Urban), 176 (Rural)	14-16 yrs.	IOTF- Cole et al.	Urban- 26%, Rural - 25.8%	Urban - 14.6%, Rural - 12.8%
7	Panda[16]	2017	Sambalpur (Eastern India)	600	10-15 yrs.	WHO	8.90%	3.40%

Nepal: Koirala et al. (2015) tried to measure the extent of obesity among children between 6-13 years at private schools in Lalitpur, a district of Nepal, which showed 14.6% overweight and 11.3% obesity.[17] Obesity prevalence was determined 3.3% among school going adolescents in Kaski district. Gurung et al. (2014) studied on 300 adolescents and pointed out overweight and obesity prevalence as 12% and 3.3% respectively in Belgaum, Nepal. Whereas in another study on early adolescents (10-13 years) Shakya et al. (2017) showed 8.8% overweight and 3.3% obesity prevalence in studied population.[18-20]

Bhutan: Norbu W. et al. (2017) investigated on 392 adolescents in Pemagatshel district, Bhutan and identified 7.1% and 1.5% overweight and obesity prevalence respectively.[21] In a study which summarized the result of the national nutritional survey from 2008, revealed pre-schooler Bhutanese have been suffering from the 'double burden of nutrition', where there are 34.9% stunting, 10.4% underweight, 4.7% severe wasting and at the same time 4.4% are suffering from overweight, well above from the average of South-East Asia.[22] According to the report of the World Bank prevalence of overweight in Bhutanese children is increasing for past two or three decades: 3.5% in 1986, 4.4% in 2008 and 7.6% in 2010.[23]

Bangladesh: A cross-sectional study across this country was done by Bulbul et al. in 2009 and reported that the obesity and overweight prevalence as 3.5% and 9.5% respectively among 6-15 years old Bangladeshi children and the urban group was more prevalent compared to the rural group.[24] Different studies on the school-going children from different areas in Dhaka district showed that the mean prevalence of overweight was 10% (10.2% boys and 9.8% girls) and obesity was 5% (4.3% in boys and 5.8% in girls). Rauniyar et al. (2018) in their study on (9-14 years) the primary school students in Dhaka found 12.9%

overweight and 10.9% obesity prevalence. Another community-based cross-sectional study in Bangladesh on pre-schoolers (4-7 yrs.) emerged that childhood obesity was perceived as a health problem by their mothers as 14% of the studied population (470) were either overweight or obese.[25-27]

Sri Lanka: Like other developing countries, Sri Lanka has also undergone nutritional transition along with socioeconomic changes, industrialization and urbanization. Study in the Colombo education zone identified the prevalence of overweight or obesity were 10.8% and 3.9% respectively within the school adolescents.[28] In a cross-sectional study in Colombo, involving 1347 children of the age group of 9-10 years explored that the prevalence of stunting was 3.8%, 16.6% underweight, 8.9% overweight and 5.1% was obesity.[29] Again in another study in the Batticaloa district of Sri Lanka, data indicated that the magnitude of obesity and overweight among adolescent girls was 9.4% and 5.5% respectively.[30]

Pakistan: Obesity or overweight and undernutrition also co-exist in Pakistani children. Warraich et al. (2009), in their study on school-going children (6th to 8th std.) in Karachi, found 6% obesity and 8% overweight prevalence and 70% of all obesity cases were present in a higher socioeconomic group.[31] Study in Hyderabad city of Pakistan reported 12% obesity and 8% overweight prevalence among students of 6th to 10th std. in both Govt. and private schools.[32] Among 293 school-going children in Lahore, Anwar et al. (2010) claimed that the obesity prevalence was 11.9% and 21.8% was overweight prevalence, whereas Mushtaq et al. (2011) who studied on 1860 school-going children of the age group 5-12 years, found 7.5% obesity and 17% overweight among those.[33-34] Another study in Karachi on school-going adolescents (11-15 yrs.) indicated 19% overweight and 10% obesity and which was more common in private schools.[35]

Associated Risk Factors Behind Obesity or Overweight Surge in South Asia

Asians have a genetic tendency to accumulate fat in abdominal regions, but not only genetics rather the interaction between genetics and environment results in this overweight or obesity prevalence. Studies of different authors from different countries reported that obesity or overweight is significantly associated with a sedentary lifestyle or physical inactivity, skipping breakfast, consumption of calorie-dense food, upper socio-economic level and urbanization. Industrialization, urbanization and globalization in developing countries over the past few decades have led to 'dietary shift' from traditional consumption of a nutritional food item to calorie-dense junk foods and also a shortage of playgrounds, having no playmate, loneliness, no outdoor game, convenient transport to schools, watching T.V. for hours or video gaming, use of smartphones all have thrust little lives to become overweight or obese.[6, 15, 17, 29, 32]

Preventive Measures

Prevention is the only way to control the current obesity surge. Preventive measures include primarily deterring obesity or overweight itself and secondarily hindering weight regain after losing weight. Preventive measures can be adopted better during childhood rather than adulthood and can be undertaken at home, school or community level. Developed countries like Australia, England, Canada or U.S.A. have implemented various health care strategies and programmes to bring changes in peoples' behaviour to combat excess fat.

Home-based strategies:

1. Restricting watching T.V. or video gaming or the use of smartphones not more than two hours.
2. Outdoor activities for at least 1 hour.
3. Restricting eating out on weekends or consumption of junk foods.

School-based strategies:

1. Providing health education to the students through the school curriculum.
2. Training to teachers regarding health education as they can play a vital role in the judicious selection of foods among their students.
3. Training to guardians on health education to build proper food behaviour at home.

4. Provision for Yoga classes.
5. Provision of playing outdoor games like basketball, dancing or swimming as co-curricular activities.
6. Organising inter or intra school tournaments of table tennis, badminton, cricket or football matches.

Community-based efforts like provision of the playground, swimming pool, children's Park in the neighbourhood will be helpful for children and adolescents to remain engaged with different physical activities. National policies and programmes could also play a pivotal role to promote healthy food consumption by countrymen.

This present analysis shows that the prevalence rate of obesity and overweight among children in South Asian countries is quite alarming. It is not only limited to any particular age group rather it has outreached to all covering from pre-schooler to adolescents and more common in private schools than government schools and associated with high socioeconomic status, high-calorie diet and sedentary life. Thus, interventions should be adopted either at home or school and community levels. National approaches are also needed to tackle this 'double burden' paradox effectively.

NOTES

1. Bray, G.A. "Medical Consequences of Obesity." *The Journal of Clinical Endocrinology and Metabolism,* 89.6 (2004): 2583-89. Print.
2. Finer, N. "Medical Consequences of Obesity." *Medicine,* 43.2 (2015): 88-93. Print.
3. Haslam, D.W. and W.P.T James. "Obesity." *The Lancet,* 366. 9492 (2005): 1197-1209. Print.
4. World Health Organization. "Obesity and Overweight." 16 Feb. 2018. Web. 17 Mar. 2019. <https://www.who.int/news-room/fact-sheets/detail/obesity-and-overweight>
5. World Health Organization. "Tenfold Increase in Childhood and Adolescent Obesity in four Decades: New Study by Imperial College London and WHO." 11 Oct. 2017. Web. 17 Mar. 2019. <https://www.who.int/news-room/detail/11-10-2017-tenfold-increase-in-childhood-and-adolescent-obesity-in-four-decades-new-study-by-imperial-college-london-and-who>
6. Sahoo, K., et al. "Childhood Obesity: Causes and Consequences." *Journal of Family Medicine and Primary Care,* 4.2 (2015): 187-92. Print.

7. Centers for Disease Control and Prevention. "Obesity and Overweight." 3 Jul. 2018. Web. 17 Mar. 2019. <https://www.cdc.gov/obesity/childhood/defining.html>

8. De, Onis M., et al. "Development of a WHO Growth Reference for School-aged Children and Adolescents." *Bull WHO,* 85.9 (2007): 660-67. Print.

9. Cole, T.J., et al. "Establishing a Standard Definition for Child Overweight & Obesity Worldwide: International Survey." *BMJ,* 320. 7244 (2000): 1240-43. Print.

10. Mazidi, M., et al. "Prevalence of Childhood and Adolescent Overweight and Obesity in Asian Countries: A Systematic Review and Meta-analysis." *Archives of Medical Science,* 14.6 (2018): 1185-1203. Print.

11. Ranjani, H., et al. "Epidemiology of Childhood Overweight & Obesity in India: A Systematic Review." *The Indian Journal of Medical Research,* 143.2 (2016): 160-74. Print.

12. Nayak, B. and Vinod H. Bhat. "Prevalence of Overweight/Obesity among School Children in Karnataka, South India." *International Journal of Public Health Research* (2011): 180-84. Print.

13. Jagadesan, S., et al. "Prevalence of Overweight and Obesity among School Children and Adolescents in Chennai." *Indian Pediatrics,* 51.7 (2014): 544-49. Print.

14. Ghonge, S., et al. "Prevalence of Obesity and Overweight among School Children of Pune city, Maharashtra, India: A Cross Sectional Study." *International Journal of Research in Medical Sciences,* 3.12 (2015): 3599-3603. Print.

15. Ahmed, M., K. Shah and V.Y. Kshirsagar. "Prevalence and Risk Factor for Obesity in Urban and Rural School-going Children of Karad Taluka, Maharashtra, India." *International Journal of Contemporary Pediatrics,* 3.4 (2016): 1389-93. Print.

16. Panda, S.C. "Overweight and Obesity and Lifestyle of Urban Adolescent School Children of Eastern State of India." *International Journal of Research in Medical Sciences,* 5.11 (2017): 4770-75. Print.

17. Koirala, M., et al. "Prevalence and Factors Associated with Childhood Overweight/Obesity of Private School Children in Nepal." *Obesity Research & Clinical Practice,* 9.3 (2015): 220-27. Print.

18. Pandey, A. and S. Sapkota. "Prevalence and Knowledge on Obesity among School Going Adolescents of Kaski, Nepal." *Journal of Nepal Paediatric Society,* 38.2 (2019): 63-68. Print.

19. Gurung, T. and V. Neginhal. "Overweight and Obesity among the Adolescent School Students in Belgaum City." *Journal of Nepal Medical Association,* 52.194 (2014): 791-95. Print.

20. Shakya, T., et al. "Overweight and Obesity among Early Adolescents from Goverment and Private Schools of Dharan, Nepal: A Comparative Study." *European Journal of Pharmaceutical and Medical Research,* 4.6 (2017): 315-19. Print.
21. Norbu, W., et al. "Obesity Prevalence and Contributing Factors among Adolescents in Secondary Schools in Pemagatshel district, Bhutan." International Journal of Adolescent Medicine and Health, 31.1 (2017). Web. 17 Mar. 2019. <https://www.degruyter.com/view/j/ijamh.2019.31.issue-1/ijamh-2016-0143/ijamh-2016-0143.xml>
22. Zangmo, U., M. De Onis and T. Dorji. "The Nutritional Status of Children in Bhutan: Results from the 2008 National Nutrition Survey and Trends Over Time." BMC Pediatrics, 12.151 (2012): 1-7. Print.
23. Atwood, Stephen J., et al. Nutrition in Bhutan: Situational Analysis and Policy Recommendations. Washington: The International Bank for Reconstruction and Development/The World Bank, 2014. Print.
24. Bulbul, T. and M. Hoque. "Prevalence of Childhood Obesity and Overweight in Bangladesh: Findings from a Countrywide Epidemiological Study." BMC Pediatrics, 14.86 (2014): 1-8. Print.
25. Sultana, N., et al. "Prevalence of Childhood Obesity and Undernutrition among Urban School Children in Bangladesh." Journal of Biosocial Science, 51.2 (2018): 244-53. Print.
26. Rauniyar, B.K., et al. "Prevalence of Obesity is Rising among Primary School Children in Dhaka city of Bangladesh." *Diabetes and Obesity International Journal,* 3.3 (2018): 1-6. Print.
27. Hossain, M.S., et al. "Is Childhood Overweight/Obesity Perceived as a Health Problem by Mothers of Preschool Aged Children in Bangladesh? A Community Level Cross-sectional Study." *International Journal of Environmental Research and Public Health* 16.2 (2019): 1-12. Print.
28. Hettiarachchi, J., et al. "Overweight and Obesity among Adolescent School Children in the Colombo Education Zone." *Journal of the Postgraduate Institute of Medicine,* 5.1 (2018): 1-7. Print.
29. Thilakarathne, R. and D. Wijesinghe. "Association between Nutritional Status and Lifestyle Practices of Primary School Children in the Colombo District: A Pilot Study." *Tropical Agricultural Research,* 22.4 (2011): 392-401. Print.
30. Karuppiah, D. and M. Markandu. "Prevalence of Obesity, Overweight and Central Obesity among Adolescent Girls in National School in Batticaloa District, Sri Lanka." *Sri Lanka Journal of Diabetes Endocrinology and Metabolism,* 8.1 (2018): 17-22. Print.
31. Warraich, H.J., et al. "Prevalence of Obesity in School-going Children of Karachi." *PLoS ONE,* 4.3 (2019): e4816. Print.

32. Ahmed, J., et al. "Prevalence of and Factors Associated with Obesity among Pakistani Schoolchildren: A School-based, Cross-sectional Study." *EMHJ—Eastern Mediterranean Health Journal,* 19.3 (2013): 242-47, Print.
33. Anwar, A., et al. "Prevalence of Obesity among the School-going Children of Lahore and Associated Factors." *Journal of Ayub Medical College Abbottabad: JAMC,* 22.4 (2010): 27-32. Print.
34. Mushtaq, M.U., et al. "Prevalence and Socioeconomic Correlates of Overweight and Obesity among Pakistani Primary School Children." BMC Public Health, 12.1 (2012): 532. Print.
35. Mansoori, N., et al. "Prevalence of Obesity and its Risk Factors among School Children in Karachi, Pakistan." *Tropical Doctor,* 48.4 (2018): 266-69. Print.

Chapter 34

Patriarchy and Female Subordination: Exploring the Equality Debate

Kauser Tasneem

Patriarchy believes in male superiority and female inferiority and is expressed in the form of male domination and female subordination. Patriarchal society denies gender equality. Individual expressions are particularly strong in areas of women's autonomy and individuality. In the public sphere, the man owns the socio-political and economic institutions of society. Man has power because of this ownership, and he uses this power to maintain his status quo in society. In the private sphere, a woman who makes a 'home' out of a house is not the decision-maker of the house. The story of mankind has been the story of this ownership and dependency which is articulately manoeuvred through the institution of 'patriarchy.' Half a section of society is subordinate to the 'other' half section of the society. A woman is perennially kept dependent by her systematic exclusion in economic organizations and in decision-making bodies of the legislature. In the private as well as the public arena, power always vests upon the male section of the society. Kamla Bhasin opines: "Patriarchy refers to male domination, to the power relationship by which men dominate women, and to characterize a system whereby women are kept subordinate in many ways" (3). At the same time, Walby defines "patriarchy as a system of social structures and practices in which men dominate, oppress and exploit women" (20).

Ethnic and religious groups strongly rally against any progressive step to bring about gender equality as they find it threatening. Patriarchy becomes more dangerous if it gets religious sanction. It is the patriarchal structure of a community that gender rules. Patriarchy also guides religious philosophy. The woman was assigned a secondary status who could not attain salvation. This assigning of the secondary role to women is seen even in religions which have female Goddesses. Manu Smriti states that is the duty of all husbands to exert total control over their wives (Chakravarty, 75, emphasis added).

The patriarchal divide between masculine and feminine has always been there. It is the divide that exists between the oppressor and the oppressed. Male and female roles are defined by society and are exercised through their culture. Women are perceived as being fragile and inconsistent. Therefore, there is a need to control them. Their sexuality needs to be controlled. Their resources need to be controlled. Men have an advantage over women by virtue of their strength. While men took charge of the finance, women were free to take care of the family without having the stress of earning an income. To be precise, Patriarchy is a socio-political system that believes in male superiority and the right of male to dominate. They do it "through institutions such as the academy, the church, the family, each of which justifies and reinforces women's subordination to men" (Millet, 35). Women were fed by patriarchy to believe that their oppression was divinely decreed. According to Aristotle: "males are active and females passive and a female was the mutilated male and because males are superior and women inferior 'the courage of man is shown in commanding and of woman in obeying'" (Lerner, 8-10).

In countries of South Asia—particularly India, Pakistan and Bangladesh acts of violence are blatantly glorified in the name of customs and traditions. 'Honor killing' is one such crime which does not have religious roots but cultural connotation. It is one of the most horrific crimes committed by family members on their own daughters. Family cannot accept their daughter defiling the family name and marrying someone from the lower caste and in order to remove the stain kill her. Ambreen 15, was dragged from her house, strangled, tied to a van and burnt because she had helped her neighbour elope. Qandeel Baloch was killed by her own brother because she had defied religious and cultural code. After her death, in October 2016, the Pakistan Government passed an anti-honour law which was an improvisation of the earlier law. In June 2002, Mukhtaran Mai of village Meerwala, Pakistan survived a gang rape which was an act of honour revenge dictated by a tribal council. She stood up against the odds to pursue the case. Her case was taken up by the international media. The death sentence was granted to six men and her crime was that her younger brother was having relation with a woman of the rival clan. Since then, she remains an outspoken advocate of women's rights. She won the North-South Prize of the Council of Europe in April 2007 and the *Glamour* magazine named her as The Woman of the Year 2005. On 13 March 2016, Kausalya of Udumalpet, Chennai married a Dalit boy. They were mercilessly killed in full public view. She survived and her testimony helped to bring death sentences against her father and five others. She asked the court to reject bail petitions 58 times (Chakravarty, 185). The 2011 draft legislation aims at preventing the honour killings and punishing the offender including the 'Khap Panchayats'. There has been a rise in the number of honour killings. The number of cases of fathers, brothers, uncles, and other relatives giving a death penalty to their daughters for choosing to marry across their caste is rising. Bangladesh has also an ideal patriarchal society. Violence against women manifests itself in various forms like honour killings, acid throwing and domestic violence in Bangladesh.

The Universal Declaration of Human Rights (UDHR), 1948 defines the family as the basic unit of society. The role of women is determined by the cultural construct of a community. Discrimination takes place in the name of religion. Personal laws are drafted by males without any participation of women. Gender relations are hierarchical in nature and are accepted as normal. Society endorses a variety of gendered practices like different sets of behaviour for men and women. The division of labour and resources is uneven. Customs and traditions, norms, and practices have limited the role of women in society. The portrayal of women in textbooks and media is responsible for building images that are difficult to erase. Men are always seen doing productive work whereas females are shown pursuing unproductive works. Boys should not cry. This asserts that boys are strong, and they should not exhibit weak emotions which are mostly associated with women. The accepted view on this believes that: "In social role theory, men and women learn femininity and masculinity through social conditions and even learn gender roles related to their biological gender through different actions with social structures" (Alsop et al., 66). Desai and Krishnaraj state that "a society gives expressions to female inferiority through symbols such as self-sacrificing, a pure image of a woman, a faithful wife, a devout mother" (Desai and Krishnaraj, 299). In order to build up a harmonious society, gender representation and portrayals should be de-stereotyped. Lim sees patriarchy as a "system of male domination and female subjugation in economy, society and culture that has characterized much of human history to the present day" (Lim, 220). So, "even when her right is legally recognized, long-standing customs prevent their full expression" (Beauvoir, 3-14).

Walby in his essay "Declining Significance or the Changing Forms of Patriarchy" says that patriarchy is "Systematically structured gender inequality" (Mogham, 21). Bhasin states "systematic deprivation and violence against women: rape, sexual harassment, sexual abuse, female feticide, Sati, dowry deaths, wife-beating, high level of female illiteracy, malnutrition, undernourishment and continued sense of insecurity keeps the women bound to home, economically exploited, socially suppressed and politically passive" (Bhasin, 13). History is witness to the suppression of women. It was the concerted efforts of the social reformers that many of these social evils were removed through legislation. The Constitution of India guarantees equality on the basis of sex. Yet, in reality, "the mobility of women is controlled and they have no right to decide whether they want to be mothers, the number of children they want to have whether they can use contraceptive or can terminate a pregnancy" (Bhasin, 6). Kate Millet introduced the concept of patriarchy to the feminist thought in the 1970s in a book called *Sexual Politics* which "opened a new discourse on a relationship between mind and body" (35-67). In the 17th century, it was used for monarchy power. Innumerable cases of domestic violence and rapes prove that even within the safe confines of their 'home', women are not safe. In the public sphere, women are exposed to sexual harassment.

Men have a large share in the economy, the corporate world and state and are parts of all the major decision-making bodies. The customs, traditions, and religious practices very effectively exclude women from socially productive work by emphasizing on their reproductive and nurturing role and this, in turn, leads to their marginalization in society. In the countries of South Asia like India, Pakistan, and Bangladesh, since birth girls are considered to be a liability. They are of less help on the farm, a threat of dowry persists and there is a strong linking of female virginity to the family honour. Gender inequality and human rights violation against women is common in South Asian countries. To undermine the patriarchal structure and reverse the process of discrimination, the legislature can be used as an effective and enabling tool. To bring about equality between men and women, the patriarchal ideology that dominates all aspects of human life needs to be removed. The Constitutional guarantee of equality should be strictly implemented. The astronomical rise in the number and intensity of crimes against women calls for heated debate and intense research on the subject and it needs to be seen through a humanistic perspective.

REFERENCES

Alsop, R., A. Fitzsimons and K. Lennon. *Theorizing Gender: An Introduction*. USA: Blackwell Publishers Inc., 2002. Print.

Beauvior, D.S. *The Second Sex*. New York: Vintage Books, 2011. 3-14. Print.

Bhasin, Kamla. *What is Patriarchy*. New Delhi: Kali for Women, 1993. Print.

Chakravarty, Uma. "Gendering Caste: Through a Feminist Lens." New Delhi. Sage Publications. 2018. 185. Print.

Chowdhury, Farah Deeba. "Theorising Patriarchy: The Bangladesh Context." *Asian Journal of Social Science*, 37.4 (2009): 599-622. *JSTOR*. Web. 15 May 2019. <https://www.jstor.org/stable/23655003>

Desai, Neera and Maithreyi Krishnaraj. "An Overview of the Status of Women in India in Manoranjan Mohanty." *Class, Caste, Gender*. New Delhi. Sage Publication, 2004. Print.

Jeyasanthi, V., S. Maheleswari and R. Abirami. "Honour Killing: A National Outcry." *College Sadhana—Journal for Bloomers of Research*, 6.2 (2014): 917-24. Print.

Lerner, G. *The Creation of Patriarchy*. New York. Oxford University Press, 1989. 8-10. Print.

Lim, Y.C. Linda. "Capitalism, Imperialism and Patriarchy: The Dilemma of Third World Women Workers in Multinational Factories." *Women, Men, and the International Division of Labor*. Eds. C.J. Nash, Fernández-Kelly and María Patricia. New York: State University of New York Press, 2001. Print.

Millet, Kate. *Sexual Politics*. United States: Columbia University Press, 2016. 35-67. Print.

Mogham, V., ed. *Patriarchy and Economic Development: Women's Position at the End of Twentieth Century*. UK: Oxford Clarendon Press, 1996. 21-29. Print.

Walby, S. *Theorizing Patriarchy*. United States: John Wiley & Sons, 1990. Print.

Chapter 35

Story of Progress: A Study of Narikuravar Tribes in Eraiyur Village at Perambalur District of Tamil Nadu

K. Subapriya

Korwa is a community who could be seen all over India and are found highly concentrated in places such as Mirzapur, Lalitpur, Jalaun, Kanpur, Etawah, Agra in Uttar Pradesh, Bihar, and Madhya Pradesh. According to a legend, Kor means men and so they believe that they were created when God created men. Two types of notions prevail that the word had its origin from the Dravidian language with the term KU standing for Earth or Mount and sometimes it represents even fortune-telling.

In general, they use both Hindi language and Devanagiri script for intra- and intergroup communications. They prefer non-vegetarian to vegetarian. They have four endogamous and four exogamous groups, namely Dih Korwa, Darn Korwa, Pahar Korwa, Agaria Korwa and Gularia, Haril, Huhar, Munda, Mura, Paari, and Lethi respectively. Mahato, the traditional panchayat heads the meetings and solves the community problems. Women and men are given equal status. Both for birth and death, ten days of strict restrictions are observed. Ancestor worship is strictly followed. The family deity is Sitladevi, the village deity is Dih and the regional deity is Jwalamukhi.

Even the Korwas follow a caste system. They accept food and water from Nai, Ahir, Bania, Chero, Panika, Gond, Kharwar and not from the Chamar, Dharkar, Dom, Dhobi, and Ghasia. Earlier they did not give priority to education but currently one could observe a sea change. All the afore-listed detail gives the general picture of Korwa community. The forthcoming section is especially an ethnographic monograph of Korwa clan in Perambalur district. This particular Korwa clan which has been taken for the study is located in the outskirts of Eraiyur village. The dwellings of Korwa clan are surrounded by hectors of sugarcane field. It is a typical traditional clan with a limited number of families and homes which are situated together for sociability and defence. They have a school, playground, and grocery shops exclusively for themselves.

The study of their lifestyle and progress gives an entirely different outlook for these people, who are in general known for their uncleanliness and ignorance. They have their own style of living which is entirely different from Korwas who dwell in North India. Even the custom and habit varies. In the forthcoming section of the article, the term Korwa has been replaced by Kuravar which is the terminology used in southern dialect. This is the success story of a clan who have mislabelled all the ill terms which denoted them previously and has emerged with a bright life filled with good ideas and notions. The study of this clan includes their tradition and believes, mode of worship, marriage and morality, language, the present state of their education and occupation.

"Oosi mani, pasi mani vangaliyo sami, vango sami, vangungo sami" (the way of address by Kuravars to sell their petty goods in public places)—this recurring voice which we hear in the train, bus or any other marketplace is passed unnoticed by us in our rushing hour. This voice which calls with respect for their hungry stomach evades from our mind in a fraction of second. How far we think about them? A study of Narikuravars in Narikuravar colony, Perambalur District reveals a story of progress. This study exposes us to a part of society which has passed through tough times and now stands on the pedestal of success. Nambiyar, the President of the Narikuravar's colony gives the history of that particular locality. Nambiyar was the first man in his clan to complete ITI in Instrumentation Mechanics as early as 1987. He had his school education at Saidapet (Chennai), which is a school especially run for Narikuravars by Mr. Ragupathy and

Ms. Gnanasundari. He is aware of the state of Narikuravars both from Tamil Nadu and about other parts of India. He gives a detailed study of the present settlement. There are nearly one hundred and twenty-six families with five hundred and eighty-seven members, out of whom seven are physically challenged. These clans of people are basically nomads. So, it is impossible for them to point out a particular place as their native town but still, they vaguely remember that their previous generation moved from Aathur (Salem District of Tamil Nadu) to the present location (Eraiyur of Perambalur District), around 1977.

Narikuravar's tradition and believes are quite interesting. It is indispensable to study one's tradition since, it is this set of customs and believes, which are passed from one generation to other often orally becomes a major case study of one's cultural phenomenon from the past. To begin with, they don't have any specific reasons for their name Narikuravars but they believe that since their favourite food is fox ('Nari' in language Tamil) they might have been labelled so. They are good at hunting. A myth prevails that during the reign of Shivaji, the Maratha ruler a certain set of people were chased to the forest. The Kuravars are believed to be their descendants. Initially, they began to hunt to appease their appetite which later became their sport too. Even now in these modern times, their offsprings show a special taste and curiosity for hunting. They have truly inherited a real enthusiasm for hunting from their forefathers. At present government has cancelled the license for using a gun, so only five in their clan have the license.

They love to walk a lot. They have a special interest in the field of dancing. They are good at herbal treatment too. They live a long life. The general life span of a man in this community is high when compared to that of all the other communities. Women of this clan have high resistance power and they do have the ability even to bear 70 kg weight on the head. They rarely go to hospitals but now they feel that one of the major reasons for their health breakdown at present is due to settlement in one place. Their way of naming the children is quite interesting. They name the children with the name of the place they are born. So, one can come across the name such as Thozhudhur, Perambalur (name of places) and Mittai which means chocolate referring to the birth of a child in a chocolate shop. Generally, these people detest having communication with the outside world. They like to remain in a cloister.

Tradition and belief also include the mode of worship. Those who believe that the Sun is a God will report that the Sun is a God. So, worship is naturally based on belief and it forms a part of the tradition. In the case of Korwa community too worship plays a major role, since a man's life is estimated worthy according to the number of worships he has conducted. Mostly they sing songs only in praising God. They primarily worship Goddesses. The two major goddesses are Madurai Meenakshi and Maakali (name of deities). They sacrifice goats for Madurai Meenakshi and bulls for Mahakali (sudukattukali). Their first sacrifice is offered to Sun God. Each and every family has their own personal God 'kuladeivam'. Nearly sixteen such gods are worshipped. They don't have temples built with great architectural works. Unlike the practice of common Hindus in Tamil Nadu who especially place their gods in Isanya moolai which refers to a particular spot at home for worship, they use the 'vadamerku' (northwest) corner for placing the Goddesses.

Only men can conduct worship. Women pay their homage to God from four or five feet of distance. They are strictly prohibited from using red skirts since the colour red is sacred for Mahakali and jasmine too should not be used since it is offered to goddesses. For worshipping, every family has its own statue made up of silver. It is systematically passed from one generation to the other. It is safely placed inside a bamboo box. These statues are exclusively made at places like Thiruvannamalai, Aathur, and Salem districts of Tamil Nadu. Their style of worship also resembles Islam and Christianity. Their God-fearing nature forbids them from committing sins. Even if they do, they confess it in front of everyone and try to overcome their guilt by some compensation. The Tamil month Chittirai (April) is the auspicious month for them. They celebrate the day of Thiruvannamalai Deepam by preparing roti (wheat bread).

Marriage is one another ceremony which is conducted in a very systematic way. In this clan, it is conducted between only two different sets of people. People who sacrifice goats are one group while the people who offer a bull as the sacrifice forms another group. A man who belongs to the set of people sacrificing goat cannot marry a girl from the same group. They are considered to be brothers and sisters. They use karugumani (black beads) as the sacred thread instead of 'thali' (thread tied during the marriage in Tamil community). Elders conduct the marriage. Love marriage is strictly prohibited, especially in the case of girls. If at all a boy elopes, he is taken back into the community after performing certain rituals. In arranged marriages, men give the dowry. Initially, it started at 12 rupees. According to economic status, it varies. In Coimbatore currently, it goes up to more than Rs. 25000. Though they are ardent Hindus, at times there are conversions, however, they come back to their original religion during the time of marriage, since it is difficult to find the bride or bridegroom.

They follow a strict moral code. Their high concerned for morality has yielded them a good result. There is not a single AIDS-affected person in this clan. Before fifty years women were strictly prohibited from staying outside after six o'clock in the evening. They state that their women were restricted not because of the distrust but because of a sense of protecting them.

Further to deal with their language, the language spoken by them is called as 'Patani' language. This language is said to be a mixture of all the other languages. Even one could trace the words from English, German, and some Dravidian languages too. The language has no script. It is only in oral form. Their language is at the brink of destruction. Elderly people of the clan alone talk this language with fluency. Younger generation talks in the Tamil language rather than using their mother tongue.

Apart from studying their tradition, culture, and language, it is now essential to study their present state. At present in this Kuravar's colony children goes to school and there are a few graduates at present. They insist that at this modern age education is indispensable for both the genders. There is a separate school which runs for them with hostel facilities. It operates under the scheme of Sarva Siksha Abhiyan.

Awareness among these people is incredible. They show a good deal of improvement in their occupation. Nearly sixteen families in the clan have stopped with a single child. Eighty percent of the people have taken a giant leap of success. They visit foreign countries with a tourist visa and develop their business both in India and abroad. They have built their own sophisticated house with all types of equipment in the land provided by the government. Though the government has just given the token for the land instead of pattas (slip denoting a recognized land), they themselves have taken steps to get the connection for drinking water facility.

There are many women who actively take part in self-employment programs. Their minimum level of educational qualification is eight standards. Almost all the family use a gas stove and they can cater to their basic needs. Mr. Nambiyar, the president of this colony has also initiated an organization called 'Sonagiri Organization' to help their clan of people. He gets the guidance from the head of Kuravar's Association.

Perambalur is basically a drought-stricken district. So, the lands are arid in nature. Due to the lack of proper experience in the field of agriculture, they could not be successful in producing a good yield. However, they are good at selling artificial jewellery which is designed with corals and pearls. They also shine in the field of selling auspicious rosaries. They usually buy accessories from Delhi. Other spots of purchase include Mathura (Uttar Pradesh), Gujarat, and Hyderabad. Their sale is good in India since the country consists of more than 65% of Hindus. Some men are good at making crackers. They are also well known for making tattoos.

Earlier they faced two major problems. They demanded the status of SC and ST and they also expected the government to settle their land disputes. According to the government order 666, Narikuravars were transferred from BC to MBC in the year 1975. And in addition, it has been stated that if the government wishes so, they can be given allowances like the SCs and the STs.

Only in case of Tamil Nadu, Narikuravars were stated as MBC while all over India they are listed in SC and ST. A group of people appealed in Delhi for transferring them to SC category. The news has been published in *The Hindu* newspaper dated 5 December 2006. Right now, they have won their demands after much patience and protest. There are few drawbacks like as they are of nomadic habit, they are not able to exercise their voting right properly. Despite their hard work, they are subdued by other caste people. At times children are ill-treated in school even by teachers. They look up for more concessions and support from the government.

To conclude, their sense of ambition and aspiration is highly appreciable. They regret that so far only two persons from their community are well placed. One works in Karur Vysya Bank while others hold the job of the surveyor. They aspire to elect a Member of Parliament from their community to voice out and solve their problems. Narikuravars of this colony present a total contrast with a few other Narikuravars who refuse to change with time. Kuravars of this clan readily accommodate themselves to sweeping changes. This clan of people is in no way inferior to others. They too have a strong sense of the religious and cultural background. One of the most celebrated siddhar of Hindu religion too belongs to this Kuravar community. From the songs of siddhar Bogar's "Bogar 7000", following information about Sri Kamalamuni Siddhar can be obtained.

Song No. 5729 gives the detail about his birth that he was born on the Tamil month of Vaikasi (May-June), while song No. 5725 tells that he belongs to Kuravar social group. Kuravars are closely associated with Tamil God Murugan. People who are ready to accept them as fortune tellers and worship them when they are called as siddhars refuses to treat them with equality when coming into the terms of society. They tend to discriminate, ill-treat and discard them. The general notions about the Kuravars are shattered by the strong will of Narikuravars from Eraiyur. The people who looked down them have raised their brows in admiration. They should further extend their support for their progress.

REFERENCES

Beteille, Andre. *Caste, Class and Power: Changing Patterns of Stratification in a Tanjore Village*. 2nd ed. New Delhi: Oxford University Press, 1996. Print.

Singh, K.S., ed. *The Scheduled Castes*. Delhi: Oxford University Press, 2002. Print.

Karthikeyan, Divya. "ST status now a reality, but long road ahead for Narikuravers and Kuruvikarans." thenewsminute.com. *The News Minute*, 1 June 2016. Wed. 26 May 2019. <https://www.thenewsminute.com/article/st-status-now-reality-long-road-ahead-narikuravars-and-kuruvikarans-44178>

"Yekalavya warriors: Indigenous people of South India." yerukaladetails.blogspot.com. Details of Yerukala, 14 Jan. 2008. Wed. 15 Dec. 2018. <http://www.yerukala.info/blogs>

Chapter 36

Scroll Paintings of Naya: A Study of the Cultural Shift from Myth to Modernity

Nabanita Dhali

The word 'Patua' can be associated with 'Pat' meaning picture or canvas. To be very precise Pat means a piece of painted cloth. In Sanskrit, 'Pattabastra' means silken cloth. It also could be the canvas made of jute to be used for painting. 'Pata' could be divided into two types, 'chauka' or square and the 'jorano' or scroll. The Patua narrates the story in the form of songs and shows the pictures by unrolling the bottom of the scroll and rerolling the top. The Patua travels from door to door and draws the attention of the villagers while begging for money or rice because they are financially weak. The most prominent subject matter of the Pat was Hindu mythological stories, the ideas of Heaven and Hell along with the God of death Yama and the physical torture inflicted by him on the sinners. The Santhal pat precisely deals with the origin of the tribe and their religious beliefs. There are Manasha pat, Ramayan pat, Gazi pat and other different pats dedicated to gods or goddesses. Here, the focus is not on the definition or technique but the attempt at interpreting the transformation of the scroll paintings of Naya (Midnapore) as a journey from tradition to modernity.

Patua is a Bengali term used to denote a particular group of scroll painters who often used the term as their surname. Patuas are also known as Chitrakarsor painters. To know the origin of the Patua community, there are no sources except mythology and oral history. The most common of them is the story of Vishwakarma and Ghritachi. Vishwakarma cursed Ghritachi to be born on earth as a low caste Shudra where she gave birth to nine sons, known as Navashakha. The Navashakha were divided into nine different low castes and nine types of artisans, and the Chitrakar is one of them. This mythic story suggests that the Chitrakars were low caste Hindus. Chitrakar and Patua were not the same at first. The Chitrakars or painters began to show their scroll paintings with the accompaniment of narrative songs for money. In the *Brahmavaibartha Purana*, it is explained that the Brahmins cursed the Chitrakar community for painting untraditional pictures and their art forms were discredited. Gradually, the Patuas and the Chitrakars became synonymous. There are plenty of other mythological stories associated with the Patuas about their origin, identity, and evolution. These stories found reflection in their earlier works.

David J. McCutchion and Suhrid Kumar Bhowmik consider the documentation of the development and styles of pat art extremely tiresome and inauthentic as there are no precise records of the actual dates of these paintings. Gurusaday Datta tried his best to record the exact stages. He divided the Patua repertoire into three categories: Heroism or epic narrative, worldliness or secular, and spiritual quests. The Patuas were inspired by Bengali Mangalkavyas for painting and composing apocryphal versions. The episodes of religious conflicts were mostly painted to depict the plight of Manasha. There are plenty of other pats in the same genre—Krishna Lila pat by Ganga Manna depicting the mischievous episodes associated with Krishna, Ganga pat by Jamuna Chitrakar about the river Ganga as a deity, Ganesha pat by Gurupada Chitrakar narrating the myth of Ganesha's Elephant head, Ramayana pat by Rahman Chitrakar, etc.

There are references to Patuas in Sanskrit plays mostly in *Harsha Charitam* and *Mudra Rakhshasa*. In these two books, the Patuas are found singing Yama patas. Yama or the God of death was a common subject matter of scroll painting from the medieval period. The Patuas were not allowed to use Sanskrit as they belonged to the lower caste. They used mostly Prakrit while singing Yama pats. In *Patua Art and the Women Patuas of Midnapur*, Suhrid Kumar Bhowmik translates a Yama pat song depicting the power of Yama as mightiest of all gods:

"You worship the feet of Yama, the king of death, what is the necessity of worshipping the other gods" (*Patua Art and the Women Patuas of Medinipur*, 11).

The Yama pat consists mainly of the after-judgment by Yama, namely sufferings, misery, and pain in hell and then rewards in Heaven. The paintings associated with Hell are usually hideous and detestable. The manner of these paintings is vulgar and crude. The visual images of the dreaded figure of Yama punishing the sinners used to torment the common people with the fear of punishment in Hell. The pat usually ended with the Hell scene. In *Charyapada*, there is a reference to the Chitrakars who painted Yama pat. Munidatta wrote: "In this world, like other animals, the artist himself is afraid of the pictures of the Yaksha (Yama) drawn by himself" (*Patua Art and the Women Patuas of Medinipur*, 12).

The Bengali pats of Naya represented sophistication as a form of art. It matured into a modern style under the influence of the Mughals and the Europeans. The earliest scrolls of Midnapore managed to preserve its tradition before the independence of India. The Patua people belonged to one of the lowest strata of Hindu caste hierarchy. The social history of Bengal unveils the fact that the domination of the upper castes backed by Royal patronage over the common people, particularly the low caste, made the latter adopt Islam in expectation of some relief from this oppression. The new Muslim rulers like Muhammad Bakhtiyar Khilji who invaded Bengal in 1202 promoted Islam as a shelter for the low castes. Most of the Patuas embraced Islam but they could not do away with the Hindu subject matter from their scrolls because of their popularity. They were well accustomed with Hindu mythologies and the main source of their income came from narrating those stories. So, the Patuas' identity was ambiguous, and they concealed their acquired Islamic ways from the Hindus. With the decline of Muslim rule and the advent of British power in India, they reverted to Hinduism. The traits of Islamic culture and the Hindu mythologies together transformed the social status of the scroll painters as more anomalous and degraded.

According to Sankar Sen Gupta in his book *The Patas and the Patuas of Bengal* (1973), from the 12th century onwards, several political upheavals helped Patua artists to witness a number of shifts in style and practice. Their artworks mirror the shifts in their religious conversion, Hinduism to Islam and vice-versa. The community is still suffering extensively from economic disparity, the oscillation between two religious identities and caste hierarchy. According to Binoy Bhattacharya in his article "The Patuas—A Study on Islamization", Patuas are a composite community oscillating "between the Hindus and Muslims" and he provides significant information from a field survey that is 90% of the Patuas had two names, two different surnames. The dubious identity of the Patuas reflects on the Pat of Gazi. A Muslim Chitrakar can paint scrolls on Hindu gods and goddesses. Gazi pat and Santhal pat remained completely traditional, while most of the scrolls of Midnapore changed.

Religious pats were the most popular with epic and puranic myths. The oral history and mythical stories were closely associated with the common people. The scroll paintings never fail to reflect the current scenario of society, the painters' role as entertainers and the impact produced by them on cultural values. This transition raises the question of the freedom of art and its capacity to relate to contemporary culture.

Rahman Chitrakar's Gazipir pat, Ganga Manna's Hindu-Muslim pats, Mantu Chitrakar's Babri Masjid pat delve deep into this fact of religious and cultural amalgamation of Hindu and Muslims. Ganga Manna showed that the villagers of Naya stayed together without any communal disturbance by painting a Hindu worshipping a god while the Muslims are performing *namaj* at the same point of time. The painting on the demolition of Babri Masjid too seeks communal harmony between the two religions and focuses on a humanitarian and secular outlook. The most popular among them was the scroll painting on Gazipir. The myth of Kalugazi and Satyapir have been depicted in Gazipata as a strategy to spread Islam. The tendency of establishing Islam over Hinduism was the initial purpose of it. Later, the Satyapir was co-related with Satyanarayana of Hindu Mythology. The Patuas of Naya combined both religions in such a unified way that one can easily find structural similarities in the case of Gazi pat and Mangal Kavya pat. The narrative song of the pat translated by Suhrid Kumar Bhowmik in the collection of songs by David J. McCutchion is identified as an attempt to unite them: "He is known as Lord Narayan among the Hindus and Pir among the Muslims. He has appeared to receive worship from both the communities" (*Patuas and Patua Art in Bengal*, 40). Even Frank Korom mentions in *Village of Painters* how Shyamsundar Chitrakar sung about the deity while showing his Gazipir scrolls: "O Satyanarayan! Where are you [...] you are Narayan to the Hindus and pir to the Muslims" (*Village of Painters*, 68).

The narrative addresses the socio-religious issue of Hindu-Muslim interaction and finally uses a secular aside with comical elements and religious instructions. The Patuas paid little attention to the doctrinaire aspects of their ever-changing religious faiths. What they embraced was to save their skin more than their souls. The establishment of British rule and the impact of Western influence replaced the old cultural values and tastes. Scroll paintings lost their popularity and Patuas began to look for other occupations. Some social reform organizations like 'Arya Samaj', the 'Hindu Mahasabha' and the 'Bharat Sevasram Sangha' reinforced the Hindu Revivalist Movement by performing purification rites known as *Suddhi*. At this point of time, the patuas were persuaded to re-embrace Hinduism. In *Village of Painters*, Frank Korom mentions that he met Dulal Chitrakar, Satish Chitrakar, and Ananda Malakar who admitted that their families had undergone purification rituals for survival. Dinabandhu Goshwami of Nabadwip, Dr. S.K. Roy of Katwa, Swami Satyananda and others initiated the reconversion of the Patuas between 1886-1929. The Hindu Muslim Riot of 1946 in Calcutta worsened the situation and the Patua families were forced to perform the rituals. Gurudas Chitrakar and his Bangiya Chitrakar Unnayan Samiti organized meetings and distributed leaflets to reunite the community and tried to provide respectable status for them in the Hindu social order by re-embracing Hinduism.

After independence and the general election in 1952 and 1957, the Patuas being low caste Hindus had the opportunity to get stipends and other facilities. Their efforts to re-enter the mainstream failed due to caste prejudices. They suffered from a feeling of estrangement from both communities. So, they chose to be identified with both religions and focused more on contemporary topics and major historical events. Dukhushyam Chitrakar and Rani Chitrakar deliberately showed the influence of British rule in their Sahib pats. The most common of them is the opening panel of the Sahib pat depicting a freedom fighter being punished for insubordination. Sahib pats represented the freedom fighters of the pre-independence period, the Bhadralok culture of Kolkata and how the disillusioned middle class was trying to adopt the Western culture. Manu Chitrakar's Tram journey pat shows different modes of transportation in Kolkata and praises the tram because it can be afforded by poor people. Rani Chitrakar painted the funeral ceremony of Mother Teresa in Kolkata and compares her with the Hindu Goddess Durga. She even tried to portray the deaths of Indira Gandhi and Rabindranath Tagore. Jamuna Chitrakar tried to present the culture of Kolkata immediately after independence where people are running to cinema halls to watch movies. Rahman Chitrakar narrates his father's story of selling pats in Kolkata in his Strange Kolkata pats. In the opening panel, a rural patua finds it difficult to cope with the modernity of Kolkata. The Bhadraloks plan to buy his scrolls at a low price and sell them abroad. Thus, the art form faced a considerable threat and the financial condition of scroll painters remained poor. Naya was quite far from Kolkata. The Chitrakars began to recontextualize the parables to make them relevant to the modern-day.

Social awareness, the importance of literacy, elections, birth control, ecological awareness and disease like AIDS gradually became parts of the subject matter of the scroll paintings. These scrolls are mostly the outcome of finding new ways to market their craft. The traditional custom of preserving scrolls became almost obsolete, song performances were neglected. Still, some scroll painters like Gurupada, Manu, Swarna, Rani continued the legacy of composing new songs in accordance with the new themes. But most of them are illiterate and unable to go beyond their mother tongue. Even the movie *Titanic* is used to create a magical pat where Swarna Chitrakar depicts the reason for the fatal crash as the retribution of love between a high-class lady with a poor painter.

The historical events became a part of their art form through juxtaposition with traditional repertoire. The patua community successfully managed to make the transition from a mere depiction of oral histories and epics to the questioning of modern events and their consequences. The local tradition thus entered the boundary of globalization and became an excellent example of evolutionary change. Gurupada Chitrakar's scroll on the Atom Bomb recognizes the power of science in destroying two cities within a few seconds. Similarly, the Tsunami pat and earthquake pat conclude the fact that humans and science are still powerless before nature. The traditional pat of Fish wedding highlights the social belief that big fishes symbolize wealth and power. It is based on the fairy tale of fish marriage where the big fish takes revenge for not being invited there. In real life, the big fish symbolizes terrorists who kill numerous innocents without any hesitation. The terrorist attack in New York in 2001 orchestrated by Osama Bin Laden played a notable role in Rabbani Chitrakar's Laden pat where Laden is being portrayed as a horse rider, fleeing to Tora Bora of Afghanistan. In such paintings, the painters had limited information about the actual events. So, they had to rely upon their artistic acumen to represent their art form interestingly as a re-enactment of events. The gang-rape case in Delhi on 16 December 2012 influenced the scroll painters of Naya to voice their protest through the Nirbhaya pat. The Nirbhaya pat undoubtedly tried to accommodate the incident and how the reality of Nirbhaya's traumatic death cracked the glass ceiling of society. People from all over the world protested against such a heinous crime. Reality and imagination are interfused in these types of pats.

The scroll painters of Naya consciously allowed new themes to expand the ideas together with their own aesthetic sensibility. The scroll painters began to work hard to connect traditional artistry with actual events, discarding the myths and oral histories. Still, they never neglected their traditional roots and moved beyond local and regional dimensions to discuss elite discourses of national and international significance. The aesthetic value and artistic merit of their pats reached the climactic point by dealing extensively with the issue of modernity.

REFERENCES

Bhattacharya, Binoy. "The Patuas: A Study of Islamization." *The Patas and the Patuas of Bengal.* Ed. Sankar Sengupta. Calcutta: Indian Publications, 1973. 95-100. Print.

Bhattacharya, Malini. *Patua Art and the Women Patuas of Medinipur.* Jadavpur University: School of Women Studies, 2004. Print.

Dutt, Gurusaday. "The Art of Bengal." *The Modern Review* (May 1932): 519-29. Print.

—. *Folk Arts and Crafts of Bengal: The Collected Papers.* Calcutta: Seagull Books, 1990. Print.

Korom, Frank J. and Paul J. Smutko. *Village of Painters: Narrative Scrolls from West Bengal*: Santa Fe: Museum of New Mexico, 2006. Print.

McCutchion, David and Suhrid Bhowmik. *Patuas and Patua Art in Bengal.* Calcutta: KLM Private Ltd., 1999. Print.

Paṇḍa, Dipak Kumar Baṛa. *Patua Sanskriti: Parampara o Paribartan.* Calcutta: Satabdi Prakashan, 1999. Print.

Chapter 37

Ritual, Body, Ecology—Interrogating Politics Involved in the Celebration of 'Menstruation' in the *Raja* Festival of Odisha

Pragnya Parimita Chayani

'Ritual', 'Body', 'Ecology' are quite distinct from each other. However, the paper ventures to interconnect these three strings by analysing Odisha's 'Raja' festival. Odisha is famous for its rich culture, festivals, Jagannath cult and religious inclination. 'Raja' is one of the famous festivals that helps in bringing a cultural uniformity among Odia. Since rituals are a display of culture, it is a vital variable to study culture and 'Raja' helps in forming a clear understanding of Odia culture. The present paper analyses the values and beliefs underlie Raja that celebrates the menstruation cycle of Mother Earth. Moreover, the paper ventures to show the politics implied in common Odia myths, beliefs surround the rituals of 'Raja', worshipping the mother Earth as the provider of food, and considering women as symbols of *Gaia*[1], yet confining their 'impure' (menstruated) body.

Ritual[2]

By looking at rituals from "historical, ethnographic or visual, grounds" (Kreinath, 75), the paper ventures to align with theorist Michel Foucault that knowledge is created. In addition, rituals create knowledge by repeated performance, over a period of time. Ronald Barthes's "myth is created" (*Mythology*, 1957) is also applied to see how meanings are thrust upon varied signs (here cultural performances), which ultimately becomes knowledge or culture.

> Banaste dakila Gaja, barasake thare aasichhi Raja,
> asichi raja lo gheni nua sajabaja.
>
> (The elephant is trumpeting in the forest since it is Raja, which comes once a year with pomp and pleasure of newness)

Raja (pronounced as raw-jaw) is an Odia festival, which is celebrated for three consecutive days (in Odia, *raw-jaw parba*), falls on *Mithuna* Sankranti (as per lunar calendar) and as per Christian calendar, in mid-June. The beginning of the solar month of Mithuna from which the 'season of rains' starts is begun with the second day of the festival. It is a celebration of the rain and it marks the beginning of agriculture. The word 'raja' means the menstrual cycle. Mythology attached to this festival is that the wife of Hindu god Lord Vishnu, the goddess Earth, goes through her menstrual cycle during these three days. Hence, women, considered as mother figures, are given a break from household chores; they wear new clothes, eat a special kind of rice cake made in this festival (*podapitha*) and chew beetle leaf (*paan*), swing, and sing songs dedicated to the festival. Since the goddess Earth is believed to be on her menstrual cycle and needs rest, women are not allowed to touch the ground on barefoot lest it hurt her (the earth). Some places allow women to wear shoes made of barks. The fourth day, which is known as "Vasumati Snan" is a day of 'purification rituals' after the menstrual cycle, owing to the traditional belief that a woman is impure during her cycle and needs to be purified once the cycle gets over. During the process, women bathe and worship a grinding stone as a symbol of the goddess Earth. Since the stone is bathed, the process is famous as *snan*. 'Raja' also marks an auspicious beginning of agriculture. So, ploughing tools are worshipped before the use. Once the festival is over, Odias believe that the earth and the sky will be united by raindrops to bless the world with crops as like as a woman becomes fertile after her menstruation cycle. In many temples of Odisha, there are idols of 'bhudevi' or the goddess Earth, which are worshipped during 'Raja' and get bathed on the fourth day, which is believed/considered as a purification process of the idol.

Body

The Anthropological study involves a careful look at the rituals since rituals form a part of the political life concerned (*Ritual, Politics, and Power*). As a result of the study, a vivid picture of the culture deepens the understanding of it. According to 'Foucauldian' discourse, which focuses on the interrelationship between power and society, rituals, which are deeply connected to emotions can be a medium, where cultural power operates. People innocently believe in their culture and consequently, offer themselves to be surveilled by the panoptic surveillance of cultural politics. Other than that, the culture creates an identity since its agenda in the form of rituals are followed. It is rightly asserted that: "We recognize that the practice of our rituals and heritage provide the basis for religious identity and community in a society that is increasingly complex, varied, and secular" (LaMothe, 54).

Since 'Raja' is celebrated by a large number of people, it has its place in the socio-cultural life of Odisha and cultural politics manifests in the mass celebration of it. To mention those politics, firstly, the festival celebrates menstruation, hence celebrates womanhood/femininity. However, this action categorizes menopausal women and girls/women with irregular/no menstruation, as un-women/unfeminine. Hence, the image of women, which underlies 'Raja' rituals, is anti-feminist. A deep inclination towards it also affects the place of Odia women in their society, both in their family, as in a private space and in public, which is a male-dominated society. These rituals have also created conservative notions that a woman is a woman if she is fertile and a menstruated woman is a dirty woman, an omen—this notion is thrust on women, who observe and who participate. Secondly, in Odisha, there is a strange custom of restricting a girl/woman to four walls if she gets her menstruation cycle during 'Raja'. On one hand, a ritual is worshipping the mother Earth for being fertile due to her menstruation cycle and on the other hand, it detests, if a woman experiences the same. Aligning with Roland Barthes, the cultural theorist whose seminal work, *Mythologies* (1957) deals with his arguments that myth is a construct, the present paper, thirdly, argues that culture is a construct. With time, cultural values, beliefs, and behaviour change due to political interventions. Subsequently, through multiple ways, these cultural changes penetrate the social life and as a result, systems are made, remade, and becomes a complex procedure, not easy to explain. Additionally, cultural politics plays a vital role in remaking or in giving new meaning to the age-old customs. This regular observation and participation create knowledge what Michel Foucault has rightly said as "historical a priori". This is a priori as Foucault has argued: "[...] is not a condition of validity for judgements, but a condition of reality for statements [...] a priori of a history that is given [...] it is defined as the group of rules that characterize a discursive practice [...]" (127).

Accordingly, it can be argued that knowledge/truth is created at some point of history and with its recurrent practice, it creates an unconscious. This unconscious helps in building a collective identity. Similarly, Odia women construct their identity from the rituals they participate in. Moreover, at the micro-level women who are reluctant to observe, are also made to believe in the sanctity and at the macro level, society gets influenced and controlled. The message is that these rituals transmitted by consistent practices, become knowledge and help in creating a collective identity. It is rightly asserted that: "Culture, therefore [...] is not transmitted genealogically. It is not, also innate but learned" (*Global Agricultural Marketing Management*, 65).

Ecology

According to cultural feminists, the oppression of women is biological. They claim that patriarchal culture suppresses and conditions women through different institutions where their body plays a vital role. Alice Echols aptly says:

> Cultural Feminism views it as a neo-Victorian ideology coming out of radical feminism but ultimately antithetical to it. Whereas the original radical feminism challenges the polarization of the sexes, cultural feminism simply embraces the positive feminine virtues. (135-37)

Following this branch of feminism, the paper asserts that a woman is confined because of her body. Her body is capable of conceiving and gets her periods. Hence, she is believed as pure and motherly. However, she is also loathed and considered impure because of her menstruation cycle. Ironically, her menstrual cycle plays a vital role in being fertile. Here, politics implied is that a woman's body, which is worshipped as a goddess, is also detested because of its certain functions. The goddess Earth or *Gaia* is worshipped because of her power to offer food. 'Raja' is celebrated, since it is believed that the Mother Earth menstruates. However, those three days are over, she also goes through a purification process or *snan*. 'Gaia worship' can go back to the days of human beings as nomads, hunters, and gatherers. Agrarian culture also has worshipped her as the provider of a good harvest. Hence, these rituals observed for a long time has been successful in creating the knowledge that a menstruating female body is dirty, impure, and needs purification. All sorts of subjugation are carried out keeping a woman's body in mind, which helps cultural politics to create knowledge, theory, or dogma to be practised that no one questions. Day by day, observation and participation in rituals create a myth.

Considering a menstruating woman fertile and worthy of worship is also a kind of injustice on women who can't bleed. Attributing essential qualities, thrusting femininity based on physical/biological features is also restricting a woman. Hence, a woman is always made (Beauvoir). With the advent of modernism, though all the rituals of 'Raja' are not performed religiously, this essentializing of women does create an identical dilemma among Odia women. This forced identity thrust on them by socio-cultural forces does make them, remake them. It legitimises all the essentialization of patriarchal culture and helps in distributing power's hegemonic theory. This interrelation between rituals, culture, and politics influence Odia women and collective identity is formed on the basis of shared belief.

'Raja' subjugates Odia women by thrusting 'femininity' on them, by imposing the idea that a menstruating woman is fertile and deserves to be worshipped. However, a menstruating woman is brought to the level of the body and a menstruating body is considered impure. A woman is a goddess for them, so also the Mother Earth, since she is the provider of food. However, the

Mother Earth is also given a *snan* after her menstruation cycle. At one point, rituals keep the society concerned intact, at the other, it is political. Rituals create beliefs and bind society culturally. Rituals also help in developing a relationship between gender and ethnicity, a cultural identity. These beliefs are "unwritten laws" and these are laws, where cultural politics play its part in creating socio-cultural norms. By consistent practice, the importance of rituals during a festival gets enhanced and consequently, the political agenda gets emphasized.

NOTES

1. In Greek mythology, Gaiais the personification of the Earth and one of the Greek primordial deities. Gaia is considered as the ancestral mother of all life (for more information please study Sharad Patil and Lance E. Nelson).
2. The rituals elaborated in the paper are the author's own experience.

REFERENCES

Carter, S. *Global Agricultural Marketing Management*. Rome: Food and Agriculture Organization of the United Nations, 1997. Print.

Chauhan, Divya. "Odisha is Celebrating a Menstruation Festival, Where Women Are Pampered & Made to Feel Special." scoopwhoop.com. *Scoop Whoop*. 16 Jun. 2016. Web. 19 May 2019. <https://www.scoopwhoop.com/Raja-Parba-Odisha-Festival-That-Celebrates-Womanhood/>

Echols, Alice. *Daring to be Bad; Radical Feminism in America, 1967-75*. United States: University of Minnesota Press, 1989. Print.

Elaine, Mary Hegland. "Religion, Ritual, and Politics." *Political and Legal Anthropology Review*, 19.1 (May 1996):131-44. Print.

Foucault, Michel. *The Archaeology of Knowledge and the Discourse on Language*. Trans. A. M. Sheridan Smith. New York: Pantheon Books, 1972. Print.

Jha, Anjali. "Raja Parba: How Odisha celebrates menstruation and honours womanhood." indianexpress.com. *The Indian Express*, 14 June 2018. Web. 25 Apr. 2019. <https://indianexpress.com/article/lifestyle/art-and-culture/odisha-challenges-taboo-around-menstrual-blood-celebrating-raja-parba-festival-5216921/>

Kertzer, David I. *Ritual, Politics, and Power.* United States: Yale University Press, 1989. Print.

Kreinath, Jens. "Ritual and Reflection: Tropes in Transformation and Transgression." *Journal of Ritual Studies*, 23.1 (2009): 73-75. Print.

L. McLaren, Peter. "Rethinking Ritual." *ETC: A Review of General Semantics*, 41.3 (Fall 1984): 267-77. Print.

LaMothe, Ryan. *Review of Ritual, Heritage, and Identity: The Politics of Culture and Performance in a Globalised World. OJS* (2011): 54-55. Web. 17 Mar. 2019. <ejournals.library.vanderbilt.edu/ojs/index.php/homiletic/article/viewFile/3625/1715>

Nayak, Radharani and Seemita Mohanty. "Reading Bruhat Tapoyi (Khudurukuni Osa): A Representation of the Socio-cultural Ethos of the Odia Community." *Lokaratna 5 and 6* (2013): 1-9. Web. 15 May 2019. <https://pdfs.semanticscholar.org/4056/1dc0abd98f8d2c7d6e0813a415a471edd42c.pdf?_ga=2.60798701.1796294627.1574181062-714991411.1574181062>

Nelson, Lance E. *Purifying the Earthly Body of God Religion and Ecology in Hindu India.* New York: State University of New York Press, 1998. Print.

Patil, Sharad. "Earth Mother." *Social Scientist*, 2.9 (Apr. 1974): 31-58. Print.